FIELDBOOK

FOR
CUB SCOUTS
SCOUTS
EXPLORERS
SCOUTERS
EDUCATORS
OUTDOORSMEN
FAMILY CAMPERS

BOY SCOUTS OF AMERICA

Second Edition
3,110,000 copies printed since 1944

1980 PRINTING
Copyright © 1967
BOY SCOUTS OF AMERICA
Irving, Texas
Library of Congress Catalog Number: 67-14537
ISBN 0-8395-3201-6
No. 3201   Printed in U.S.A.   50M780

BOOK WITH A PURPOSE

The *Fieldbook* has a past and a future. Almost a million copies of the original *Scout Fieldbook,* written by William Hillcourt, were used and treasured by Scouts and Scouters. This second edition not only captures the spirit and flavor of the first edition but also has the latest information on outdoor living.

Preparedness, outdoor living, nature lore, and self-reliance have been an important part of the program of the Boy Scouts of America since 1910. Preparedness leads to confidence and self-reliance—a knowledge that come what may, you're prepared. The *Fieldbook* is a guide to preparedness. In it you will find many things to help you serve others and take care of yourself.

The *Fieldbook* is a book of action. You won't sit very long in an easy chair reading it—you'll want to get outdoors to try all the exciting things described.

In using this book, may your trails be exciting, your experiences challenging, and your opportunities unlimited as you enjoy and live these great outdoor adventures.

> *Who hath smelt wood-smoke at twilight?*
> *Who hath heard the birch-log burning?*
> *Who is quick to read the noises of the*
> *night? Let him follow with the others, for*
> *the young men's feet are turning to the*
> *camps of proved desire and known delight.*
> Rudyard Kipling

IDEALS

SLOGAN
Do a Good Turn Daily

MOTTO
Be Prepared

SCOUT OATH
On my honor I will do my best to do my duty to God and my country and to obey the Scout Law; to help other people at all times; to keep myself physically strong, mentally awake, and morally straight.

SCOUT LAW
A Scout Is TRUSTWORTHY. A Scout tells the truth. He keeps his promises. Honesty is part of his code of conduct. People can depend on him.

A Scout Is LOYAL. A Scout is true to his family, Scout leaders, friends, school, and nation.

A Scout Is HELPFUL. A Scout is concerned about other people. He does things willingly for others without pay or reward.

A Scout Is FRIENDLY. A Scout is a friend to all. He is a brother to other Scouts. He seeks to understand others. He respects those with ideas and customs other than his own.

A Scout Is COURTEOUS. A Scout is polite to everyone regardless of age or position. He knows good manners make it easier for people to get along together.

A Scout Is KIND. A Scout understands there is strength in being gentle. He treats others as he wants to be treated. He does not hurt or kill harmless things without reason.

A Scout Is OBEDIENT. A Scout follows the rules of his family, school, and troop. He obeys the laws of his community and country. If he thinks these rules and laws are unfair, he tries to have them changed in an orderly manner rather than disobey them.

A SCOUT IS CHEERFUL. A Scout looks for the bright side of things. He cheerfully does tasks that come his way. He tries to make others happy.

A SCOUT IS THRIFTY. A Scout works to pay his way and to help others. He saves for unforeseen needs. He protects and conserves natural resources. He carefully uses time and property.

A SCOUT IS BRAVE. A Scout can face danger even if he is afraid. He has the courage to stand for what he thinks is right even if others laugh at or threaten him.

A SCOUT IS CLEAN. A Scout keeps his body and mind fit and clean. He goes around with those who believe in living by these same ideals. He helps keep his home and community clean.

A SCOUT IS REVERENT. A Scout js reverent toward God. He is faithful in his religious duties. He respects the beliefs of others.

EXPLORER CODE

As an Explorer—

I believe that America's strength lies in her trust in God and in the courage and strength of her people.

I will, therefore, be faithful in my religious duties and will maintain a personal sense of honor in my own life.

I will treasure my American heritage and will do all I can to preserve and enrich it.

I will recognize the dignity and worth of my fellowmen and will use fair play and goodwill in dealing with them.

I will acquire the Exploring attitude that seeks the truth in all things and adventure on the frontiers of our changing world.

CONTENTS

1 HIT THE TRAIL

"Afoot and light-hearted I take to the open road,
Healthy, free, the world before me,
The long brown path before me leading wherever I choose."

Walt Whitman wrote his "Song of the Open Road" just about the time the forty-niners were shoving off across the wide Missouri in their lumbering prairie schooners, and not many years after Boone and Lewis and Clark had died. Jim Bridger, the first white man to see the Great Salt Lake, was still around, as was Kit Carson, but Jedediah Smith was gone. John C. Fremont and Brigham Young were exploring California and Utah respectively. San Francisco was still known as Yerba Buena.

Actually, not far beyond the outskirts of Boston or Savannah or St. Louis or New Orleans, people found real brown-pathed wildernesses and sometimes no path at all. "Go West" was the word, and go they did. America was on the move. So a poet could talk about walking out to anywhere and people would know what he meant.

And the way West meant penetrating forest, fording streams, rafting rivers, threading gaps in barrier peaks, and spanning plains and deserts. Adventure became our heritage, it got in our blood.

Today, the interstates net the land, forests have shrunk, bridges arch the "wide Mizzoura" *and* the Mississippi, peaks are strung with cables, and flooded deserts produce lettuce. Shadows of supersonic planes ripple over mountains. Dark lakes mirror the passage of a starlike satellite.

Still there is for us Americans a drive for personal high adventure—not just the exploits that hit the front pages (except maybe our hometown papers) but an answer to the challenge of nature and to the invitation to share in the good things the outdoor life has to offer.

So the poet was singing for us, too.

And there is still wilderness enough for those who want to slug it out toe-to-toe with nature. After all, how much wilderness can you cover in a lifetime? You go a little further to find it now, but it's there.

Two great trail systems, the Appalachian and the Pacific Crest, stretch over 4,000 miles of grand wilderness on the East and West. In 39 States and Puerto Rico there are 154 National Forests with 182 million acres and 150,000 miles of forest trails. The remotest areas are more accessible than ever. The jumping-off places are only hours away now. What's wanted chiefly is the adventurous spirit to seek out the lonely places.

Since 1910, the Boy Scouts of America has tried to encourage the adventurous spirit in boys, along with an appreciation and love of our country. It has worked for physical and mental fitness through a vigorous program of outdoor activities centering on hiking and camping. Its people have developed facilities for Scout camping near to home and off in the wilds. The rugged road to adventure has always been of more interest to us than the superhighways to boredom.

Scouts find in their advancement plan the incentive and skills to make hiking and camping the enjoyable means to the outdoor life. Explorers include all kinds of outdoor recreation in their activities—camping, swimming, water-skiing, canoeing, sailing, rafting, spelunking, fishing, hunting, and you-name-it. They master camping skills to enable themselves to follow these adventurous pursuits. They find not merely enjoyment but personal fitness and strength of character. They learn to value the good things our country has, the great things it has done.

To help Scouts and Explorers in their pursuit of the outdoor life, a little of the wealth of experience accumulated by those who have gone before has been put in this book.

Now nobody in his right mind thinks of a book as a substitute for experience! There are many fine books on camping and the outdoors, but reading them will not guarantee instant success as a woodsman. Books can only take you so far . . . right to the brink of experience.

Now, if you're lucky enough to have as a friend someone who has "been there," someone who'll show you the way and initiate you in the mysteries of the outdoors, you have it made. A Scout troop or Explorer post may have the experienced leaders and the seasoned campers you'd like to have help you in your quest for adventure.

However you do it, get out and enjoy the wonderful things this land of ours has to offer. Stop being a spectator—get out of the chair; find your walking shoes; pack up your pack; grab your hat and get out-of-doors! Sure, read the books—but don't just settle for them. Try some things you've only read about. See if you can make it on your own.

Afoot and lighthearted, take to the open road . . . healthy, free, the world before you . . . the long brown path before you leading wherever you choose. . . . Hit the trail!

2 READY FOR HIKING

IF YOU want to see through the eyes of the early scouts and pioneers, you'll do it best on your own two feet! This means you can get to the places rarely visited by others and you can take time to explore and observe as you move at a leisurely pace. You'll see more really interesting things and can afford to stop and take a good look. Travel doesn't have to be boring, you know.

Walking has another advantage: It's the best general exercise known—good for people of all ages. To make yourself physically strong, *walk; don't ride!* Build up those leg muscles and keep them strong by walking at least an hour a day. Develop your own walking pace, point your toes straight ahead, and walk tall and fast. Your natural walking pace won't develop automatically; you must walk with determination. When you see something that interests you, you can move at a leisurely pace; but walking for exercise isn't a stroll.

When does a walk become a hike? A hike is *a walk with a purpose* lasting, say, more than an hour; often a hike will last all day.

What do you do first? Well, planning a hike includes where you're going, when you'll leave and return, equipment, food, parental permission, and what you'll be doing on the way. What's the purpose of the hike? What do you want to do, what do you want to see, what do you want to prove?

You aren't a real hiker if you only hike in fair weather. Not until you've hiked through the wind and showers of spring, the heat of summer, the chill of autumn, and the cold of winter can you really be called a hiker. A hiker has faced brambles and thorns, sudden downpours, steep climbs and descents, slogging through swamps, and braving the raw cold of a winter wind. He has faced these things, overcome them, and looks back on them as part of the better hikes he has taken. Why? Because faced with problems, he overcame them. His preparation and equipment were up to the test.

You can be a hiker. You can learn how to be prepared.

foot care

Hiking can be fun or pure misery depending on the condition of your feet. So, wash your feet at least once a day; use foot powder to control athlete's foot or prevent its occurrence; and trim your toenails straight across. Then, wear clean socks and broken-in well-fitted shoes. And finally, try to walk a little farther and run a little faster each day to toughen your tender feet.

Why should you bother about washing your feet and trimming your toenails? The misery twins, athlete's foot and ingrown toenail, will make it painfully clear if you don't. Athlete's foot, as you may know, is a fungus that thrives in the dirt and dampness between your toes; your feet itch and burn, cracks develop in the skin that will not heal. The other misery twin, the ingrown toenail, becomes a problem when you trim your toenails as though they were your fingernails. When you round off the corners of a toenail, it may grow into the skin and jab that tender spot at every step. Convinced?

Socks should fit perfectly. If they're too long they will wrinkle and rub; if too short they'll bind your toes. Holes in toes or heels let sores develop on your feet. A neatly darned sock is almost as good as a whole one— almost. But try to wear only whole socks on a hike. On a long hike, carry an extra pair of socks with you and change them at midday. Use the tops of the soiled socks to wipe the moisture from between your toes.

When you buy shoes remember that hiking shoes, those good-looking thick-soled glove-soft beauties are every bit as comfortable as they look.

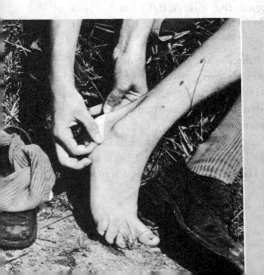

Don't ignore a sore spot caused by a shoe that rubs. When you feel the first signs of irritation, stop and cover the sore spot with an adhesive bandage. This will stop the friction that caused the irritation to take place between the shoe and your tender skin.

6

Your Scout or Explorer field uniform is tops for hiking. One good reason that makes it so is the respect people have for the uniformed members of the Boy Scouts of America. Another good reason is the brush and bramble protection that it gives you when you wear it.

With your uniform you can be prepared for the season and the weather. Layers of clothing help you keep warm and let you cool off. In the morning and afternoon you may need an extra layer—a jacket, sweat shirt, or parka—which you can shed in the middle of the day. If it rains, you can pull your poncho and rubbers from your pack and stay relatively dry.

Leggings are an important part of a hiker's clothing when the ground is wet or covered with snow. They keep the bottoms of your trousers from getting muddy and wet on rainy days and keep the snow out of shoe tops and from crawling up the inside of your pant legs.

The broadbrimmed hat protects your head from the sun and rain. The winter cap with its earflaps keeps your ears from freezing in the icy winds. Beneath your field uniform wear ordinary underwear in cool weather and change to winter underwear when the weather becomes extremely cold.

The summer uniform of short-sleeved shirt, shorts, and stockings is the cool way to dress for hot-weather hiking. But even then, carry a light jacket or poncho just in case the hot weather changes into a summer storm. Some hikers use a 4-foot square of plastic in place of the poncho to sit upon when they rest and hold over their heads when it rains.

The poncho is man's best friend in a downpour. With water-repellent hike shoes and your waterproof poncho you move inside a walking tent. And, man, that's a smart place to be; only green-horns don't know when to come in out of the rain.

7

time and distance

From dawn to dusk are the outside limits of your hiking day. A few exceptionally vigorous and well-trained individuals have walked 50 miles in that time, but most veteran hikers must push themselves to cover 20 miles in a day. Your walking speed will not vary as much as you might think. The average walking speed of 3 miles an hour will be pretty close to yours and to the veteran hiker who covers 20 miles in a day. How long did it take the veteran to walk 20 miles? The problem is simple arithmetic and the answer can be exact: 6 hours 40 minutes of continuous walking. No time out for rests, no time out for lunch, and no time for looking.

How far you go on a hike, then, depends on how much time you can spend. Your watch can measure the miles: 1 hour is 3 miles, 20 minutes is 1 mile, 10 minutes is a half mile, and 2 minutes is a tenth of a mile. If you want to hike to a point 5 miles from your home, it will take 1 hour and 40 minutes of your walking time. Add three rest periods of 5 minutes each, and you can determine your outbound time of 1 hour and 55 minutes. And of course, your return trip will take just as much time. You can manage to cover 1 mile in 12 minutes—5 miles in 1 hour—if you alternate 50 running with 50 walking steps. It's a good trick to use in an emergency. Rough trails and steep hills, though, will cut your speed sometimes by half; so when you plan your hikes, allow more time than you think you'll need. Before you leave, *tell someone where you are going* and *when you expect to return*. Then stick to your schedule.

The hiker's basic instrument panel is a watch; some sports models have pedometers. What model are you? What's a watch have to do with hiking? Time and distance is the hike; and time is distance, if you read your watch correctly. Too complicated? Buy a pedometer. It keeps track of your miles, and with it and your watch you can check to see if your walking speed is better than 3 miles an hour.

Always keep away from railroads and avoid hiking along a highway. Use the secondary roads that parallel the main road. When you hike on a road, get into single file along the left shoulder and hike toward oncoming traffic. In this way, you can see what is coming and can be prepared to move out of the way. If for some reason you must walk along a road at night, hike in the same manner as during the day and tie a white handkerchief around your right knee. The headlights will pick up the white flashes as you walk along and warn the driver that you are on the shoulder of the road. If you have another handkerchief tie it around your right wrist to double your protection. A flashlight should be aimed down and never flashed directly at a car, because you might blind the driver and cause an accident.

Hitchhiking has no place in Scouting. A fellow who goes hiking and resorts to "hitching" instead doesn't know what Scouting is. It is illegal in most States; and, furthermore, it's a real risk, because you don't know the character of the driver of the car.

If you are hiking where poisonous snakes are prevalent, learn to identify the dangerous varieties and then avoid them. Look and listen carefully. Don't climb rock ledges in known snake country.

Learn to identify poison ivy, poison oak, and poison sumac and stay clear of it. If you are exposed, wash with soap and water and apply rubbing alcohol to the exposed area.

If ticks are a problem in your part of the country, check yourself often to see if any have attached themselves to you. If you find one, cover it with grease or oil. This will close its breathing pores and cause it to drop off.

Chigger bites will itch all the more if you scratch them—and they might become infected. Cover each affected area with clear nail polish for relief. It's better to prevent chigger bites by using an insect repellent before entering infested areas or by dusting sulfur powder around the ankles, under the arms, and around the waist.

If you are caught in a thunderstorm, don't seek shelter beneath a large tree or a lone tree or stay on a hilltop or a rock ledge. Lightning strikes these targets; while dense woods, groves of young trees, ditches, and ravines are relatively safe from lightning bolts.

food and drink

When you are not permitted to build fires and cut green sticks for kabobs or broilers, carry a lunch of sandwiches, fruit, and cookies. In winter, you may want to fill a vacuum bottle with hot soup or cocoa. At other times your canteen filled with water from home should give you enough liquid for the day. Never fill your canteen with anything but water. Fruit drink powders can be sprinkled into your cup, add water from your canteen and stir. This is a particularly good trick when your drinking water is heavily chlorinated. But remember, flavoring in your cup and only water in your canteen.

If you can't take time out for a regular lunch, the following hike snacks are ideal. No time is lost in meal preparation on the trail, you don't even have to stop hiking to eat unless you want to. Prepare these snacks at home before you leave, pack them where you can get to them easily, and munch on them while you're walking along.

HONEY BARS. You'll need a half cup of each of the following: raisins, figs, dried apricots, and peanuts or almonds. Put the fruit through a grinder, chop the nuts and mix together. Add a half teaspoon of lemon juice and enough honey to bind the fruit and nuts together. Shape into bars and wrap in aluminum foil; lick your fingers for a taste of what's to come on the trail.

HIKER'S NOSEBAG. Horses used to be fed from a bag of oats that hung over their heads. A horse didn't need to go back to the barn for his lunch and you won't go hungry away from home if you carry your own "nosebag." Get a plastic bag, put in an apple, a half cup of raisins, a half cup of chocolate, and a quarter pound of cheese. Simple?

BIRDSEED. Next to some hikers, birds are the hungriest of creatures. Make your own "birdseed" to munch for lunch. Do you like sugar-coated cereal, candy-coated chocolate, roasted peanuts? If you do, pour equal parts into a plastic bag. Mix and munch.

NUTS AND BOLTS. Do you fall apart when you're hungry? Here are some "nuts and bolts" to hold you together until mealtime: Mix together equal parts of raisins, peanuts, chocolate and graham-cracker pieces and pack in a plastic bag.

Soda pop is great for parties, but it wasn't made for hikes. It won't help your thirst, and you'll only have to carry the sticky bottles or containers back home with you in your tote-litter bag.

On hot days, you may want to drink more water than is good for you. Even on a "scorcher" a canteen full of water should last the day. Don't let yourself think about how hot and thirsty you are, because your mind can play tricks on you and the easiest trick is thirst. Pour a little water in your cup and sip it slowly. If you drink directly from your canteen, you cannot judge your water intake; and, furthermore, this unsanitary practice makes your canteen as personal as your toothbrush. Who wants to use someone else's toothbrush? So, don't pass your canteen around to others, and don't drink from theirs.

A hiker has to be prepared for emergencies, so just in case: *Never drink all of your water or eat all of your food.*

If everyone tossed papers from his lunch on the trail, our country wouldn't be America the beautiful. You can do your part to keep America beautiful by carrying your trash home with you in a tote-litter bag. You won't walk by litter no matter who scattered it, if you're a real hiker. There's room in that bag for a cleaner America.

hike fun

Could you direct a person to any point within a 2-mile radius of your home? Have you walked every road or street? Do you know the parks, factories, schools, streams, swamps, ponds, and woods within your neighborhood? Have you been there? Here are some ideas for you and your friends.

FLIP-A-COIN HIKE. Start down a road and every time there's a fork or side road flip a coin: heads we go right; tails we go left. Better keep track of your turns by sketching your route so you'll have something to guide you back to your home.

TRACKING HIKE. Follow the track of an animal in new fallen snow. No snow? Then find wet ground and search for tracks; make plaster casts of the fresh ones or make sketches. No animals? Let a friend be the "hare" and you be the "hounds." In city or town, the "hare" puts his mark (! !) on the sidewalks in chalk; in the country, the "hare" wears tracking irons or pulls a whifflepoof, (a log with nails driven part way in) after him.

STALKING. One fellow sets out ahead of the others, he does not look back as he hikes along. But when he stops, he can whip around on the count of five to spot anyone following him. The "stalker" who is spotted becomes the man to follow.

NATURE SCAVENGER HIKE. Before leaving on the hike, make a list of nature objects that you are apt to find along the way: leaves, flowers, nuts, seeds, feathers, and similar collectible items. The idea is for each Scout to collect as many of the objects as possible. The fellow with the most wins.

SEALED ORDERS. Make up a set of orders that can be carried out along a route that you've scouted. First envelope directs your gang to a stopping place where they may open the second envelope that tells them to count the windows in the building in front of them, for example, and directs them to the second stopping place where the third envelope is opened that may order the gang back to the starting point. Make the orders practical and reasonable—ask yourself: Can I do it?

PHOTO FUN. If you and your pals like to take pictures, try to take pictures of one another while trying to avoid having your picture taken while in the field. Another challenge is to get a picture of a wild bird or animal, because you'll have to be a patient stalker to get close enough to snap a good picture.

FOLLOW-THE-STREAM HIKE. Whether you go up or down stream, you'll find wildlife or at least the signs of wildlife. Trees and shrubs are thicker and sometimes the going will get tough and swampy. A follow-the-stream hike may show you that following a stream is adventurous, but it isn't the quickest route or a wilderness turnpike.

Hike fun leads to more adventure farther from home because when you have the ground-level view of your neighborhood you are ready to look at and use the topographic maps described on page 15. A map, as you know, is a picture of the land showing the roads, streams, swamps, lakes, and hills. It's the big picture very much like the view you would get from an airplane that flies above your home. See pages 16 and 17.

what you need

IN YOUR HEAD
- [ ] common sense*
- [ ] compass and map know-how (study pages 15-31)
- [ ] imagination

IN YOUR HEART
- [ ] respect for property*
- [ ] cheerful disposition
- [ ] adventurous spirit

ON YOUR WRIST
- [ ] wristwatch*

IN YOUR POCKETS
- [ ] adhesive bandages*
- [ ] matches
- [ ] pad and pencil
- [ ] telephone dime
- [ ] compass and map
- [ ] hike snack
- [ ] knife and string

IN YOUR PACK
- [ ] poncho or 4-foot square of plastic*
- [ ] rubbers
- [ ] canteen and cup*
- [ ] extra socks*
- [ ] field guidebook
- [ ] camera and film
- [ ] binoculars
- [ ] tote-litter bag*
- [ ] lunch
- [ ] toilet paper*

*Essential items

3 MAP AND COMPASS

FOR CROSS-COUNTRY TRAVELING, you need to know the use of map and compass, also useful for such practical jobs as sketch mapping.

The best maps for hiking are topographic ones. To get such a map, send a postcard to Map Information Office, U.S. Geological Survey, 1200 South Eads St., Arlington, Va. 22202, requesting a free *Topographical Map Index Circular* of the State you expect to hike in and a free folder describing topographic maps.

The index circular has a small map of the State divided into sections termed "quadrangles." For each quadrangle there is a separate map. Find out which quadrangle you plan to hike in; it might take more than one. Also, there may be both *7.5-minute* and *15-minute* maps for the area. (The latter cover four times the area and, hence, are less detailed.) Then order the maps, naming the quadrangles and including a money order or check for the proper payment. For a map of any area east of the Mississippi River, send to the Geological Survey in Arlington; for areas west of the river send to U.S. Geological Survey, Box 25286, Federal Center, Denver, Colo. 80225. Sometimes maps of your locality are sold in sporting-goods or other stores.

There are many, many kinds of compasses on the market. The official *Polaris* compass, used for many illustrations in this chapter, is good for both hiking and mapping. It is a dampened-needle compass that calms down quickly to give faster and more accurate readings. The compass dial rotates on a baseplate so that you can use it as a protractor and direction pointer in the field. The edge of the baseplate has measuring scales in centimeters and in inches—a help in reading and making maps like the one illustrated on page 31.

You must first learn how to read a map correctly, and then use it with a compass for cross-country traveling. Try some beeline hikes; then take on a full-scale hike or an orienteering race that will really test your skills.

details

Terrain details are shown on a topographic map by means of *map symbols.* There are several types, often printed in code colors for quicker reading.

Items in *black* are the work of man — roads, railroads, cities, bridges, boundaries, names. A good road is shown with two solid lines; a poor one, by two broken lines; a path, with a single broken line. On some maps highways are in *red.* A railroad is one or more lines with many crosslines, suggesting railroad tracks. Black rectangles are buildings, and a rectangle topped by a cross shows a church; if topped by a flag, it's a schoolhouse.

Blue shows water: a blue line is a brook; a blue band, a river; a blue blotch, a lake.

Contours of hills and valleys are indicated by *brown* lines. Every point on one has the same altitude. Follow a heavy brown line on the map, and you'll find a number—for instance, 100. Everything on that line lies 100 feet above sea level. The "interval" of height between lines is stated on the map — usually 20 feet. Where lines are far apart, the ground slopes gently — maybe a good campsite. Where they are close together, the hill is steep — hiking may be tough. Where lines are crowded, they show a cliff.

The top of a prominent hill may be indicated by a number, the altitude of the crest.

Woodland areas are sometimes printed in *green.* As this may be useful, specify "woodland copy" when you order your map.

16

Open pit, mine	✗
Index contour	
Intermediate contour	
Fill	
Cut	
Power line	
Telephone line, etc.	
Railroad	
Hard surface roads	
Improved road	
Unimproved road	
Trail	
Bridge	
Footbridge	
Perennial streams	BLUE
Water well · Spring	o ⌒
Lake	BLUE
Marsh (swamp)	BLUE
Buildings (dwelling)	
School·Church·Cemetery	
Buildings (barn, etc.)	
Sand area	
Woods	GREEN
Orchard	GREEN
Scrub	GREEN

distances

You will often need to know how far you have to travel to your destination or how far away a certain landmark is.

The scales at the bottom of a topographic map afford several means of measuring distances on the map: (1) a ratio—1:24000 or 1:62500, (2) a scale divided into miles and fractions, (3) a scale in thousands of feet, and (4) a metric scale.

On a map in the scale of 1:24000, 1 inch on the map represents 2,000 feet in the field. So you simply measure the number of inches and multiply by 2,000 to get the distance in feet. Even simpler are maps in the scale 1:62500, where the number of inches on the map gives you roughly the number of miles on the ground. For finding your way in a limited area within a radius of about 4 miles and for general orienteering practices, the 7.5-minute series map at a scale of 1:24000 should be your choice. If you plan to cover your area extensively or do advanced orienteering, the 15-minute maps at a scale of 1:62500 would be more useful. For the orienteering distance computer, see pages 565 and 566.

To estimate how far it is from one point on the map to another, use a rule of thumb. Place your thumb on the scale to see how wide your thumb is. Now place your thumb on the map so that a little of point A shows to the left of your thumb; notice the spot on the trail to the right of your thumb and slide your thumb to that spot, so that it is to the left. Now point B is to the right of your thumb. Point A to point B is two thumb widths apart or six-tenths of a mile or I kilometer.

To use the scale ruler of the map itself, mark off the map distance between the two points for which you want to find the actual distance along the edge of a piece of paper, then measure against the scale ruler in the bottom margin of the map. Or copy the scale on the map along the edge of a piece of paper and use this homemade ruler. On page 18 are the distance rulers of the 1:24000 map scale, as shown in the bottom margin of topographic maps.

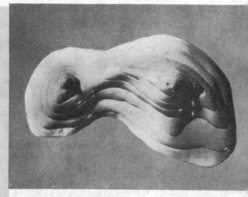

Contour lines indicate the elevation above sea level. To get a good idea of what contours are like, make a relief map of an actual hill. Copy the contour lines from a map through carbon paper. Cut a piece of plywood to the size of each contour. Slant the edges, stack the pieces on top of each other, and paint. These two photos are the side and top views of such a model.

You may find the contour lines a bit confusing in the beginning, but you'll soon be looking at each hill and mountain in terms of contour lines. Then you'll immediately recognize a steep hill or cliff by close lines and a gentle slope by lines which are far apart. Where would you camp, at A or at B?

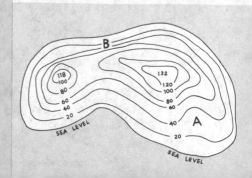

directions

A quick glance at a map will show you the relative direction in which any point lies from any other point. But when you want to find the actual direction between two points, as related to the north and the south of the landscape, you need to know first of all what is north and what is south on the map as a whole.

When you place a topographic map before you with the reading matter right side up, you can be pretty certain that what's up is north and what's down is south. This means that the left margin as you look at the map is west, and the right margin, east.

You can locate where you are on a map, if you know how to use a compass. Suppose you were backpacking not far from a firetower that is shown on your map. At one point on the trail you can see the firetower. You read the bearing as 158. Now all you have to do is place the compass on the map as shown below and you can pinpoint your position on the trail. However, it won't be all that accurate unless you have taken your magnetic declination into account. See pages 22 and 23.

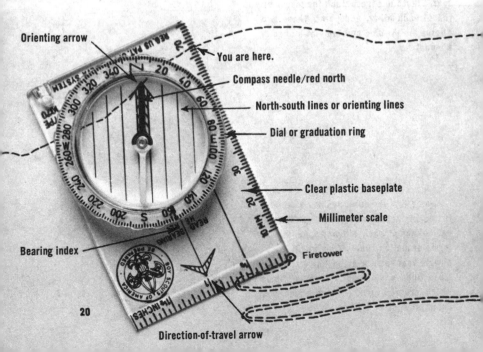

Orienting arrow

You are here.

Compass needle/red north

North-south lines or orienting lines

Dial or graduation ring

Clear plastic baseplate

Millimeter scale

Firetower

Bearing index

Direction-of-travel arrow

20

To orient, turn map and compass until needle points to N.

Map oriented.

Face firetower, hold compass level against your chest.

Turn dial until compass needle points to N. Read bearing 158°.

21

declination

As iron filings align themselves with the magnetic currents between the ends of a bar magnet, so your compass aligns itself with the magnetic flow over the earth. This magnetic flow is toward the north magnetic pole in Canada, some 1,400 miles south of the North Pole. So there is a difference between magnetic north and true north. This difference is called variation or declination. Depending on where you are, your compass needle will lie east or west of true north by as much as 20° westerly in Maine and more than 30° easterly in Alaska. On a thin strip from Lake Superior to Florida there is no declination.

The map on page 23 shows lines on which compasses will show the same declination. As you will not be traveling great distances by compass, you need to know only the local declination, usually shown on a topographic map.

One way to solve the problem is to line up the north end of the needle to the degree of error east or west instead of bringing the needle in line with the orienting arrow. The compass to the left is indexed to 346°, the one on the right to 13°.

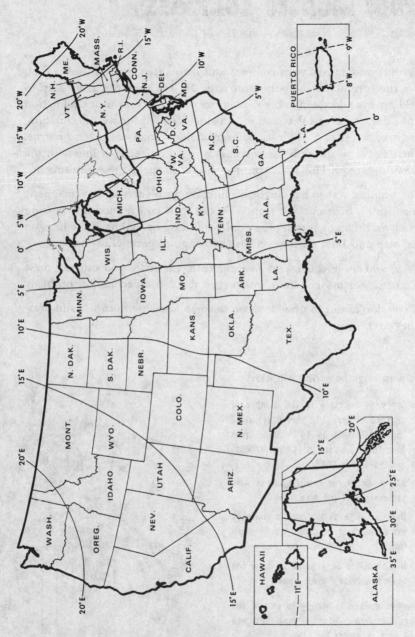

From map to field: West declination add; East declination subtract.
From field to map: West declination subtract; East declination add.

from map to compass

Another way to make the compass and map agree is to adjust the dial. Use the formula at the bottom of page 23. For example, from map to field always add the number of degrees of error from west declination and subtract for east declination. Advance the dial for west declination. Set it back for east declination. From field to map the reverse is true. Then as you work with the compass bring the needle in line with the orienting arrow. However, you may forget to make these adjustments.

The simplest way to handle the declination problem is to draw magnetic north-south lines on your map. You can then take an accurate bearing from your map by turning the graduation ring or dial until the lines on the map and lines on the compass housing are parallel or match.

Now, whenever you take a bearing from the map, you can use these magnetic north-south lines and forget about the declination problem.

If you don't want to draw lines on the map, use a photocopier and draw lines on the copy.

To draw magnetic north-south lines:

1. Set your compass to the number of degrees of error. In this illustration the declination is 14° west. From field to map subtract 14° from 360°. Set the dial to 346°.

2. Align one of the orienting lines with the margin of the map.

3. Use the edge of the plastic plate to draw the first magnetic north-south line.

4. Use that line as a guide to draw the others, a ruler's width apart.

Another method is simply to extend the magnetic arrow into the map and use that as a guide for the others.

PROBLEM—You are on Record Hill and must get to the top of Anthonys Nose. On a clear day that would be easy, but a fog has rolled over the hills. You can see just a short distance ahead.

STEP I—Place the compass on the map so that Anthonys Nose and Record Hill are lined up on the edge of the baseplate. Note that the direction of travel is from Record Hill toward Anthonys Nose.

STEP 2—Hold the compass baseplate firmly on the map. Turn the dial until the orienting lines match the north-south lines on the map.

STEP 3—Read the bearing 270°. Don't change the setting of the dial. Hold the compass firmly against your chest. The compass needle should swing freely as you face in different directions. Turn until red end of the needle points to N. Look up and find something in the fog to walk toward. When you get there repeat the process.

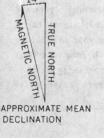

14°

MAGNETIC NORTH

TRUE NORTH

APPROXIMATE MEAN
DECLINATION

cross-country

A fascinating kind of hiking is to follow compass and map cross-country.

Then, after you have done some simple compass-map work with the gang or a buddy, you may want to pit your orienteering skills against others.

Try to get into an orienteering event arranged by your district or council, an individual Scout troop or Explorer post, or an athletic or outdoor club.

In orienteering, speed alone does not determine the winner — it takes a combination of four things: (1) exact understanding of instructions, (2) correct use of compass and map, (3) best choice of route between points, and (4) speed, of course, in covering the entire route.

An especially fast runner may speedily get off to a bad start by failing to follow instructions. Or he may be careless in his compass setting or in correcting declination or in orienting his compass. He can run into unnecessary obstacles by picking a poor route. So take it easy—especially in the beginning. By the time you are seasoned in the sport, your speed will increase with your skill in using compass and map.

Some of the more common orienteering events are shown on these pages, but there are many others. If you really want to get into this sport, read Bjorn Kjellstrom's book *Be Expert With Map and Compass* or the *Orienteering* merit badge pamphlet.

For speed in orienteering, use roads and paths where possible. Wherever a beeline course crosses a steep hill or thick underbrush, study the map to see whether it might be faster to dodge it.

Use common sense in orienteering. Don't attempt to cross a marsh or shallow pond. Instead, take a bearing to a landmark on the other side and run around.

A good orienter picks the most efficient route. Strike for a "catching" landmark such as a lakeshore, to get closer to your destination, then go by compass from there. Avoid using the compass where possible, to save time.

orienteering

ROUTE ORIENTEERING. In this type of event you follow a route decided on by the organizers of the event—part of it along roads, part of it cross-country. This route is indicated on a master map put up in camp, and from this map you copy off the route on your own map. As you follow the route with map and compass, you pass a number of stations *not* marked on the map. The object is to mark the location of each of these stations on your map. The winner of the event is the participant who has found the most stations and has indicated them correctly on his map; speed is not counted, but a time limit should be set.

PROJECT ORIENTEERING. A cool event that not only tests your map-and-compass skills but other outdoor skills as well. As you follow the route, laid out as for route orienteering, you arrive at various stations where signs tell you what to do. Projects may be anything from collecting a number of different leaves or boiling a quart of water to deciphering a Morse code message or chopping through a log. The separate scores you receive from the judges located at the different project stations are added to your orienteering score.

POINT ORIENTEERING. Something different—you are not given a definite route to follow but only the location of a number of points which you have to reach one after the other in numerical order. You must figure out your own route from one point to the next, and decide on the quickest and easiest way of getting there. The organizers of the event may show you all the points on a master map so that you'll know all of them before setting out, but it is more common to have each point revealed one at a time on a marker at each station.

SCORE ORIENTEERING. This event is a variation of point orienteering. For this the map is put up at the starting point with a number of stations marked on it. Next to each station mark is a figure which indicates the score you'll receive if you succeed in hitting that station. The nearby, easily reached points give you low scores; the faraway, tough-going points, a high score. You have to layout your own route, planning it in such a way that you'll get the biggest possible score within the specified time limit.

In route orienteering, the route is shown on a map at the starting point. Before going out, you plot the route on your own map. Then at each station you come to, study your map, decide where you are, and mark the location.

It is possible to vary route orienteering in a great many ways. In a Scoutcraft orienteering race, for instance, your team stops at each of the stations to do some kind of Scoutcraft project.

For point orienteering, all station points to be reached may be marked by numbers on a master map; or each point may be indicated by a score figure; or points my be revealed on route. You have to figure your own route and try to cover each leg in the least possible time. Brain and legs together win.

In score orienteering, the object is to reach as many high-score stations as possible. Each station has a code figure you must copy to prove that you've hit that point.

locating objects

You were fishing on a shallow lake and it was getting dark. Just as you made that "last cast," you dropped the whole rig overboard—and it was your Dad's! Too dark now to see it on the bottom, but you know you can get it by diving . . . in daylight. There's no float you could anchor on the spot, but you have your compass in the ditty bag.

You can see a prominent tree that's unmistakable. It's on a bearing of 224° magnetic. No telling how far away it is—but no matter. There's a farmhouse on the hill, and it's on a bearing of 314° magnetic.

So the next day you row out to where you get the house on a bearing of 314°, and row on that bearing until you get that tree on a bearing of 224°. Anchor and dive. Bet you'll find that rod.

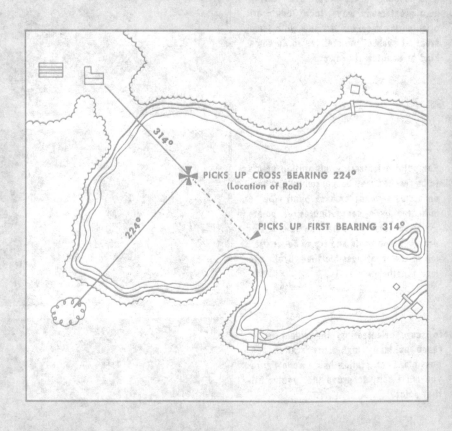

You'll have to cache a heavy pack in the woods while you accompany an injured person down to the highway. You'll take the easiest—but, in this case, longest—route down. But naturally you want to get back to the pack directly, which means over the hill instead of around—which should be a cinch for a woodsman like you. So from your pack you take a sheet of lined notebook paper, and you've got a pencil and the Pathfinder compass.

Hang the pack in a tree so you can spot it on your return. Now pick a landmark for the first leg of your journey. Set the compass on the line of travel and align arrow with needle. Use the blue lines as magnetic north-south lines; draw the first leg of your travel from the cache. As you travel, count your PACES (each step of your right foot); at the landmark, lay off the distance on the map line—one millimeter for each pace you took. Mark it off.

Reset your compass for the next leg to a new landmark. From the mark for the first landmark, lay out the line on the proper bearing. Jot down the bearing. Again, beginning with the left foot, count the PACES until you reach your second landmark. Now lay off the distance on the second leg on your map.

Repeat the process until you find the road. Now, to return you could just follow back azimuths or your own trail; BUT, for the shortcut, project a new route between pack and road on paper. Set the compass and get the bearing, then scale off the distance. All-OK!

31

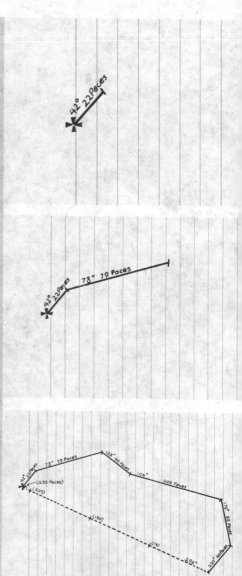

4 CAMPING GEAR

WHAT DO YOU NEED for camping? A simple question — without a simple answer. If you've ever been camping you'll know why. Think back to the last time: you took some things you used every day, some items you used once or twice, and other things you didn't use at all. (Then there were a few things you wished you *had* taken.) And some of the things you didn't use at all — like the first aid kit and the raincoat — leave them out? Hardly. Take heart — even old-timers search on for the ideal rig, a better answer to the question "What *do* you need?"

Some men could cross a wilderness with little but an ax, knife, gun, blanket, a little salt, with maybe some dried corn or jerked beef, in case hunting was poor. But that was long ago, and there were very few of those men; their tastes were simple, and nobody claimed it was much fun. Today it's almost impossible and not much point to it. So what kind of camping are you figuring on? An overnight with your troop? A week at Scout camp? A 10-day expedition with your post? Can you get where you're going by car or canoe or pack animal? Or is this real backpacking, maybe above timberline?

Now we're getting down to cases! You'll have to cope with these problems (no matter where you're going or how): *clothing* to protect yourself; *food and water* for sustaining yourself; *cooking gear* to make food edible or acceptable; *tools* for work, play, maintenance, and emergencies; *bedding* for rest; *shelter* for protection; and a *pack* or something for storage and carrying. Don't worry about which of these categories is most important—it'll be the one you haven't coped with properly!

Now, as to *what* clothing to take, *what kind* of pack you need — it all depends . . . on where you're fixing to go, for how long — and where you draw the line between necessity and luxury. If you just *must* have some item with you, carry it if you can; but if you're part of a group, don't forget, you must carry your fair share of the common needs too. Study this section for specific suggestions; try to look at the total trip, your responsibilities, and plan far in advance, if you can.

personal gear

Your gear will dictate where you can go and how you can get there. You can't very well go backpacking across country with just a tiny shoulder hike bag or go winter camping with a thin summer sleeping bag. Assemble your personal camping gear so you can do what *you* want to do in the out-of-doors. Now if you don't mind being bound to the highway, don't worry about the bulk and weight of your equipment — but if the sky's literally the limit for you and your gang, study your equipment needs carefully.

Analyze and plan, weigh and discard, check catalogs, snoop in stores, and study plans for making your own gear. Pounce on those ounces that add up to pounds of misery on a long trek. Don't even consider giving up the freedom of backpacking—concentrate on cutting weight.

Some fellows will look at a checklist, like the one opposite, and groan just at the length of it. But look at each item shrewdly — figure how *it* rates being lugged — would you be in a bad way without it during *this* trip? Naturally you have to use judgment, but, if you're still a little low on experience, don't be too quick to leave out suggested items — just a change in the weather can change your mind about what is worth carrying! And of course, you'll carry your own gear plus your fair share of group equipment and food.

Should you make your own camp gear or buy it? The answer is "yes." Confusing, isn't it? It really depends on lots of things—how much you have to spend, whether you can buy exactly what you want, and whether you have the skill you need to do a top job of making your own gear. You'll probably take greater pride in homemade equipment because it's all yours, but only if you do a good job.

Wear (or carry in top of pack)
—Complete uniform
—Hiking shoes
—Sweater or jacket
—Rubbers, lightweight
—Raincoat or poncho
—Rainhat or rainhood

Carry in Pockets
—Jackknife
—Matches in waterproof case
—Handkerchief
—Wallet and money (include dime for phone call)
—Personal toilet paper in plastic bag
—Compass
—Two or three Band-Aids

Top or Outside Pockets of Pack
—Repair kit containing:
  —rubber bands —shoelaces
  —safety pins —cord
  —extra plastic bags
  —fire starter
—Pair of extra socks
—Eating utensils: —knife
  —fork —spoon —cup
  —deep-sided plate
—Flashlight

Inside Pack or Secured to Pack or Frame
—Sleeping bag or two or three warm blankets (if outside pack, covered completely with waterproof plastic)

Inside Pack
—Waterproof ground cloth, plastic
—Moccasins or sneakers
—Plastic or cloth clothesbag containing:
  —extra shirt —extra pants
  —pajamas or sweat suit
  —extra handkerchief
  —extra socks
  —change of underwear
—Toilet kit containing:
  —washcloth —comb
  —soap in waterproof container
  —hand towel —bath towel
  —metal mirror
  —toothbrush and paste/powder

Optional Items
—Watch —Map —Songbook
—Camera, film —Dark glasses
—Notebook, pencil
—Personal first aid kit
—Survival kit
—Binoculars —Canteen
—Nature books
—Scout handbook or field book
—Insect dope and netting
—Swim trunks
—Rope or line
—Air mattress or foam pad
—Washbasin, plastic or canvas
—Air pillow —Personal tent
—Bible, Testament, or Prayer Book, according to faith

group gear

Most Scout or Explorer camping involves patrols or groups of boys in contrast to personal camping where a couple of buddies go camping together. There are items of patrol or group gear that are quite different from personal gear. Tentage, cooking gear, and basic camp tools are considered to be group gear. This shared equipment, plus the food needed for the group, is divided up into piles of about equal weight for each camper (a little extra for the big guys — a little less for the smaller ones) and added to the personal pack of each one. Take into account the size of each camper's pack, and try to allocate gear to fit the packs available. Thus patrol or group members share about equally in carrying the food and equipment that each will use.

A patrol food box is a real asset in a permanent camp. Your patrol cooking gear and staple foods can be stored and carried in the box, and when you set up your camp kitchen you have ready-made storage shelves and work counter. When you're going out for only a weekend camp, or traveling light, take what you need out of the box, and carry these items in your packsacks.

Your patrol dining fly and camp tools are important items of camping gear, but there's no need for each camper to duplicate those items that can be used by the whole group. Sharing cuts down on the amount and weight of equipment and spreads it out among all members.

HEADQUARTERS EQUIPMENT

___Small American flag, halyard
___Patrol flag (for Scouts)
___Dining fly — Trail Tarp,
  10' x 10'
*___Fly, 12' x 16'
___Poles, pegs, and rope for fly
*___Food chest

COOKING EQUIPMENT (add as needed for size of group)

___Pots (4)
___Frying pans (1 or 2)
___Serving plates (2 or 3)
___Serving—measuring cups
___Spoon, large ___Fork, large
___Pancake turner or spatula
*___Can opener, roll type
*___Potato peeler
*___Carving knife *___Paring knife
___Match container, waterproof
*___Sugar container, waterproof, unbreakable
___Salt and pepper container, waterproof, unbreakable
___Hot-pot tongs *___Cooking gloves
*___Plastic food containers (3 or 4) with screw lids, 16 to 32 ozs.
*___Roll aluminum foil
___Sanitizing tablets

CAMP TOOLS

___Ax ___Bow saw
___Camp shovel
___Mill file for sharpening ax
___Sharpening stone ___Nails

___Cord ___Wire
___Sewing kit
___Side-cutting pliers
___Safety pins ___Rubber bands

HEALTH AND SAFETY

___Plastic sheets (2), at least 4' x 4'
___First aid kit ___Toilet paper in plastic bag
___Screw-top water container, collapsible plastic, $2\frac{1}{2}$ gal.
*___Rubber scraper
*___Dishmop, cellulose
*___Scouring pads, nonrusting
*___Soap/detergent in plastic screw-cap container
___Paper towels in plastic bag
*___Galvanized mop buckets for dishwashing (2), 14-qt.
___Tote-litter bag, extra plastic liners
___Water purification tablets

TENTAGE

___Two-man tents
___Poles, pegs, and guylines

OPTIONAL ITEMS

___Dutch oven ___Reflector oven
___Griddle
___Mixing jars, plastic, 1-qt.
___Metal tent pins
___Extra canteens
___Plastic bags, various sizes
*___Electric lantern
*___Table cover, oilcloth or plastic

Unstarred items are basic to overnight/short-term camping. Add starred items for long-term camp (6 days and nights or more).

tents

There's no such thing as the all-purpose tent — the ideal tent for a long-term camp would be too heavy and bulky for packing, while the ideal trail tent is too confining for many days at a time. The Boy Scouts of America recommends two-boy tents, with 30 square feet of floor space per boy. So a 9- by 7-foot tent with 63 square feet has little more than the minimum, which isn't excessive considering lost usable space under slanting sides. Tents should have sufficient headroom to permit dressing or undressing in a standing position—about 6 feet high, depending on the shape of tent. The tents shown here meet these design specifications, although they differ in other advantages. As tents are a major investment, it pays to be very careful in making your choice. Once you have decided on design, shop with an eye for *value* as well as price, using the criteria suggested on these pages. Then *take care* of your investment. The great enemies of canvas are fire, rain-shrunk ropes, poor pitching, clumsy feet, and mildew. Good construction and quality materials can resist much of this kind of abuse, but there's a limit. A tent-repair kit for immediate repair of damage is worth carrying—small rips become catastrophes if not caught at once. Pack wet canvas (if you must) loosely and dry thoroughly as soon as you can.

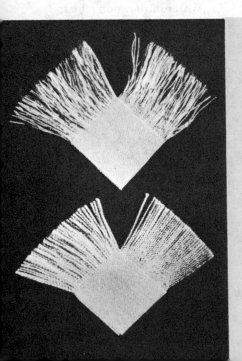

The fabric used in the manufacture of your tent determines its weight, durability, and ability to keep out the rain. Tents distributed by the Boy Scouts of America are made from two fabrics: lightweight tents are made of 5.18-ounce jean and heavier tents from 10.10-ounce army duck. The duck has heavy yarn and a low thread count, while jean material uses light yarn and higher thread count. Most tents have a finish over the basic material. Avoid finishes that have a heavy waxy feeling—they tend to seal the air spaces, making a tent that won't "breathe." Dry finishes that don't chip, crack, or rub off are best. Modern tents should be flame-retardant.

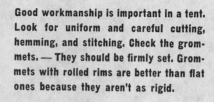

Good workmanship is important in a tent. Look for uniform and careful cutting, hemming, and stitching. Check the grommets. — They should be firmly set. Grommets with rolled rims are better than flat ones because they aren't as rigid.

Look for reinforcements at stress points like the peak, eave, and corners. Every place exposed to extra wear should be reinforced. Where tabs or ties are attached to the canvas, they should be supported with one or more layers of extra canvas stitched in place to spread the strain over the fabric.

Several kinds of tent poles are available — some sectional, some one-piece. Poles may not be included in the price of the tent, because the buyer may wish to make or buy his own. Make sure your poles are sturdy. A strong wind places tremendous pressure on the pole; and, if not strong, it might collapse at a poor time — right in the middle of a storm.

The sod cloth helps fill the bottom gap caused by uneven ground. It gives a seal between tent and groundcloth, giving your tent a built-in floor. National Supply Service tents can be ordered with or without sod cloths.

backpacking tents

THE OVERNIGHTER is light, easy to pitch, and a good wind tent. It requires a front rope that might be in the way of your fire unless you use a two-rope front tie-down. The wide front panels give privacy when closed; they tie down in foul weather.

THE ADVENTURER I is a maximum protection nylon tent complete with floor, fly, and screen. It is big and roomy. There's a smaller version, Adventurer III, that weighs about the same as the Overnighter.

THE VOYAGEUR is an improved "A" or "wedge" tent. The ridge is reinforced with heavy webbing to eliminate the need for a ridgepole. This tent is available with floor, vent, and netting. Side pullouts give extra usable interior room. The Voyageur is an excellent snow tent.

THE NYLON TRAIL FLY is used mainly to protect the dining area. It can be set up in a number of ways to give temporary shelter. It also comes in a larger size for use in permanent camps.

40

permanent camp tents

THE BAKER is tops in ventilation, headroom, and front area protection. Because of its wide-open front, the Baker isn't a good high-wind tent. Its flat roof makes it a poor snow tent.

THE ADVENTURER II is ideal for group camping or backpacking. Lightweight, it has plenty of room for four adults. Four-way ventilation is provided by two side windows with screens and flap, rear vent with screen, a zippered door, and front screens. Made of nylon.

THE ADVENTURER IV is an ideal nylon backpackers tent that sleeps two and weighs only 5 pounds, including poles and pegs. It features an "A" frame pole assembly in the front and "I" pole in the rear. Includes zippered entrance and vent window with screens and a breathable roof.

THE WALL TENT is the old standby of camping through the years. It comes in a variety of sizes. The Wall has lots of usable space, good headroom, and can be ventilated by rolling up the sides.

NOTE: All tents pictured on these pages are flame-retardant, water-repellent, and mildew-resistant. Nylon tents are made of rip-stop fabric.

pack facts

A limiting factor in camping is the size of your pack; it's a serious matter, having too small a pack. Sure, when you're a brand-new Tenderfoot that first pack looks awfully big. But the first time you try to get all you need for even a short pack trip in, you find it just won't work — it isn't big enough for all *your* stuff, say nothing of your share of the group gear. You've seen 'em straggling into camp—the guy with the little pack on his back, patrol cook kit in one hand, cardboard box bouncing along from the other hand, trench shovel under one arm, and the patrol dining fly rolled under the other. Pathetic. And no need for it — but, once you're stuck with a small pack, what can you do? *Any* pack worth considering is not going to be cheap — but figure all the times you'll be living out of that sack; the difference in cost per mile will be negligible compared to the annoyance of making do with skimpy gear. Aside from size, no one pack is going to be best for all situations — hiking, canoeing, mountain climbing, and so on—that's why there are different kinds. For even a medium load, for instance, a pack frame feels better than just the pack; but a pack frame is a nuisance in a canoe. So when you're on the trail, see what the old-timers are carrying. They *could* be stuck with what they have, of course, but chances are it won't be the first pack they've owned. Packs have improved lots over the years—take advantage of progress.

THE RAYADO is big enough to handle the camping job. It has outside pockets for carrying items you might need on the trail. The Rayado on a Cruiser Pack Frame is a man-size rig for large loads, but it fits any official pack frame.

42

WIDE STRAPS make your pack seem lighter. They spread the weight of the load and prevent cutting into your shoulders. Padding under the straps at stress points will help your comfort.

THE CRUISER PACK FRAME is made of tubular aluminum. It's light and strong. The straps are wide and padded. The webbing keeps the load away from your body, allowing perspiration to evaporate. The pack frame lets you carry the load high on your back.

HOMEMADE PACK FRAME can be fun to make; but be sure you are following a sound design that will be light, comfortable, and still do the job required. Thin tough wood is usually the basic material for a homemade frame, but you can use aluminum tubing if you have the proper tools to work with.

HORIZON I on the Astral Pack Frame with a Deluxe Padded Hip Belt is the backpacker's complete outfit. Horizon I comes in red or blue nylon. The hip belt takes the weight off your shoulders, and the pack frame has room for your sleeping bag.

43

sleeping gear

Ever wake up to the ring of axes hacking away? At 2 a.m.? You tried to get back to sleep, but those characters with the cold, uncomfortable beds wouldn't let you. Next day everybody was grumpy and all they wanted to do was flop in their tents. Sad story. Understandable.

You need your sleep, especially when camping, and old hands insist on it. The problem is — comfort you can *carry!* But people differ greatly in what they call 'comfort' — softness of bed and warmth of bedclothes — so you can't go much by others' experience. (The differences are mostly ones of degree—not principle.) Air mattresses aren't perfect, but they're a practical means to a lump-free, resilient bed, and some pack quite well. (Dump the air *first thing* on mornings you're moving!) Put yours on a ground cloth to ward off ground moisture, snags, and dirt. Your bedroll or sleeping bag goes on top. Sleeping bags are so common now that choosing the "right" one is a problem. Consider the cost of a good mattress and bag, though, an investment in comfort, sleep, *and* good humor!

Only thing warm in a sleeping bag is YOU—all the bag can do is insulate you from the cold around you. When the bag isn't enough insulation for the temperature, you add more. A liner is a help, and will serve to keep the bag clean, too. Of course you can add a blanket or two, but they add weight and bulk, if that's important. A neat and effective solution is wearing a Camp Warmer which is a two-piece insulated suit, and just the thing for fighting that frosty feeling. Smooth quilted finish combats getting all snarled up in the bag lining, too. Add wool socks and a stocking cap for real warmth from head to toe.

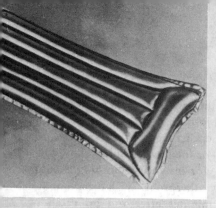

Air mattresses are usually plastic or rubberized cloth, plastic being lighter but not as durable. Inflate mattress until your body barely touches ground when you lie on mattress; you should then be comfortable on it. Too much air makes mattress too "lively."

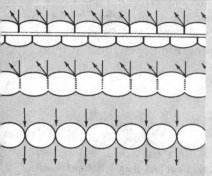

Sleeping bag fillings are now mostly synthetic fibers or waterfowl down—label must state what and how much, although these aren't the only factors affecting comfort. Good down is very expensive, but very light for backpacking; synthetics may compress less, with less heat loss to ground. Diagrams show even-comfort quilting; I-beam construction giving superior insulation; and sewn-through quilting with cold spots.

Rectangular bag is most common type. It is roomy and economical to make, but extravagant of space and weight. With a full zipper it is easy to open for airing. It can be rolled lengthwise to a horseshoe for lashing to a pack, or folded and rolled for lashing to a pack frame. Keep clean by using a light, washable insert. Bags should be machine washed and air dried. They should not be dried in a drier or dry cleaned.

Barrel—or mummy—bag is really a robe; formfitting to conserve heat, it moves with you. Light and efficient, it is favored by backpackers though some find it confining. It can be had with synthetic or down filling; needs smaller amounts than other shapes.

45

packing

So — now you've got your gear all together, with a sack to put it in, and maybe a pack frame to tote it on. Well, just put it in shape to carry and to live out of! Use the personal-gear checklist, heeding the suggestions for situating stuff. (Some things you — or the guy behind — should be able to fish out at once, like a poncho, for instance.) Nothing should rattle, bang, or flop. The rig should be weatherproof. With forethought, the pack won't look mixmastered 5 minutes after you hit camp— you'll be able to lay hands on just what you want. Organize! Leave room for your share of group stuff. If you don't use a frame, pad the back of your sack by packing soft things next to it; you'll get to appreciate it.

A proper pack is a sack of sacks. You'll find it easier to pack—and to find stuff in— if you use a set of bags for grouping related items; not just clothes, but underwear, socks, dirty clothes—like that. There's a set of plastic bags made for this use, but you can use cloth or plastic bags from the kitchen or laundry, or make 'em. Plastic is cheap, transparent, and waterproof.

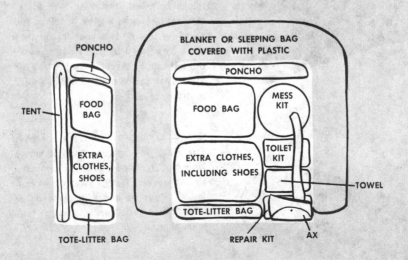

The famous diamond hitch of the Old West is still holding many a pack snug on a packsaddle or frame. Its advantage is that the entire length of the rope can move to be self-adjusting and with six projecting pegs or hooks on the frame you throw the hitch without pulling the free end through bights.

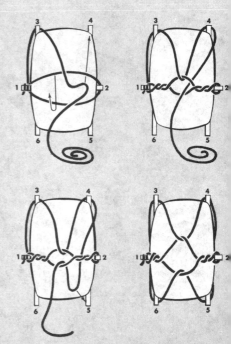

Lay your sack or duffel on the frame, flat, and secure one end of your rope to a center tie. Run the rope across the duffel and around the opposite tie and back across to the snubbed end; pull this loop tight and then twist it twice or three times. This is the key to the whole thing, the diamond. Now, using only bights of the running part of the rope, loop the rope over the upper-left peg and pass a bight through the center twist and up to hook it over the upper-right peg, opening the upper side of the diamond. Pull the running end down around the lower-right peg and pass a bight up through the center and back down to the lower-left peg, opening the bottom of the diamond. Now finish the hitch off by snubbing the rope around the left-center peg. Hold it and pull the rope taut. Tie it off.

Shock cord is great for securing an ax, bedroll, sleeping bag, or tent to the outside of your pack or on a pack frame. Make loops as desired; when loading, snap around gear, and stretch to remove. No knots to tie and untie. It's self-adjusting, convenient, and strong.

47

5 CAMPING

YOU CAN BUILD a backyard shack using a hammer and saw, but a skyscraper requires dozers, cranes, riveting equipment, and hundreds of other pieces of complicated equipment. What's that got to do with camps? Well, it's a bit exaggerated, but the principle is the same.

You don't need the same camp equipment to go on an overnight camp that you do for a long-term camp of a week or more. A chuck box, for example, is a wonderful convenience in long-term camp but it is not really essential for a weekend. Why not? Because it would sure cut back on your choice of places to go.

Heavy equipment tends to make station-wagon campers out of those who can't get along without it. The best camping takes place away from roads. Don't let your camping gear keep you close to civilization.

Similarly, major camp improvements are important when camping for a week, but hardly worth the effort for a weekend. Unless it's to gain experience, why take the time and trouble to build patrol tables and kitchens when you'll only use them for three or four meals? Better use the time for nature adventuring, stalking, tracking, trailing, or any other activities that would be more fun or more productive.

So, in planning your activities and preparing your gear for camping, keep in mind the shack and the skyscraper. Decide what you want to accomplish, how long you'll be out, and where you really want to go. It's pretty hard to beat a checklist for making sure you have what you need when you need it. You might develop *two* of these lists — one for backpacking trips, and the other for long-term camp. In either list, label items as "essential" or "optional."

Don't shackle yourself to heavy gear (and the automobile) for short-term camping; on the other hand, don't ignore the comfort that this kind of equipment can provide when you're long-term camping. Common sense is a mighty fine guide to deciding what is needed.

the site

A few years ago, you could be choosy in picking a campsite. It's still possible in some areas of the country, but in much of the Nation you take what you can find and make do with less than the ideal. Don't let problems of finding the ideal site spoil your camping activities. If there isn't water on the site, bring it with you. The same with fuels for fires. Learn to live with and make the best use of what's available. Scouts and Explorers across America have learned to camp in sandy deserts, on open plains, on rocky outcroppings of mountain slopes, and even on a bit of high ground in a swamp. They have learned to live with what they have, and to go camping in spite of campsite problems.

As you hike the trails in your area, keep your eyes open for the ideal campsite. When you find it, get permission to camp on it, and then live up to all agreements reached in obtaining that permission.

The ideal site has trees, water, grass-covered ground, gently sloping terrain, protection from severe weather, and a view. The possibility of finding all of these in one campsite is quite remote, but the more of them you can get in one site, the better it will be. Avoid natural hazards in picking any campsite. What's ideal in fair weather may be dangerous in a thunderstorm. Don't pitch tents directly under trees. Nearby trees afford wind protection, wood, shade, and cover for wildlife; but trees overhead will continue to drip water long after a rain, and heavy branches or whole trees can come down in a windstorm.

If a number of patrols or groups of campers are to use the site, rope off the area to establish fair shares in the camping area. Eight 20-foot lines linked together will make a ring 50 feet across—the recommended area for a patrol site.

On knolls or gentle slopes rainwater drains away from, instead of through the tent. Be sure the slant of the ground isn't too steep; because, if you camp there, you'll wake up in the morning outside your tent.

You ought to have some time to sit and dream. A campsite with a view of a beautiful lake, mountain, waterfall, or forest helps a camper to appreciate the wonders of God's great plan. Sit with your back against a stump and look across the land. Watch cloud shadows playing tag as they race across the hills and valleys. You'll see things and think thoughts you didn't have time for before.

Well, here we are! The hike into our campsite is over, and we're ready to make camp. Let's get at it—pitch our tents and clear our fire area. Hold it, gang—don't be too anxious to get started! You don't build a house without a plan, nor should you set up camp without one. Time spent before setting up facilities can avoid later problems. A smart outfit takes a good look at the total area, using eyes and horse sense to pick the logical locations for dining fly, kitchen, latrine, and tents. Check wind direction, weather probability, and terrain. Plan your campsite for convenience and comfort. Four patrols can camp close enough together for troop administration and far enough apart for independent responsibility.

setting up

Once you've decided where to put things, the whole gang pitches in on the jobs that need doing. The first thing you'll want to do, whether it's raining or not, is to set up a dining fly for the protection of packs and equipment and even for the fellows if it's really pouring. When the fly is up, packs can be opened and equipment readied for use. If a latrine must be built, a couple of fellows get started on this, a couple get wood and water, and a couple ready the cooking area. With every camper doing his share, the total job of setting up camp is simple.

Scout troops camp by patrols. The Scoutmaster or troop leaders' council usually designates the general area to be used by each patrol. The patrol under the direction of the patrol leader is then free to select tent, kitchen, and dining locations within its assigned area. A staff area for adult and nonpatrol troop leaders is also reserved.

Explorer posts camp in a different manner. While Explorers usually form into small groups for cooking purposes, they don't necessarily set up tents in formal groups. Tent occupants usually pick their own locations in the general tenting area of the campsite.

Make it a habit to fly the flag of the United States of America. No flagpole? A branch of a tree will proudly bear our country's colors and mark your camping headquarters soon after you select it.

Once the dining fly is set up, it serves as a base of operation for establishing the rest of the patrol camp. It provides shade and shelter permitting the rest of the camp making to go ahead at a more leisurely pace than might be the case without it.

Where public rest rooms aren't available, dig a latrine trench 6 to 8 inches wide, 36 inches long, and 18 inches deep. Keep away from trees to avoid roots and chop the dirt out a little at a time. Put the topsoil along the right side of the trench, heap the subsoil on a plastic sheet so that you can carry it to your fireplace to make a dirt hearth.

If privacy isn't afforded by nature, make your own with a tarp or some brush stuck in ground around the latrine. Place toilet paper nearby, with a plastic bag over it to protect from rain. Hang lantern near latrine to mark its location in the dark. Use light covering of dirt after each use. Provide scoop to scatter dirt.

Use the plastic sheet to carry mineral earth from the hole to your fireplace. In addition to protecting the sod, the earth mound makes it easy to position rocks just right for any size kettle or pan in your camp kitchen.

53

First check your site to be sure you won't be setting your tent up in poison ivy or on a root, rock outcropping, or some other hard-to-remove obstruction. If the tent has a door, tie it shut before going any further. Now using tent pins or pegs that can be pushed or driven into the ground, peg down the corners, making sure that the edges are pulled tight between the tent pins.

Put tent pegs out for whatever guy lines are needed to support the tent. In most soils drive tent pegs at right angle to pull of line. Fasten line to peg at ground level to gain most leverage from the ground. Fasten the guy lines, but leave plenty of slack in the lines. Then raise the tent pole, lifting the tent into position. Repeat this process for the other tent pole.

Retie guy lines or reset guy-line pins as necessary to give proper shape and support to your tent. Use taut-line hitches at upper ends of guys for no-stoop control of tension. As you know, canvas tightens in damp weather and loosens in dry. You'll need to adjust the tension during the day, because a trim looking tent in the afternoon will pull out its tent pins or tear itself apart in the night.

Now go around the tent. Peg the sides to the ground, making sure that your sod cloth is properly spread out on the inside of the tent. Change the position of the tent pins to remove folds and wrinkles from the canvas for a trim appearance. When properly located and pitched, there is no reason to ditch your tent. Ditching is not permitted on many camp grounds because it causes soil erosion.

comfort

You've set up your dining fly, taken care of your kitchen and sanitation, pitched your tent, made your ground bed, and spread your sleeping bag or blankets. This is all you have to do to get along OK on an overnight — but maybe you want a little more in the way of comfort, or perhaps you'd like to practice some of the skills necessary for comfortable living in a longer camping period. The amount of camp development you can do with native materials depends on availability and the landowner's permission for use. If there's a willow or bamboo thicket nearby, the property owner would probably be happy to have you thin it out, but ask him first. The same is true of thick underbrush in much of the northern part of the country. In the National Parks and Forests, however, *no* cutting is permitted except in the development of an area under the supervision of a ranger. You'll be safe if you make it a practice to do *no cutting whatsoever* without the permission of the owner of the property on which you are camping. Even if you can't cut live trees, dead-and-down branches often can be used to make camp comfortable.

A length of line fastened to the back of your pack or pack frame provides an easy method of attaching your gear to a tree so you don't have to rummage around on your knees on the ground to get at things in the pack. If the ground is wet, too, the bottom of your pack is apt to get soggy if it just sits there.

Wire coat hangers can be twisted into S hooks for heavy-duty pothooks. Twisting the wire into this shape is a two-man job. First straighten the wire then bend it in half. While your friend clamps pliers on the center, twist the wires around each other. Cut off ends and bend into shape.

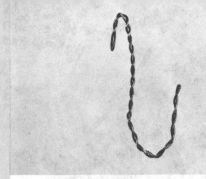

A tripod from which you can suspend pots over your fire is easy to construct and can be made of down branches just as well as from green wood. Bring coathanger wire to form the S hooks on which to hang the kettle. A few lengths of light sash chain are very useful for making adjustable pothooks.

Pull small loops through the grommets. Then shove short sticks into the loops. Pull the line back so that the sticks press tightly against the grommets. In this way, you can fasten a ridge line to a dining fly, secure the flag to a halyard, and hold your chef's cooking tools against a tree.

This one-legged fire crane demonstrates the strength of a well-made dovetail joint that can support a full kettle of water over a fire. For detailed information about the dovetail notch see the next chapter.

57

Placing your ground cloth over the sod cloth of your tent gives you a tent with a removable floor. The sod cloth seals out drafts and crawling critters. Before setting the ground cloth, check the ground for rocks and twigs that might make bumps in your bed.

In soft ground, tent pins have a tendency to pull loose. This can be prevented by overlapping two tent pins so extra support is added to the pin to which the tent is fastened. Taut-line hitches are tied at the end of the line near the tent rather than at the stake.

Use a clove hitch to secure a guy line to a tent fly support pole if the pole doesn't have a small point which can be slipped through a grommet. If it does, tie a bowline in the line and place the loop over the tip of the pole after the tip has been put through the grommet.

58

Tension on canvas and tent ropes must be relieved when tightened by rain. This can be done by loosening all taut line hitches, but a simpler, and drier method is to dig a small hole to the side of each tent pole. Moving the pole into the hole in wet weather will give slack in all lines and in the canvas.

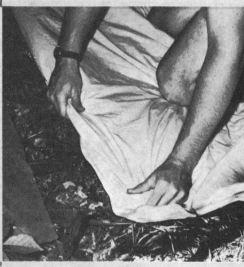

Instead of digging hip and shoulder holes before making your bed, collect leaves, grass, pine needles, or similar padding. Build your bed so extra padding is located in the small of your back, under your head, and under your middle thighs. Tuck your ground cloth around the padding to hold in position.

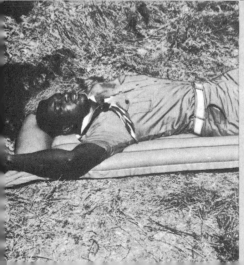

If you have an air mattress you won't need a leaf bed, but you'll still need to make it comfortable. Lie on the mattress after it's blown up. Let out air until you can just feel your tail touch ground. If you don't have an air mattress, test your ground bed for comfort and add more padding where needed.

A blanket-airing pole or line is a real asset to your camp. Dry, aired-out blankets or sleeping bag will help in giving you a warm night's sleep. Clammy, musty blankets are small comfort.

Set up your woodpile where it's handy to your fire. Sort wood by size and stack it accordingly, so you can burn the right size as needed. You can peg in your woodpile to keep it from sprawling out by driving two stakes at each end.

Be sure to have a plastic sheet or light canvas tarp to throw over your woodpile during wet weather. Weight the edges with rocks or sticks of wood to hold it secure in a blow.

Never take a chance by drinking water not known to be tested and safe. The clearest spring imaginable can be polluted. Your safest water source is a canteen of water brought from your home water tap. When purity of water isn't known, use water purification tablet or boil it for 5 minutes. Since this drives the air out and gives the water a flat taste, aerate it by pouring rapidly from one clean container to another several times.

Insects and animals have a way of finding your food supply if you don't protect it. A line over an overhanging branch will let you raise and lower your food as needed, and the food will be out of the reach of varmints. Keep the line out away from the trunk because some animals can climb and reach.

Refrigeration isn't required in a short-term camp if you plan your menu properly. Use any spoilable items very early in the camp period. Some foods do taste better when cool; if near water, you can make a simple cooler by shaping a holding basin with rocks at the edge of the water. Place articles to be cooled in watertight containers, and weight them with rocks to hold under water.

adventure

Stalking animals and each other, tracking and trailing, fishing, and nature expeditions will lead you away from the campsite to adventure, if you are prepared; and misadventure, if you're not.

KNOW WHERE YOU ARE. You are prepared when you know the lay of the land around your campsite for 3 miles in all directions. That's a tall order when camp is miles away from home, but a map gives you the big picture and you can explore at ground level when you study and follow the map of your camping area.

WHAT TO DO IF LOST. Suppose, just suppose that in spite of all your precautions you find yourself following a deer trail that fans out into no trail at all.

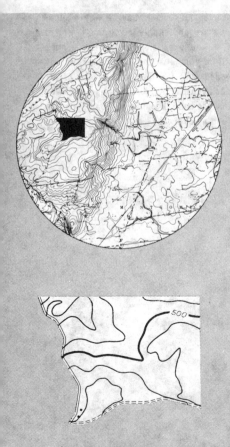

A 6-mile circle on a topographic map gives you an eagle's-eye view of the territory, the same 6-mile circle on a road map can show only the main and secondary roads. If the only map you have is a road map, take 30 minutes to scout the base lines before you enter the woods. Below is a half mile square from the map above. Let's begin where the trail meets the road. Walk north on the road for 10 minutes then return to the starting place. Before you go down the trail tell someone where you are going. Then walk down the trail for 10 minutes. The trail is your east west base line and the road your north south base line. You can explore north and west without worrying about getting lost. Why? Because you will come to the road if you go west, and the trail if you go south. A base line can be a river, lakeshore, or powerline. Base lines work best when the two are different and are obvious enough so that you can't cross one of them without recognizing it.

You begin to feel completely helpless; but you are not, because you have a memory and some reasonable assumptions. Relax, lean against a tree or sit down, give your mind a chance to think. That mind of yours works something like a tape recorder and, like a tape recorder, it works best when you turn it back to the beginning and let it unwind. As you let your mind begin where you started the hike, scratch a line in the dirt to represent your progress. Pay particular attention to the intersections. Did you go left or right? Were there streams along the way? Did you cross them or follow them? Show them on your map and when the map is finished that is the point where you are now. The last leg of the hike will not be lined up with the lay of the land. If you have a piece of paper and a pencil, you can copy your sketch map on the paper and then can turn the paper to make it *agree with the land* or *orient* it. No paper? Then make another sketch on the ground that is oriented. This should help you pick the right direction to retrace your steps.

So much for memory, what about the reasonable assumptions? The first one is that you cannot be more than 3 miles from a familiar spot. Three miles is an hour's walking time and about as long as any reasonable hiker would hike without knowing where he was going. The second assumption is that searchers will find you if you stay right where you are, build a smoke fire, and call out from time to time. The third assumption is that if you follow a straight course in any direction you will come to a road within 30 minutes. The *last assumption* holds true only for the populated sections of the country and *cannot be assumed for the wilderness areas.*

Walking a straight course in the woods without a compass is not as simple as it sounds, because you will tend to walk in a circle—a big circle that tires you out and gets you nowhere. When you can see the sun, you can use it as your guide; walk toward it or keep the sun to your left or your right or follow your shadow, if the direction you choose is away from the sun. To avoid walking in circles on a cloudy day, use the principle that two points make a straight line. From where you are (point one) to a distinctive tree or "target" (point two) is a straight line. When you get to the tree, stand on the far side with your back toward the point you came from; pick out another "target," walk to it and continue picking out distinctive landmarks until you reach a road.

breaking camp

By following an orderly procedure you can leave behind you a campsite that will earn you a welcome back and you'll take with you *all* your equipment in a condition that will ensure it a long, useful life. Think ahead and allow yourself time. For instance, when you wake up, pull the plug on your air mattress. The weight of your sack should collapse it completely by packing time. Now gather up the odds and ends you have in the tent; get 'em in the pack or on your sack. You're responsible for your own gear, of course, so look to it. Dirty clothes go in one plastic bag, damp stuff in another—but you know how to pack your sack.

Brush any dirt or leaves off your bed sack or take it off the line if you had a chance to air it (you'll air it again at home, of course). Roll, waterproof, and pack it. That mattress must be flat now—stow it. The ground cloth, though, is probably damp on the bottom, so dry it. Now get your pack under the dining fly with the others.

Two fellows working together can quickly fold dry tentage. As you make each fold, brush dirt, leaves, and debris from the exposed canvas. Press excess air from the tent with each folding so it won't balloon the tent and prevent your making it compact enough to fit your pack or the tent bag. Take time to make a neat package with all ropes and flaps tucked in.

Damp canvas must be thoroughly dried before it is stored for any length of time. You may have to carry it home wet, but just as soon as you get there hang it up or spread it out in the garage or cellar. When weather permits get it on the clothesline to dry completely.

The dirt hearth under your fire came from the latrine pit. Use it to cover the ashes and charred wood from your fires which you put into the hole during your final cleanup. Although it is to be buried, make sure the fire debris is dead out by sprinkling with water and stirring it with a stick before putting it in the latrine pit.

The last thing to come down before you hit the trail is our country's flag. It can be a ceremony for the post, troop, patrol, or just you two.

As soon as the tents are as dry as possible, strike them and collect all poles and pins—don't leave pins or pegs in ground; they're hazards. Be careful to clean tents of mud, leaves and grass as you fold them. Stash them under the fly. The fly is the last thing to come down so you'll have shelter for yourself and gear in case of a shower—if it gets wet that's only one piece of canvas to dry. Assemble group gear for checkoff before it goes in the packs. Have the pots sparkling, the tents clean, pins counted, and woods tools sheathed.

Improvised structures should be taken apart and the poles piled or scattered naturally, according to the wishes of the property owner. Do the same with firewood. Scatter natural materials used for ground beds instead of leaving them piled. Carefully replace sod removed for any purpose. Except for trampled grass, there should be no trace of your having camped in the site. Inspect! OK? Now strike and pack the dining fly. Heist your packs and move out.

6 WOODS TOOLS

". . . AND WITH TRUSTY KNIFE AND AX he hewed his way through the wilderness!" Sound familiar? True, many a pioneer did just that. Today, though, you'd better go slow with that idea. Not that the knife and ax aren't trusty as ever—it's this wilderness isn't what it used to be . . . someone may not be too keen about your hewing your way through what's left of it.

But let's not forget what the knife and ax are all about. They're part of our heritage, as well as our basic woods tools. The saw belongs with them, too, for our earliest colonists had saws. Anyone relying on wood as fuel knows a saw is the only tool to keep the woodshed full. That's true today, and the smart camper uses saw *and* ax *and* knife in working up his firewood. You have some advantages over the pioneer, though.

What the "trusty" really meant was that the old-timer picked the best tools he could get and, more important, knew how to use them. He was dependent on them day-in day-out, so if they weren't good they didn't last long. An old guide bragged on his ax: "That there is a *real* good ax! She's had nine handles and three heads!" And no doubt it had.

Quality in a knife, an ax, or a saw—or any other tool—has to be judged on proper design, suitable material, and honest workmanship. To the expert, just "hefting" a tool—trying its weight and balance—and running an eye along its edge tells him a lot. The maker's name may influence his opinion—some—but the test will be in the using: will the knife take and hold a keen edge, does the ax hang right and swing true, can a saw bite deep and smooth and not chatter or run out of the cut?

There are many makes and patterns for each of these basic woods tools. Some are favored in one locality, foreign in another; some best for one kind of wood or certain special uses. And, of course, there are always cut-priced imitations of the real thing. Shun them; the price is *never* right for a poor tool. Don't be tempted by the gawdy novelty—the all-purpose tool really good for no one purpose. Stick to the tried and true.

knives

Of man's crudest tools, the knife is still one of the most useful, especially in the primitive environment of camps, what with daily fires to be built, food to be prepared, rope to be cut, items to be repaired, and useful articles to be made. The knife is a sharp wedge good for severing or for planing off thin strips of materials softer than that of the knife. Blunt or nicked, the knife can do only a crude job at best and is a hazard to the work, the worker, and bystanders. Most knives are sold with a coarse, machine-made edge; the smart owner immediately refines this with stone and strop to a smooth, thin edge that will show not at all when held edgewise to the light. Draw it lightly across the edge of a sheet of paper—a proper knife will cut it smoothly. Keep the blade keen and clean; keep it dry and don't stick it in the ground; keep it out of fire. Clean dust and grit from slot of a folding knife and oil joint and spring now and then. Keep folding knives folded, sheath knives sheathed when idle. Don't throw or fool with knives—this is hard on knives . . . and people!

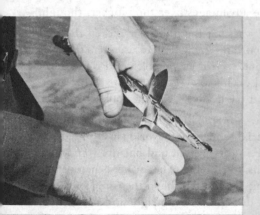

For cutting only—this major blade of famed Scout knife. It takes and holds a keen edge for fine-to-medium work. To save this blade from abuse (and basis of reputation as most useful outdoor tool) this knife has separate leather awl, screwdriver-bottle opener, and can-opener blades. Shackle is for lanyard or belt clip.

Carving of useful or decorative articles is possible with the Scout knife; however, the special whittling knife or the Handi-Kraft Knife with curved blades would be more practical.

68

Any knife is safer, will work better when kept keen. Use coarse stone to shape blade, remove nicks; fine stone gives final shape to edge. Oil lubricates, keeps stone from clogging with metal bits. Use push-pull strokes.

As edge gets thin, a flexible "wire edge" may form. This must be removed lest it break off and spoil the edge. Finish edge by stropping on hone made of 180-grit cloth stretched over rubber pad on wood strip. This wears off wire edge leaving good, hard edge. For delicate carving, use 400-grit. A mirror finish comes with stropping on denim or leather on back of stick. This is commonly called a slipstick.

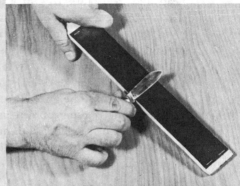

Patterned on skinning knives of trappers and hunters, the sheath knife has more romantic appeal than practical value for most people. Because it is at hand and does not need to be opened, it is fine around camp kitchens when you can't reach fork, spatula, or a cook's knife. Wear it over hip pocket — never at the front — for safety.

If kept sharp, sheath knife is useful for slicing. Shape of blade makes a draw stroke work better than a sawing motion. Keep it sheathed when not in use—don't stick it in tables or trees.

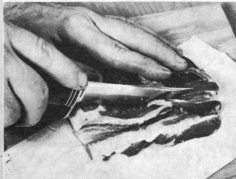

axes

Unless you're cutting big logs for a project, the small *pack ax* is about the best for camp chores—mainly firewood. Light, yet heavy enough to be worth carrying, the 1¼-pound head has real authority in expert hands—correction—*hand*. It's a *one*-hand tool, clumsy and dangerous otherwise. (If you just can't use it with one hand, stick to a saw!) On the other hand, the *three-quarter ax* is a *two*-hand ax. The greater weight and longer helve requires the control only possible using both hands and a free swing. It is designed for medium-duty work.

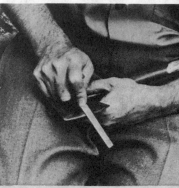

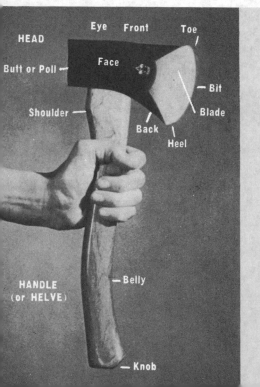

HEAD — Eye — Front — Toe
Butt or Poll — Face — Bit
Shoulder — Blade
Back — Heel
HANDLE (or HELVE) — Belly
Knob

The names for the parts of an ax are the same for pack ax or three-quarter. These names are useful for clearly describing the part of the tool you are talking about. It's really not so important to be able to talk about any tool, though, as to know what it is for, how to use it, and how to take proper care of it.

If your ax has a wooden handle, keep the head on tight with proper wedging; and, if the wood dries out, swell it with linseed oil or a commercial preparation. Sand down nicks or scratches that may raise blisters and keep it free of pitch or gum that may do the same. Replace warped helves at once.

70

When your ax is dull, you can sharpen it with an 8-inch file. Cradle the ax in your lap and run the file away from you over the toe of the bit, working an inch of the bit at a time toward the heel. When the edge of the blade is bright, turn the ax over and work from heel to toe. Then draw the bit across a piece of wood to remove wire edge. See page 538 for method to use at home between trips.

When not in use, the ax should be masked. Don't let the open end of a sheath lead you to using your ax as a hammer. The business end of the axhead is the bit and the handle is shaped in that direction only. Your ax was made to cut wood or split it. Use a rock or a chunky piece of wood to drive pegs or stakes. When using the ax, mask it temporarily in a log—handle inward. Never drive your ax into a live tree to mask it. Always keep your ax off the ground.

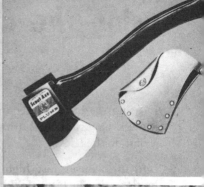

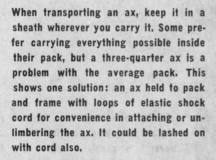

When transporting an ax, keep it in a sheath wherever you carry it. Some prefer carrying everything possible inside their pack, but a three-quarter ax is a problem with the average pack. This shows one solution: an ax held to pack and frame with loops of elastic shock cord for convenience in attaching or unlimbering the ax. It could be lashed on with cord also.

71

using the ax

In using the hand ax, keep in mind that brute force is not necessary. It is the keenness of the cutting edge and the weight of the axhead behind it that do the trick.

Lift the axhead just high enough with a smooth wrist-and-forearm motion, aim the bit by looking at the point where you want it to hit, then let the axhead fall in a guided drop. Easy does it!

Before starting to chop or split, get yourself a chopping block. This can be a tree stump or the thickest piece of downed wood you have found. Then, when chopping and splitting, make use of the contact method. In this, you keep the bit of the ax and the wood you want to cut in contact with each other throughout the cutting, bringing both of them down against the chopping block at the same time.

For CHOPPING a stick by the contact method, set the ax bit on about a 45 degree slant to the stick and raise the stick and the ax together . . .

. . . then bring them down together onto the chopping block. A stick should come apart in one cut; a branch may take more, depending upon its thickness.

72

If you need to cut a thick branch in two, use a V-shaped cut. The idea is to make the top of the V as wide as the thickness of the branch.

"Strike four!" Four cuts only — and the result should be a perfectly square, pointed tent peg — if you have reached that point in your training.

Cut brush by bending it with one hand, thus straining the grain. A quick, slanting blow close to the ground will then make it come apart easily.

In SPLITTING, place the bit parallel to the grain in the end of the stick — in a crack if there is one. You will then lift the stick and ax together . . .

. . . bring the stick and ax down on the chopping block together. Just as they hit, twist the ax slightly — this will tend to break the wood pieces apart.

lopping and logging

LOPPING or "limbing" is the process of removing branches. Always chop toward the top of the tree—if you strike down into the crotch your ax will very likely stick. Stand on the side of the trunk opposite the branches being cut.

LOGGING or "bucking" is the term for cutting a tree trunk into suitable lengths. Logging is done with two "flying cuts," each as wide as the tree is thick. Make the first of these two cuts to the center of the tree . . .

. . . then make a similar flying cut from the other side of the tree. If your log is very heavy, make the cut with a series of three strokes — at the top, bottom, and in the middle. Done in this way, your ax will not stick.

Aim to have a neat-looking cut when the two parts separate.

74

You can make eight tent pegs from one chunk of wood. Split each quarter piece of wood in half.

Rest the piece on the log, bark side down, and clip the top to prevent splitting the notch when the peg is driven into the ground.

Tap the blade across the edge to make a crosscut for the top of the notch. Cut halfway through.

Rest the peg on the log and slice down to the crosscut to finish the notch. Shave the other end to a blunt point. If your ax won't cut wood like this, see page 539.

felling a tree

When it comes to using a felling ax, there are a couple of points you need to consider beyond the rules you follow in using a hand ax:

• *Clear the ground an ax-length around.* An "ax-length" is the combined length of your arm and your ax. Anything in the way of the ax when you swing it may catch and deflect it; and it may end up in your leg instead of in the tree.

• *Onlookers stay two ax-lengths away*—not just so they won't get hit by the ax, but so they will be safely away from flying chips.

• *Hit the same spot again and again.* Whether felling a tree or chopping a log, the work calls for cutting V-shaped notches into the wood; and those require numerous hits, one on top of the other. It's only by practice that you will learn to hit the same spot repeatedly, at an even rhythm, cutting out large chunks of wood each time.

• *Rest when you are tired.* You have no control over your ax when you are tired; and an ax out of control is a dangerous weapon.

Before felling a tree, decide where you want it to fall. It is advisable to fell it in the direction in which it is leaning. Find this lean by dangling the ax in front of you, using it as a plumb line.

Before you start cutting, remember the rule: "Clear the ground an ax-length around." Remove underbrush and overhanging branches within reach of your ax so that they will not catch hold of it and cause it to deflect.

76

Grab the helve of the ax with both hands near the knob. Extend your arms and touch axhead to tree to get the distance. Bring the ax up and slide your left hand about three-quarters of the way up the helve, bringing the ax well up over the shoulder. Keep your eyes fixed on the spot you intend to hit. Swing the ax down, sliding the left hand down the helve until it touches the right hand.

The felling is done with two "box cuts." The top of a box cut should slope down into the tree at a 45-degree angle; the bottom should be almost horizontal. Make the first of the two box cuts on the leaning side of the tree (top picture), close to the ground.

Make second box cut (photo just above) on the opposite side of the tree, slightly higher up. Cut downward with a straight stroke. Cut horizontally with same kind of stroke, but with twist of your shoulder.

When tree begins to totter, yell "Timber-r-r-r!" and run to the side. Occasionally, a tree, in falling, overrides the stump toward the last box cut you made. So be alert and move into the clear when the tree falls to the ground.

saws

Novices may admire the skill and grace needed for good axmanship, but the real timberbeast knows that for serious felling and bucking the saw is a champion tool. The old two-man crosscut, though, is heavy and unwieldy except in expert hands and difficult to pack. The Swedish bow saw with its ribbon blade under tension changed all that—the saw is now a very practical tool for the camper. It is light to carry, highly efficient, and enables neat, precise cutting. It is safer, tidier, and less wasteful than the ax, even for beginners.

Saws are great for felling trees — as lumbermen from Paul Bunyan on all know. The work goes fast with a minimum of sweat and chips and both stump and butt are neat. Get rid of nearby saplings or pesky stump sprouts that may catch the saw. Cut close to ground on the falling side, then back-cut higher.

Limbing is smoother with a saw. Cut so weight of limb doesn't bind saw in the kerf. If it does, you may spoil the blade by kinking it—if it slows down, stop and get the blade out immediately. To limb a standing tree, undercut first, then cut from top. Don't try to saw branches under ½ inch thick—they'll snag saw.

Bucking is simple with saw—just don't bind saw. Even small stems will pinch, so hold or prop one end up so cut wood will fall clear. Don't dig saw into dirt.

For simpler bucking, use a sawbuck of some kind, even two stakes driven into the ground and lashed for a cradle. One higher than this one would make for easier work.

Even the small Scout pack saw does a surprisingly good job on occasional cutting, although the 21-inch bow saw is better for working up a woodpile. The pack saw folds to stow in pocket or pack and masks its own teeth; the blade is locked in place with a spring pin and wing nut. Blade is replaceable.

The traveling safety saw uses the same blade as the bow saw—even carries two extra blades in the frame. Unfolded, the blade is held under tension with a screw device, and it is used exactly like the familiar "Swede fiddle" bow saw. Folded, the saw takes little space in the pack and blade is safe. Great for backpackers.

Those teeth can bite; be very wary and keep hands away from the blade whether the saw is in use or you are just carrying it or storing it. For packing or storage, mask the bow saw with a piece of slit rubber—not plastic—hose tied or taped in place on the blade.

Carry masked saw inside large pack or strap it to frame or outside of small pack. Rubber shock cord can be used for convenience, but simple lashing will do.

dovetail notch

When you must hold two pieces of wood together, and you don't have rope for lashing and there are no nails or wire, you can do it with a dovetail notch. The dovetail joint, as you know, is a familiar cabinet-maker's trick. However, you don't have to be a skilled carpenter to make this dovetail notch. Four cuts by a saw and a few strokes with your knife to pry out the wood in the notch is all there is to it. The notch will hold slender unshaped round sticks for quick work and thicker tight-fitting dovetails for heavy loads.

Make a cut with the saw that slants to your right, not quite halfway through the pole. Avoid knots (a branch is a knot). Begin the notch in from the end of the pole to prevent splitting when the dovetail is driven in tight.

Now make an equal cut to the left. Notice that the cuts are almost at a right angle to each other. On thicker pieces the notch angle can be sharper.

Cut straight down to the depth of the side cuts and make another vertical cut to one side of the first.

The side cuts outline the dovetail and the center cuts break up the fibers so your knife can pry them out.

Pry out the wood in the notch, first on one side and then on the other. If you haven't cut into a knot, the wood should chip out easily.

The cleaned-out notch is ready for a fitting—round stick or dovetail.

With the piece to be fitted held over the notch, shape the base and sides. Make the end a little smaller than the notch.

Drive the dovetail into the notch until it jams. If you wish a very rigid joint—one that will support a heavy load—shape this dovetail some more so that it fits through the notch.

file your saw

The bow saw or the safety-folding saw works just fine when it's sharp. With a little bit of practice you can develop a skill to keep your saw sharp. Of course, you can buy a new blade when your saw refuses to zip through the wood. However, the blade you throw away can be sharpened easily. All you need is a 5-inch ignition file. That's not a specialty item only good for one job. This light little file fits into your pocket and will sharpen most anything that needs an edge from pocketknife to ax.

Hold the saw in your lap and look at the blade; notice that the teeth are in sets of four. The second tooth and the fourth tooth are filed. Turn the saw over and look at the other side and you'll see that again the second and the fourth tooth are filed from that side. There are 15 sets of four and usually only the teeth in the middle of the blade need attention. That's about eight sets and you can do the job in a few minutes.

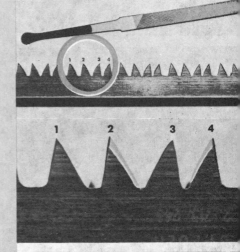

With the saw across your knees, hold the blade in your left hand and tip it up slightly, pressing down with your thumb and pushing up with your index and middle fingers. File the second tooth in each set. Keep the same angle. You'll see the metal brighten, which will guide you as you work. Only a few short, forward strokes of the file are needed.

Turn the saw over and repeat the process for the other side. File only on the forward strokes.

Now, hold one end of the saw and rest the other end on the ground or a bench. Slant the saw a little to the left and file the fourth tooth in each set.

Turn the saw end for end and repeat the process for the other side. It won't take you very long to become an expert. You'll soon be able to tell whether a saw needs sharpening by looking at it.

7 ROPEWORK

ROPE IS ESSENTIAL to many outdoor activities, and the fellow who is unfamiliar with its qualities and use is sadly handicapped. It's a basic in camp making, sailing, water-skiing, mountaineering, trail riding, and pioneering—and very useful in many other pursuits. Experts in the use of rope make it all look so simple that it's easy to overlook their careful choice of just the right kind and size of rope and type of knot or lashing for the job at hand. But they know it's *their* neck, and they wouldn't risk it without confidence in proper rope and knot.

Only a fool or a greenhorn figures any old rope or any old knot will do. Ropes are made of vegetable, animal, or mineral fibers skillfully combined to get maximum strength, flexibility, and uniformity for specific purposes. Its adaptability can fool you—you're tempted to consider only whether it's *long* enough, especially if you don't know rope.

Now common sense is often a poor substitute for real knowledge; what you don't know *may* hurt you. A nice thick rope may be rotten to the core. That thin, strong nylon may slice your hands as it slips through. Manila is the standard fiber, but it does rot if mistreated; sisal is less costly, but is coarse; nylon stretches, Dacron doesn't—is that good or bad? Binder twine is for binders; it's abominable for other uses.

In backwoods engineering—*pioneering,* if you will—rope is essential; it is ideal for fastening the odd sizes and awkward shapes of logs used for temporary or semipermanent structures. Pioneering, by the way, is *not* playing at Dan'l Boone—the word refers to the work of old-time military engineers who slipped ahead of an army on foot to build bridges and roads—like our Seabees. They got there first, often in the wilderness, and made do with what they could find or carry. With an ax and rope they could do wonders. The logs were there, and rope they could carry or make. Naturally, *you* won't just cut logs on the spot for your projects without written permission from the landowner—but judicious cutting can actually improve a woodlot, so a cooperative owner might let you have the makings for a bridge or tower.

rope

Rope ordinarily used is made of manila, sisal, or synthetic fibers. Cotton and other vegetable yarns are also used—clothesline, sash cord, mason's line, and the like—but are inferior though widely obtainable. As mentioned, manila is the standard against which others are measured. But if synthetics overcome some defects of manila—such as rotting—they do have their own shortcomings or peculiarities. All good rope is a major investment worthy of careful maintenance. Keep it clean and free of mud or grease. Replace worn spots by splicing. Uncoil and coil it properly and watch for kinks. Prevent its untwisting or frazzling with whipping. Above all, "red tag" all rope unsafe for normal use or loading. The safe use of rope can only come with *learning* rope.

LAID ROPE. Natural and synthetic fibers are often twisted into yarns, the yarns into strands, and then the strands twisted into ropes in such a way that the twists are equalized so the rope is stable but flexible. This is called "laying." This construction permits using the shorter lengths of natural fibers to make uniformly strong rope, but it's fine for synthetics, too. Such rope comes from twine size up to ship's hawser size. Sizes are given in diameters or circumferences according to custom in certain usages.

WOVEN ROPE. Synthetic fibers are often woven or braided into line or rope in smaller diameters.

SASH CORD or **CLOTHESLINE** is woven of cotton and glazed with starch or other filler. It is unreliable and clumsy for pioneering. **BINDER TWINE** is unsuitable and should be avoided.

The strength of rope in a given situation is a complex calculation. Before you risk *your* neck, or anybody else's, with bridges, towers, slings, or manropes, you'd better bone up on it. The pioneering projects outlined specify safe rope sizes *provided* your rope is fairly new and in good condition, without kinks or knots from faulty coiling.

APPROXIMATE BREAKING STRENGTH (*In Pounds Dead Weight*)

Diameter (inches)	Sisal	Manila	Polypropylene	Dacron	Nylon
1/4	480	600	1050	1600	1800
3/8	1080	1350	2200	3300	4000
1/2	2120	2650	3800	5500	7100
3/4	4320	5400	8100	11000	14200
1	7200	9000	14000	18500	24600

You can see that great variation in the same size rope made of different fibers. All of them seem very adequate for the average use, so why go to great expense to buy the larger sizes and more expensive materials?

Well, the *safe working load* of a new rope is only one-quarter of the breaking strength, and with average rope you'd better figure only one-sixth with a steady strain. Jerking the rope or dropping the load will *double* the strain. Any knots or splices to lengthen the rope will reduce its strength by a certain amount (that pesky overhand knot that somehow just slipped in will cut it by more than half!)

Now, looking at the chart and roughly thinking over the weight of the fellows in your outfit, you might think that 600-pound break-strength manila, that is, 1/4 inch, ought to be plenty strong for general use. Maybe so, but suppose you decided to lower a 125-pound boy over a cliff; would it be safe? Probably not. If brand new, the rope would have a safe working load of 125 pounds—but with no knots . . . what good is that? Knots put the rope in shear—that's how knots work—and that shearing action tends to break the fibers or weaken them tremendously. An *overhand knot* reduces rope strength to 45 percent of normal. A *bowline* or a *square knot* will halve the strength. A *sheet bend* or a *bowline on a bight* leaves your rope at 60 percent efficiency. *Splicing* is the best way to join ropes as it cuts the strength only 5 to 10 percent, but of course ropes nearly always have to have knots in them for other reasons. So instead of 1/4-inch rope, even new, it would be best to go to 3/8 inch or better.

using rope

To make rope do what *you* want it to do—like staying put or forming a noose or joining another rope—you use only *three* ways of arranging it; all knots, bends, and hitches are merely combinations of *bights, loops,* and *overhand knots.* Think of ropework in these terms and it'll come a bit easier! Avoid frazzled rope ends by *whipping* them—that helps too.

BIGHT. A bight is formed by turning the rope end so that the end and the standing part (the rest of the rope) lie alongside each other. A square knot consists of two interwoven bights.

LOOP. A loop is made by crossing the rope end under or over the standing part. A sheet bend is made up of a bight and a loop; so is a bowline. A clove hitch consists of two loops.

OVERHAND KNOT. An overhand knot is a loop through which the rope end has been passed. A slipknot is an overhand knot tied around a rope. A timber hitch and two half hitches are variations of an overhand knot.

WHIPPINGS are laid around ends of ropes to keep them from unraveling. Ordinary thin twine may be used, but waxed sail twine or electrician's twine is better.

AMERICAN WHIPPING. Make a loop in a 3-foot length of twine and place it at the end of the rope with one end of the twine pointing in the same direction as the rope end, the other pointing the opposite way. Wrap twine tightly around rope, starting about $\frac{1}{2}$ inch from the rope end. Continue until whipping is as wide as rope is thick. Pull the two ends out to either side. Cut off ends of twine near whipping.

SAILMAKER'S WHIPPING. Unlay the rope 2 inches. Make a bight in a 3-foot length of twine and place it around one of the strands. Re-lay the rope. Wind the twine tightly around the rope end for a sufficient number of turns. Carry the bight originally formed back over the end of the same strand around which it was laid. Pull twine ends tight and tie them with a square knot between the rope ends. Trim ends of twine.

Synthetic fiber rope can be prevented from unraveling by fusing the ends with a flame or a hot iron. Beware of the dripping hot synthetic! In an emergency, an overhand knot in a line will keep it from unraveling.

89

SQUARE KNOT. Put the two rope ends together, left over right, and twist the lefthand one behind and around in front of the righthand one.

Bring the ends up and even with each other. Now place the end in your right hand over the other and twist it behind and down through the bight.

Grasp both ends with fingers and thumbs and pull ends out to form the knot. (To loosen the square knot, push the ends toward each other—or "upset" the knot by pulling back on one end, then pull the other end through the loops.)

knots for joining

The most popular knots for joining two ends of two ropes or lines are the square knot, the sheet bend, and the fisherman's knot.

The *square knot* is used for tying two thin ropes of *equal* size together. It is *always* used in first aid for tying bandages. It is called square because it seems to have four "sides" to it.

The *sheet bend* has its greatest value for joining ropes of *different* thicknesses, but it is equally good for joining ropes of the same thickness. It got its name from its use by sailors to bend (attach) the sheet (the ropes used to rig a ship).

The *fisherman's knot* is used by fishermen to join strands of gut. It is one of the best knots for tying *fine* lines together.

SHEET BEND. Form a bight on the end of the heavier rope and hold this firmly in your left hand. You will then pass the end of the thinner rope from below up through the bight.

Bring the end of the thinner rope over, around, and under the bight, then slip it under its own standing part where this enters the bight. (Note that both rope ends are on the same side.)

Hold the bight with one hand and tighten the sheet bend by pulling in the other rope's standing part. (The sheet bend is easily untied by straightening the bight and pulling the other rope over it.)

FISHERMAN'S KNOT. Tie an overhand knot in one of the ropes (or lines), but do not pull it taut. Pass the other rope end through this overhand knot and alongside the first rope's standing part.

Tie an overhand knot in the second rope around the standing part of the first rope. Pull each of the two overhand knots taut separately.

Pull the whole knot taut by pulling in the two standing parts thereby interlocking the two overhand knots. (To untie the fisherman's knot, pull the two overhand knots away from each other and untie each separately.)

SLIPKNOT. Throw the rope in a large loop over the item around which you wish the slipknot to be tied.

Tie the end of the rope around the standing part with an overhand knot. (It will be more secure if an overhand knot was first tied in the end itself.)

Pull the overhand knot taut. Then push it up against the item to be tied and tighten the whole knot by pulling the standing part.

knots for loops

Sometimes you may want to throw a loop — a "running" loop or noose or a permanent loop — around something. For this you use a slipknot, a taut-line hitch, or a bowline.

The most common use for the *slipknot* is for tying a string around a package or for tying up a rolled-up tent.

The *taut-line hitch,* as the name suggests, can be tied on a line that is taut. When used for tying a tent guy line, you can tighten or loosen the line by pushing the hitch up or down on the standing part.

The *bowline* (pronounced bō-lin) is fundamentally a rescue knot that you tie around yourself or throw to someone who needs a lifeline. The knot was originally used to tie a line in the bow of a ship.

TAUT-LINE HITCH. Pass rope around the peg, then bring the end over and under the standing part and twice through the loop formed.

Make another turn with the rope end around the standing part by bringing the rope end over, under, and through loop formed.

Work the hitch until it is taut around the standing part. The hitch can be moved by pushing it up and down the standing part.

BOWLINE. Place the end on the standing part. With a twist of the hand, carry the end around, forming the loop in the standing part.

Bring the end around the standing part and down through the small loop just formed and alongside of its own continuation.

Tighten the bowline by holding on to the bight formed by the rope end and pulling hard in the standing part.

knots for attaching

The most commonly used knots—or hitches—for attaching a rope to a pole or some other kind of timber are the clove hitch, two half hitches, and the timber hitch.

The *clove hitch* is the most widely used and is an important knot for pioneering. You use it for starting and finishing most lashings. It probably got its name from the Dutch word *kloof* that means "cleft"—it seems to be cleft or divided into two parts.

Two half hitches are good for fastening a rope to a post or a ring.

The *timber hitch* is another pioneering knot. It is used when two timbers need to be "sprung" together. It is also fine for raising logs, for dragging them over the ground, or for pulling them through water.

CLOVE HITCH. Pass the rope end in front of the pole and around it. Then bring the end forward over its own standing part.

Pass the rope end once more around the pole below the first turn. Then bring the end in under the rope itself.

Tighten the clove hitch by pulling hard on the end and the standing part of the rope after first pushing the loops close together.

TWO HALF HITCHES. Pass the end of the rope around the pole, then over and under its standing part and through the loop formed.

Make the second half hitch in front of the first by repeating the process of bringing the rope end over, under, and through the loop formed.

Push the two half hitches close together and up against the pole. Then by pulling in the standing part you will tighten everything.

TIMBER HITCH. Pass the end of the rope around the pole, then under and over its own standing part and through the loop thus formed.

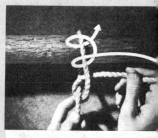

Make a bend near the rope end and twist the end a number of times around the part of the rope next to it.

Push the timber hitch firmly up against the pole. Then make it taut by pulling hard in the standing part.

95

other knots

Don't imagine that the knots shown here are the only ones in existence. Over the years hundreds of knots have been invented for joining ropes or attaching them to other objects. Many are ideal for given purposes—often reflected by their names—but others are useful generally. No matter what they are called, they're all *knots, bends,* or *hitches.*

Properly, a *knot* is a knob made in a rope to serve as a stopper—such as a figure eight or an overhand knot—but the term is used very loosely. A *bend* is a way of fastening one rope to another (or to a ring) by passing the rope through a loop and fastening it back to itself.

A *hitch* is a temporary noose made by tying a rope to itself or around a timber, usually to anchor the rope or to tether an animal or boat. As there are special knots for special purposes, there are sometimes different names given by different trades to the same knot; for example, a sheet bend, weaver's knot, and weaver's hitch are the same thing.

SHEEPSHANK is used to shorten a rope temporarily without cutting it. It holds only as long as there is sufficient strain on it.

ROLLING or MAGNUS HITCH is tied like the taut-line hitch to attach rope to a stave, pipe, or another rope. Won't slip easily.

STEVEDORE'S KNOT is one of the stopper knots. It is used, for instance, to keep a rope from being pulled through a pulley.

96

CARRICK BEND is the best knot for joining heavy, stiff ropes. The ends should be lashed to the cord standing part with string.

BOWLINE ON A BIGHT may be tied in the middle or at the end of a rope. It is superior to the regular bowline in an emergency.

PIPE HITCH is thrown around a pipe that you want to pull vertically out of the ground. The hitch itself is tied just like two half hitches.

HITCHING TIE is a good knot for fastening a halter rope to a post or ring. It doesn't work loose, yet is very easily untied when no longer needed.

MILLER'S KNOT is a valuable one for tying up sacks of grain in a mill or on the farm, and it is closely related to the clove hitch.

LARIAT LOOP as a running knot turns an ordinary rope into a lariat. It's an overhand knot with the end put through, then pulled tight.

97

splicing

Splices are used to mend a damaged rope or to fasten one rope to another. A good splice has up to 95 percent of the rope's strength, while a knot's efficiency varies from only 45 to 60 percent of the rope. The *long splice* allows a rope to run through a block, and should be made only with two ropes of the same size; however, the long splice is time consuming to make and uses up considerable rope. The *short splice* is the strongest way to join two ropes, can be made quickly, and involves little rope waste—the disadvantage is that it cannot pass through a block. The *eye splice* is used in the end of a rope for mooring, or in place of the honda knot for lariat making. The eye splice is the strongest rope loop. In splicing synthetics, add at least one extra tuck per strand.

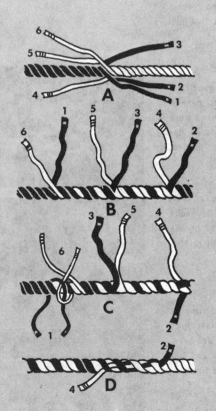

THE LONG SPLICE. A. Unlay each rope end about 15 turns and place ropes together, alternating strands of each end. **B.** Using opposite pairs, unlay one strand (4) and fill its place with its "partner" strand (2). Repeat operation exactly with another pair of strands (1 and 6) in opposite direction. **C.** Trim the longer strand (4) and tie each pair of opposing strands (2 and 4) with an overhand knot, tucking each strand twice. The tuck goes over one strand, under the second, and out between the second and third. Strands 3 and 5 are simply tied with an overhand knot. Strands 1 and 6 are halved, and opposite strands are tied with an overhand before tucking. **D.** Roll and pound tucks into the rope and clip the strand ends.

98

THE EYE SPLICE.

A. Unlay the strands for a short distance and double the rope back to form a loop, with the unlaid ends pointing across the lay of the rope. **B.** Take one of the ends and tuck it under any of the main strands. Arrange the next one to it on the loop side across the rope and push the third one behind out of the way. **C.** Take the second one under the next strand to the first one, going in where the first one comes out. **D.** Turn the splice over. There is one end left, and one main strand without an end strand under it. The end does not have to go in the way it is pointing, but must go under the strand against the lay, so that it is pointing the same way around the rope as the other ends. See that all three ends come out level with each other and are equally tensioned. Tuck each end again, over one and under one, in the same way as in the back splice. Even up the tension, then tuck once more. Taper a further tuck, if you wish, and roll smooth between two boards or under your shoe.

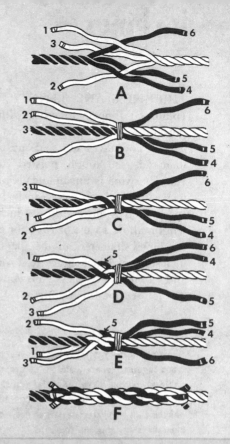

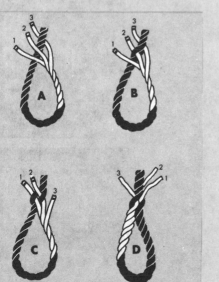

THE SHORT SPLICE.

A. Unlay each rope a few turns and alternate the strands. **B.** Tie the strands down to prevent further unlaying. **C.** Tuck one strand (1) over an opposing strand, and under the next strand. **D.** The tuck of strand 2 goes over the first strand 5, under the second, and out between the second and third. **E.** Repeat operation with the other two strands (1 and 3) from same rope end. **F.** Remove tie and repeat operation on other rope end. Make two more tucks for each strand, roll tucks, clip ends.

lashings

THICKNESS AND LENGTH. When lashing (binding) timbers together with rope, it's important to use ropes of correct thickness and length. For staves and spars up to 1¼ inches in diameter, use tough twisted or braided line (binder twine is unsuitable). For spars up to 3 inches in diameter, use ¼-inch line or rope. For spars over 3 inches, use ⅜-inch rope. As for length, allow 1 yard of rope for each inch of the combined diameters of the spars. For example: in lashing a 3-inch brace to a 4-inch leg, add 3 and 4 to make 7 inches. Thus you need 7 yards or 21 feet of rope for lashing.

Knowing how to attach two pieces of wood together securely and at the proper angle gives you a real advantage in the woods. You can then make things for convenience, to meet emergencies, or sometimes just for the fun of it.

SQUARE LASHING is started with a clove hitch around the upright, immediately under the spot where crosspiece is to be.

DIAGONAL LASHING begins with a timber hitch around the two timbers at the point of crossing, springing, or binding them together.

Twist the end of the rope into the standing part, then "wrap" the rope around crosspiece and upright binding them together.

Take three turns around both timbers, alongside the timber hitch. Place turns beside each other, not on top of each other.

In wrapping, rope goes on outside of previous turn around crosspiece, on inside of previous turn around the upright.

Take three more turns, this time crosswise to the previous turns. Strain each turn to be sure of getting a taut lashing.

After three or four right wrapping turns, make two or three "frapping" turns between the timbers. Strain them tightly.

Make a couple of frapping turns between the timbers, around the diagonal lashing turns. Pull them as taut as you can.

Finish with clove hitch around end of crosspiece. Remember: "Start with clove; wrap thrice; frap twice; end with clove."

ALL lashings finish with clove hitch. In the case of diagonal lashing, hitch may be laid around any convenient timber.

Shear lashings are used when the construction calls for "shears" or "shear legs" of two timbers with their butt ends spread apart. *Tripod lashings* are made in the same way as shear lashings, except that three timbers are used and two frappings are made to separate the timbers, one from the one next to it.

If the flooring for a bridge or a platform is to consist of a few crosspieces only, you can use square lashings for fastening them to the stringers. But if you intend to lay a complete floor, you'll be better off using *floor lashings*.

TRIPOD LASHING. Place three timbers next to each other and attach rope to outside leg with clove hitch at proper place.

Bind poles with seven or eight loose wrapping turns and two frapping turns between the poles to form the hinge pivots.

Finish off lashing with clove hitch on the other outside leg. Spread the legs to proper positions for use.

102

SHEAR LASHING. Place the two timbers next to each other. Tie clove hitch around one of them, at right place from top.

FLOOR LASHING. In floor lashing, start with clove hitch around stringer on which the flooring spars are to be laid.

Make a pigtail of the running and standing ends of the rope and pull it snugly over the first spar of the flooring.

Bind the two timbers together by laying seven or eight turns of the rope around them, loosely, one turn beside the other.

Pull a bight under the stringer and up between the first two spars and slip the bight over the end of the first spar.

Make two frapping turns around the lashing turns between the timbers. Fasten rope with clove hitch around either timber.

Now pull rope under the stringer and up over the second spar—on the outside of the stringer—then repeat third step.

Open out the timbers. NOTE: Two shear lashings without frappings are used to lash two timbers into one long one.

Continue this way until all spars have been laid firmly in place. Finish the lashing with a clove hitch around the stringer.

pioneering

With your knots and lashings down pat, you're ready for one of the most exciting outdoor crafts going: *pioneering*—building structures of timbers for practical purposes. It tests many skills, including teamwork.

Probably your first try ought to be a simple project—but you may get your gang really steamed up by the notion of a bridge to avoid a long walk around a gully, stream, or pond on your campsite. So bridge it!

You'll need timbers 3 to 4 inches thick at the butt, reasonably straight, sound, and not too springy. See "Lashings" for proper ropes to use.

LOCK BRIDGES are used for spanning streams with steeply sloping sides. If the stream is narrow, use a single-lock bridge (top right), consisting of two trestles and two roadways. For a wider stream, build a double-lock bridge (center) in which the two trestles that are placed in the water are locked into a horizonal trestle that carries the center section of the roadway.

TRESTLE BRIDGES are used to span fairly wide streams with shallow beds and gently sloping sides. The trestles are of different heights, depending on the depth of the water at various points. Bridge is constructed by placing first trestle, lashing two "road bearers" to the top of it, and anchoring the other ends of the bearers to the bank. Other trestles are then placed in the water and connected with road bearers.

single-lock bridge

A pioneer bridge is an honest-to-goodness engineering job. It requires careful planning and good workmanship.

The single-lock bridge is the simplest to construct. After you have made one of these, you should have no trouble building the others.

The two trestles of the single-lock bridge are built in such a way that the top of one fits into the top of the other as shown by the dotted lines in the diagram.

Notice also in the diagram that the slope of the legs of the wider trestle is "20 over 1." That is, for each 20 feet the trestle is high from ledger to transom each leg should slope in at the top 1 foot from the upright. If the trestle is 10 feet high, each leg should slope in ½ foot.

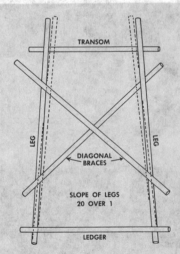

In making the trestles, notice that the transom and the ledger go on the opposite sides of the uprights. Also that while one diagonal brace has both ends on the same side of both uprights, the other diagonal has one end under one upright, and one end over the other upright.

As soon as you have built the two trestles, float them out in the water and raise them into position. Adjust them so that they face each other squarely and stand securely on either bank. Bring the tops together with transoms on the outside. Lock the narrow-topped trestle into the wider trestle. If bridge is intended for heavy traffic, lay a crosspiece in the V's formed by the uprights and lash it firmly into position.

Run two timbers (road bearers) from each bank to the transoms and secure them by lashings near the uprights. Lash crosspieces to road bearers about 2 feet apart (or lay a complete flooring of crosspieces, lashing them in place with floor lashings).

Roadway may be made from old boards or from saplings. Lash them down securely to the crosspieces. (If the bridge is to be more or less permanent, it is advisable to creosote the timbers and tar the lashings before you put the trestles in the water.)

monkey bridge

The monkey bridge consists of three ropes stretched over a river from two shear legs. This kind of bridge has the advantage over the usual pioneering bridge in that it can be used to span a much greater distance— up to 100 feet. To do a quick job, divide the gang into two teams; one to make the shear legs, the other to work on the ropes.

For shear legs, use two 12-foot logs, about 4 inches thick at the butt. Place the logs side by side with ends even. Lash them together 5 feet from top with shear lashing. Spread the legs apart. Lash a 4-foot crosspiece to the legs, 2 feet from butts, with square lashings.

Three manila ropes are required: one 1-inch foot rope and two ½-inch hand ropes, 30 feet longer than the stream is wide. Place them on ground, 4 feet apart, foot rope in the middle. Attach 9-foot "stringers" (¼-inch rope) to foot rope and hand ropes with clove hitches.

Drive three 3-foot stakes into the ground at 60-degree angles to act as holdfasts. Hammer them down in line with the bridge with their tops pointing away from the bridge. Tie the stakes together in pairs.

Put the rope assembly in place across the river and secure it temporarily to the holdfasts. Raise the shear legs with the butt ends in shallow holes to prevent shifting. Hold each shear leg upright with two guy lines from top of legs.

Make the pads of two pieces of burlap. Place them in the two shear crotches. Lay all three ropes up into the crotches. Lead ends of the foot rope in two turns around the first stakes on each side of the river, then tie them with two half hitches, pulling the rope taut.

Send two fellows up to stand in the two shear leg crotches, one on each side of the river. Attach one hand rope to one shear leg with clove hitch, then pull taut and fasten it to shear leg on opposite shore. Then tie the other hand rope in position in the same way.

Tie the ends of the hand ropes to the first stakes on each side of river with two turns and two half hitches. Then go over all the ropes, tightening them as much as possible — and your bridge is finished, ready for crossing.

signal tower

For a 20-foot tower, you will need:

Four uprights, 20 feet long, 4 inches thick at butt

Four lower crosspieces, 8 feet long, 4 inches thick

Four middle crosspieces, 6 feet 6 inches long, 3 inches thick

Four upper crosspieces, 5 feet long, 3 inches thick

Eight lower diagonals, 10 feet 6 inches long, 4 inches thick

Four upper diagonals, 8 feet long, 3 inches thick

Fifty-four 21-foot lengths of 1/4-inch or 5/16-inch rope, whipped at both ends, for lashing.

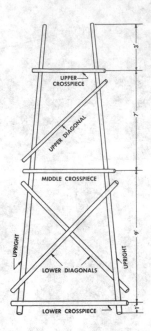

Get all necessary timbers together and arrange according to length for ease in handling. Peg down a string for a center line, then lay out one side of the signal, carefully following the diagram above.

Lash all the pieces together with square lashings, except where the two lower diagonals meet: Here the diagonal lashing is in order. To simplify the lashing, block up the timbers so that the lashing ropes can slip under them.

110

Make two sides. Prop them up facing each other, 7 feet apart at lower crosspiece, 4 feet at upper crosspiece. Lash them together temporarily with diagonal brace between them. Connect them by crosspieces and diagonals, following diagram used for original sides.

While you still have the tower resting on its side, lash the flooring pieces onto two opposite upper crosspieces to form a platform. Square lashings or floor lashing should be used here.

Now for the raising! Make a large loop in a rope and throw it over the tips of two of the uprights. Throw a similar loop over the other two. Lift tip of tower a few feet, then raise tower by one gang pulling in one rope, another gang holding back on the other.

It goes without saying that not a stick of timber is touched unless you have the owner's permission to cut it. Under proper guidance, a wood lot is not harmed but, on the contrary, improved when the right kind of cutting is done. When you know how, it is possible to improve a stand of timber and at the same time use the timbers for pioneering.

III

Fires 8

FIRE! This can be a word to express unbounded joy in the heart of the Tenderfoot learning the ancient process; it eases the anxiety of a wet woodsman shivering in the cold; it can strike terror in the vitals of city dweller and countryman alike when it rings out in alarm.

To primitive people fire was a god—as well it might be, for it raised them above animals and made civilization possible. The old Greeks regarded fire as a gift from the gods—or rather they said that Prometheus stole fire to give to the mortals he had created. At any rate, from time out of mind fire has been revered by man—even men who do not directly use it for warming themselves, cooking their food, lighting their way, melting their metals, or any of the basic needs. One has only to stare into the curling flames to be lost in formless dreams of comfort, comradeship, and security in the dark.

Our American pioneers used fire as their basic tool, as did their Indian predecessors. In places within our country fires burn today that were kindled hundreds of years ago. Indeed, fire was "borrowed," carried from the old homestead to the new hearths of young married people.

If you must eat, if you are wet or cold, if you wonder what crouches in the night nearby, if you would make tools, if you would signal to others, or just enjoy the close company of friends, you can use fire. And if you can provide fire *when* you need it, despite wind and weather, you're on the way to being a woodsman worthy of the name.

Technology—the kind that provides gas, electricity, and the exotic fuels that put rockets into their journeys to other worlds—has not entirely removed man from the need to know how to kindle a simple fire. The astronauts are thoroughly trained in starting fires with primitive means. (Most of them were Scouts, so they probably only needed refresher courses!) Fire! A trusty friend—and a terrible enemy. Constant vigilance is the key. Let the flames leap high, and spirits soar. But be sure, when it's time to turn in, your fire is out—*cold out!*

safe fires

Firesafety depends on three things: a safe spot for the fire, a safe fire, complete extinction of the fire after use.

Pick a spot in an open space more than 10 feet away from brush and the nearest tree. Then clear a 10-foot circle down to mineral dirt—free of dry leaves, dry grass, twigs, and pine needles.

On grassy soil cover the turf with a mound of mineral soil. Carry half of the dirt from the latrine pit. Replace when fire is out.

If ground is wet, build your fire on a floor of sticks or bark of dead trees. In winter, scrape the snow away before laying this floor.

WIND DIRECTION

Arrange tinder and a few sticks of kindling in the shape of a cone or Indian tepee or in one of the other ways shown in this chapter. Be sure to light the fire from the windward side, and close to the ground. You should be able to do your fire lighting with one match — certainly never with more than two.

FEED FROM LEE SIDE

Feed the fire lay from the lee side, first with small sticks, then gradually with larger sticks. Make your fire just large enough to meet your needs — that's one of the main secrets of proper fire building. The smaller the fire, the safer it is. REMEMBER: Once the fire is started it is criminal to leave it unattended.

114

10-FT

If you are using a pot for boiling, hang it as soon as the fire is started, making use of the flames. For a simple meal you can push a dingle stick into the ground to act as a crane. When fire has burned down to coals, it is suitable for frying.

DINGLE STICK

To extinguish the fire, kill all embers and douse all sticks with water. Sprinkling is more effective than pouring and requires less water to do the job effectively. Hold your hand on the remains to be sure the fire is "cold out." Then "garden" the dead coals into the ground. Replace the turf if you have dug it up.

115

SPRINKLE
DON'T POUR

materials for fires

You need three kinds of material for making a fire:

• *Tinder* — some kind of flammable material that will flare up when touched with the flame from a burning match.

• *Kindling* — thin branches or split wood that will catch the flame from the tinder and, in turn, ignite the heavier fuel.

• *Fuel* — for doing the real job of providing heat or light. This can range from thumb-thick branches for cooking a simple meal to heavy logs for keeping a fire going throughout a long night in winter camp.

The kind of tinder, kindling, and fuel you will use depends on the part of the country in which you live. By keeping your eyes open and by experimenting with native materials, you will quickly learn what to use.

TINDER. If you happen to be in a place where evergreens are the most prominent trees, look for the tiny dead twigs that seem to sprout right from the bark. The tips of the dead branches of many other kinds of trees are also usable. Spicebush and sassafras make good tinder.

In birch country, you have the ideal tinder. Peel a piece of bark from a DEAD tree—never off a live one. Light it, and you will find it burns furiously, wet or dry. Many old-time campers carry a tiny roll of birchbark in their packs.

If everything else is wet, split open a fairly thick dead log, and you are pretty certain to find it fairly dry in the center. Cut the center part into small sticks and "fuzz" them up, leaving the long shavings attached to them.

KINDLING. In dry weather, there are plenty of dry sticks on the ground. Dead branches still on the tree — the so-called "squaw wood" — are better. Break off a couple of handfuls of pencil-thin sticks for quick fire making.

FUEL. For fuel for preparing a simple meal, use the heavier pieces of squaw wood or dead branches from fallen trees. You can break it easily underfoot. If it only bends, it's too green for use.

Before starting a fire, line up the material you need: tinder, kindling, fuel. Have enough of everything on hand so that you do not have to leave your fire for more after you have once started it.

When you are camping for several days on the same spot, you'll need wood for campfires as well as for cooking fires. To keep your campsite neat and to have wood on hand, make a woodyard. Drive sticks into the ground a foot apart and place fuel neatly between them, sorted out in different sizes.

117

LEAN-TO FIRE LAY. You start this fire lay by pushing a green "lean-to stick" into the ground at a 30-degree angle. The top of the stick should point in the direction from which the wind comes.

Place a good amount of tinder well in under the lean-to stick. Then break the thin sticks, the dry weed stalks, and the other kindling into short lengths and lean them carefully against the lean-to stick.

Continue building up the fire lay by leaning thicker fuel sticks against the thinner kindling wood. Strike a match. Let it burn into a real flame while you cup your hands around it for protection. Apply it to the tinder.

quick fire making

It's a joy to see a real woodsman lay and light his fire. He knows exactly how much tinder and kindling to use. He knows exactly how to build up his fire lay to secure the best draft. And he knows how to light it with a single match. In a few moments he has it going and is ready to cook his meal or to settle down in front of it for a quiet hour of rest.

One of the most common mistakes in fire making is to lay the fire so that the fuel collapses the moment the tinder has burned out with the result that the small flame is smothered, and the fire maker has to start all over again. There are several different ways of preventing such a "calamity." They are known to every real outdoorsman. Here are three of them.

FIRE-STICK FIRE LAY. For this fire lay, you start by placing two small rocks on the ground, about 10 inches apart. If there are no rocks, use two thick sticks instead. Then lay a "fire stick" across the two rocks.

Push a large handful of dry tinder in under the fire stick. Next lean a number of thin kindling sticks against the lee side of the fire stick—that is, the side opposite to the direction from which the wind comes.

Build up the fire lay with thicker and thicker pieces of fuel wood — enough to provide you with the amount of flame or coals you need for your cooking. Then strike a match and ignite the tinder close to the ground.

CROSS-DITCH FIRE LAY. Prepare the ditch by scratching a cross in the ground, 3 inches deep. This shallow ditch makes it easy for the air to sweep in under the fire lay and thereby provide a good draft for the fire.

Put a large wad of tinder in the middle of the cross ditch, then lay several foundation sticks diagonally over the cross. Build up on those, in crisscross fashion, enough wood for a speedy bed of coals for broiling.

For a job of quick boiling, put a layer of foundation sticks diagonally over the cross ditch and place your pot on them. Then, in log-cabin style, build fuel up around the pot. When completely laid, light the tinder.

kinds of fires

The experienced camper builds his fire to fill his needs. If you are planning to cook, a horizontal bed of coals is your best bet. For baking, you will need flames that radiate heat. For your campfire, you will want a fire that lights up the whole circle and goes on burning throughout the evening campfire program.

COOKING FIRE. Use any kind of fire lay you want, then continue feeding the fire until you have the amount of coals you need. Broiling and frying can be done directly on a bed of glowing coals. For boiling you will be better off if you contain the fire in some simple fireplace.

BAKING FIRE. As in the cooking fire, use any kind of fire lay to produce flames. Heat radiates directly into your reflector oven and bakes your meal.

FRIENDSHIP FIRE. The best fire for your gang's evening campfire is built in a modified log-cabin style. Place two logs on the ground, then two others crosswise on the first. Next lay a whole row of heavy sticks and add layer upon layer to a height of a couple of feet. Place the tinder on one of the upper layers and ignite the whole fire lay from the top.

fireplace

TRENCH FIREPLACE is dug in the ground. Make it wide enough to fit your pots, about 1 foot deep, 3 to 4 feet long. Widen the windward end and slope it. The trench goes light on fuel and it is safer than above ground, especially on a windy day. If trench is dug in grassy ground, keep the sods and replace them carefully.

ROCK FIREPLACE is quickly built from rocks. Use even-sized flat rocks and arrange in two rows, close enough to accommodate your cooking utensils. Beware of sandstone or rocks containing moisture as they may explode when heated.

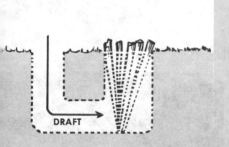

DRAFT

DAKOTA FIREPLACE is used only in mineral soil. It is used mainly on the prairies of the midwest where high winds make surface fires dangerous and impractical. Be sure to replace dirt and sod when through.

TENT PIN FIREPLACE uses the principle that a pot or pan will rest firmly on three points of even height. Stones are natural supporters, but tent pins are simpler. Push three tent pins into the ground so that the pot will rest squarely on them. Then build your fire.

cooking with charcoal

Wood for cooking is increasingly hard to get in many camping areas; so we turn to charcoal. It is quite readily obtained in convenient packages. It takes different management, though, than wood—for instance, adding fuel will not increase the heat for some time. It burns clean with little smoke and no wild flame, giving a steady, long-lasting heat.

In camp cooking you need three kinds of fire: (1) intense, lasting fire for boiling; (2) slow, steady heat for frying, broiling, or roasting; (3) quick, low fire for heating. Charcoal is best for the second kind, more difficult for the other two.

A proper stove helps solve these problems by concentrating heat, by permitting fanning the coals to high heat, and by allowing you to decrease heat by lowering firebed or raising the grate. You can reduce heat also by sprinkling coals with water. Putting aluminum pots or pans directly on hot coals is risky, because a fresh breeze over the coals can produce heats that will melt holes in the aluminum. Try to guess the amount of fuel needed for the whole meal and use that much from the start. Figure on about 20 minutes to obtain a working heat.

Where wood is not readily available or when you want to simplify your cooking, you can use charcoal for your fuel.

Charcoal is an important fuel in the West Indies, in South America, in the Orient, and around the Mediterranean. People in those places use mostly stoves made of clay, which have an upper, basin-shaped part with a perforated bottom. The lower part has an opening for draft and a solid bottom for catching ashes.

Spread out the fire to broil, but stack up the fire to boil. How do you pile up a charcoal fire? Simple. Use heat localizers —sheet metal collars that put the heat where the pots are.

Closest imitation of a native stove is a tin washbasin with a perforated bottom, placed over a galvanized pail. Cut a draft opening on side of pail. Make sheet-tin damper that can be raised or lowered.

Cut semicircular draft opening in a 1-foot length of 10-inch stovepipe. Circle of perforated sheet tin is held at various heights in three pieces of jack chain, resting in small slits at top of stove.

A charcoal grill with adjustable heat levels gives you control. Lift the tray to speed things up; lower the fire tray to prevent burning or to keep food hot.

123

9 COOKING

HAPPINESS IS A GOOD CAMP MEAL. An old hand can make it look easy, but actually he's juggling menus, recipes, ingredients, utensils, techniques, and teamwork. Wonderful, what practice will do for you!

Now *menu planning* is a skill you can learn. You want enough of the right food to be sure everyone has the energy to get the most out of your trip. Unbalanced meals on an overnight won't kill you; on a long, strenuous trip you'd better pay attention to nutrition and quantity—outdoor appetites are BIG. Don't have the "same old stuff" all the time, but do get agreement on menus—don't plan things no one likes.

About *recipes*—follow them! Check them in making your shopping list (so there will be an onion for the stew) and read 'em *twice* before starting the meal. They clue you on ingredients, utensils, fire, techniques, and timing—all important. Don't improvise unless you're desperate.

As for *ingredients*: Food's more expensive than you think, especially for camping where there's no refrigeration and weight has to be kept down. A cheap price per pound may include waste fat or tops or feathers you can't use. Maybe you should consult an expert—like Mom?

Your *utensils* are limited—use the "pot test" on menus: If a dish calls for too many pots or ones you don't have, forget it! Don't carry every pot in your cook kit if they're not needed for your menus.

Techniques? Camp cooks aren't born—they're developed from guys who can read, will follow directions, use judgment, have taste, and take pride in turning out a good job. The toughest thing is getting everything done at the proper time—that takes *practice*. If you're smart you won't practice on the gang, either. Start in your own kitchen where you don't have to worry about the fire and can get coaching. Then move outside and learn to manage a charcoal or wood fire while you cook.

Teamwork is important—you can't do it all yourself. If all help with fuel, water, sanitation, and food preparation (according to an agreed, written schedule) it will go fine. Then you yell, "Come and get it!"

the buddy system

A good camp cook takes pride in turning out first-rate meals with a minimum of fuss—but he sees to it that everything he needs is at hand, he won't wash dishes, and he's often considered crotchety. Now if he's *hired* for it, like a hunting or fishing guide or cook for a lumber or cattle camp, why what's one thing—you let him be. But *your* situation's different; you're all out for a good time in camp and figuring to come back good friends. So you share the load and take turns.

The jobs connected with meals boil down to three areas: *fuel and water, cooking,* and *cleaning up.* How much of a job any of these is depends on your location, menu, the weather, and your organization plan.

Most people like company in doing a job and often they need two sets of hands. So a buddy system for getting the job done seems natural enough. "Too many cooks spoil the broth," but you'll probably find that *two* cooks are not too many, especially when one is more experienced than the other, which, if you're clever, you'll probably arrange for on-the-job training. The buddy system permits flexibility in assignments because it's the job, not the system, that's important. Whether you have five, six, seven, or eight in the gang, you make the assignments to get the job done, not to use up the people. Who needs a title?

If you are a natural Scout patrol, you're used to each other and have elected a leader to keep things moving. You buddy up on the jobs and leave the patrol leader free of regular assignment so he can give a hand where needed; it's his job to see that everything gets done.

The problem is not so different for an Explorer post except that you usually don't operate in regular small groups. But you'll find that 6 or 7 make a better-sized cooking group than 10 or 12 would, so split up for the trip. You'll find the buddy system works equally well for you.

Once you're organized, *don't keep it a secret!* Put your schedule on a card big enough, and write black enough, to be read several feet away. Hang it near the kitchen area so everyone knows who has the duty—a scoring point at camporees, you know. Buddies change jobs after lunch cleanup—*their first meal is supper,* then breakfast and lunch. Adapt the sample form opposite to your situation—it's very flexible.

Fellows going for Cooking skill award or merit badge will find this system of doing three meals in a row a help—schedule *them!*

duty roster

Assign buddies to duties, but adjust assignments to share duties fairly. Keep the system flexible to get things done—the job is the big thing. Assignments change daily after lunch cleanup.

If you're out for only a few meals, change duties after each meal.

DUTY	FRI.	SAT.	SUN.	MON.	TUES.	WED.	THURS.
FUEL AND WATER	Rory	Eddie	Mark S	Cal	Eddie	Mark S	Cal
	Cal	Ricky	Mark D.	Paul	Ricky	Mark D.	Paul
COOKING	Mark S	Rory	Eddie	Mark D	Cal	Ricky	Mark S
	Mark D	Paul	Ricky	Mark S	Paul	Eddie	Mark D
CLEANUP	Eddie	Mark S	Cal	Eddie	Mark S	Rory	Eddie
	Ricky	Mark D	Paul	Ricky	Mark D	Paul	Ricky

FUEL AND WATER BUDDIES maintain water supply; maintain supplies of tinder, kindling, and firewood/charcoal protected from weather; start fires in time for cooks to have meals ready on time.

COOKING BUDDIES assemble food supplies; follow menus and recipes exactly; serve meals on time; put away food; put cook pots to soak; have cleanup water supply on fire before serving meals.

CLEANUP BUDDIES set up wash and rinse water for dishwashing; clean cooking pots and utensils; clean up kitchen and dining areas; store all group equipment; dispose of garbage and trash; put out fire.

buying trail foods

Think *nutrition,* think *economy* when you buy food. For trail foods, think *weight, bulk,* and *keeping quality,* too. Anything inedible or unusable, anything fragile or bulky, or anything needing refrigeration must be eyed with the suspicion that maybe it's not worth carrying.

Trail foods are the most difficult class of foods to buy. So if your gang can feed itself with what you can carry on your backs, you needn't worry about other less-critical situations in camping.

Specially packed trail foods are offered in great variety by many manufacturers and distributors. You can learn much by studying the catalogs of such foods; send for them.

What *is* available from your local store—*if you know what you're looking for*—is a surprising number of items quite suitable for backpacking, and there are advantages to using these foods: Most of them are familiar and you can choose favorite brands; you can examine them firsthand; you can ask the grocer for recommendations. Also, since they're not specialty items, the prices are likely to be reasonable and you eliminate the postage and minimum-order costs of ordering by mail.

Maybe you never really thought of them as trail foods, but you will find your store has *naturally dry* foods, *dried* foods, *dehydrated foods* (all water removed), and *concentrated* foods (some water removed). Then there are *canned* foods that range from raw to completely cooked. Now *how* the food has been prepared or packaged is not important except as it affects their weight, bulk, or keeping qualities, although with foods available in more than one form you may prefer one way over another.

To help in menu planning, here are suggestions listed by food groups:

MILK AND MILK PRODUCTS. *Whole milk,* dried, evaporated, condensed; *skim milk,* dehydrated; *hard cheeses,* dry; *instant puddings,* dehydrated; *cream sauces,* dehydrated; and others.

MEAT GROUP. *Eggs,* dehydrated; *fish (tuna, salmon, herring, sardines, anchovy, cod, and others),* dried and canned; *fish and clam chowders,* concentrated, canned; *shrimp,* canned; *oysters,* canned; *clams,* canned; *beef stew,* canned; *roast beef,* canned; *dried beef,* dry, canned; *corned beef,* canned; *roast-beef hash,* canned; *corned-beef hash,* canned; *precooked ham,* canned; *bacon,* canned; *Canadian bacon,* canned; *Smithfield ham,* dry; *hard sausage,* dry, canned; *hamburgers,* canned; *liver paste,* canned; *tongue,* canned; *potted ham,* canned; *luncheon meat,* canned; *minced ham,* canned; *turkey paste,* canned; *turkey meat,* canned; *boneless whole chicken,* canned; *gravies,* dehydrated, canned; *meatballs,* canned; *meat sauces,* canned; *bouillon,* dehydrated, concentrated; *soups,* dehydrated, canned; *mushrooms,* dried, dehydrated, canned; *omelets,* dehydrated; *gelatin desserts,* dehydrated; *peanut butter,* canned; *shelled nuts (peanuts, almonds, walnuts, pecans, pistachios, cashews, piñon nuts, Brazil nuts, and mixtures),* dry or canned; *shelled beans (navy, pea, kidney, pinto, soldier, lima, and the like),* dry, canned; *baked beans,* canned; *split peas,* dry; *lentils,* dry; *nut bars,* dry; and others.

VEGETABLES AND FRUITS. *Whole-kernel corn,* dried, canned; *cream-style corn,* canned; *peppers,* dried, canned; *pickles,* canned; *whole onions,* canned; *onion flakes,* dried; *chopped onion,* dehydrated; *peas,* canned; *green beans,* canned; *beets,* canned; *soup greens,* dried; *potato slices (au gratin),* dehydrated; *mashed potatoes,* dehydrated; *spaghetti sauce,* dehydrated, canned; *catsup* (repack); *soups,* dehydrated, condensed, canned; *dates, figs, apricots, apple slices, pears, peaches, prunes, raisins,* all dried, some dehydrated, some canned; *fruit jam,* canned; *fruit pie fillings,* canned; *fruit drinks,* concentrated, dehydrated, canned; *fruit juices,* concentrated, canned; and others.

CEREAL AND BREAD GROUP. *Oatmeal, wheat meal, cornmeal, farina, hominy grits, barley, white rice, brown rice, converted rice, wild rice,* all dry; *cold cereals,* all dry; *macaronis (elbow, spaghetti, seashells, lasagna, and the like),* all dry; *egg noodles,* dry; *chow mein noodles,* canned; *flour (granulated, enriched white, or whole-grains),* dry; *mixes for pancakes, biscuits, piecrust, muffins, gingerbread, cake, or others,* all dry; *Melba toast,* dry; *zwieback or rusk,* dry; *tortillas,* dry; *cookies,* dry, canned; *pilot biscuit,* dry; *graham cracker,* dry; *saltines,* dry; *milk biscuit,* dry; *Boston brown bread,* canned; *rye crispbread,* dry; *plum pudding, fig pudding, date pudding,* all canned; and others.

FATS, SWEETS, AND MISCELLANEOUS. *Hard margarine, butter,* canned; *vegetable shortening,* canned; *sugar,* cubed; *brown sugar,* granulated; *corn syrup* (repack); *molasses,* canned; *maple syrup,* canned; *mixed table syrups* (repack); *semisweet chocolate; jellies* (repack); *maple sugar; spices (cinnamon, nutmeg, paprika, pepper, worcestershire sauce, red-pepper sauce, garlic salt, mustard, chile, and the like);* and others.

Make it a habit to look at the shelves, read the labels of new things.

canned goods

Napoleon had a problem. He had armies all over Europe and they had to be fed. They could forage and seize food from farms, but by winter and spring they were suffering. For years the government had offered a prize of 12,000 francs for some way to preserve food. If soldiers had food that wouldn't spoil, they could go forever (Napoleon thought). In 1809 a Paris candymaker named Appert sealed food in glass. It didn't spoil. Later, the Englishman Durand did the same thing with a plated-metal canister—the "tin can." It was all too late for Boney, but the rest of us have been eating out of cans ever since.

To some people, "living out of cans" means being downright shiftless. The picture of a glum greenhorn spooning cold beans out of a can *isn't* very appealing. But there are times when canned food is a lifesaver, and often it is the only *practical* way of carrying certain foods—which is what we're thinking of, after all.

You'll find many canned foods useful on pack trips where you have no refrigeration and where your water supply is scarce or uncertain. It does not make much sense to carry a lot of dehydrated foods if you also have to carry all the water needed to make them edible. On the other hand, the liquids (broth, gravy, gelatin, juice, syrup, water, or oil) in most canned foods are edible, nourishing, tasty, or at least *wet*.

Cans add but a modest amount of weight to dense foods, like meat or fish, which are high-value foods hard to find or carry other than canned. Although inedible, the can is not *useless* if it is the price of having necessary foods on hand at all. So keep your eyes open—compare canned goods with other ways of packing the same foods.

For instance, a soup maker uses a 2-ounce tin for 10½ ounces of condensed soup to make 21 ounces when added to 10½ ounces of water. The same firm has a half-size, ½-ounce aluminum can for 2 ounces of dry soup; you add 24 ounces of water to get 24 ounces of soup. Which would you rather carry? Where will you get either 10½ *or* 24 ounces of water? Carry it? If so, should you consider just carrying 24 ounces of ready-to-heat soup?

Don't automatically rule canned goods out of your food list, then. You carry canned goods when they make good sense—like anything else. What you carry isn't as important as why you are carrying it.

It's true, there were (and probably still are) men who could work all day at a back-breaking job and live on voyageur's rations of a pound of pemmican, a pint of flour, and a handful of tea. But the romantic who idealizes this Spartan existence probably can't or wouldn't if given the chance—and he forgets that this wasn't the voyageur's choice. That was what the company "found" for him—and it was about the best it could do in the circumstances.

Suppose you pulled out of your pocket a little foil packet and showed that voyageur a disk about as hard as a hockey puck—then you put it in water and watched it swell into a nice-size steak, lean and trim and ready for the pan! And when it was cooked, with all the delicious aroma one expects of a steak, and he had eaten it, do you suppose that voyageur would ever touch pemmican again? Not if he could help it!

One does as well as one can—within the circumstances, *non? Oui!* So, although the previous lists of foods concentrated on the ones you might find on your grocer's shelves, it was mentioned that special foods could be found that were particularly suited to situations where weight, bulk, or refrigeration were problems. If your circumstances are such that you must absolutely pare every ounce, you *must* consider the use of special trail foods available from specialty houses or camp outfitters.

Freeze-drying has been used to produce such little miracles as that beef steak and many other products nearly as good as the original and much more convenient. Because these products are being increased so fast as to obsolete any list, you are urged to consult the manufacturers' catalogs and your dealer's offerings.

At the last reading, however, you could obtain: *beef,* patties, hamburger, steaks, swiss steaks, stew, and combinations with vegetables and noodles; *pork,* chops and patties; *ham,* sliced, diced, patties, and with scrambled *eggs; chicken,* diced, with rice, and a la king; *bacon,* precooked; *hash; meat bars; meatballs; shrimp; chili* with beans; *potatoes; omelets; mushrooms,* sliced; whole-kernel *corn; peas; fruit cocktail; peach* slices; *apricot* slices; whole *strawberries;* and probably many more items.

Some makers have special packs of 4- and 8-man rations, with all items in a menu for one day or several. Check catalogs, trading posts, or camp stores. Time for you to try these, *non? Mais oui!*

menu making

Take a guy with all sorts of imagination and daring . . . ask him what he'd like for a cookout. He thinks maybe five seconds and comes up with hamburgers! Great! Hamburgers are the staff of life—but *every* meal?

Variety is the spice of life and the key to good diet. Your body needs not just something to fill the stomach, but a replacement of *all* of the chemicals you use running around or just growing. No one food has everything you need, so the answer has to be *variety* . . . every day.

In camp you use about 4,000 calories of energy a day—in winter, 6,000! But the *kind* of calories is the important thing: about 1/5 should come from *proteins* (1/3 vegetable, 2/3 animal), 1/5 should come from *fats,* and 3/5 from *carbohydrates*. This gets technical—so just use the chart below in setting up your menus and check them as shown at the right. When your friend says, "Hamburgers!" you say, "OK; what else?" With suggestions. Give'm a choice—but make sure his choice is right! P.S. If you do take hamburger, eat it first thing—it spoils very fast.

EVERY DAY YOU NEED THESE:

**MILK GROUP—
4 OR MORE CUPS**
fluid and in foods like these:
cheese, soup, pudding, ice cream

**MEAT GROUP—
2 OR MORE SERVINGS**
meat, eggs, poultry, fish, soup, dry
beans, peanut butter, cheese

**VEGETABLE/FRUIT GROUP—
4 OR MORE SERVINGS**
one citrus fruit or tomato daily;
dark green or yellow vegetables

**BREAD/CEREAL GROUP—
4 OR MORE SERVINGS**
whole-grain or enriched breads,
cereals, macaronis, rice, grits

MENU CHECKLIST	FOOD GROUP				FOOD GROUP				WOLF PATROL
	1	2	3	4	1	2	3	4	
									FRIDAY
SUPPER									**SUPPER**
Meat/fish/fowl		x				x			ROAST CHICKEN
Potatoes/rice			x			x		x	RICE & GRAVY
Vegetable (cooked)			x				x		GREEN BEANS
Vegetable (raw)			x				x		COLE SLAW
Bread/butter/jam	x			x	x			x	BISCUIT & BUTTER
Dessert	x	x	x	x			x	x	PEACH COBBLER
Beverage	x				x				MILK
									SATURDAY
BREAKFAST									**BREAKFAST**
Fruit			x				x		APRICOTS
Cereal/milk/sugar	x			x				x	PANCAKES & SIRUP
Meat or eggs		x				x			BACON
Bread/butter/jam	x			x					
Beverage	x				x				COCOA
									SATURDAY
LUNCH (TRAIL)									**LUNCH**
Soup (optional)		x	x		x		x		
Sandwiches, meat or equivalent	x	x		x		x		x	CHEESE SANDWICHES
Fruit			x				x		ORANGES
Vegetable			x				x		CARROT STICKS
Dessert	x	x	x	x		x			CANDY BARS
Beverage			x				x		LEMONADE
Minimum servings daily	3	2	4	4	4	5	8	5	

Use the checklist to suggest usual menu items; you may not want all, of course. Now put a check in the proper column for each item; some rate more than one; peach cobbler, for example, would be both fruit *and* cereal. Fats and sweets, good fuel foods, aren't counted but are listed if important on the menu. Now add the checks in each column. If less than minimum servings show for any group, see if the number of servings per meal make up for it. *Cocoa* for breakfast and *milk* for supper show as only two servings—but they'll drink more!

sample menus

Hundreds of suitable foods have been suggested for your use on the trail and your gang should have no trouble dreaming up some nifty ways to get your proteins, carbohydrates, and fats (what an awful way to think of such delicious stuff as food!) Further on, you'll find a number of recipes that may help when you get down to cases. At any rate, you have menus to make whether you're out overnight or off to high adventure for a week. Now you know how to go about ensuring a good diet, so your problem is to avoid monotony, keep it lightweight, and stay inside your budget. Pick main dishes that appeal for each meal and build the menus around them; use perishables early in the game. Here are a few samples:

SUPPER MENUS

First Day	Second Day	Third Day
Creamed chipped beef on biscuits	Spaghetti and meatballs	Macaroni and cheese
Peas	Corn cakes with sugar and cinnamon	Grilled ham loaf
Peach cobbler (in foil)	Chocolate pudding	Carrot strips
Milk	Milk	Fig bars
		Milk

SUPPER FOOD LISTS

Chipped beef	Spaghetti	Elbow macaroni
Margarine	Spaghetti sauce (canned or dehydrated) or tomato paste	American cheese
Powdered milk		Powdered milk
Biscuit mix		Ham loaf (canned)
Peas	Cream-style corn	Margarine
Sliced peaches (dried or canned)	Hamburger (canned)	Carrots (raw)
Sugar	Sugar	Fig bars
Powdered milk	Biscuit mix	Powdered milk
	Cinnamon	
	Chocolate pudding mix	
	Powdered milk	

Breakfast Menus

Stewed or dried prunes	Quick oats with raisins	Stewed peaches
Quick oats	Grilled bacon	Cornmeal mush
Pancakes, camp-made syrup	Hot biscuits, jelly	Sausage
Hot chocolate	Hot chocolate	Pancakes, camp-made syrup
		Hot chocolate

Breakfast Food Lists

Dried prunes	Quick oats	Dried peaches
Quick oats	Seedless raisins	Cornmeal
Pancake mix	Bacon or jowl	Sausage
Sugar	Biscuit mix	Pancake mix
Maple flavoring	Jelly	Chocolate mix
Margarine	Powdered milk	Powdered milk
Chocolate mix	Chocolate mix	Sugar
Powdered milk	Sugar	Maple flavoring

Lunch Menus

Bouillon (beef)	French onion soup	Split-pea soup
Cheese sandwich	Peanut butter sandwich	Corned beef sandwich
Luncheon meat sandwich	Jam sandwich	Apple butter sandwich
Raisins	Carrot sticks	Dates
Apple	Butterscotch pudding	Instant fruit drink
Instant fruit drink	Instant fruit drink	

Lunch Food Lists

Beef bouillon cubes or granules	French onion soup (dry)	Split-pea soup (dry)
American cheese	Peanut butter	Corned beef
Luncheon meat (canned)	Strawberry jam	Apple butter
Raisins	Carrots	Dates (seeded)
Apples (fresh)	Butterscotch pudding mix	Bread/margarine
Bread/margarine	Bread/margarine	Fruit-drink crystals
Fruit-drink crystals		

shopping

OK, you got your menus all doped out—now just go buy the food, right? Wrong! First, go over the staples leftover from the last trip—cocoa, cinnamon, salt, sugar, dry milk—and foil, paper towels, toilet paper, matches, soap powder, and other stuff not on the menu.

Now make your shopping list after checking out the menus and *recipes.* Allow time for making an accurate list; check the recipes for "hidden" items you'd never guess and for *actual* quantities needed for the number of guys going out. Take small quantities of seldom-used spices and the like from home, rather than buying a package you'll never use up. Food normally is packaged for family use—which may not be right for you since you don't want a pantry full of odds and ends. You'll have to be very aware of quantity—weight, volume, and servings per package. See if different brands of an item give a better break on quantities than the one you usually buy. Maybe one will prove to be a "better buy."

But why worry about costs? Few mothers could tell you the meal cost per member of the family. Their problems are different—*you* have to divvy everything fairly, you can't handle leftovers easily, and the kinds of food most suitable for camping are apt to lean toward the expensive. If your costs get unreasonably high, some guys are going to quit going.

All right, you're in the store with a good list and enough money . . . now what? If you're an old hand at shopping, go to it! Maybe divide the list with the others to shorten the job and spread the experience. But if you're new at the game, take it easy. The average store has many dif-

If some of the newer fellows squawk about the cost of food, take them along to help with shopping; they'll get educated. Don't let yourself get trapped into doing all the shopping for every trip—you'll get good at it, but the others won't. Same thing happens when you let a lady do it for you—she already knows how. Shopping for camp food is a man's job!

When you get up to the cash register you have to get up the dough. Better take care of that little matter in advance. Some groups bankroll the shopping from a treasury and then divide the cost among those going on the trip to repay the treasury. Some estimate the cost, set a price, and collect in advance from those going. (Take extra money in case you guessed wrong—don't louse up a good shopping list for lack of cash—and a rebate will be popular.)

ferent packages and brands of the same item, often with different price tags. Both quality and quantity should affect prices, but sometimes it is competition. Anyway, start to READ THE LABELS! Start with labels you recognize, but READ THE LABELS. Find out what's in the package, how many or how much, what condition it's supposed to be in, any other ingredients you'll need ("add one egg"), the time it takes to prepare it, and so on. Don't forget that "serves 4 to 6" may mean *serves 3 hungry campers!* If you're not sure, tend to buy on the hearty side.

READ ALL OF THE LABEL. Pineapple comes canned in slices, chunks, and crushed. Just try skewering crushed pineapple for ham shish kebab! On the other hand, don't buy expensive slices when you, could use chunks. Fruits packed in heavy syrup are higher priced than if in light syrup; if you have no use for the syrup, buy the cheaper. But, how would that heavy syrup go on fritters? Now and then you get a "plus."

Now and then you get a minus, too. How many loaves of bread do you need to make 12 sandwiches? (Bakers count the heel slices—do you?) A nationwide bakery has a family loaf with 18 slices, a "big sandwich" loaf with 26 slices, and a "Pullman" loaf with 28 slices—the weights don't matter. You may calculate your meat need by the pound but serve it by the slice; check the package or specify your need to the butcher so somebody isn't shy his share . . . that somebody might be *you*.

• *Avoid the need for refrigeration.* This limits menus, true, but counting on perishables requiring cold storage is begging for trouble. Even the most efficient, convenient refrigerator is cumbersome—anything less just isn't worthwhile bothering with. Maintaining the low temperatures needed for safe food storage is difficult or impossible. CHECK THIS: If held *under 32°F.,* fresh seafood is safe for only 24 hours. If kept *under 36°F.,* large cuts of fresh meat will keep for 3 or 4 days, but hamburger is safe for only 24 hours; poultry may keep 2 days. If held *below 45°F.,* bacon, ham, smoked meats, eggs, butter, cheeses, vegetables, fruits, and fluid milk may keep from only a few days to several weeks (depending on the item). Maintaining such temperatures in portable coolers in summer weather is difficult in camp. Finding spoiled food is bad—*not* finding it can be fatal! Plan on substitutes for perishables.

Meat. It ought to be a chapter in itself. It's your most expensive and critical item. It isn't uniform and price doesn't tell everything you need to know. Most stores carry graded beef, veal, and lamb; pork isn't graded. Usually you have no choice as to grade—if you do, "good" or "choice" grades would be best for you. Except for stew, you need quite tender meat for your kind of cooking. The whole animal is graded, but the cuts of meat will vary in tenderness, texture, and flavor. Some include considerable waste; some have little waste but are overpriced—in particular the popular outdoor-barbecue items campers go for. Discuss this with a butcher, if possible. He should be able to guide you. Tell him what you want it for, how you plan to cook it, and how many you have to feed.

With these few examples it is easy to see that shopping is no easy matter. Get all the advice you can—from mom, from other fellows, and from food people. Try not to make the same mistakes twice, and be sure to pass your hard-won experience on to others who'll have to shop for your gang. It will pay off in satisfaction and lower food bills.

Watch that batch of new campers setting up. They unload the car (naturally) of lots of grocery bags and boxes, a picnic cooler, and some water jugs. Now starts the mealtime game—where did the checkout girl put the raisins (or whatever)? Their meat, soggy gray lumps, floats in the melted ice in the cooler. Bread dries out in squashed, torn wrappers. Butter becomes a gooey mess of thumbprints and bits of grass. Labels have shed from three cans of . . . ravioli? . . . pears! Pears?

Now a seasoned crew moves into the next campsite. They hiked in with everything on their backs. As others get busy setting up camp, one fishes a plastic bag from his sack. Inside it are several smaller bags—everything for supper, measured in portions, labeled, with instructions. All their meals are that way. It took some doing, but it all has to be done sometime—why not at home with nobody breathing hard?

There's no one best way to handle food packing and storage; it depends on your situation. When everything's on your back, you have to do a lot of homework, carry a lot in your head. Working from a car or in a fixed camp, your problems are easier or different. The point is to *have all the food you need for each meal in its most convenient form.* If it doesn't come that way, take the time to put it in that condition.

"Most convenient form" means this: The food is in good condition; there is enough of it, but not too much; waste has been trimmed; its identity is clearly marked; preparation instructions are on or in the container; the container permits easy packing or storage, protects the contents, and won't leak, puncture, spill, shatter, seep through, stain, contaminate, or blow away. This may mean repackaging the food.

Take all you need for each meal in its most convenient form—light, flexible for easy packing; premeasured, premixed for no-waste, no-sweat preparation. It is essential that dehydrated food be packaged in waterproof containers.

packing tips

- *Look for special packs of foods.* Cruise the stores or ask food people for leads on small packets of catsup, mustard, jelly, sugar, syrup, salt, pepper, and drink mixes so handy for packing. Trail-food suppliers often list these in catalogs with other specialties; read their magazine ads. Prepackaged small portions will save you much time and trouble.

- *Avoid leftovers.* Eat it up or throw it out is the usual rule to avoid trouble in safe storage. But some things like bread, cookies, peanut butter, jelly, butter, and syrup will keep a short time if packed to avoid drying out, melting, molding, or attracting vermin. Sealable bags and plastic or metal containers are a help. Food-safe metal or plastic tubes (like toothpaste tubes) are good for packing squeezables like jelly, jam, butter, cooking fat, and so on—if you can locate a source of them.

- *Avoid glass.* It is heavy and hazardous and can usually be replaced by plastic. (A popular table syrup comes in a jug that weighs as much as its contents! A screw-top plastic bottle would weigh 1/10 of that.)

- *Prevent contamination.* Foods must be protected from dirt, water, and tainting from soap, cleaners, oils, and strong foods such as onions, garlic, oranges, melons, and cucumbers. Seal these in plastic or foil.

- *Label everything.* When you're repackaging, label everything with name, quantity, and clear instructions—if they're long, cut them from package and put them in the trail pack. Remove loose labels on cans; use surgical tape labels or felt-pen directly on cans. Use big letters.

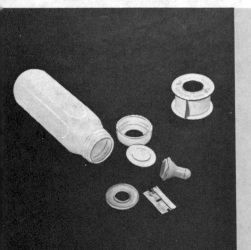

BABY BOTTLES? Right. These wide-mouthed, screw-cap, unbreakable plastic containers are fine for dry, semidry, and liquid foods and come in 4- and 8-fluid-ounce sizes. Make a snug gasket (needed) by slicing ring off rubber nipple. Completely washable, bottles can be sterilized by boiling before reusing. Good shape and size for packing. Label with tape.

Plastic boxes, jars, tubes, bottles, flasks, and bags for repacking foods from break-able, oversize, heavy, or inconvenient original containers. Clean and sanitize before using. Check security of caps; insert foil to make tight seals. Tape box lids.

• *Compact the load.* Fill empty spaces, cooking pots, canisters, and the like with small flexible or fragile items. Eggs can be snugged (wrapped in paper) into a cup in your personal cook kit, or bury them in oatmeal in the cocoa pot for travel if you have no noncrush egg case. Original food containers are often oversized—repack to obtain better shapes for packing. Rearrange foods for convenience when you are camped.

• If you *are* going to carry perishables, buy them as late as possible before departure. If you do all your shopping at once, sort out the stuff so perishables don't hide with nonperishables in the shopping bag. Check your food list to be sure any perishables are refrigerated at once until load-up time. Chicken, fresh meat, and seafood may have to be removed from store packages and repacked even for refrigerator storage. Even sitting around in a warm car for long may cause it to spoil.

• *Be alert to progress* in foods, containers, and techniques. Experiment!

a packing plan

In backpacking, with all food supplies carried in individuals' packs, a system to keep track of things is essential. But this novel and practical scheme works for you right from the menu-planning stage through marketing, packing, and up through meal preparation. All but cooks for you! It fits in fine with the buddy system of organizing to get things done. So you gear everything to *start with the first evening meal,* even if you go before lunch because that will likely be a nose-bag lunch. So make your system go from supper to breakfast to lunch.

Now, using a big game table or a large bare floor without much traffic, lay out a big grid with masking tape with a square for every meal of the trip. With a felt pen, write the name of the day and meal on a piece of tape and stick it in the square, according to your plan.

Write out the menu for each meal on a small card, "A," and put it in the proper square. On another card, "B," list the exact food quantities for each menu. Put it with the "A" card in the square. You're started. Now consolidate the food lists for each meal to make up your shopping list, checking unfamiliar recipes for those "hidden" items you'll need. Now if you can get individual portion packets of some foods, fine;

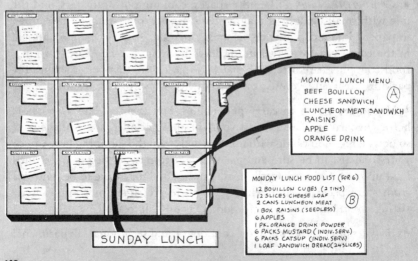

MONDAY LUNCH MENU
BEEF BOUILLON Ⓐ
CHEESE SANDWICH
LUNCHEON MEAT SANDWICH
RAISINS
APPLE
ORANGE DRINK

MONDAY LUNCH FOOD LIST (FOR 6)
12 BOUILLON CUBES (2 TINS)
12 SLICES CHEESE LOAF Ⓑ
2 CANS LUNCHEON MEAT
1 BOX RAISINS (SEEDLESS)
6 APPLES
1 PK. ORANGE DRINK POWDER
6 PACKS MUSTARD (INDIV. SERV.)
6 PACKS CATSUP (INDIV. SERV.)
1 LOAF SANDWICH BREAD (24 SLICES)

SUNDAY LUNCH

if you can't, buy a larger quantity and repack enough for *each* meal. Be sure to label each item and include adequate instructions . . . don't assume that anybody knows how to cook anything.

Put the food for each meal in its square. When you have all of the food for all of the meals, pack all of the parcels for each meal in one bag (more if necessary) together with the cards. Label the bag clearly with the name of the meal and the day.

The object of this system is to avoid frantic clawing through all the packs to find the necessaries. So put the good things for one supper, the next breakfast, and lunch in one fellow's pack. Then the next set of rations go in the next pack, and so on. You might make a master list of who's got what. Then, comes Tuesday night, Old Jim had better haul a bag out of his pack marked "Tuesday supper." Now if he has another marked "Wednesday breakfast" and another marked "Wednesday lunch," you're in business. It really works!

About lunches: In the morning the cooks make up the trail lunches in individual bags for the gang to carry on their persons since lunch is seldom fancy. If the weather calls for something hot, locate the pot and the soup or whatever *before* you go out on the trail.

As the food is used, trade equipment items to equalize pack weights.

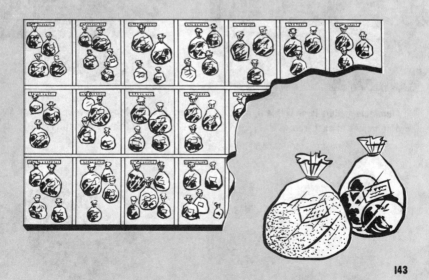

utensils

Check the hardware when you set up shop—you'll have no time for hunting a potato peeler when supper's afoot. Check *before* the trip, too. The Trail Chef kit is standard, plus or minus items to suit your needs. Some want a griddle for French toast, pancakes, or sandwiches—so they drop a frying pan; others need a Dutch oven for baking—they substitute it for a large pot. Same with the tool kit—you may want to add measuring spoons, a rubber scraper, chef tongs, or a boning knife—so the ladle stays home and you use a cup. Measuring cups and serving dishes, you'll need. Pot tongs and gloves are very handy. Keep water and a washbasin near. Spread your plastic "workbench" and you're ready!

The standard 4- to 8-man cooking rig.   **Most-needed chef's tools in handy kit.**

 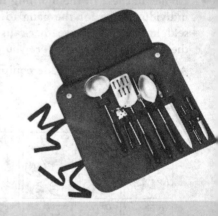

Aluminum griddle is convenient, light. Also comes in cast iron.   **Versatile Dutch oven now in aluminum as well as the old reliable cast iron.**

Some recipes use traditional words to describe operations in cooking—unfamiliar perhaps, but good words. You should learn them so you can read any recipe and know just what you are expected to do.

BAKE	To cook by dry heat, as in a reflector or Dutch oven.
BASTE	To moisten food while cooking, by spreading with melted fat, drippings, or special sauces.
BOIL	To cook in water or other liquid hot enough to bubble ($212°F$. at sea level, $-2°$ for each 1,000 feet elevation; *double* given cooking time at 5,000 feet).
BRAISE	To cook meat tender by browning in hot fat, then cooking in covered pan, usually with added liquid.
BROIL	To cook meat directly over or before an open fire.
CUT IN	To blend cooking fat with flour to make dough, by pressing in with fork or cutting in fine chunks with knife.
DEEP FRY	To cook by immersion in boiling or very hot fat or oil.
DREDGE	To coat meat with flour, often seasoned, before frying.
FRY	To cook in an open pan with small amount of fat.
MARINATE	To tenderize or flavor meat (usually) by covering with spiced vinegar and oil, salad dressing, or the like.
PAN BROIL	To cook meat in a very hot skillet with a minimum of fat.
PLANK	To fasten meat to a slab of wood and broil before a fire.
POACH	To cook just below the boiling point of (usually) water.
ROAST	To cook meat or vegetables in hot air, as in an uncovered pan in an oven, without water. Also to cook in hot ashes.
SCALD	To heat to just below boiling temperature (as of cocoa).
SEAR	To seal surfaces of meat by exposing to intense heat so juices are confined.
SIMMER	To cook in liquid held just barely at the boiling point.
STEEP	To extract the value by soaking food in hot water.
STEW	To cook meat by searing, then simmering until tender, usually with vegetables added. Also to cook vegetables and fruit (often dried fruit).
TENDERIZE	To render meat easier to cook or chew by softening the tissues by pounding or with chemicals or by marinating.

reading recipes

Now you're the cook. There's this pile of food, a going fire, lots of water on hand, and some of the guys are casting an eye at their watches. What now? How about washing your hands, for a starter? Now put on the apron and the chef's cap. No kidding—they keep stuff off your uniform and out of the stew. Besides, they give you a certain air.

Now glance casually at the menu—in fact, read it thoroughly. Read off the food list as your buddy takes the "makings" out of the bag. You two had better hang together on this, lest you hang separately. Now read the directions or the recipes for the menu. Now *read them again*—OUT LOUD—so your buddy gets the word, too. Don't get mysterious.

Unfortunately, all recipes are not written the same way (there is no standard form), which is only *one* reason for reading them twice. As you gain experience you'll know what size pot is needed or realize that someone copied a recipe wrong (it happens); you'll know when the fire isn't hot enough or what "salt to taste" really means. Meanwhile you can hardly do better than follow instructions. It might be prudent to read over the instructions for cooking the dishes you're going to have to cook *before* you leave the house. (You had the schedule and menus?)

Besides the names and quantities of ingredients, recipes give you some idea of *time,* like "cook 3 minutes" or "cook until tender" or, unhappily, "until done" (!) You'll need a watch *and* some idea of what you're doing. Some menus have food lists and directions for the whole meal—with timing so it all comes out right. But not all. Most recipes are just for one dish—the timing of the meal is up to you. And you may as well be aware: *Timing is the toughest part of cooking.* More on timing later.

The *next* toughest part of cooking is probably *measuring.* Maybe your ancestors always used a pinch or a dab or a fist of this or that—but you had better *stick to level measures* if possible. Most cook kits have a cup with marked fractions—if not, get one. For less than a quarter of a cup, though, you'll need measuring spoons. If you're caught without them, measure the number of spoonfuls of water to fill a quarter of a cup—which is two fluid ounces—and go on from there. (There's a helpful table of measures further on.) Especially with baking powder, spices, herbs, and flavorings don't guess! You can spoil a whole lot of food for a lot of guys with one little error. Stick to the recipe.

measurement

You'll run into a great-sounding recipe, but it's for the wrong quantity. Usually it's too small, so multiply the ingredient quantities (watching out for salt and spices) by the appropriate factor; don't overlook the old proportion bit—A:B::a:? After the figuring, check it out to see if it seems reasonable. If not, check with a cook or a computer.

Dash	= 6 or 7 drops
Pinch	= less than 1/8 teaspoon
15 drops	= 1/4 teaspoon
1 teaspoon	= 1/3 tablespoon
1 tablespoon	= 3 teaspoons
2 tablespoons	= 1 fluidounce
4 tablespoons	= 1/4 cup or 2 fluidounces
5 1/3 tablespoons	= 1/3 cup
6 tablespoons	= 3/8 cup or 3 fluidounces
8 tablespoons	= 1/2 cup or 4 fluidounces
16 tablespoons	= 1 cup or 8 fluidounces
2 cups	= 1 pint or 16 fluidounces
4 cups	= 1 quart or 32 fluidounces
4 quarts	= 1 gallon (U.S.)

The spoon of the larger Vitt-L Kit is 1/20 cup; a tablespoon is 1/16 cup. These are measures of *volume,* not weight. Canadian cups, pints, quarts, and gallons are 25 percent greater in volume.

Temperature measurements are often expressed: "Bake in slow oven" or "preheat oven to 375°." What do you do in camp? You can't watch food baking in a Dutch oven without opening it, which cools it and retards the baking. And how do you preheat it to a proper temperature? Try putting a teaspoon of flour (or a piece of white unglazed paper) on a pan in the oven. The colors will give you a clue:

Light tan	in 5 minutes	Slow oven	About 250°
Medium tan	in 5 minutes	Moderate oven	About 350°
Dark brown	in 5 minutes	Hot oven	About 450°
Dark brown	in 3 minutes	Very hot oven	About 550°

Aluminum Dutch ovens respond very rapidly to changes in fire.

With a reflector oven, of course, you can see the progress and adjust by moving oven or building up the fire; experience alone can prompt you.

timing meals

Some menus for camp meals include specific directions telling you exactly what to do, and when, to prepare the entire meal—like the one opposite. If you are working with these, fine. On the other hand, most recipes confine their remarks on timing to that particular dish without regard for whatever else you're doing at the same time.

Now here's where you can get in a bind unless you *think the whole thing through*. The idea is to have everything finished at once, or at least so you can serve the meal in its proper course. (No one will want your beautiful omelet after they've finished their peaches and cookies!)

Cooking is a serious business—especially with a pack of hungry wolves standing around waiting to fall to. So take it seriously. Look ahead on the schedule and see what meals you're responsible for. Then look at the menu. See if you're sure you know just how each dish is prepared and check it with your cooking buddy, too. That way you can divide up the responsibility agreeably and go about the meal efficiently. If there are no directions for the whole meal, maybe you should write some.

Many faults in the timing of camp cookery can be traced to poor fire control. Things just won't cook if the fire dies down while you're busy rolling out biscuit dough. Don't yell at the fuel and water buddies—their job is to see that your fire is started on time and that you have plenty of fuel on hand. As cook, *you* want to be in charge of your fire without somebody else tinkering with it.

With most camp fuels, especially charcoal, you have to think way ahead and not wait until the heat is gone before adding new fuel or poking the fire up—first it will cool down and then get too hot, before it is just right, especially for frying, broiling, or baking.

Don't let people get in your way while you're cooking—they may not mean to interfere, but they may disrupt your operations, and you'll get the blame if meals aren't on time. Keep everybody away from your fire and work area—it's positively unsafe, what with sharp knives, forks, fire, and boiling water around. Nothing like having some guy throw paper in the fire while your back is turned. *He* walks off while your biscuits get a nice golden black. Don't let anyone put *anything* in the fire but fuel until the meal is cooked. Eggshells stink, water sends ashes all over, grease may throw flames in your face. Unh unh—keep 'em away!

typical procedure

Baked Glazed Ham
Boiled Rice
Green Beans   Bread and Butter*
Pineapple   Milk

FOOD LIST

This list is for eight campers; adjust for smaller groups.

2-pound canned ham	1¼ cups rice (uncooked)
2 No. 2 cans green beans	2 No. 2 cans crushed pineapple
1 loaf bread	¼ pound butter/margarine*
4 1-quart packets dry milk	

UTENSILS

8-quart pot	4 serving plates	bowl
4-quart pot	50-ounce pitcher	Chef's Tool Kit

DIRECTIONS

1. Wash hands and **READ DIRECTIONS TWICE.**

2. Open ham and put in 4-quart cooking pot along with fat and jellied juices. Cover and heat. When juices have liquified and the ham is hot, add some of the pineapple juice and 2 tablespoons of sugar; baste ham occasionally (spoon juices over ham). Brown sugar or maple syrup could be used instead.

3. If processed rice is used, follow directions on the package; otherwise, add rice to 6 cups furiously boiling water in 8-quart pot. Cook until tender and water is absorbed, or drain boiling water and rinse with warm water. Drain and hang near fire to fluff up and keep warm.

4. Open green beans and place cans near the fire to heat.

5. Make up a quart of milk now, more as needed later.

6. Set the table and slice the ham. Call the gang. Put water on for dishwashing. Set out food. Say grace and serve family-style.

*NOTE: Wherever butter or margarine are mentioned it is assumed that either may be used; margarine is regarded as less perishable in camp.

supper

Supper should be the best meal of the day—and the high spot of the day! It ought to furnish about half of the nourishment for the day. You should have a meat dish (red meat, fish, or fowl), potatoes or rice or macaroni or noodles, at least one cooked vegetable and a raw vegetable or salad, bread and butter or margarine, a beverage, and dessert.

The meat is most important—somehow, if that's good, people tend to forgive small errors in other things. But don't slight the vegetables, because they're needed for nutrition (whether they're worth mentioning depends on how well you manage them). Naturally, you want *everything* to be good. Your reputation as a cook depends on it.

Allow plenty of time to prepare the meal, eat it, and clean up before dark. This starts way back at menu-planning time—give a thought to the time of sunset and the day's schedule of activities. A roast or a stew may have to *cook* for 3 hours, with preparation beforehand—that's OK, but not when you won't even be in camp then. Doing dishes in the dark is no fun (it's a little hazardous) and neither is waiting for supper after a strenuous day. So schedule a "fast" supper for a jam-packed day and save the feast for an opportunity to do it justice. A last-minute emergency may be met by switching supper menus around—but with all the considerations of menu-making, be sure you don't create more problems than you solve. The idea is to be sure the gang is well-fed.

You'll find all kinds of ideas for supper dishes farther along.

Sizzling hamburgers on toasted rolls, the all-American dish—and very fast for a first-night supper. Add, maybe, scalloped potatoes (from a dehydrated "mix") and stewed tomatoes. Crisp carrot sticks are always welcome on the side. For dessert, Apple Betty, and a mug or two of cocoa if it's cool, or cold milk if it's warm.

Chicken "goes pretty good" with most people, especially fried chicken. It should be used early in the game as you can't keep it long in camp. Wipe cut-up fryers with a paper towel and then dredge them in seasoned flour. Heat margarine or cooking oil in pan and lay pieces in the hot fat until one side is golden brown—then turn. It should be done in 20 to 30 minutes.

In this day of precooked wonders, remember the old camp favorites now and then. Baked potatoes—"Mickeys"—are such, and no big thing to make. Scoop a pit among the embers of the fire, put the spuds in and cover them with ashes, then live coals. In an hour they should be light and fluffy inside and not too black on the outside. Pierce with a fork, crisscross, and squeeze the potato to open. A dab of margarine, some salt, and you're living!

OTHER WAYS WITH SPUDS

BOILED. Scrub, don't pare, a couple *new* potatoes for each person; boil in salted water to cover in a covered pot for 20 to 30 minutes; old potatoes should be pared, quartered, and boiled 30 to 40 minutes.

MASHED. Prepare instant mashed potatoes as directed on package; or boil old potatoes. Drain, then mash thoroughly with peeled wooden club. Add 1 teaspoon of margarine, 1/4 teaspoon salt, and 1 tablespoon hot milk for each potato. Stir with fork until fluffy.

HOME FRIES. Slice peeled, cold, boiled potatoes into enough hot fat to keep them from sticking to the pan. Add onion for zing. Salt.

STEAM FRIES. Cut pared raw potatoes in $\frac{1}{8}$-inch slices; keep under cold water to avoid discoloring. Melt fat in covered pan. Dry slices on towel before slipping into fat. You may add onion. Add fat if potato seems dry. Cover pan but stir to avoid sticking. Salt.

SCALLOPED. Preheat Dutch oven to *hot*. Pare and slice 6 cups of old potatoes; keep them under water—dry before use. In large frying pan (without handle) put a layer of cracker crumbs, then a layer of potatoes. Dab margarine (1 stick/$\frac{1}{2}$ cup in all) on the potatoes and salt lightly. Add another layer, more margarine and salt—repeat until pan is full. Add onion or slivered cheese, if you want. Cover pan with foil and rest on three pebbles in oven. Cook 45 minutes. You may find dehydrated scalloped and au gratin potatoes at your grocer's.

INSTEAD OF POTATOES

MACARONI. In a large pot bring 3 quarts of water to a rolling boil; add 1 tablespoon salt. Sprinkle in, to keep pot boiling, 3 cups elbow or other macaroni. Prevent boiling over, but keep it enthusiastic for about 10 minutes. Don't overcook—it should be a *little* chewy. Drain completely and serve buttered, with sauce, or in other dishes.

SPAGHETTI. A pound should feed three or four. Use large pot and cook like macaroni, but put a handful of the pasta into center of the water, slowly pushing it in endwise—allow to spread like jackstraws. Keep pot boiling to separate the strands. If necessary, stir occasionally with a fork to keep things moving. Thin spaghetti should be done *al dente*—chewy—in 8 to 10 minutes. Drain and serve with sauce. Good dry sauce mixes are on the market, and many canned ones. Making a sauce from scratch takes time, fresh meat, and cans of tomatoes and paste—unless you have a jewel of a recipe, you may as well buy a prepared sauce.

RICE. As there are short-grained and long-grained white rice, brown rice, instant rice, converted rice, and wild rice (not rice), check out any instructions on package carefully. If none, try this: Start with a large pot (rice swells fearfully) and for each cup of grain (yielding 3 to $3\frac{1}{2}$ cups) put in 1 quart of water and 1 teaspoon salt. Wash and drain rice at least once in cold water; pick out discolored grains. Into furiously boiling water, sprinkle rice in slowly to keep pot boiling and to separate grains. Watch pot doesn't boil over. Do *not* stir unless rice seems in danger of sticking to bottom. It should be tender in 20 minutes (double for brown rice, less for others). Drain completely and hang pot high above fire to swell and keep warm. Serve with margarine and salt, sugar and milk, with a sauce, or in other dishes.

VEGETABLES

CANNED. It is only necessary to *heat* canned vegetables in their own juice as they are cooked in canning. Simplest way is to *open* the can and set in coals. This gets boring if overdone, but as there is a big variety available, this shouldn't be too serious—nor should you have to fancy them up much for a second go-around. Drain hot vegetables and add margarine and salt. Unless you're positive your gang dotes on certain spices or herbs (or won't challenge your taste), avoid the exotic.

DEHYDRATED. Few vegetables, except onions and mixed soup greens, can be found in ordinary stores. Specialty houses list dozens; they vary in cooking time, but may take an hour of soaking before cooking. Follow instructions on package. If you have an extra screw-top plastic jar, you can save time by soaking vegetables in your pack while traveling to your campsite; a good way to have raw salad vegetables.

BOILED FRESH VEGETABLES. Getting enough raw vegetables in camp is the usual problem, but if you happen on some that must be cooked, keep these points in mind. Clean thoroughly, discard inedible parts, peel and cut up as necessary. *The rule* is to boil until tender in as little water as possible in a covered pot over a medium fire. *Exceptions* are onions, beets, greens, and cabbage and its cousins which should be cooked covered with water in an open pot over low heat—quarter *cabbage* and cook 15 minutes; *cauliflower,* 20 minutes; *broccoli,* 10 minutes; young *beets,* 1/2 to 1 hour; *greens,* 20 minutes. Among others going by the rule: *corn on the cob,* 5 to 10 minutes; *carrots,* 25 minutes; *okra,* 10 minutes; *peas,* 15 minutes; *lima beans,* 35 minutes; pared *sweet potatoes,* 15 minutes.

A few celebrated combinations of vegetables, such as succotash and red-flannel hash, will be accorded the dignity of a recipe. Otherwise, you may combine vegetables—after cooking or heating—that are traditional with you or that suit your fancy—like peas and carrots! Combine them because you like them, not because they're leftovers—*they shouldn't be!*

supper dishes

In other parts of this chapter you will find several ways to cook main dishes for supper according to the methods used. These are important undertakings—but having a tasty, filling, nourishing supper can be a simple and quick thing if you go to the one-pot meal or a simple meat with perhaps a casserole combining noodles or pasta with vegetables. You may know these dishes by other names, but don't worry about it; it's the eating that counts. If you have no favorites, try these.

QUICK STEW

2 pounds hamburger or equivalent in canned meatballs   4 cans condensed vegetable soup   1/2 stick margarine or 1/4 cup oil

Not a stew, but it *is* quick. Heat meatballs or make: Ball the hamburger and brown in fat. Pour undiluted soup over them and allow the mixture to heat thoroughly. Correct seasoning with salt and pepper.

MACARONI AND CHEESE

Cook 3 cups of elbow macaroni as instructed. Drain and return to the pot. Add 3/4 cup milk (if skim, add 1/4 stick of margarine) and 1 cup American or cheddar cheese, slivered and crumbled. Reheat over low fire until cheese is melted. Or bake in *hot* Dutch oven until top is browned.

CHIPPED BEEF ON BISCUITS

2 cans cream soup—celery, mushroom, asparagus, cheese, or mix   2 8-ounce packages chipped beef   3/8 cup milk

Combine undiluted soup, milk, and beef (you can use diced corned beef instead) and heat the mixture. Check flavor—add salt if needed. Serve over hot biscuits, bannock, or (in a pinch) pilot biscuit.

HURRY HASH!

2 cans condensed cream of mushroom, celery, or other cream soup
4 sliced hard-boiled eggs
16 pilot biscuits, rusks, or Melba toast
1/2 cup milk
2 cups diced canned ham loaf, corned beef, frankfurters, hamburgers, or the like

Heat soup slowly, stirring; add milk gradually. When smooth and hot, add meat and eggs. Heat. Season if needed. Serve over biscuits.

TIP-TOP TUNA

2 cans condensed cream of celery soup

1 pound noodles (or macaroni)

2 7½-ounce cans shredded tuna

1 can peas

Boil noodles or macaroni as directed; drain and add ¼ stick (2 tablespoons) margarine to coat noodles. Heat undiluted soup and add heated, drained peas. Drain tuna; spread over noodles. Pour soup over tuna. Hang covered pot over low fire to heat mixture.

A.O.C. SLURP

½ pound lean salt pork or slab bacon

2 medium onions, peeled, sliced

16 pilot biscuits or other hardtack

1½-2 pounds hamburger

3 green peppers, diced

1 No. 2½ can tomatoes

Dice and fry pork to even tan; remove meat and save. Pour off half the fat and add onions and peppers; fry until onion is transparent, stirring to avoid burning. Crumble hamburger in skillet with onion and pepper; turn until hamburger is brown. Add heated tomatoes and mix. Salt and pepper to taste. Simmer 15 minutes. Serve over hardtack.

SUCCOTASH

1 can whole-kernel corn

¼ cup (½ stick) margarine

1 No. 303 can lima beans, drained

1 teaspoon salt

Combine ingredients in small pot and heat in double boiler until margarine is completely melted. You may add ½ cup milk before heating if you like. Make double boiler by putting rocks in large pot to hold the smaller pot above boiling water in large pot. Cover smaller pot.

CORN CHOWDER

8 slices bacon, 1-inch lengths

1 medium onion, minced

3 cups milk

2 small cans whole-kernel corn

4 medium potatoes

1 teaspoon salt

Pare and dice potatoes in ¾-inch cubes. Boil with a tablespoon of onion in salted water. Meanwhile, fry bacon until light brown; remove and save. Fry balance of onion in fat until light yellow. Pour off all but a cup of the potato water when potatoes are cooked. Add bacon, onion, corn, and milk to pot and heat for 10 minutes. Do not boil. Serve over pilot biscuit broken into each bowl.

Recipes are given for eight campers—adjust to your group's needs.

Red-Flannel Hash

2 cans corned beef, ½-inch cubes   1 No. 303 can beets
1 medium onion, minced   4 medium potatoes
2 slices bacon (or 1 tablespoon fat)   1 teaspoon salt

Pare and dice potatoes in ¾-inch cubes and boil in salted water. Fry bacon in large frying pan, save bacon, and fry onion in fat until light yellow. Add meat and stir to brown lightly. Add potatoes and drained beets. Crumble bacon and add. Hash with turner and allow to brown lightly on one side. Turn hash to brown other side.

All-Purpose Fried Rice

8 slices bacon, 1-inch lengths   1 medium onion, minced
1½ cups uncooked rice, culled   2 cans corned beef (1½ pounds
1 can beef or chicken consomme   hamburger; 2 cans tuna, salmon,
   (or equivalent in bouillon cubes   shrimp, or boned chicken)
   or granules, dissolved in water)   1 No. 303 or larger can tomatoes

This is a flexible recipe; you can make a number of quite different dishes—it's your choice. In a large frying pan, fry bacon until light brown. Add rice to the hot fat and stir until it is thoroughly browned, but not scorched. Put in onion and continue to stir until onion is light yellow. (If using hamburger, cook now.) Add the bouillon or consomme (beef with beef or chicken with chicken or fish). Cover pan and cook, stirring now and then, for about 5 minutes. Add meat, chicken, or fish; stir. Add tomatoes and stir. Heat uncovered until entire mixture is simmering.

Jambalaya

1 cup instant or regular rice   2 slices bacon, 1-inch lengths
   (boil as instructed)   1 tablespoon all-purpose flour
1 No. 303 can tomatoes   1 12-ounce can ham loaf, lunch
1 medium onion, minced   meat, corned beef, frankfurters or
   whatever you have

Boil the rice and keep hot. Meanwhile, fry bacon until almost done, then add onion and fry until light yellow. Add flour and stir until smooth. Add the tomatoes and juice. Bring to a boil, then add your meat, cut into bite-size chunks. Add rice. Simmer, stirring the while.

Topsy-Turvy Shepherd's Pie

1½ to 2 pounds hamburger
2 medium onions, minced
1 tablespoon fat

instant mashed potatoes (amount and preparation as directed)
2 tablespoons all-purpose flour

Melt fat and scramble hamburger in large pan. Salt to taste. Meanwhile, prepare potatoes and keep hot by putting pot in pot of hot water. Add onion to meat and stir. Mix flour with ¼ cup water—easiest way is to shake violently in screw-top container. Add to meat and stir until mixture thickens. (Add a can of drained peas and carrots if you wish.) Serve over helpings of mashed potato. Real shepherd's pie is a meat-and-vegetable hash with mashed potatoes atop as a crust and baked in an oven until lightly browned. Try it that way, too.

Desserts

FRUIT CUP. Peel, cut up 3 oranges, 3 apples, and 3 bananas in small chunks. Add 2 tablespoons sugar and ½ cup shredded coconut. Allow to blend during supper. Serve with pinch of coconut on top of portion.

APPLE BETTY. Put down ¼-inch alternating layers of cornflakes and applesauce sprinkled with sugar and a little nutmeg or cinnamon. Two No. 303 cans of sauce should do it. If you want it hot, put the ingredients in a frying pan, dot the top with margarine, and bake in an oven for about 20 minutes.

PIES AND LIKE THAT. See sections on foil and oven baking.

MAGIC LEMON PUDDING. Mix 2 cans sweetened condensed milk with ¼ cup lemon juice . . . don't be surprised by what happens. Mix with a few handfuls of crushed graham crackers, chocolate wafers, vanilla wafers, or gingersnaps. The grandfather of instant puddings.

LEMON OR ORANGE SAUCE FOR DESSERTS. Over low heat, melt ¼ cup (½ stick) margarine and blend in 2 tablespoons of flour. Add 1 cup of sugar, blend thoroughly. Slowly add 2 cups of hot water and stir until thickened. Add ¼ teaspoon salt and stir. Add ½ cup lemon juice or 1 cup unsweetened orange juice. For Goldfish Sauce, add only 1½ cups hot water and add 1 can mandarin oranges and syrup. Serve sauce over gingerbread, plum pudding, crushed gingersnaps, vanilla wafers, graham crackers and small marshmallows, or the like.

breakfast

Well, no wonder you're hungry—what's it been . . . 14 or 15 hours since supper? And it's chilly. Now's the time and this is the place for a real "loggers' breakfast," even if you skimp or skip it at home. Here's where you pick up 1,200 to 1,500 calories for a start on the day—and you can't do that on a gulp, a swig, and a hope that lunch is early. Check this: fruit or juice, hot or cold cereal, ham 'n' eggs *or* a stack of wheats and bacon *or* French toast and sausage, toast or biscuits and jam, with milk or cocoa! Why so many things? *Variety,* remember? That's how you get all the proteins, fats, and carbohydrates (plus vitamins and minerals) your body needs. Fruit, cereal, jam, and cocoa provide eye-opening energy with carbohydrates, but the long-burning fuels come from the fats and proteins of those mainstay dishes. (Has something to do with blood-sugar levels and all that good stuff.) So plan and serve and eat enough to hold you until supper—that way you don't really *need* lunch —you eat it just in case you get hungry later.

LIGHTWEIGHT? This fellow is having applesauce; hot cereal with raisins, milk, and sugar; scrambled eggs and salami; fresh biscuits, margarine, marmalade; cocoa. Everything but the biscuit spreads was packed dry, which makes it a lightweight breakfast in every way but in the punch it packs! This is real nourishment with very few "empty calories." As studies of high-school-age boys showed, those who had egg or meat for breakfast got off to a faster start and stayed "with it" much longer than those who skipped that vital protein early in the morning. So when you have so many things to do you hardly know where to begin—begin with a really first-class breakfast.

OATMEAL. Bring 2 cups of water to a rolling boil and add ½ teaspoon of salt. Sprinkle—don't dump—1 cup of quick-cooking rolled oats into the water while stirring it; don't let the water stop rolling. Then move it to a spot where it will simmer for the next 5 minutes, stirring occasionally to keep the oats from sticking to the bottom. This is only enough for two; multiply for a group—be sure your pot is big; the stuff tends to boil up.

PANCAKES. Use mix as directed or mix 1 cup of all-purpose flour, 1 teaspoon baking powder, 1 teaspoon sugar, a pinch of salt, 1 tablespoon oil or melted shortening, and a beaten egg if you have it. Enough for about 10 cakes. Mix and add milk or water to make a thickish batter that will pour easily. Heat your pan or griddle on coals until a drop of water will dance 3 seconds before evaporating. Grease lightly. Pour batter. When bubbles form, turn the cakes. A flapjack is frying-pan size—it is turned by flipping in the air. It flaps, Jack.

FRIED EGGS. Easiest and most popular breakfast eggs are fried "sunny-side up." Melt a teaspoon of margarine or bacon fat in a pan over coals; grease entire pan. Before it smokes much, break eggs into the pan. Salt and pepper lightly and fry gently until the white is firm and the yolk has a film of white—baste yolk with hot fat to glaze. Don't overcook or scorch.

159

JUICES AND SUCH. You must renew your supply of vitamin C daily — your body can't store it. Fruits, juices, and some "breakfast drinks" are rich in it—so they aren't just frills. Orange, lemon, grapefruit, and lime juices are high in "C"; tomato juice with lemon is good. Dry artificial drinks are convenient to carry; some juice concentrates need no refrigeration; small tins of pure juices are on baby-food shelves. Many juices come in big cans. (Don't mess with the frozen—read the label.) In camp you can easily stand 8 ounces of "C"-rich juice per day.

CANNED FRUITS. There are even more canned fruits than juices. No use listing them—you just take your pick.

DRIED FRUIT. Eat dry or soak overnight in plenty of water and stew with some sugar while breakfast is cooking. See directions on box.

HOT CEREALS. Follow directions on package or sprinkle 1 cup of cereal in 1 quart of furiously boiling salted (1 teaspoon) water; don't slow the boiling. Stir slowly; cook 15 minutes or to right thickness.

BOILED EGGS. Put eggs in cold water and bring to boil. Lift from heat, cover pan. In 3 minutes eggs will be soft-cooked; in 4, medium-cooked; in 15, hard-cooked. Put hard-boiled eggs in cold water to arrest cooking at once; it also makes them easier to peel.

DRY-CAMP FOIL-BOILED EGGS. Put egg on 10-inch edge of 10- by 12-inch piece of foil and roll egg into foil; twist ends of tube tightly. Nearly cover in ashes amid coals; in 5 minutes it will be soft-cooked.

SCRAMBLED EGGS. Add 1 tablespoon water and a pinch of salt for each egg in the bowl; beat vigorously with fork. Melt margarine to completely grease the pan; when it bubbles, pour eggs in; cook gently. As eggs thicken, scrape from bottom with fork quickly until all is cooked. Add diced browned bacon, ham, lunch meat, cheese, onion, peppers, peas, or combinations of these for variety and interest.

FRIED BACON. Lay slices separately on cold griddle or pan and fry over slow fire; turn often and pour off fat often. Don't overcook; it will be crisp when it dries on paper towel. Keep sliced bacon cold, slab bacon cool; unopened canned bacon need not be cooled. Use fat same day.

FRENCH TOAST. For 16 slices, beat lightly 2 eggs, 1 teaspoon salt, and 2 cups milk; dip both sides of bread in mix (don't soak) and fry on greased griddle, turning bread only once. Don't squash it. Serve with table syrup, heavy fruit syrup, or applesauce and cinnamon.

SYRUP. Melt 2 tablespoons margarine in pot, add ½ cup brown or white sugar. Stir to melt and brown *a little;* slowly add 2 cups of boiling water, stirring. Simmer 5 minutes; add flavoring, if desired.

MILK. Fresh, cold *pasteurized milk* is OK—but do not use *raw* milk! Dry whole or skim milk is convenient to carry. Buy sealed packets that make a quart; mix only enough for one meal at a time. To make a single cup, add 3 to 4 tablespoons to a cup of water (experiment with taste) or as directed on package. Whip with fork to mix and aerate the milk.

COCOA. Use instant cocoa as directed or mix ½ cup cocoa, ½ cup sugar, ¼ teaspoon salt; stir with enough hot water to make a paste. Add 2 cups boiling water. Simmer for 3 minutes, stirring. Scald and add 6 cups milk. Stir and keep warm but do not permit it to boil. Cocoa has a high fat and sugar content—if used *constantly* in place of milk, it can cause problems with an otherwise good diet.

For other suggestions for breakfast menus, see again the sections on suggested foods and menus. See other sections for breads and baking.

For a change sometime, you might try this way of coddling eggs. Clean the segments from half an orange skin or cut a large onion in half and remove all but about the three outer layers. Crack an egg into the shell and set it in the coals to cook the usual time. When done, eat it right from the container—after removing the scorched onion layer, you can even eat the container! Onions have vitamin C, too.

Most eggstraordinary method of cooking egg is on a spit. Pick a tiny hole in each end of shell and push a thin wood skewer (square it off) through the egg. Put over the coals, turning occasionally, for perhaps 10 minutes.

trail breads

Store-boughten breads don't take very kindly to packing; attempts to squash them succeed only in rendering them helpless. After a few days you'd better convert them to French toast or bread pudding. What do you do then for the "staff of life"? Make your own. You're no "sourdough"? Nothing wrong, then, with good biscuits from a reflector or Dutch oven or foil or made in one of the primitive ways shown here. Keep dough cool, handle as little as possible; flour hands before handling; add liquid at one time instead of dribbling it; bake slowly but thoroughly to an even golden brown. Use your favorite mix or this:

BAKING POWDER BISCUIT MIX

4 cups all-purpose flour	8 teaspoons baking powder
1½ teaspoons salt	⅜ cup (¾ stick) margarine
¼ cup dry skim milk	(1½ cups cold water for whole amount)

Sift or thoroughly mix dry ingredients. Cut in shortening until mixture is like coarse cornmeal. Store in plastic or waterproof food bag. To make dough for rolled biscuits, add entire amount of water and stir for ½ minute or so to gather all solids. Turn out on floured pan or foil and lightly knead or roll to desired thickness—about ½ inch thick. Cut with knife or sharp can. Or mix smaller quantity for cakes or twist.

You can mix dough right in your flour bag—pour water right into a pit made in the mix and stir it with a pencil-size clean stick until a ball of dough forms around the stick. When the ball revolves in opposite direction, remove it.

DAMPER or ASH BREAD. How primitive can you get? Pat dough into an inch-thick cake and put it on several sweet green leaves. Sweep coals and ash to one side and lay cake and leaves on hot hearth. Cover with leaves, then with gray ashes and hot coals. Test in 10 minutes by pushing dry stem of grass into it— if it comes out clean your bread is done.

TWIST. Peel a club of sweet wood 2 inches thick and 2 feet long—point ends. Preheat club near fire. Make dough. Wet the hot club and then roll a long "sausage" of dough and twist it around the club. Stick end of club in ground so dough bakes over fire. Keep turning as it browns —reverse ends of club to even out browning. You can keep an eye on this bread, so don't let it bake too quickly or burn.

BANNOCK. Canoe-country standby is this frying-pan loaf. Recipes vary, but the biscuit dough works fine. Make an inch-thick loaf as big as your pan. Don't grease the pan. Bake for 7 or 8 minutes over slow coals to brown the bottom, then tilt pan almost upright before a brighter fire to finish off the top. Test with stem in another 7 or 8 minutes. No hurry—it'll wait.

163

meat

BROILING. Steaks and chops are often broiled, and they should be tender and cut about an inch thick. Marinate or brush with oil and add seasoning *except* salt—salt when done. Hold about 4 inches over bright coals or to one side to avoid oily smoke or fire from drippings. Turn only once, and cook 9 minutes each side for medium well-done. Pork and veal should be cooked thoroughly and slowly; no pink juices from pork!

PAN BROILING. Better than frying. Heat ungreased pan or griddle over hot coals. With lean meat, rub pan with a bit of meat fat to prevent sticking. Sear meat on one side for 1 minute and turn; cook 8 minutes per side for medium well-done. Pour off fat as it accumulates, otherwise you're *frying* the meat. Season after cooking.

BRAISING. Moist heat is best for thin cuts of tough beef (Swiss steak), thick pork chops, and veal cutlet. Dredge meat in seasoned flour and brown in hot fat in pan. Add some water, cover pan tightly, and cook gently: 1 hour for beef, 30 minutes for pork chops, 20 minutes for veal; turn once halfway through cooking.

POT ROASTING. Exactly the same as braising except with large cuts of meat. Specific recipe is given in "Dutch Oven Cooking."

ROASTING. For better cuts of meat. Dry heat radiated from fire or walls of Dutch oven does the trick slowly. Don't sear or dredge meat; place on upturned metal plate in oven. Start with *hot* oven, then cut heat somewhat. You can use a reflector oven if it's big enough. Try dangling leg of lamb from wire between two fires; allow it to twist and turn; catch drippings in pan. Rule of thumb: roast ½ hour per pound.

Sirloin on a grill—what more can be said? That's what happiness is!

KABOB or SHISH KEBAB. Use a metal skewer or a 2-foot straight stick (from unwanted growth) about as thick as a lead pencil and point one end. Better peel it. Cut tender beefsteak or lamb shoulder into I-inch squares; it may be marinated if need be. Peel onions and cut lengthwise once; separate the layers. To get fancy, cut up bacon, quarter tomatoes, slice cucumbers, or quarter green peppers, as you wish, too. Alternate slices of meat with vegetables on skewer, then put over or beside hot coals, turning to broil evenly. Let everybody do his own. Eat right from stick.

FOIL ROASTING. Wrap a 4-pound rolled chuck roast in heavy foil; sprinkle with dehydrated onion soup as you roll it. Place in large Dutch oven preheated *very hot*. Be sure foil is sealed and untorn. Cook 25 minutes per pound with reduced heat. To roast over coals, first skewer lengthwise with 1-inch peeled stick long enough to prop on rocks so roast is 6 inches over coals; roll in foil, twisting ends securely at stick. This cooks in own juices. Turn often. Open carefully. Salt.

STEWING. A long process to make meat tender; allow 3 hours. Use a Dutch oven or 4-quart pot and fry fat from 1/2 cup of diced salt pork (or use 1/2 stick margarine or 1/4 cup oil) to brown meat in. Dredge 1-inch or smaller cubes of trimmed lean beef, veal, or lamb in seasoned flour and brown *all* sides in fat. Add enough water to cover; cover pot and put it to simmer for 2 hours, checking water level occasionally. Meanwhile wash, peel, and cut up 1 medium potato, carrot, onion, turnip, and tomato per person. Add these for last 3/4 hour of stewing or boil separately 1/2 hour and add for last 1/4 hour.

fish

Ever have the grand luck to show up in camp with a mess of trout just in time for breakfast? You know how good fish can be, then. They lose flavor about as fast as they lose their color, though. It takes proper handling and cooking to know trout at their best; otherwise you wonder what all the shouting about trout is for.

Don't soak or overwash them. Use only fresh fat when pan frying them. That's the commonest way of cooking trout, and it can be good. However, it can be bad, spoiling even the best fish. It also gets monotonous, especially on a long fishing trip. So if you're able to swing a fish from pond to pan in one flip, try these new ways of cooking them.

If the trout aren't cooperating, don't turn up your nose at crappies, bluegills, perch, bullheads, or other panfish. They can be delectable.

No fishing? OK, so bring the canned variety, like salmon, tuna, sardines, or cod. Or luxury items like shrimp, crab, anchovies, or lobster! Fish may not be "brain food," but it's a smart camper who makes use of this handy source of high-protein food.

With canned fish you can't follow the recipes shown here for fresh trout, but you can make a whole list of fine fish dishes from a simple sardine sandwich to a seafood Tetrazinni with canned fish.

For a seafood salad on the trail, use canned condensed cream of celery soup instead of mayonnaise or salad dressing (which is dangerous without refrigeration) and add minced onion, sweet pickle, and a dash of lemon juice to give tuna, salmon, or shrimp a real jolt. Good in sandwiches. Use chopped olives instead of pickle and use the same mix in a casserole on a bed of noodles, with peas or hard-boiled egg.

PAN FRIED. Wipe trout dry and remove head, tail, and fins after gutting, if you prefer. Heat 1/8 inch of margarine, butter, cooking oil, or bacon fat in the frying pan. Coat the fish with seasoned flour and fry until golden brown, rocking pan now and then to prevent sticking.

POACHED. For the delicacy blue trout, you must have freshly caught fish. Do not wipe off slime—this is what turns blue—handle as little as possible. Add ¼ cup of vinegar to just enough water to cover fish. Slip fish one at a time into boiling water, so boiling won't stop. Poach 6 minutes.

STAKED. Simplest way to cook trout. Cut a stick for each fish, 4 inches or so longer than fish. Point one end. Tie trout to stick at tail and gills, head toward the point. Push stick into shallow coals until heads are partly covered. Cook for about 10 minutes.

FOILED. Gut and wipe, but don't skin or scale. Take 2 feet of foil and double it. Rub margarine or bacon fat on the foil and roll fish singly, crimping ends of foil packet. Place packets on glowing coals. After 5 minutes, turn packet over, cook 5 minutes more. Open and salt fish. Simple and neat.

SMOKED. Chop up red cedar twigs and put 2 inches deep in large pot. Behead and clean fish. String fish by tails on sticks and hang from pot rim. Cover pot and put it over fire. Fish should be done in about an hour—the flesh tender and juicy, the skin tough.

167

chicken

A bird in the hand is worth two in the bush, as the saying goes. But even one in the bush can be very fine when roasted to juicy splendor before your very eyes. Most everybody likes chicken and the price is usually reasonable. You can treat it in several interesting ways.

However you do it, make it a first-night performance because it's hard to keep it safe for long. Keep it cool until used. Presumably it is minus head, feet, feathers, and innards—if not, get it that way. Be sure it is completely cleaned; that is, all kidneys and doodads inside removed. Don't soak it long in water, but wipe it all over inside and out with a clean damp paper towel or cloth. Remove pin feathers.

Now, how to cook it? Simplest way is to spit it and rotate it to one side of the coals (so you can put a pan or foil under it to catch the drippings for basting so it won't dry out). Turn to an even "tan." To prevent the breast drying out before the legs are done, you may be able to rig a foil "bib." Baste the whole bird often to keep it juicy.

You can cut apart a young fryer or broiler for pan frying or foil roasting or oven frying in a Dutch oven (which is OK for a small whole bird). Melt fat in pan and thoroughly dust bird or parts in seasoned flour.

A way out of baby-sitting with the chicken is to make an *imu* (ee-moo), that practical Polynesian picnic. Heat a stone-lined pit red hot, rake out the coals, and put in a thickish layer of moistened sweet leaves. Then comes a layer of whole chickens, sweet potatoes, corn rewrapped in the husks, greenish bananas, and maybe a whole pineapple! Cover with a layer of moistened leaves and a wet burlap bag. Now fill in the hole with earth up to ground level. After 2 hours, have a little luau.

Primitive way is to spit chicken on a peeled stick run from vent to neck. Truss bird securely so it will turn with spit. If wings or legs stick out, they'll burn before bird is done. Test doneness by twisting leg; when thigh is loose, the entire bird should be OK.

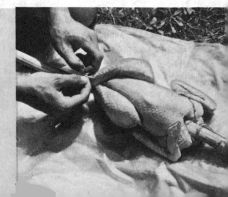

Another way to do it is to suspend the bird from a dingle stick to one side of the fire over a foil or other drip pan. Prepare bird as usual and truss the legs and wings. Then run skewers through wings and upper body and the thighs and lower body. Be sure the drumsticks are snugged down and that the wing tips don't stick out. Now hang the bird from the dingle stick by running a thong under the skewer. While cooking, turn it now and then so both back and front get the heat, and when about half done, swap skewers so top and bottom are done equally. Baste the breast particularly, as it tends to dry out before the rest cooks.

Now here's an inside-out imu that will work while you're traveling—and be there when you get there! Prepare the fowl as usual except for trussing. Meanwhile, be heating up a batch of stones that will go into—and fill—the cavity of the bird. When they're red hot, fill the bird and quickly truss the legs and wings securely. Wrap the bird in foil, sealing it, and then be prudent and put it in a plastic bag to catch stray juices. Put the package in the center of a packsack loaded with dry leaves for insulation; fill with more leaves and strap the pack. Stash the pack in your canoe or even carry it. In 3 or 4 hours the bird should be ready—and so should you.

foil cookery

Want a good hot hike meal without lugging pans or washing dishes? Take foil! Don't take the whole roll if it doesn't fit your kit—take as much as you need, carefully folded to convenient size. Or carry your food (except eggs or biscuit dough) already packaged ready for the fire. Be careful, though, it's tender and easily torn or punctured, which spoils it. Use two thicknesses to make the packets for steam baking—or make utensils for frying or boiling from two layers when you're ready to cook. Shape foil for small pots over your fist and roll and crimp the edges to make them sturdy; improvise larger ones by folding or pinching the foil. Keep it simple; you needn't mess around with wire to make handles or a frame; you can manage, especially around the coals needed for foil cooking. Temper the live coals with hot ashes to avoid incineration of the food. Check the progress of sealed food packages until you learn timing, even though steam will escape and slow things down. You'll get the hang of it. Carry a plastic bag to carry home the used foil. *Don't leave it!*

BURGER IN ARMOR. Wash, peel, and cut in ⅛-inch slices a medium potato and a large carrot. Double foil into an 18-inch square and spread the vegetables on one-quarter of it, leaving a 2-inch margin around them. Pat ¼ pound of hamburger into a ¾-inch cake and put it beside the vegetables. Salt the vegetables but not the meat; pepper if you like. Add slices of onion and a dab of butter. Fold empty side of the foil over until edges are even. Turn a ½-inch fold over and crease; fold twice more, pressing flat. Do the same at both ends to seal packet. There is (or should be) room for expansion. Set on tempered coals and cover with more. Cook 15 to 20 minutes. Eat from foil.

BISCUITS or SHORTCAKE. Use mix or favorite recipe and make dough, adding 1 tablespoon of sugar per cup of dry ingredients for shortcake. Mix with water right in the carrying bag, stirring with stick until dough makes ball on stick. Flour hands, pat dough into ½-inch-thick biscuit with minimum handling. Grease a 12-inch square of doubled foil, and fold as for burger recipe. Bake in coals 10 minutes, turning packet to even browning. Leave plenty of room in packet for dough to rise. Eat as is or save to combine with fruit.

BAKED FRUIT. Wash and cut a lid off the top of an apple. Remove the core and sprinkle in a teaspoon of sugar or cinnamon sugar for zip. Add a generous chunk of butter. Center in large square of doubled foil and bring corners up over apple. Twist to close foil tightly. Bake 10 minutes or so in coals. To bake a banana, wrap it, skin and all, in doubled foil and twist ends to seal. Bake it about 10 minutes. Serve the fruit in the foil—it's less messy to spoon out that way. Try adding berries or fruit to foil-baked shortcake.

bean hole

A bean hole is for cooking beans (and other things). First, the beans:

BAKED BEANS

1½ pounds pea beans	½ pound salt pork,
1 large onion, chopped	cut in inch cubes
(¼ cup catsup, optional)	½ cup brown sugar
1 tablespoon dry mustard	*or* ⅜ cup molasses
1 teaspoon salt	¼ teaspoon pepper

Don't start an argument—if you don't like the recipe, change it. (Nothing like a bean recipe to start a hassle!) Wash, cull (watch for stones), and soak beans overnight, covered by 3 inches of water, in a large pot. Then bring to a boil and simmer about 45 minutes until a bean skin pops when you blow on it. Drain beans, saving 2 cups of water. Mix everything thoroughly in your bean pot, Dutch oven, or whatever, saving a few extra chunks of pork for the top. Add bean water. Cover pot tightly. Bake 6 to 8 hours in hole. Uncover cautiously. Open lid humbly. Eat!

Bean holes aren't just for beans. You can cook lots of one-pot meals while you're off having a good time. Heated stones do the job. Dig a hole 1½ feet wider and a foot deeper than your pot after it is lined with dry, flat, nonexplosive stones. Bridge it with some sticks and lay a big crisscross to get a good fire going. Keep feeding it until you have a hole full of embers so the stones are white-hot. Your pot should be ready now. Shovel the coals out and set the pot in on the stones. Replace the embers around the pot and over it, then mound it over with the excavated dirt. Mark the spot well!

ONE-POT FEAST. Get a large cut of beef, veal, lamb, pork, chicken, or fish ready for roasting. (Dredge and sear red meats in hot fat first.) The vegetables you use perhaps depend on the meat, but use raw ones as they will be cooking a long time. Clean and cut up the vegetables and arrange them in the pot around the meat. Add 1½ cups of hot water and cover the pot securely. That's the last time you'll see it until you dig it up, so check the estimated time of cooking the meat and scoop the embers out of the pit.

Lower the bucket and surround it with embers. Cover over with embers, then a layer of dirt. Of course, you left the bail of the pot up so you can locate it when you excavate. Cover snugly and mark the area to keep oafs off. When it is time, find the bail and dig gingerly. Haul up the pot and don't tip the lid; it's too great for grit in it!

173

dutch-oven cooking

Boiling and frying are OK, but for something fancier—especially in long-term camping—you'll want to be able to roast and bake foods too. Best all-round utensil for this is the Dutch oven. This deep, thick-walled pot has flaring sides and a close-fitting flat lid with a turned-up rim for holding coals on top. It sits on coals, on legs, or on a separate rack. Old-time ovens were heavy cast iron, but now you can get aluminum ones, too, that are lighter. The 12-inch size holds 7 quarts; the 10-inch one, 3 quarts. The rack of the smaller one stores inside it, and the whole thing goes inside the larger oven for storage or travel. Neat. Except when used as a regular pot, the oven is usually *preheated* before food is put in to bake. The trick is getting the heat just right—you regulate it by adding or taking away coals, so you have to experiment. It's not too difficult, but the tendency is to get it too hot. Check progress of cooking by lifting lid, with tongs or hook, and testing. The Dutch oven is well worth mastering—it's the camp cook's friend.

Dutch ovens are naturals for one-pot meals, but if you want to get spoiled, try the luxury of a whole battery of ovens: one for meat, one for vegetables, others for bread, pies, cake, cobbler, or you name it. This is real living. Yes, Sir!

POT ROAST. Dredge a 4-pound roast and brown all sides in hot fat in oven. Add ½ inch of water, put on lid; add coals to lid. Simmer 2 to 3 hours, adding water as needed, until tender; add peeled potato, onion, and carrot per diner for last 45 minutes.

OVEN-FRIED CHICKEN. Use ½ fryer per person, cut into two pieces. Dip in cold water, wipe dry; shake in seasoned flour in paper bag. Put 2 tablespoons of fat or cooking oil in hot oven, and brown chicken pieces all over. Then turn skin-side down. Cover with lid; add coals. Bake, basting occasionally, for 15 minutes. Turn pieces over and cook until tender, about 25 minutes.

BAKED POTATO. Scrub well one big potato per person. Prick skin with a fork and grease lightly. Wrap tightly in foil and put on plate set on pebbles in hot oven. Cover; add coals to lid. Bake for an hour or so. Test with splinter—mealy crumbs sticking to wood show potato is done. Slash an X in foil and potato and pinch to push it open. Add butter and salt.

BAKED APPLE. Wash, core large apple per serving. Fill hole with sugar, raisins, and dab of butter—cinnamon, if desired. Put apples on greased plate and add some water. Put plate in hot oven on three pebbles to prevent burning. Cover and bake for about 30 minutes.

175

dutch-oven baking

Baking in a Dutch oven is a piece of cake—also bread, rolls, biscuits, muffins, gems, pone, cookies, pie, tarts, cobbler, or what would you like? Start with a mix, a family "scratch" recipe, or some in this book.

PIECRUST *(For 9-inch double-crust pie)*

2¼ cups all-purpose flour	6 tablespoons (¾ stick) margarine
1 teaspoon salt	¼ cup (about) cold water

Thoroughly mix salt in flour. Cut in shortening to size of peas with edge of fork or two knives. Sprinkle water on mixture, mixing with fork, until you think dough can be formed into a ball. Handle very lightly. Follow commercial-mix directions exactly; to make a 9-inch double-crust pie, in small frying pan of Trail Chef kit, use one and a half 10-ounce boxes of mix; two packages for a double-crust pie in large frying pan. Roll out bottom dough about 3 inches wider than top diameter of pan.

BISCUITS. Use mix or biscuit recipe. Preheat oven. Turn dough out on lightly floured board and knead 30 seconds. Roll to ½-inch thickness. Cut squares with knife or remove ends from small can to cut round biscuits. Flour edge of can. Press, don't twist.

Don't roll or reknead dough scraps; press them together gently to make a biscuit-sized piece.

Handle dough tenderly or biscuits get "sad." Put cut biscuits in bottom of ungreased oven with some space between. Put lid on and set oven on coals; add coals to lid—it must be quite hot. Check in 10 minutes; test with straw. They may take 12 or 15 minutes to bake.

176

DEEP-DISH PIE. Start with a mix or recipe opposite. Divide dough in two parts. Roll out bottom ⅛ inch thick and 8 inches wider than oven. Fold once and lay in cold oven; unfold and tuck into shape. Don't stretch it or it will shrink on baking.

Bake pie shell in oven for about 10 minutes, then have a look. Starting with a cold oven, the shell should be firm but not done. Rub bottom lightly with margarine. Now add a prepared fruit pie filling (unless you have fresh fruit at hand)—about two cans—up to the rim of the shell. Don't break the crust or the filling will leak through and burn on bottom.

For a lattice crust, customary with some pies, roll out rest of dough ⅛ inch thick and an inch wider than the oven. Cut into narrow strips and cover pie as shown. Moisten ends with water and press to crust lightly — leave some slack for shrinkage. (Other pies are completely covered with upper crust which must be slit to vent steam. In this case, both bottom and top crust are baked, with filling, at the same time, starting wih cold oven.)

Replace hot lid and bake pie until the lattice is browned. The filling should be hot by then—prepared fillings don't need cooking. With raw fruit, bake entire pie all at once to cook filling. A closed crust is best for firm fruit, but don't forget to make steam vents.

177

reflector-oven baking

A reflector oven is something well worth having in camp. It's great for baking biscuits, bread, pies, and cake, or for roasting meat, fish, or poultry. Its big advantage is that it is lightweight and the folding or take-apart types are very compact, compared to a Dutch oven. It works on the principle, as its name implies, of reflected heat, rather than radiation from the heated walls of an oven. It won't hold heat and being open loses heat quickly if the fire is not kept up. But because it uses a bright fire, you needn't wait for coals to start cooking; it's especially good where hardwood for coals just isn't. It starts to work immediately, but you must be quick to adjust it to varying fire conditions. You do this by moving the whole oven close to or back from the fire or by adding fast fuel. Check distance with the back of your hand—hold your hand in front of the oven and slowly count to eight. If you can't keep it there that long, it's too hot—more is too cool. Fortunately, you can watch your food through the open front, and turn it to avoid scorching and to ensure thorough cooking. You can even improvise a reflector out of sticks and heavy aluminum foil—it works! Folding ovens are bent out of line somewhat easily—so pack in a bag and stow carefully; don't lose small parts. All ovens must be bright to work well—so keep them clean and well scoured. They're a real joy.

This fresh berry pie is the kind of thing that makes worthwhile the getting or making (and toting) of a reflector oven. Get camp off to a real start or buck up spirits for the way back. With a reflector oven you can see the progress and adjust baking conditions. If anticipation is half of fulfillment, you've got it made!

Make pastry dough right in the baking pan: Use a mix and make half quantity for the bottom; gently pat dough thinly over pan. Or use piecrust recipe; divide in two, and roll out bottom crust.

Now fill crust with washed, culled, and hulled berries. To a pint of berries add ½ cup of sugar, 2 tablespoons of flour, and a dash of cinnamon, if you like. (Be sure to bring some along if it's berry season, for goodness' sake! After all, you brought the oven.)

Mix the other half of your pastry on a sheet of foil, lightly floured, and pat it out with floured hands (or roll it) to ⅛-inch thickness, an inch wider than the pan. Keep it uniform and avoid patching, if possible. An aluminum tent-pole section makes a pretty good rolling pin. Keep it clean.

Flip the whole business over on top of the pie, centering it carefully on the pie. Now peel back the foil from the crust, and trim and crimp the edges to seal it off. Slash the crust to vent the steam, or prick it here and there with a fork if you'd rather.

Put your pies (why stop at one?) on the oven shelf. Build up your fire; you're using reflected heat, so keep that fire bright. Keep an eye out for scorching, and turn occasionally.

fish fry

For a real way down South fish fry, complete with hush puppies, you need *catfish*. But if you can't get 'em (and why not—they're everywhere), use any firm-fleshed fish. Get yourself a pan big enough and enough vegetable fat to submerge the fish completely. Keep it smoking hot. Just follow directions and you can hardly lose. Then make the hush puppies. *Hush puppies?* Sure. Seems a good Southern hound dog can smell a fish fry for miles and come yawping and begging. Now the fish is too good for 'em, so somebody got smart and fried up some bitty cakes of meal in the fish pan to fool them. You'd throw one to the dog and say, "Hush, puppy!" See? Now don't waste these on dogs—they're *people*food!

You don't scale catfish—you skin them. Stick the head on a hook or nail, cut the skin around the "neck," and then pull the skin off with pliers. Watch out for the dangerous spikes on the fins, they're sharp and poisonous, too. You know, catfish is much better eating than looking!

Cut large fish in serving-size chunks; fillet medium-size fish; fry small ones whole. Have fat hot enough to brown a 1-inch cube of bread in 20-25 seconds, about 375° F. Keep the fat that hot all through the cooking, if you can. You'll want a good supply of fast fuel on hand because the heat is important.

Dip cut-up fish in clean water, then coat it thoroughly all over with the "crumblin' mix" that will put a golden shell over that succulent morsel. See recipe for mix on opposite page.

Lower coated fish carefully into fat, a few pieces at a time so fat won't cool down and make the fish too greasy. Cook and turn until the whole outside is golden brown, the inside all flaky.

Make your hush puppies from a rather stiff dough, using a mix or the recipe given. Dip a teaspoon in grease and scoop up some dough. Drop it in the hot fat. This should be enough for one hush puppy. From time to time, dip the spoon in fat so the dough won't stick to it.

Now with hush puppies in the fat, turn them and keep an eye on them. Fry until the dough is crisp and brown—keep the heat up to prevent sogginess. Remove from the fat and dry on a paper towel or brown paper. They should be eaten while they're still hot, along with those delicious chunks of fish.

CRUMBLIN' MIX *(For 10 pounds of fish)*

1 cup medium-fine cornmeal	1 cup flour
2 tablespoons salt	1 teaspoon pepper

HUSH-PUPPY DOUGH

4 cups medium-fine cornmeal	4 tablespoons flour
4 teaspoons baking powder	2 teaspoons salt
2 large onions, finely chopped	4 cups milk
2 eggs, lightly beaten	

Mix dry ingredients thoroughly, then add onion, milk, and eggs to make a fairly stiff, sticky dough. If using prepared mix, follow directions.

salmon bake

Chinook salmon, right out of the water, baked Indian-fashion over red-alder coals is something you'd never forget. But try *any* big fish—shad, pickerel, walleye, or whatever you're catching—by this method. Not only is it easy, there's no better way, really.

As usual, a lot depends on how you build your fire. Start with a criss-cross lay of sound hardwood. Put on all the wood you'll need—you want *coals* and plenty of 'em, so don't count on adding any fuel later.

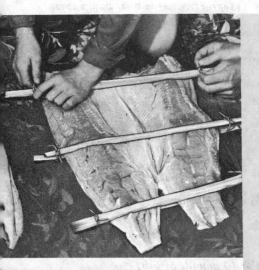

Note that this salmon was cut through from the back, and the backbone taken out, leaving the belly intact to hold the sides together, Chinook-style. Now spread the fish on three stout peeled sticks, with three more added on top of the fish, so they're paired. Tie each set of sticks together at the ends to clamp the fish firmly. Use only "sweet wood" for making the rack, those with a neutral taste.

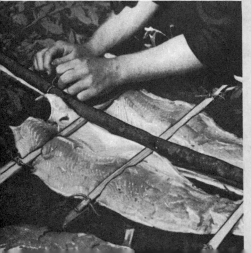

Split a 2-inch stick 3 feet long to make the upright for your broiler rack. Wire the two halves together on the outsides of the three pairs of cross sticks. If you are smart you will have already dug a hole big enough and deep enough to hold this upright, with room for rocks to adjust it to the right angle. This would be very hot or impossible to do after the fire is started. And you had best get the brace rocks now.

182

So, you have a hole for the broiler, you have the rack built around your fish, and you have a large, deep bed of coals going that will last long enough to cook the fish. Naturally this depends much on how big a fish you have. Set the rack beside your fire, flesh-side-to and leaning in over the pile of coals. Brace it sturdily.

From time to time, test the progress of your bake by pushing a sliver of wood into the flesh. When it comes out clean or with small crumbs of dryish meat on it, the fish is done. The 11-pound salmon shown here was cooked in about an hour. But a great deal depends on your fish, your bed of coals, how the wind blows, and maybe the phase of the moon . . . but you know how you like your fish done. The thinner section of the fish, of course, will be done first. If it tends to dry out, brush it with melted margarine.

Now lay your fish on a clean bed of boughs and yell, "Come and get it!" The simplest, best way to serve it is to use fingers for forks in the ancient Chinook way, as this Explorer demonstrates to the Scout. Fish prepared in this way has a terrific flavor with the addition of the usual fish sauces.

183

clambake

How about a Down East clambake? You don't have to be lucky and live on the coast—today you can have one most anywhere. The menu is authentic, the method true—although you may have to tinker it up a bit. Get one lively lobster, 30 clams, a couple of roasting ears, and a sweet potato apiece, and have a pound of melted butter for every 10 people. Butter goes on everything but the pickles, watermelon, and lemonade!

You want plenty of good kindling to get 'er started, and have on hand all the wood you'll need for the whole thing. Use a crisscross lay of kindling and pile on about two bushels of fist-sized, dry rocks so's not to cut off the draft. Touch 'er off!

When she's going real good, stack your cordwood—an eighth of a cord or so—around the fire and on it. It'll take an hour to get stones red-hot, which is the idea. An eighth of a cord would be 2 feet wide and 2 feet high and 4 feet long. Quite a bit.

Now get busy with the candidates. Scrub the clams clean of all sand. Husk the corn; pick the silk, and snap off stalk stubs. Put the butter in covered cream cans or cocoa pots to melt in the steam. Calm the lobsters. Stones ready?

GO! Don't lose the heat while you build the bake. Rake out smoking embers (steam, not smoke, does it). Level the rocks. Cover them with 8 bushels of wet seaweed (rock-weed is best) or wet corn-husks. Save some for the top layer.

Quick—put the ingredients on top of the steaming seaweed in layers: potatoes on the bottom, then the lobsters, then the corn, and last, the clams. Cover with wet husks or more seaweed. But hurry, you want to catch all that steam!

Throw a canvas tarp over the whole heap and haul it down tight. If steam shows along the edges of the tarp, close it off with sand. Now go do something—like swim—for 45 minutes or so. Carefully open up a corner and test a potato; if it's done, all is ready.

Uncover the bake from one side to get at the good things while the rest stays hot. Watch the sand! One lobster, 30 clams, a tater, and a couple roasting ears to a customer. Who forgot to put in the butter? No watermelon for him!

after the meal

Instead of sticking a couple of guys with the dishwashing chore for the whole group, it's a lot faster for each camper to do his own in a kind of "assembly line" setup. Two of the campers will still be responsible for doing the pots and pans, and since that's a pretty good job in itself, a couple of other fellows who don't have a job for that meal usually do their own dishes plus those of the two men busy with the pots and pans. Dishwashing may be a chore, but a good case of ptomaine from dirty dishes is a very convincing argument in favor of thorough cleansing. The secret of good dishwashing in camp is plenty of hot water. Modern detergents do a good job of cleaning the utensils, but it takes hot rinse water to sterilize the utensils and give them enough heat to dry by themselves when set aside. Throw away that old dish towel. It's not needed if rinse water is hot, and at best just spreads germs from one dish to another.

Disposal of dishwater will vary according to the campsite you are in. In a camping area that is lightly used, with periods of several weeks between use by another group, dishwater can be carried to the edge of the camping area and poured out on the ground.

In a heavily used area such as a permanent camp or where many other troops are involved such as a camporee, a permanent dishwater-disposal sump should be installed. The old individual patrol hole-in-the-ground disposal method was never very satisfactory and should not be used.

A steady supply of hot water is important to every good camper. As soon as your fire is built, set a pot of water close to the edge where it will be heating throughout the time you are cooking. If it isn't boiling by the time you need it for dishwashing, place the pot over the fire to bring to a boil. As long as your fire is still burning, keep the pot warming. You'll then enjoy warm water for cleaning hands and face.

The "assembly line" dishwashing method will speed up the process while forcing each camper to do an adequate job. The line won't be long since each cooking group has its own setup to take care of garbage disposal, washing in soapy water, rinsing in hot water with a sanitizing agent, and finally air-drying on a plastic sheet.

Have a rubber plate scraper or supply of paper towels at the refuse pail at the first station of the line. Each camper in turn scrapes the scraps and goo from his plate so they won't go in the dishwater. There should be no food floating in the dishwater and only a few soap bubbles on the rinse water at the end of the session.

Next stop is the dishwater pot with detergent-loaded water. A dishmop (cloth or sponge on a stick) is used by each camper to clean off his own plate, cup, and utensils. Hot-pot tongs are best for handling dishes in this very hot water.

Rinse water must be nearly boiling so dishes will be degreased, sanitary, and hot enough to dry without wiping. A chemical sanitizing agent available at your local Scout distributor will ensure proper sanitization even if rinse water cannot be maintained at proper heat. Allow dishes to remain in rinse water at least I minute. Handle them with tongs to avoid scalding yourself.

Spread a plastic sheet at the end of your dishwashing assembly line. Put a stick under it, if you wish, to make a ridge to lean dishes against so they will drain; aluminum cools quickly and will air-dry only if water drains rapidly, so stack 'em on edge. Sunlight is beneficial, but as soon as the dishes dry each camper should pick up his own gear and store it. Put group gear away.

Disposal of dry garbage is simple in camp. Just save it until you are through cooking and burn it in your fire. Such things as onion skins, dried biscuit dough, and paper can be put directly in the flames or on hot coals. Don't let them smolder in the ashes; the stench is most unpleasant. Burn them up and leave a clean fire pit.

188

Wet garbage is another story: The problem can be solved, though, by drying the garbage before burning. Put it close to the fire at one edge, preferably spread on a hot flat rock that will transmit heat up through the garbage and help dry it out. As the part nearest the fire dries, push it into the fire to burn. Move the rest closer to the fire replacing that which has been burned. Carefully pour grease from a skillet or other pan directly on the fire but watch for flare-up.

Put empty tin cans directly on the fire when you are through cooking. The remaining food will burn out. Remove from the fire with a stick, and when cool, flatten the can by stepping on it. Wash out empty jars and put them with the flattened cans in your tote-litter bag.

An item of equipment that should be on every hike or camping trip is a tote-litter bag. This bag is for carrying out foil, burned and flattened tin cans, and washed-out jars. These are not to be buried at your campsite. You carried them in when they were full and heavy—it's no real problem to carry them back out when they are empty and light. Put them in the nearest trash can.

189

10 PHYSICAL FITNESS

NATURALLY you want to be physically fit. But are you willing to make the effort? It may not be easy. Physically, it costs some sweat—maybe even some agony. Mentally, it takes a lot of self-discipline. But you're the one—the only one, you know—who can do it.

Just about everybody knows the importance of fitness . . . it's the basis of personal well-being. And for your efforts the payoff begins right away with increased strength, agility, and stamina for today's jobs and fun. The dividend is a sound physique for the long tomorrows ahead.

To begin, you should have a health examination by a physician once a year. Underscore this as the most important step in your personal fitness program. If the physician finds your body in good working order, he'll give you a clean bill of health; if he finds any weak points, he can advise you on what to do about them.

So much of good health is a matter of good habits. Good or bad, your health habits are pretty well fixed in the days of your youth. Fortunately, there's no big mystery about practical rules for good health—they involve such common-sense factors as cleanliness, good nutrition, exercise and physical activity, balanced by adequate sleep.

There's no lack of free advice on health habits—it is available from your leaders, teachers, and parents, and even if not always backed up by a good example, it is likely to be factual and helpful. (For instance, any adult who smokes would probably advise you not to smoke because of the health hazards involved.) But be wary of free advice from people of any age who are not known to have sound values, experience, and mature judgment. This is *your* life you're talking about! And it is *your* decision and *your* willpower and *your* effort that will establish personal health habits vital to your physical fitness.

So give yourself a body with muscles and nerves ready for action—with plenty of reserve energy—to carry you through a lifetime. The man you will become is being built today. How're you doing?

nourishment

The food you eat should do three things: it should help you grow; it should give your body tissues and organs (liver, spleen, and others) the material they need to maintain themselves; it should provide you with the energy for your many activities.

The four food groups form the basis for such a balanced diet. They contain all the proteins, fats, carbohydrates, vitamins, and minerals necessary for good health.

Besides solid nourishment and milk, you need plenty of water during the day. Water is necessary for the digestion of food and for carrying away waste. It is also important for regulating the heat of the body.

If you eat a variety of foods, get a reasonable amount of exercise, drink plenty of water, you'll develop a regular time for elimination. Don't worry about how often your bowels move—worrying is a frequent cause of constipation. And don't take a laxative if you feel constipated—it throws your automatic mechanism out of gear. Simply drink three glasses of water before breakfast. The idea that your bowels should move once a day is out of date. The only right schedule is your own schedule.

1. **Meat, poultry, fish, and eggs.** Eat at least two helpings every day and three or four eggs a week.
2. **Milk and milk products.** Drink a quart of milk a day and eat cheese and ice cream.
3. **Vegetables and fruits.** Eat citrus fruits or tomatoes daily and dark-green or deep-yellow vegetables at least every other day. Eat potatoes, other vegetables, and other fruits twice a day.
4. **Bread and flour products.** Eat at least four helpings a day.

A tanned look is a healthy look. But take precautions to get a *tan*—not a burn. If your skin is quite sensitive to the sun, follow this system: The first day, expose your skin to the sun for only 10 to 15 minutes. If your skin is red the next day, wait for the redness to disappear before you expose it for another 10 to 15 minutes. After this, you can usually add 15 minutes' exposure a day. In a few weeks you will have a deep tan and will be able to withstand exposure to the sun most of the day. Of course, if you tan easily, you may increase the length of exposure much faster.

To live and grow, each cell of the body must have a steady supply of oxygen from the air. The oxygen must reach the lungs through the nose —not through the mouth. Breathing through the mouth supplies the lungs with cold, dry, dirty air, whereas breathing through the nose gives them warm, moist, filtered air. If you keep your mouth shut for breathing, you must keep the nasal passages clear. But be careful when you blow your nose or you may cause painful ear trouble. Always blow it gently, one nostril at a time, never both together. If you have any trouble breathing through your nose, see your doctor.

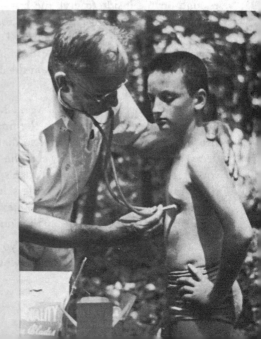

Nourishment, fresh air, and sunshine help you grow like other living things. Life, a priceless gift, is guarded by a doctor who listens to the beat of your heart, thumps your chest and back, looks down your throat and in your ears. Checkups are necessary. If the doctor finds your body in fine working order, he will give you a clean bill of health. If he discovers any weak points, he will tell you how to strengthen them.

193

cleanliness

Bathe regularly—every day, if possible. If you are unable to get a daily bath or shower, you should at least wash your body every day with a wet cloth. Follow the sponging with a brisk rubdown until your skin tingles. In addition to this quick daily bath, take a more leisurely bath— with plenty of soap and warm water—twice a week and after any hike or strenuous game that leaves you grimy and sweaty.

Get into the habit of washing your hands with soap and a nailbrush morning and night, before every meal, after each trip to the toilet, and any other time your hands are dirty. Make sure you dry them thoroughly. Remove all dirt from under your fingernails. If you do work that causes dirt to collect under the nails, scrape them over a piece of soap before you start working. The soap keeps out dirt and makes washing easier. Trim your fingernails regularly to a proper length with a nail file or small curved nail scissors. After cutting the nails, use your thumbnail to push back the cuticles.

Keep your feet clean at all times. Cut your toenails straight across to prevent ingrown toenails. If you have sweaty feet, frequent washing and thorough drying are particularly important. If you have athlete's foot, see your doctor and follow his advice. Wear shoes that are straight enough on the inside to give the big toe room to point straight ahead and wide enough to give all the toes room to move. Wear the right size socks, and change them frequently. To walk correctly, bring the foot down almost flat. The toes should point straight ahead or even slightly inward. Toeing-in and walking on the outer edges of the feet strengthen the arches of the feet.

Wash your hair about once a week. Every day exercise your scalp by brushing and massaging it with the fingertips. Keep your hair combed. Brush you teeth after every meal so that all the food particles that cause decay are removed from between the teeth. In a pinch you can keep your teeth clean with a woodsman's toothbrush—a 6-inch-long dry stick frayed at one end—and table salt or baking soda. In addition to keeping your teeth clean, have them examined by a dentist twice a year —he will arrest or repair decay that might cause serious disease.

Use a mirror to see if the pupils of your eyes are black and bright and if the whites of your eyes are a clear white, as they should be. If your eyes are bloodshot or if they hurt or get watery, you may be suffering from eyestrain, which may be caused by too little sleep, too much reading in inadequate light, or an eye defect. If your eyes bother you in any way, don't delay seeing an eye specialist—and follow his advice. You only have one pair of eyes.

Keep the outside of your ears clean by using a damp cloth over the end of a finger. Never dig in your ears with any kind of hard object. You might break an eardrum, even lose your hearing. Eardrums are sometimes broken by headfirst high diving, and ear trouble is sometimes caused by diving feetfirst into the water without holding the nose. If water bothers your ears while you are swimming, use rubber earplugs or tightly rolled tufts of absorbent cotton. If you have a constant ringing in your ears, a running ear, an earache, or wax in the ears, see a doctor.

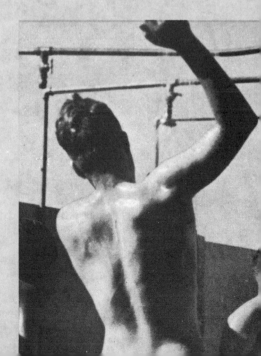

A hard driving shower puts zip back into your spirit, and washes off some of the trail that stuck to you. You'll look better, feel better; and . . . you'll be welcome anywhere.

sleep

Without adequate sleep, your growth may be retarded. The greatest growth occurs between the ages of 11 and 16, the very years when large demands are made on people's energies. It is, therefore, the time when sufficient sleep is an absolute necessity. Between these years you should get 9 to 10 hours of sleep every night.

Sleep outdoors as often as you can—under the open sky or in a tent, but don't close the tent door. At home, sleep with your windows open, but out of a direct draft.

Do you wake up raring to go; or do you stretch and slowly pull yourself out of the sack? Fast starters and slow movers all have one thing in common—another day of adventure. Get-ahead guys sleep—at night.

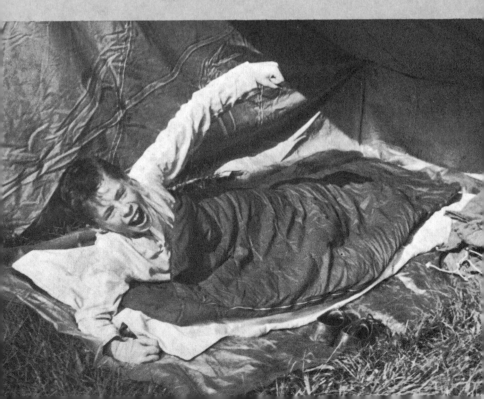

guard against disease

Keep away from people who have a communicable disease—that is, a disease spread from one person to another. Avoid people who are coughing or sneezing. Never use cups or eating utensils that someone else has used until they have been properly washed. Never put anything in your mouth that has been in anyone else's mouth. Use only your own bath towel, washcloth, and handkerchief. In camp, keep flies off you and your food. In tick country, check frequently to see that none are attached to you. Use insect repellent to ward off mosquitoes and other insects.

health taboos

As far as your health and growth are concerned, certain things are taboo —to be avoided. Anything useless, harmful, or unnatural—such as stimulants and narcotics—should be considered taboo.

Stimulants are drugs that excite the nervous system and speed up the action of the heart. Coffee and tea are stimulants, not food. The chief objection to coffee and tea is that they crowd milk, a food and a good one, out of the diet. They also raise the blood-sugar level temporarily— producing a quick sensation of well-being—but cannot sustain it.

Narcotics are drugs that have the ability to relieve pain and bring sleep. They include opium and its active ingredient, morphine. They also include heroin, which is a form of morphine. The dangers of narcotics use are extreme. An overdose can kill. Many diseases are caused by using dirty needles for shots. A person on narcotics can't fight diseases such as tuberculosis and pneumonia.

testing physical fitness

To find out if you are physically fit, try the five tests pictured on these pages. First check the accompanying chart for the standard you should be able to meet at your age in each test. Now take the tests. After you have written down the results, go in for exercises that will improve your performance in the tests in which you are weak. Retest yourself until you are up to par.

Your Age	SIT-UPS		PULL-UPS		LONG JUMP		50-METER DASH* *50-YARD DASH*		600-METER RUN/WALK* *600-YARD RUN/WALK*	
	Number of times		Number of times		Meters (feet/inches)		Seconds		Minutes:Seconds	
	Good	Excellent	Good	Excellent	Good	Excellent	Good	Excellent	Good	Excellent
11	41	45	5	6	1.75 (5' 9")	1.83 (6')	8.2 *7.5*	7.8 *7.2*	2:24 *2:12*	2:18 *2.06*
12	43	48	5	7	1.83 (6')	1.90 (6' 3")	8.0 *7.3*	7.6 *7.0*	2:16 *2:04*	2:08 *1:57*
13	47	50	6	9	1.96 (6' 5")	2.08 (6' 10")	7.6 *7.0*	7.3 *6.7*	2:08 *1:57*	2:00 *1:50*
14	48	52	8	10	2.08 (6' 10")	2.18 (7' 2")	7.2 *6.6*	7.0 *6.4*	2:00 *1:50*	1:54 *1:44*
15	49	52	10	12	2.21 (7' 3")	2.32 (7' 7")	7.0 *6.4*	6.8 *6.2*	1:55 *1:45*	1:49 *1:40*
16	49	52	10	12	2.29 (7' 6")	2.41 (7' 11")	7.0 *6.4*	6.8 *6.2*	1:52 *1:42*	1:47 *1:38*

* 50 m (54½ yd.) 600 m (656 yd.). Times for 50-yard dash and 600-yard run/walk are set in italics.

SIT-UPS. Lie on your back; have someone hold your ankles or put feet under a heavy object; clasp your hands behind your neck. Sit up; touch the right elbow to the left knee; lie down again. The next time, sit up, touch the left elbow to the right knee, and lie down.

198

PULL-UPS. With the palms facing forward, grasp an overhead bar. Hang there, with the arms and legs fully extended and the feet off the ground. Pull the body up with the arms in a smooth movement—without kicking the legs and without swinging—until you can place your chin over the bar. Now lower yourself. Do as many pull-ups as you can.

STANDING BROAD JUMP. With the feet comfortably apart, stand on a level surface. Flex the knees; swing the arms back and forth; then jump, swinging the arms forcefully forward and up. Measure the distance from the takeoff line to the spot where the heel or any part of the body has touched the ground.

50-YARD DASH. Measure out a 50-yard course. Have someone with a stopwatch stand at the finish line to act as the starter. He raises one hand, then brings it down smartly. As he hits his thigh, you start to run. As you cross the finish line, the starter notes the time in seconds to the nearest 10th.

600-YARD RUN (WALK). Measure out a 600-yard course. On the starter's signal run the distance. You are permitted to walk if necessary, but the idea is to cover the distance as quickly as possible. Record the time in minutes and seconds.

199

individual exercises

When you are out with your troop or post, you get plenty of exercise through hiking, games and contests, swimming, rowing, and axmanship. Carry some of these activities over into your daily life. Play good swift games—baseball, football, basketball, or handball. Swim in the old swimming hole or the local pool. Try skating or skiing, tennis or golf. Go in for simple gymnastics. If you want strong arms, you must push and swing them in work and play, lift with them, and throw with them. If you want strong legs, you must walk and hike, run and jump. If you want an agile supple body, covered with flat firm muscles, you must bend and twist it. Every day spend at least 15 minutes exercising at home, and you will soon be a prime specimen of physical fitness.

PUSH-UPS. Lie facedown on the ground or floor. Keep the back and arms straight while you lower and raise the body. To build strong arm and shoulder muscles, do 20 push-ups every day.

BUTTERFLY. Lie facedown on the ground. Raise the arms, chest, and legs. Spread the arms and legs 10 times. Return to the starting position. Repeat the exercise; this strengthens your back.

SQUAT THRUST. Assume squat position, hands in front on floor. Thrust legs back until body is straight from shoulders to feet. Return to squat. Stand up.

HORIZONTAL BAR. Helps builds arms and shoulders. Use hands to move across bar, ladder, or pipe. Practice on a pipe, hung securely in cellar or garage.

STRETCHER. Lie with your back on the ground. Curl up the body slowly until the knees touch your chin. Count five. Now return to the starting position, and repeat the exercise slowly.

ALL THE WAY. Lie with your back on the ground and with your hands above your head. With the arms and legs straight, raise your body, and touch your toes with your fingertips. Repeat.

HALF KNEE BEND. Stand up straight with your hands on your hips. Draw in your abdomen and buttocks. Rise on the toes, and bend the knees slowly halfway to the squat position, extending the arms out straight. Stand up. Repeat.

201

dual contests

Exercising to build up your strength and endurance will really seem worthwhile if you demonstrate to yourself its effectiveness in a contest of physical fitness with someone your own weight and size. The only equipment you need is a broomstick—and determination, of course.

STICK PULL. Sit on the ground facing each other, with the soles of your shoes braced. Grasp the stick and try to pull opponent to his feet.

INDIAN ARM WRESTLE. Lie flat on your stomach. Lock inside elbows. Try to force the other's hand to the ground or to raise the other's elbow without raising your own.

DUCK FIGHT. Squat and grasp your ankles. Butt with head or shoulders to upset your opponent or make him release his ankles.

BACK PULL. Stand back to back and lock your hands over your shoulders. Try to pull the other fellow off his feet onto your back and carry him forward 10 feet.

CHEST PUSH. Mark two lines 10 feet apart. Between the lines, stand chest to chest, arms extended to the sides and hands locked. Try to push the other over the line.

STICK FIGHT. Face each other and grasp the stick firmly with both hands. Force the stick held by your opponent's left hand down to the ground.

INDIAN LEG WRESTLE. Lie on your back and link your right elbows. Raise inside legs three times. On the third count, try to catch the other's heel and flip him.

PUSH BACK. Mark two lines 20 feet apart. Between the lines, stand back to back with your arms linked. Push your opponent back over the line.

games for fitness

Building physical fitness doesn't have to be a solitary activity. It also doesn't have to be a chore. You can do it by playing games with your patrol and troop or post. The games may be played anywhere—both indoors at meetings and outdoors at a campsite.

LASHING RELAY. Learn fitness skills of agility and coordination by completing this lashing problem. Teams must lash poles with lashings that hold. First team finished wins, if all of their lashings are tight and resist a reasonable testing by impartial judges.

JUMP THE SHOT. The fellow in the center swings the shot—a long rope with a soft weight on the end. Contestants must jump as he swings it around below their knees. If hit, they are penalized one point. Scout with least number of penalties wins.

TUG-OF-WAR. A real arm and leg builder, this game is only one of the many you can play outdoors with equipment. For this, use a long rope at least I inch in diameter. Teams should be evenly matched as to weight. Tie a piece of string or cloth to center of rope above the line. On signal, each team tries to pull the opposite across the line. Set a time limit.

THREE-MAN TUG-OF-WAR. Try to grab an object near your corner of the rope before your opponents can snatch theirs.

ANNIHILATION. Teams face each other, about 50 to 75 feet apart. On a signal, the teams rush toward each other. Each fellow picks an opponent and tries to pin his shoulders to the ground. If a fellow is pinned to the ground, he is out of the game. If two players pin a man, it is a foul, and he is automatically free. Team that pins all opponents is winner.

205

11 SWIMMING

YOU'RE NORMAL (with plenty of company) if you like swimming. It tops all activities in popularity at camp and year-round.

Just getting wet is fine, but as with other skills, the better you are at swimming, the more fun you can have—which is one reason why coaching and practice in swimming skills have high priority in camp.

This is a sport that lasts a lifetime. From early youth to old age, it benefits heart, lungs, and muscles more than almost any other exercise. Few people have physical problems that prevent their swimming; but for your own protection have a health examination—know for sure that neither the exercise nor being in the water will be harmful to you.

Take these tips for getting the most from swimming:
- Swim defensively—learn the rules and obey 'em for your protection.
- Swim with a buddy, never alone. (And keep an eye out for him, too!)
- Don't be a show-off—bad anywhere, it can be fatal in the water.
- Avoid horseplay or running on decks, docks, rafts, or diving boards.
- Taking a dare may be courting disaster—show judgment, play it cool.
- Stay in depths you can handle—watch waves, weeds, and bad currents.
- Never dive headfirst into the unknown. Even in emergency, *feet*first!

Keeping cool is more than just being in up to your neck! Being at home in the water is born of self-confidence, the mark of a first-class waterman. But you needn't be an expert swimmer to develop this confidence—even a nonswimmer who has learned to cope with his condition can show a cool head. He can survive when expert swimmers may die, by following a "drownproofing" procedure—conserving energy and using a "bobbing jellyfish float" that sounds crazy—only it works!

From survival to expert swimmer is a matter of a progressive program to increase your skill and stamina. For Scouts there is the First Class requirement, testing for camp swimming privileges, and the Swimming merit badge. For Explorers and Scouts there is the goal of Mile Swim BSA. Now try for Lifeguard BSA, the ultimate for watermen!

safe swim defense

Summertime is the time when the newspapers are full of reports of swimming accidents. Yet you seldom hear of a swimming accident in a Scout camp. The reason? The Safe Swim Defense. This plan has been most successful throughout the years in making unit swims safe and in giving Scouts an understanding of the basic principles of group swimming under adequate supervision and safe conditions. If every swimmer thoroughly understands it, he can cooperate in its operation and help teach others its basic principles. The plan consists of a qualified supervisor, physically fit swimmers, a safe swimming area, lifeguards, a lookout, ability grouping, the buddy plan, and maintained discipline.

An adult supervisor or his trained assistants are in charge of all Scout swims. The supervisor must have qualified in water-safety training at a Scout aquatic course or at Red Cross or YMCA classes.

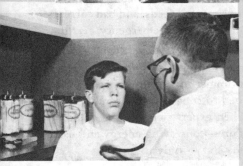

Each swimmer should have an annual medical examination to make sure that he's physically fit. Most swimming accidents are caused by physical handicaps or defects, such as fainting spells or a weak heart.

Bottom is cleared of hazards and areas are set: no more than 3½ feet deep for nonswimmers, just over the head for beginners, deep water for swimmers.

208

The good swimmers act as lifeguards. They stand on shore with a lifeline. In an emergency, one carries out the line, while the other feeds it out and then pulls in his partner and the swimmer who's being helped.

The lookout has a responsible job. He stands at a point where he can see and hear all areas. He directs any assistance needed during the swim.

Before a swim, swimmers are divided into ability groups: nonswimmers, who are just learning; beginners, who can swim 50 feet, and swimmers, who can swim 100 yards—25 yards on the back—and who can float. Each group stays in own area during swim.

In buddy plan, each Scout is paired with another boy of same swimming ability. Buddies check into water together, stay within 10 feet of each other in the water, and check out together. At buddy signal, buddies raise grasped hands high so lifeguards can check the number of buddy teams.

With good discipline, everyone has a good time. Pay strict attention to the rules, and you're sure to become a better swimmer.

swimming events

Would you like to earn the Mile Swim BSA badge with the embroidered red seahorse? Start by increasing the lengths of your daily swims — from 50 yards to 100, 200, 300, up to a quarter mile. When you've built up your strength and your lung power, you strike out on the swim itself. You're accompanied by a boat that always stays within easy reach. You may use any stroke or combination of strokes. You're allowed occasional short rests, but only by keeping yourself afloat in the water. There's no time limit and no competition. You'll have plenty of that in races some other time.

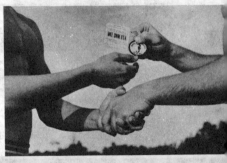

The mile swimmer is escorted by a boat within easy reach of him. In addition to the rower, there is a guard who holds a long pole. He sits in the stern to give any needed help.

The buddy tag shows the mile swimmer's progress. He should aim for a quarter-mile nonstop swim as early as possible.

Look-Ma-No-Hands Race: Only legs are used. In addition, the hands must be above the water, with the index finders pointing straight up.

The sidestroke and the breaststroke are the most popular strokes for long-distance swimming, but any stroke may be used in the event.

Egg Race: In this speed event, a dropped egg is regained by surface diving, and race is resumed at the spot where the egg was lost or dropped.

The successful completion of the mile swim is marked by the awarding of a Mile Swim BSA certificate and emblem for swim trunks.

Obstacle Race: Tread water, dive through inflated inner tube, slither over log, and surface dive under another log.

Leapfrog Race: Patrol treads water in line. The second man leaps over the first man, and the third man leaps over the first and the second men until everyone has leaped over—and has dunked—everyone else.

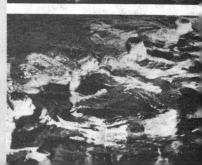

Two-Arm Buddy Race: This is a breaststroke speed event. Buddies link arms; their free arms are used for swimming. Good coordination is necessary to keep each team from circling.

rescues

About 6,500 people die every year in drowning accidents. Some of them might still be living if someone nearby had known what to do. If you should be that bystander, keep calm, and remember these key words: *reach, throw, row,* and *go.* Look for something to *reach* out or something to *throw* to the victim. Be prepared to *row* or to *go* out to him, and bring him back safely.

REACH: In an accident close to shore, look for a stick, board, rope, shirt, paddle, or oar to extend to the man in the water.

THROW: To reach a victim far from shore, throw a ring buoy or rope to him. Learn the technique of throwing a ring buoy beforehand.

212

ROW: Use any available boat. Approach the victim with the stern first. In a canoe, pull up so the victim can first grab an extended paddle, then the gunwale.

GO: Swim to a victim's aid only when you have no choice. Undress quickly, removing your shoes and dropping your trousers. Put your shirt between your teeth. Jump out as far as possible, feetfirst, to keep from hitting your head on any underwater objects.

When you're near the victim, hold one end of your shirt in one hand, flip the other end into his hands, and tow him to shore.

213

strong swimmer rescues

Effecting a safe, successful rescue of a person in trouble in the water requires more than just wishful thinking. You must be a capable swimmer to help somebody else, and you must have good judgment. Most of all, you must be skilled in the techniques of lifesaving. Start practicing right away.

Keeping your eyes on the victim, jump far out and up, with your legs wide open. Now snap your legs together and bring your arms down fast and hard after you hit the water. Level off and swim out.

Approach the victim from behind whenever possible. Reverse your position to be ready to tow him to shore. Reach over his shoulder, grasp his chin, and level him off.

Pull his shoulder under your towing arm and clamp your elbow down on his chest. Shift your grasp under his arm; reach as far around him as possible.

A pair can always do it easier and safer than one. The "two-on-one" rescue combines the foot push with a cross-chest tow. This technique would be specially helpful if the victim were fully clothed.

A front surface approach is used when the victim is unconscious. Swim in and grasp his hand. Shift your grasp firmly to his wrist.

Using the wrist, tow twist him around so that he is faceup and tow him ashore.

If the victim tries to grab you, use a straight-arm push to keep him away. Then swim around him, and get hold of him from the rear.

Use the tired swimmer's assist to aid a swimmer who has become exhausted or has a cramp. Have him float faceup, his hands on your shoulder. Swim with a breaststroke to safety.

215

skin diving

Nothing compares with the sensation of feeling free as a fish in water. This sensation may be yours if you try skin diving—underwater swimming with special equipment. Before you start, you should get your doctor to certify to your health, and you must line up a buddy to skin dive with.

Fins add nearly 60 percent to the thrust of your legs. The flipper part should be rigid and not too large, with adjustable straps that fit comfortably around the foot.

The face mask should have a shatterproof glass lens and should fit firmly, covering only the eyes and nose. The snorkel (breathing tube) should consist of a semiflexible plastic tube with a well-fitting soft-rubber mouthpiece.

A float—which may be an inner tube painted bright orange or yellow—should be anchored in the diving area as a marker and as a place for frequent rests.

Train to skin dive by distance swimming and practice diving. Be able to swim 300 yards easily, to swim underwater 15 yards without a pushoff, and to stay afloat 15 minutes by treading water and sculling. Practice snorkel breathing by swimming just underwater.

Dive only in clear water, and always enter the water feetfirst. Walk in from the beach or slip in smoothly from the pier. If you must jump, hold your mask and snorkel.

Your arm motion can be a regular breaststroke, sidestroke, or crawl—for covering distances—or a simple dog paddle —for moving slowly underwater.

Your leg motion can be a forceful scissors kick. Often you will also use a strong flutter kick, with the knees bent more than they are when you are doing the ordinary crawl.

12 WATERCRAFT

Perhaps, even before he learned to swim, early man tied together a couple of logs and rode them on the water. Some believe this discovery to be as important in history as inventing the wheel. As methods of propulsion developed from the paddle to use of the wind and eventually to motor-driven craft, explorers have used boats to locate new continents and move whole populations. They have made possible world commerce and influenced world power.

Watercraft are important to history, but to you boats are for adventure, fun, and fitness. To launch a boat or canoe and move away from the shore gives you the same thrill known to that early man. But the modern man has an advantage. So much has been learned about boats during these past few centuries. Progress from a rustic raft, moved by the current or push-pole, to a dugout canoe propelled by paddle, to the boat moved by wind pressed against its sail, and finally to the sophisticated motor craft of today—it all adds up to a knowledge and skill of handling them much more safely and efficiently. All of it is available now to the modern boatman. Yet even though the variety of water sports in use of boats is expanding, the use of primitive skills is of equal interest and value to everyone attracted to the water.

No one could ever say that "learning how to paddle a canoe is easy." But today, the same techniques learned in order to pass Rowing or Canoeing merit badge, took the Indian and sailor many generations of trial and error to perfect. With a little bit of work you can master them soon and ride a wild river on which no Indian canoe could have ever survived. Because you can learn better paddling methods, launch a sturdier craft, and be protected by a modern life jacket, you may reach the unspoiled wilderness on lakes and streams and recapture the same exhilaration of man's early challenge to adventure. Or you may gain a mental relaxation from the complexities of modern-day living best found in deep woods and quiet waters.

row your boat

The first thing to learn in rowing is to sit where your weight is equally distributed between the length and width of the boat. Brace your feet against the stretcher (the crosspiece on the boat bottom). Place the oars in the rowlocks and adjust them so the handle ends come close together, directly in front of the center line of your body. Now for the rowing stroke. It has four parts: the *catch, pull, feather,* and *recovery.*

To launch a boat alone, place the oars on the the thwarts, grasp the boat with both hands, and shove off. As soon as the boat is afloat, go aboard, sit down, and put out the oars.

To launch a boat with a buddy, have him sit down in the stern. Shove the boat outward until the bow is just resting on the shore. Get in and move back to your seat. As you move toward the stern the bow will lift so that you can back away from the shore.

To trim a boat properly, your weight should be equally placed between the bow and stern, with the bow about 3 inches higher than the stern. Trimming cuts water and wind resistance.

Keeping your back straight, bend your body toward the stern of the boat. Raise the oar handles slightly, and drop the blades edgewise into the water —not too deep.

Swing your body backward until it is leaning toward the bow, with your arms straight. Bend your arms, and pull. Bring the body erect, with the elbows tight into the ribs.

Lower your wrists to turn your knuckles up—just a little—enough to make the oar blade turn flat with the water's surface. The flat blade decreases the wind resistance.

Move your oar blades into place for the next stroke by swinging your body toward the stern. Your hands turn, ready once again to assume the catch position.

221

land your boat

You've learned how to get into a boat, how to trim it, and how to launch it. But you can't just stay out there—you must also learn the technique of *landing* a boat properly, which means more practicing. It is customary to land a rowboat bow first, but lifeguards working on surf-washed beaches may reverse this order and land their boats stern first. This gives them greater efficiency when they move out to the trouble spot when there is an emergency.

When you are ready for a landing and the water is rough, carefully watch the waves and allow the big ones to pass under you while your boat is in deep water, then row directly to shore. As you near shore, hold your boat back a little to avoid hitting it too hard.

The last lesson is: what to do if the boat gets swamped or overturns. That's not so tough—just stay with the boat, which will float, until someone comes to your rescue!

Many fishermen stand up and face the bow while they move ahead by sculling. This is done with only one oar, set in a U-shaped sculling notch or rowlock in the stern of the boat. Care must be taken because standing up in a boat is always dangerous.

In sculling, the oar is moved back and forth at the stern in a figure-eight motion —almost the same motion you use to scull with your hands while you swim on your back.

222

To row a straight course, point the bow toward your destination and pick a landmark on the opposite shore over the center of the stern. Keep it there, looking over your shoulder to make sure you don't drift too far sideways.

To pivot, row ahead with a strong pull on one oar, backing water equally with the other oar. The boat's center turns around as the boat comes about.

Practice approaching the pier correctly. Begin your landing maneuver 20 or more feet from the pier. Try coming against the wind. Watch where you're going.

The bow is a few feet from the pier. Let the oar on the landing side trail for one stroke, and give the other oar an extra-hard pull. Quickly ship the oar on the landing side.

If you go overboard: HANG ON!

launch your canoe

Canoeing is a rewarding experience. And the greater your knowledge and skill, the greater will be your reward. The tool of this pleasure—your canoe—therefore merits special care. In handling a canoe on shore, always carry it. It won't stand being dragged over rough ground. Speaking of roughness, learn your canoeing techniques on a quiet lake or slow-moving stream. Get into the habit of using the proper paddling position. This is a kneeling position, with knees kept well apart on a light, but adequate, kneeling pad under each knee and with the buttocks resting against a thwart (crosspiece). The kneeling pad is an important part of the canoeist's standard equipment. It will contribute greatly to his comfort and the experienced canoeist never tries to to get along without it. The paddling position is the safest position because it keeps the center of gravity low. It is also the best position for speed and for keeping the canoe steady and under control.

An aquatic star performer and almost everyone's favorite watercraft is lightweight on land and graceful on the water.

In camp, canoes are generally stored in racks. One canoeist grasps the bow; the other canoeist takes hold of the stern. They lift the canoe off the rack, turn it, and carry it to the edge of the water.

The canoe is eased into the water without touching the ground. The bowman and sternman "walk" their hands along the gunwale to the middle of the canoe, put the bow in the water, "walk" the gunwale toward the stern.

The bowman enters the canoe first and stows the duffel. He then places the paddle tip against the lake or river bottom and braces the canoe while the sternman enters. The sternman takes his paddle, and they're off.

The canoe must be properly trimmed —that is, the weight of the duffel and the canoers must be evenly distributed over the canoe. Tie the duffel to the gunwale or thwarts so it won't be lost if canoe upsets.

225

paddle your canoe

When there are two paddling a canoe, the bowman generally uses a straight paddling stroke, while the sternman paddles on the opposite side and finishes his stroke with a hook that steers the canoe. When you are paddling alone, you act as both sternman and bowman, while you sit in the middle of the canoe. In either case, you must know the four parts of the paddle stroke: the *catch, pull, recovery,* and *feather.*

Cup the grip of the paddle with the upper hand close to the shoulder, and grasp the throat of the paddle with the lower hand. For the catch, face the blade squarely aft as it enters the water. The pull and power really starts by pushing the upper hand forward.

The lower hand follows through on the pull. With the lower arm comfortably straight, recover the blade, swinging it forward again with a feather that is almost parallel to the surface of the water.

When there are two in a canoe, the bowman uses a straight bow or power stroke. The sternman follows his rhythm and tries to match the power of his stroke with that of the bowman.

The sternman is responsible for keeping the canoe on course. Turning the fist of his upper hand down, he finishes the stroke with an outward hook (the J-stroke). When paddling alone, use the J-stroke for steering a straight course.

In swift water, the bowman has to look for obstructions. To move the bow quickly toward the side where you are paddling, brace the blade at a 30° angle from the keel line for a bow rudder.

The bowman can give the canoe a wide turn by making a quarter sweep, while the sternman continues the straight paddle. To stop, brace the paddle vertically, with the blade square against the direction of motion.

To bring the canoe sideways closer to the dock or shore, use a drawstroke, drawing the blade of the paddle flat toward the canoe. In sculling for the same effect, the blade is at a 45° angle to the canoe.

canoe rescues

Although the good canoeist is not likely to upset his canoe there is always the possibility of his being in such a situation. It is therefore important that he know what to do at such a time. The first rule is to stick with the canoe and then try to get it back to shore. Always remember that your canoe is an excellent life preserver and it can save your life. It has been demonstrated many times that a canoe filled with water can keep a number of swimmers afloat merely by their holding onto the gunwales. If you are alone get back into the swamped canoe and paddle it back to shore.

It is possible to vault out of your canoe and climb back into it again without shipping water and without losing contact with the canoe. To get in again, grasp the canoe amidship near the gunwale and reach across to the other; kick your legs vigorously in a crawl motion until your body slides over the gunwale; turn your body; sit down; swing your legs in; and assume the paddling position.

If your canoe is submerged, roll it over right side up. Hold onto one gunwale, and reach for the other.

Pull yourself across the gunwale with a slow, easy motion, keeping your body well submerged. Now slide in like an eel.

Get yourself seated on the bottom of the canoe—in the water. Now paddle slowly toward the shore.

228

To empty a swamped canoe, swim to one end, put your hands on it, and push forward, then bring your weight down hard.

As the end goes down, push the canoe forward and upward without letting go. This will make the water surge out. Repeat until the canoe rides high in the water.

Move to the side, grasp the gunwale, press down, and shake out the remaining water.

To help someone else with his swamped canoe, have him hold onto your canoe. Grasp one end of his canoe.

Swing the water-filled canoe at a right angle to your own. Turn it over slowly as you pull it across your gunwale.

Turn the canoe right side up, and slide it back into the water. Hold it while the other canoeist climbs in.

229

power afloat

That itch to get out on the water is rarely better satisfied than when in an outboard motorboat. Whether it's leisurely trolling down the lake, heading upstream for a camping trip, or bouncing along on a speedy runabout—every outboarder shares in a great feeling of power and pride in man's mastery of the waterways.

A great deal of pleasure in motorboating depends on selecting the right combination of boat and motor for the particular purpose or sport which interests you.

Make sure to get a basic knowledge of its operation, safety measures, and traffic requirements in your cruising area. Good training can be obtained from merit badge counselors, the Coast Guard Auxiliary, or Power Boat Squadron and frequently from an experienced dad.

When preparing to cast off secure your boat snugly, both bow and stern. Install the motor and chain and carefully check gas, life preservers, oars, anchor, ropes, and fire extinguisher. Do not overload.

If your motor has a gearshift, start it before casting off. Don't stand up while starting the motor. Slow up when passing docks, other boats, and swimmers. Avoid taking waves broadside; head bow to meet them at a slight angle.

Observe the rules of the road. Know and obey all navigational aids. Give right-of-way to rowboats, sailboats, and canoes. Keep to the right in narrow channels and when meeting a boat head on.

If your' boat should ever become swamped or capsized remember to stick with your boat; it can save your life. You should also know how to approach and rescue a person in water, using an oar or a piece of clothing.

If you go overboard: HANG ON!

If your motor is running and in drive gear, but the propeller doesn't turn, you've probably broken the shear pin. Always carry a spare. Put it in by first pulling the cotter pin on the hub of the prop shaft. This releases the streamlined housing so it can be removed.

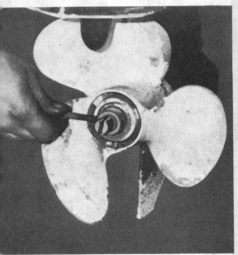

The next step is to knock out the broken shear pin, and replace it with the spare. Put back the housing, and secure by putting the cotter pin back in place. The shear pin is of soft metal, designed to break if the prop hits a solid object.

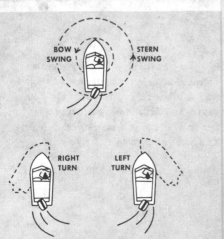

Boats don't steer like cars. The rudder or turning mechanism is in the rear of a boat, while in a car it's up front in the wheels. Thus, in a boat the stern responds to the steering impulse and in the opposite direction of the way you want to turn. In close quarters, give your stern enough room to swing.

232

The design of outboard motors permits them to tilt forward or backward to compensate for the difference in transom angle of various boats. When in correct position, the line of thrust through the propeller should parallel the bottom of the boat.

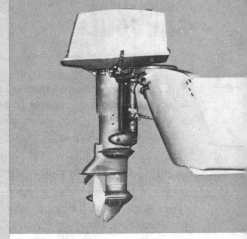

This motor is tilted too far forward and will cause the bow to plow the water. The line of thrust will lift the stern. Similarly, if the thrust line is too far in the other angle, it will depress the stern and the boat will porpoise. Either extreme cuts efficiency, handling ease, and speed.

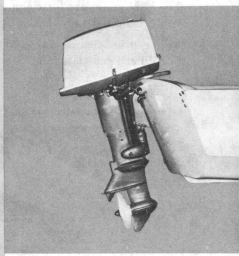

In docking at a pier, approach from the downwind side. Throttle the motor back and ease up nearly parallel to the pier. Cut motor or put in neutral and allow momentum to carry you to the pier. If there is a current, approach the dock heading into the current.

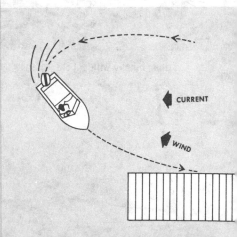

CURRENT

WIND

233

sailboats

Sailing is a complicated business. Seagoing language for all parts of a boat would require a course in seamanship. A rope is never a rope on a boat. It is a halyard, sheet, painter, line, hawser, or something else, depending upon its use.

If you must sail a boat and need the minimum information to operate it, you'll find these few pages will help. We will be talking about boats under 16 feet with either a lateen or a marconi rig. There are many other types of boats and rigging which you will probably not have enough nerve to tackle for a first try.

The instructions are for rigging a small sloop, but the basic principles apply to a catboat or a lateen-rigged craft.

Sailing principles are universal, but a boat's reaction to the wind and tide differ from class to class and even in boats of the same class.

Sailing surfboard with lateen sail

Sailing canoe with lateen sail

Sailing dinghy with cat rig

One design sloop

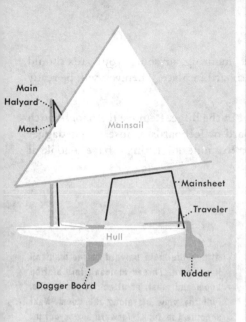

Sailing surfboard with lateen sail

Labels: Main Halyard, Mast, Mainsail, Mainsheet, Traveler, Hull, Dagger Board, Rudder

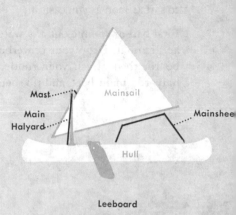

Sailing canoe with lateen sail

Labels: Mast, Main Halyard, Mainsail, Mainshee[t], Hull, Leeboard, Rudder

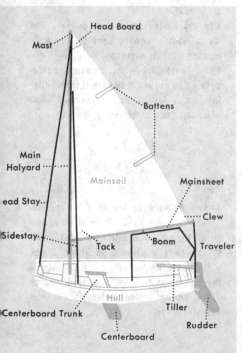

Sailing dinghy with cat rig

Labels: Mast, Head Board, Battens, Main Halyard, [H]ead Stay, Mainsail, Mainsheet, Clew, Sidestay, Tack, Boom, Traveler, Centerboard Trunk, Hull, Tiller, Rudder, Centerboard

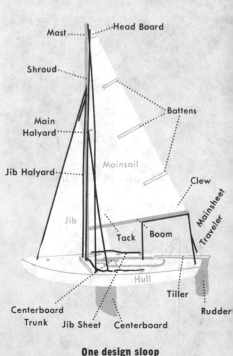

One design sloop

Labels: Mast, Head Board, Shroud, Battens, Main Halyard, Jib Halyard, Mainsail, Clew, Jib, Mainsheet, Traveler, Tack, Boom, Hull, Centerboard Trunk, Jib Sheet, Centerboard, Tiller, Rudder

Before your boat leaves the dock, mooring, or shore, your sails should be up and your rudder and centerboard in place. Then you will be ready to sail as soon as you cast off.

First bail or sponge out any water in the bilge. Remove the boom crutch and stow it. Drop your centerboard or leeboards or insert your dagger board, then attach your rudder. Examine all fittings; have a look at halyards, mainsheet, and jib sheets.

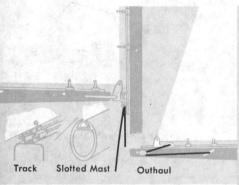

Track   Slotted Mast   Outhaul

Attach the main halyard to the mainsail headboard. Thread mainsail into slotted boom and mast, or attach to the tracks. Pull the clew aft along the boom. Next shackle the tack (forward lower corner of the main) to the boom fitting, attach the clew to the outhaul fitting, and haul it out toward the end of the boom and make fast.

Slip the battens into their pockets and tie in with a square knot or use self-closing pockets or snaps.

Put a loose furl in the mainsail and secure a line around it to keep it from bellying out or falling into the cockpit while you turn your attention to the jib.

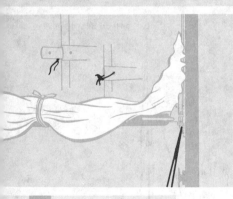

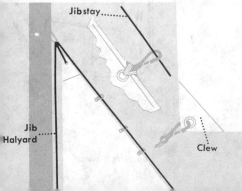

Jibstay..........

Jib
Halyard ....

Clew

Attach halyard to the head of the jib. Attach clips or hanks to head stay. Run sheet through the fairlead. Most small sloops have a divided jib sheet. Check if it should be led aft inside or outside the side stays through a fairlead, snatch block, or cam action device, both to port and starboard.

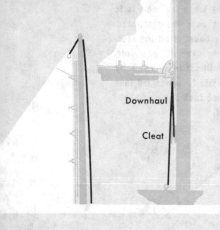

Downhaul

Cleat

Hoist the mainsail with main halyard to its peak, attach the down haul to the base of the mast, haul down and make fast to the cleat. Make sure your mainsheets are free so that the sail will flap in the wind, but cleat the end so it won't go overboard.

After making certain the jib sheets are free, hoist away on the jib halyard. Be sure to set it up taut. Then make fast on the cleat. You are now ready to sail.

If you are leaving a dock, be sure your boat is on the lee. If necessary, tow the boat into position before you hoist your sail. You should leave a mooring on the leeward, also. Cast off your buoy and line to windward so you will not run over it. Leaving a dock, have your crew push the nose away from the dock and pull your tiller to windward. Then gradually push it to leeward. Trim your mainsheet until you are close-hauled.

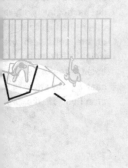

Look carefully in the direction you plan to travel to be sure you have enough room to maneuver.

A boat is on a starboard tack when its boom is to port and the wind is coming over the starboard. It is on a port tack when the boom is on the starboard and the wind is coming over the port side. Since it is impossible for a sailboat to sail directly into the wind, progress is made to windward in a series of tacks or zigzags, each tack being at about a 45-degree angle to the wind.

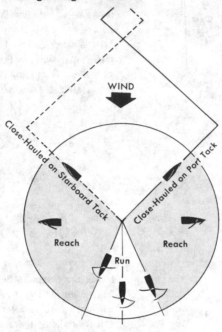

WIND

Close-Hauled on Starboard Tack

Close-Hauled on Port Tack

Reach

Reach

Run

STARBOARD TACK

PORT TACK

REACH

When running free (the most difficult point of sailing), many factors must be considered. Carelessness on the helm or a sudden wind shift could cause an accidental jibe with disastrous consequences. Keep a sharp eye on sea and wind conditions and be ready to meet any changes.

Sailing on a close bea or broad reach pose no particular problem other than proper tri of the sails and cre weight distribution. Th boom should be at near a right angle to th direction of the win

RUNNING FREE

Close-hauled on
starboard tack.

Adjust sheets to best trim,
crew weight to windward.

Filling away,
trim jib and main,
begin to ease helm back
to center line.

In the eye of the wind,
jib and main slatting,
helm still over,
crew weight in center.

Hard alee,
ease jib sheet,
helm over slowly
about 45°.

Ready about,
prepare to tack.

Close-hauled
on port tack.

Unless the breeze is very light, the crew weight should be on the windward side. You will see as you sit to windward that pulling the tiller toward you causes the boat to swing away from the direction of the wind. Pushing the tiller away from you causes the boat to head into the direction of the wind.

Now look at the sails. They have a graceful curve because of the pressure of the wind. Correct trim of the sails is essential to their effectiveness. It can be learned only by practice.

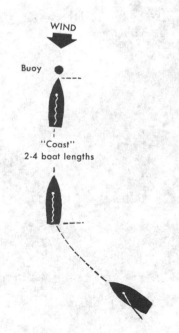

WIND

Buoy

"Coast"
2-4 boat lengths

The mooring pickup buoy is approached from downwind with sails luffing and just enough way on the boat for her to reach the buoy.

Take into account how the boat carries her way when headed into the wind. Does it move slowly or quickly?

Obviously you would "shoot" for the buoy sooner in light air and a foul current than you would if the current were running with your boat and the breeze was fresh.

Land at a pier on the leeward side only. Gauge your speed so that the man on the foredeck can jump to the pier or the float with the dock line in his hand and then turn to fend off the boat's bow.

If you go overboard: HANG ON!

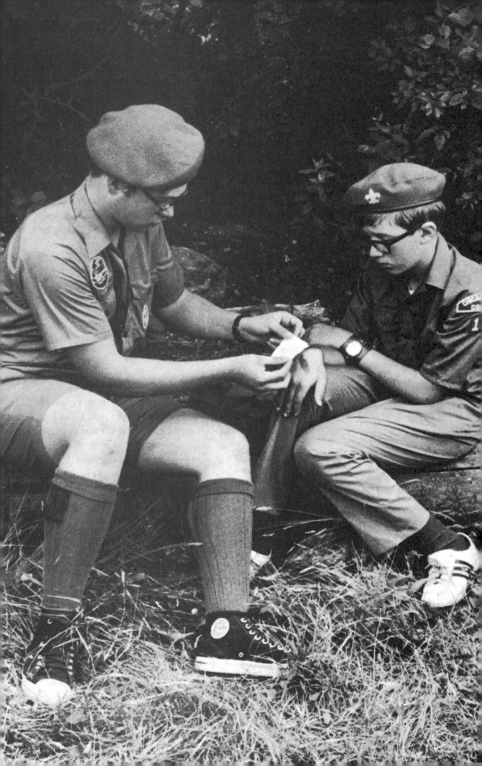

13 SAFETY AND FIRST AID

YOU NEED TO KNOW basic first aid so you can care for yourself and others when accidents happen. But, wouldn't it be wonderful if you never had to use it? Most accidents don't happen—they're caused. How many times have you cut yourself, tripped, or burned your finger? Didn't you really cause the accident to happen? It wasn't just bad luck.

If you're serious about hiking, camping, and high adventure, don't trust to luck; you must recognize the results of carelessness. Perhaps you've always been careful and have never had an accident. Wonderful! But read—*no study* this chapter because there can be a first time, and besides you'll want to be able to help other people.

Poor planning, inexperience, and carelessness can make you a danger to yourself and your companions. Safety comes from skill and knowledge, practice and preparation, caution, and common sense. Even with these, though, you can have an accident. You'll get in trouble when you're angry and lose your temper. Studies of automobile accidents show that often the drivers are angry at something or someone. These drivers lost judgment as a result of their emotions.

What about you? Do you get mad at trivial things and have to blow off a head of steam? Are you upset when things don't go the way you want them to? Do you argue a lot just to get your own way? Anytime you are really upset about something, you are accident prone.

Another cause of accidents to the normally careful guy is haste. You're in such a hurry to do something, you forget some of the precautions. You're in a rush to get a supply of wood for a fire—a cut foot. The pot's boiling over and might put out the fire. You hastily grab at it—a bad burn. You didn't allow enough time on the trail to reach your camp before dark, and so you hurry along—a sprained ankle. All caused by haste, and the need for this haste is usually lack of planning.

Be Prepared is the motto of the Boy Scouts of America. Preparedness is the key to success in avoiding accidents and in meeting emergencies.

prevention

Cuts, burns, and broken bones cause suffering for no good reason. Almost every accident can be prevented. Keep these ideas in mind and practice them on every field trip:

Don't drink from strange wells or springs, except in an emergency, and then purify tne water with iodine tablets or by boiling it.

On rough or unfamiliar trails, hike in parties of at least three so that two can help a disabled hiker.

On the trail, stick together but not so close as to be hit by branches that snap back.

Avoid railroads, construction projects, and excavation areas. Observe all signs and barricades.

Don't disturb beehives or hornets' nests.

In snake country, wear high-topped shoes or boots.

Never place your hands over or behind an object that you cannot see the surface your hands will touch.

If you meet a stray dog or wild animal, stay still or out of sight until the animal moves on. *Never run.*

Test roots, branches, and stones carefully before relying on their strength when climbing. Wherever possible distribute your weight between your hands and feet so there will be support even if you slip or if an object gives way.

Before cutting wood be sure cutting tools are sharp. Make sure that all surrounding brush and branches are cleared away and that no one is standing close by before you start using an ax. Be sure, too, that the ax handle is dry and not slippery and that the head is tight. Trim branches from the opposite side of a fallen limb and cut away from the butt.

At camp, shake out shoes and clothing before dressing to avoid insect bites.

In lightning storms, remember that lightning takes the course of least resistance and tends to strike isolated objects on high ground or above the ground. Lightning is also attracted by metal, so put your equipment away from you and, if no shelter is available, sit in a low crouch with your feet close together. Keep away from cliffs and caves.

Ax guards keep the blades sharp and ready for work. Ax blades should be covered as soon as the job is done. A homemade hickory sheath on an old ax and the manufacturer's leather sheath on a new one both keep the blades safe to store and to handle.

The razor-sharp sawteeth cut through wood with very little pressure and motion. Unwary campers find out that sawteeth can bite into flesh even easier. Mask the bow saw with a piece of split garden hose and tie it securely. The folding safety saw has its own guard built in. When folded for travel, the sawteeth are safe within its frame.

The folding safety saw opens up to a businesslike looking woods tool that zips through wood for the fire. Work gloves give you a little extra protection if the blade jumps. Take it easy, though, the gloves aren't sawproof.

When your hands are not used to rough work, blisters develop rapidly. When the cook is yelling for firewood and when you're hungry for food, you may not notice the blisters until after dinner. Work gloves save your hands.

243

wind-chill factor

It was an unusually hot, sticky day when a young couple left their sports car in a notch in the White Mountains and started up the highest peak. They were comfortable in sneakers, shorts, and T-shirts, even warm as they scrambled up the trail. When they got up to the timberline it was cooler traveling as the wind moved freely over the rocks. They were near the top where tourists picked postcards in the lobby of the summit house, when a cloud moved in on the rising wind. Even the stone cairns showing the trail were blotted out. Later the couple was found, their bodies huddled against a stone, about 10 feet off the trail, some 100 feet below the summit. They were not frozen—it is surmised they died of dehydration, the wind relentlessly drawing the moisture from their bodies.

It is now thought that many people supposed to have frozen probably died of *dehydration*, the same condition that kills in the hot desert.

Strangely, a moderate breeze can make the desert heat tolerable. Why? Our skin is one large radiator by which our body rids itself of excess heat. A breeze carries off the heat. Our sweat glands moisten the surface of the skin, and the wind evaporates the sweat, further cooling us. More wind dries the sweat as fast as it comes to the surface—we no longer sweat, but we keep on losing water or moisture. It may be refreshing, but there is a limit. If we lose 10 percent of our body moisture, we die. The more skin exposed to wind, the quicker we succumb.

As you can figure from the chart opposite, actual chilling can begin at a normally comfortable temperature with only a moderate wind—that is, your skin quickly gets down to the freezing point of water. The relative humidity of the air affects the sensation and the effect, too. One result is that surface blood vessels shut down (the skin turns white) and blood distribution in the body becomes unbalanced, which can cause problems when large areas are affected. Strong, steady winds that you may easily encounter in mountains or at the beach even in summer, can produce dramatic losses of body heat that can be disagreeable or damaging.

Apparently your head is the most efficient radiator of heat, with your feet a close second. Moral: Keep your head covered and your feet dry and warm if you want to avoid chilling the entire body.

Even crude estimates of wind velocity and air temperature, applied to the chart opposite, should convince you that proper clothes are needed.

ESTIMATION OF WIND VELOCITY IN MILES PER HOUR

INDICATIONS	Velocity	INDICATIONS	Velocity
Calm; smoke rises vertically.	0-1	Large branches in motion; whitecaps on most waves; tents billow and strain.	25-31
Smoke shows wind direction.	1-3		
Wind felt on face; grass or leaves rustle; snow eddies.	4-7	Whole trees in motion; walking against wind difficult; loose snow rises in air.	32-38
Leaves and small twigs in constant motion; light flag extended by breeze.	8-12	Twigs break off trees; walking generally difficult.	39-46
Dust or snow or leaves are raised; branches move.	13-18	Branches break off trees. High waves and tides.	47-54
Small trees in leaf sway; crested wavelets form on inland waters; tents flap.	19-24	Seldom experienced inland; trees uprooted.	55-63

TO READ THE WIND-CHILL TABLE: Estimate the wind velocity in miles per hour from the table above or other data, such as Weather Bureau forecasts. Read, estimate, or get probable lowest temperatures from forecasts. Locate wind speed in left-hand column and read right to column for thermometer reading or forecast temperature—number will indicate effective equivalent temperature.

WIND CHILL ON DRY BARE SKIN (Read as equivalent temperature at 0 mph.)

Estimated Wind Speed (mph)	Actual Thermometer Reading (° F.)									
	50	40	30	20	10	0	—10	—20	—30	—40
	EQUIVALENT TEMPERATURE (° F.)									
calm	50	40	30	20	10	0	—10	—20	—30	—40
5	48	37	27	16	6	—5	—15	—26	—36	—47
10	40	28	16	2	—9	—22	—31	—45	—58	—70
15	36	22	11	—6	—18	—33	—45	—60	—70	—85
20	32	18	3	—9	—24	—40	—52	—68	—81	—96
25	30	16	0	—15	—29	—45	—58	—75	—89	—104
30	28	13	—2	—18	—33	—49	—63	—78	—94	—109
35	27	11	—4	—20	—35	—52	—67	—83	—98	—113
40	26	10	—4	—22	—36	—54	—69	—87	—101	—116

(wind speeds greater than 40 mph have little additional effect.)

Little Danger (to properly clad person)	Increasing Danger	Great Danger

Danger of Freezing Exposed Flesh

first aid

On a hike, you or your pal may develop a blister, sprain an ankle, or get something in your eye. In each case, you may be the one to give the necessary first aid. It feels good to have a thorough knowledge of first aid. It is good to know that you can take care of yourself if you get hurt. But even more important, it is good to know that you are able to help other people who may be in trouble.

What is first aid? First aid is very definitely aid given *at first* in case of injury or sickness. That word "first" suggests that there is more to follow—the aid given by a person who has many years of training for the job—the doctor. If a case is at all serious, get him to a doctor.

Hikers who don't stop to examine a heel when it hurts are forced to sit down when the blister breaks and the heel is rubbed raw. A hole in the stocking started the trouble. Wash the heel with soap and water and resist telling this hiker what you think of him.

Use a sterile dressing and adhesive tape or cut a hole in moleskin to the size of the broken blister.

Cover the moleskin with the hole in it with a moleskin cover patch. Tape the moleskin around the heel. Replace the stocking and help the hiker home. A doctor's treatment may be needed.

Poison ivy, poison sumac, and poison oak can spoil a camping trip. When you know that you've touched either one of these plants, wash now or scratch later. Common yellow laundry soap worked into a good lather can help you avoid or reduce the effects of poison ivy. Rubbing alcohol will also flush away the toxic oils from these plants.

Something in the eye is painful and can be dangerous particularly if you rub it. If the object is under the upper eyelid, grasp the lashes of the upper lid and gently pull the lid out and down. Tears may wash it out. If the object is below the lower lid, place a finger just below the lower lid and pull down gently. Someone may locate the object and remove it with the corner of a clean cloth moistened with water. If the object cannot be located, cover your eye with a sterile pad and bandage, and go to a doctor.

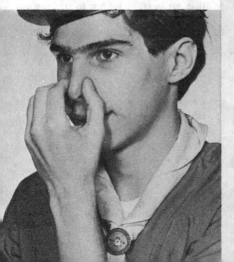

Nosebleed is usually from a small vein in the middle partition of the nose. Pinch your nostrils together. Check from time to time to see if bleeding has stopped.

247

shock

Every accident is accompanied by shock—a sudden lowering of the vitality caused by pain and fear and loss of blood. A shock victim is very weak. His face gets pale, his skin cold and clammy, his breathing shallow. He shivers from chills, may even vomit. He seems dazed, does not know what is happening about him. In serious cases he may lose consciousness entirely. Shock may come immediately with the accident, or soon after, or may even be delayed for several hours.

Keep the patient lying down. If he has a head injury, keep him level; otherwise, raise his feet on a packsack, a log, or whatever else you may have. In cool weather, put enough blankets under and over the patient to protect him. If the weather is hot, do not cover him. The idea is not to make him warm, but to prevent him from getting cold.

If your shock patient is conscious, let him sip a little water. If he is unconscious, do not attempt to force a liquid between his lips—it may choke him.

Fainting is "blacking out." It may occur when a person has a sudden fright, has been standing on his feet too long, is sick to his stomach or suffering from hunger, or is overtired. If you see that your partner is getting pale and wobbly, have him lie down with his head lower than his body, or get him to sit down and put his head as low as possible to get the blood back to his brain.

One way to help restore blood balance is to press down on the back of his neck with the web of your hand. This tends to slow the flow of blood from the head. Keep him quiet. If he fails to snap back, treat for shock and call a doctor.

248

Heat exhaustion hits suddenly. A fellow's face turns pale and he breaks into a cold sweat when he suffers from heat exhaustion. He is sick at his stomach and his breathing is shallow.

Because heat exhaustion may be considered shock from heat, treat for shock. Place him on his back with head and shoulders low and cover him with a rescue blanket, if available. Give him sips of salted water.

Sunstroke is usually caused by long exposure to direct sun. Your face feels red, hot, and dry. Your breathing is slow and noisy—sounds like snoring.

If you're alone, lie down in a shady spot and pour water on your head and body. If sunstroke happens to someone else, try to keep him as cool as possible by dousing him with water. When he regains consciousness, let him drink all the water he wants. Check with your doctor for further instructions.

249

artificial respiration

Rescue breathing saves lives. When breathing stops, life hangs in the balance. If you are there and know how to administer rescue breathing, you may save that life.

There are other methods of artificial respiration but the most effective —the method that saves more lives—is rescue breathing. In this, you breathe your own breath into the victim's lungs through his nose or his mouth or, in the case of a child, gently into nose and mouth both.

Time is of the utmost importance. Place the victim faceup. If there is foreign matter (food particles, blood) visible in his mouth, wipe it out quickly with your fingers. Tilt the victim's head back, pushing his chin

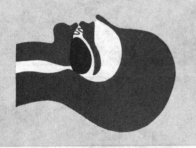

The head of an unconscious person slumps forward, and the base of his sagging tongue blocks the airway. The first job is to open up the airway. This is done by tilting victim's head back.

When victim's head is tilted back until his chin points almost straight up in the air and the skin over his throat is stretched taut, the base of his tongue is raised off the back of his throat.

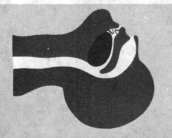

After head has been tilted far back, airway can be opened even more by pushing up the victim's chin—part way for mouth-to-mouth breathing, the whole way for mouth-to-nose breathing.

250

up so that the skin is taut over his throat, and start breathing into him. For mouth-to-nose breathing, hold the victim's mouth closed with your hand against his chin and seal your lips around his nose. Now, blow air into the victim until you see his chest rise. Remove your mouth and let the air escape from the victim's lungs while you take a deep breath.

Blow into his lungs again, and again let the air escape. Continue blowing about 12 times a minute for an adult, 20 times for a child. For mouth-to-mouth breathing, lift up under the patient's neck with one hand in order to tip his head far back. Pinch his nostrils with fingers of the other hand, seal your lips around his mouth, and blow as described above.

When the victim's breathing starts, time your efforts to fit his efforts to breathe for himself. Keep him lying down, and make him warm with blankets or other coverings. Get him under a doctor's care during the recovery period.

Of course, in training for this method it is not necessary for you to do the actual blowing. Learn and demonstrate the correct way of tilting the victim's head back, pushing the jaw up. Explain how you would clean foreign matter out of his mouth, place your mouth, and give rescue breathing.

The six steps for giving mouth-to-mouth resuscitation as illustrated in the "Rescue Breathing" poster, No. 3186.

1.—Clear victim's mouth of all foreign matter.

2.—Tilt head back, lift neck to open air passages to lungs.

3.—Pinch nostrils; place mouth on victim's mouth, blow 12 times for adult or 20 times for child per minute.

4.—Let victim exhale naturally; watch rise of chest to see if your efforts are effective.

5.—If breathing is obstructed, turn victim on side, slap back to clear throat of possible foreign matter.

6.—If air passage is still blocked, try mouth-to-nose breathing; hold mouth closed and blow through nose.

cuts and burns

Most of the first aid cases you will handle will be cuts and scratches. These are wounds—openings in the skin. Even the slightest wound should be given prompt care. Otherwise, germs may get to work and cause a dangerous infection. Clean the wound and protect it.

Burns and scalds are among the most painful of all injuries. In mild burns and the usual form of sunburn, the skin gets red. These burns are called *first-degree burns.* For mild burns use cold water immediately. Keep burn under water until there is little or no pain.

If blisters form, you are up against a *second-degree burn.* This is considerably more serious than a first-degree burn, because the blisters may break and become open wounds. Do not rub greasy ointment on blisters. Protect them by covering with dry, sterile gauze. Keep the gauze pad in place with a bandage.

Third-degree burns are the worst of all. In these, the skin may be burned away and some of the flesh charred. Do not try to remove any clothing—it may be sticking to the flesh. Keep in mind that shock is certainly present. Wrap a clean sheet around the victim, cover him with blankets if the weather is cool, and rush him to a hospital.

SMALL CUTS can become infected if not cared for properly. Wash the cut with soap and water. Let it dry, then apply an adhesive bandage. **PUNCTURE WOUNDS** are dangerous because of tetanus infection. Squeeze gently around the wound to get it to bleed. If a splinter or a nail is in the wound, pull it out. If it is a fishhook, it must be pushed in and around until the barb comes out. Cut off the barb with pliers and back the hook out of the wound. Clean and bandage. See a doctor.

LARGE CUTS may bring on shock. Watch your patient for signs of fainting. If he appears pale and unsteady, help him lie down. Wash the cut with soap and water.

Remove a sterile gauze dressing from its package. Handle by the corners.

Apply the dressing over the cut.

Use a roller bandage to hold the dressing in place.

Slit the bandage, then tie the ends with a square knot. Check again to be sure that your patient is not suffering from shock.

253

CRAVAT can be made from a triangular bandage, neckerchief, or large handkerchief. Start with the point close to you.

Fold up the point to about 2 inches from the long edge.

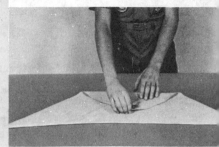

Fold the long edge down over the point.

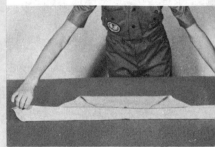
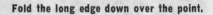

Fold once more from the long edge.

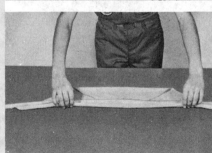

Make final fold to make the cravat.

The cravat is used to hold a dressing in place over a wound.

For a wound on an arm or leg, place the dressing over the cut. Hold with one hand while putting the cravat in place to secure the dressing.

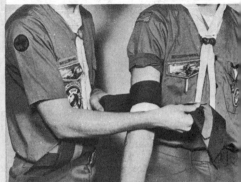

Wrap the cravat tightly around the limb. Continue until ends remaining are just long enough to meet so a square knot can be tied with them.

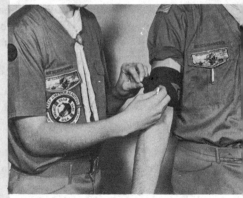

Tie securely with a square knot.

The same procedure is followed for a cut on the head. Wrap the cravat around the head and tie in place.

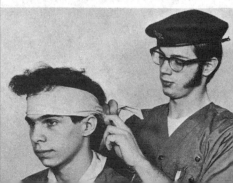

severe bleeding

When blood is gushing from a wound, grab at the wound with a bare hand and PRESS—HARD! Stop that blood! Then use your free hand to reach for your neckerchief or handkerchief or tear a piece off your shirt —or, if someone is near, call for a cloth folded into a pad or for a sterile gauze pad. Let go of the wound for the split second it takes you to slap the pad on it, then press again. Finally, tie pad firmly in place with some kind of bandage. If pad gets blood-soaked, don't remove it. Just put another pad on top of the first, and another bandage. Then get the victim to a doctor or a hospital!

Usually, direct pressure on the wound will stop even the most severe bleeding. There is only one extreme case where it probably won't— where an arm or leg is almost or completely cut off and where the artery gushes blood. In such cases—and ONLY WHERE THE CHOICE IS BETWEEN LOSING A LIMB OR A LIFE—you may have to apply a tourniquet.

To make a tourniquet, twist your handkerchief into a bandage about 2 inches wide. Wrap this bandage twice around the limb on the side nearest to the heart, leaving about an inch of skin between the wound and the tourniquet. Tie an overhand knot. Place a strong stick on the knot and tie it in place with a square knot. Turn the stick until the blood stops. Tie one end of the stick to the limb to keep it from slipping. Cover the wound with a dressing and bandage it. Note the time. Then get the patient under a doctor's care as soon as possible. Do not loosen the tourniquet—let the doctor do that.

Learn to make a tourniquet—but use it only in case of extreme emergency.

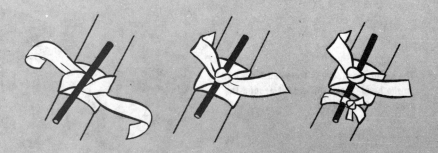

Rip clothing clear and press down hard on the wound with your bare hand.

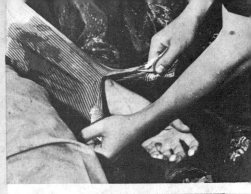

Grab clothing or sterile pad and press against wound.

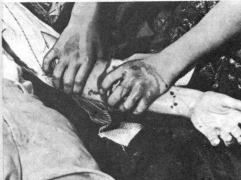

Add pads of clothing or compresses as blood soaks through. Keep pressure on; don't let go!

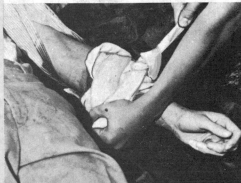

Tie compresses in place with whatever you can reach and apply. Treat for shock and send for help.

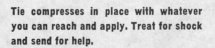
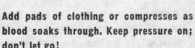

pressure points

If the tourniquet is so dangerous to use that it is to be applied only where there is a choice between loss of life or loss of a limb, isn't there anything else that can be done to stop severe bleeding? The answer is use of pressure points. Arteries carrying blood to the parts of the body are quite similar to a hose carrying water. If a car tire stops on top of a garden hose, it will cut off the flow of water. Pressure of the tire, squeezing the hose to the pavement, shuts off the water supply to the end of the hose. Similarly, if an artery is pressed against solid bone in the body, the flow of blood through the artery will be checked.

There are four places in the body where this pressure can be applied to stop bleeding. These places, two on each side of the body, can be used to control bleeding in the arms or legs.

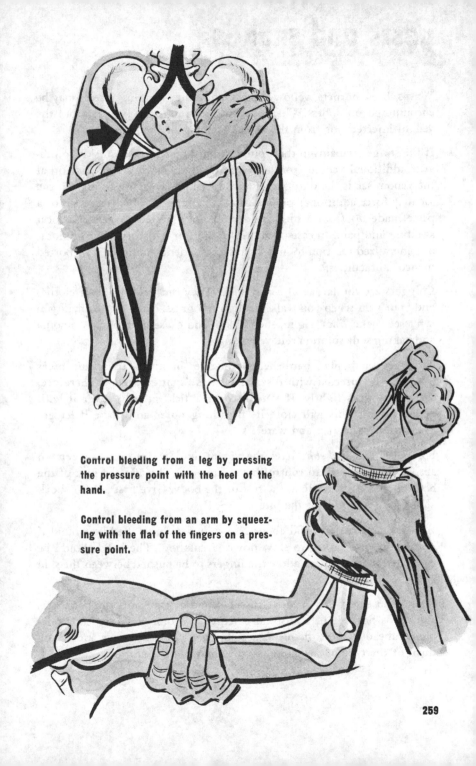

Control bleeding from a leg by pressing the pressure point with the heel of the hand.

Control bleeding from an arm by squeezing with the flat of the fingers on a pressure point.

pests and snakes

Wasps, bees, hornets, yellow jackets, and other stinging insects may be encountered outdoors. When a person is stung, the pain is from the venom injected not from the actual piercing of the skin.

If the stinger remains in the wound, it must be removed quickly to prevent additional venom from entering the system. However, flicking at the venom sac is the only suggested procedure, as trying to dig out the sac may force additional venom into the system. Local applications of a paste made up from a meat tenderizer is suggested to decrease local swelling and pain. In case of multiple stings or a history of severe local or generalized reaction to insect bites, the patient should be transported to medical facilities.

Chiggers are the larvae of a tiny mite. They can get onto your clothes and your skin when you walk through tall grass. They are so small you can't see them. They dig in, suck blood, and cause irritation. Ammonia and baking soda solution relieve itching.

Ticks are small, flat, hard-shelled relatives of mites. In certain areas ticks may be infected with disease, such as "spotted fever." Therefore, don't take ticks lightly. If you discover a tick on you, cover it with grease or oil. This will close its breathing pores and make it let go. Then wash with soap and water.

For poisonous *snakebite* have the victim lie down at once and remain absolutely quiet; try to control his excitement. The affected part of the body should be lower than the rest of the body. Give first aid for shock along with first aid for the bite.

Apply a constriction band about 2 to 4 inches above the bite wound if it is on an arm or leg to slow down circulation. The band should be tightened moderately to allow the fingers to be pushed between the skin and the band.

Contact an emergency medical rescue squad or transport the patient as quickly as possible to a hospital emergency room. Have someone telephone ahead to alert the medical staff when you will arrive and advise them of the type of snakebite, so they may get the antitoxin.

frostbite and exposure

When you are out skating or skiing, someone in the crowd may complain of his ears, nose, fingers, or toes feeling numb. Or you may notice that a fellow's ears or nose or cheeks are looking grayish-white—sure sign of frostbite. Get the frozen part thawed out. If part of the face is frozen, have the person remove a glove and cover the part with his hand. If a hand is frostbitten, bring it under the armpit next to the skin. Then get the victim into a warm room, give him a warm drink, and rewarm the frozen part by holding it in lukewarm but not hot water, or by wrapping it in warm blankets. Do not use rubbing or friction, because this will damage tissues. When the frostbitten part is rewarmed tell the patient to exercise injured fingers or toes.

When a person is exposed to severe cold he may become unconscious. If his breathing stops, give artificial respiration. Bring him into a warm room. Wrap him in warm blankets or place him in a tub of warm *but not hot* water. When he reacts give him a hot drink. Dry his body thoroughly if water was used to warm him.

Anyone who falls through the ice will need treatment for exposure.

sprains and fractures

Sprain or fracture? Only a doctor can tell. The fellow who is disabled knows that it hurts. Swelling can start immediately. What do you do? If in doubt treat for fracture. *First,* let the patient lie exactly where he is with as little motion as possible while you render first aid— making him as comfortable as possible with something over and under him. *Second,* call a doctor or an ambulance. *Third,* treat for shock.

In case of extreme emergency—when an accident has happened in a faraway wilderness—it may be necessary to move the patient before the doctor gets to him. In such a case, DO support the broken limb by making it immovable between well-padded splints. *Do not* move the patient before this splinting is completed—*splint him where he lies!*

A splint is some stiff material that can be tied to the fractured limb to make it rigid and prevent the bone from moving and tearing the flesh with its sharp edges. A splint should always be longer than the bone to which it is applied. Before applying, the splint should be padded with soft material.

THIGH FRACTURE. Use two padded splints, one for outside of leg extending from heel to armpit, and one for inside from heel to crotch. Bind together, using four binders around splints and leg and three around part of the outside splint and the body. Because of the strength of the muscles of the upper leg, they often pull the broken parts of a bone out of line and into the flesh. Therefore, use only for early emergency care.

SPRAINED ANKLE. If your partner thinks that he has sprained his ankle, don't let him take his shoe off. Fold a triangular bandage into a narrow band.

Bring the bandage from the instep around the heel.

Cross the ends over the ankle and loop each end through itself.

Pull the ends through and tie in a square knot. Be careful. Not too tight!

If the sprain is not severe, the patient may be able to walk with this extra support.

COLLARBONE FRACTURE. An arm sling may be used to relieve strain on a broken collarbone. Support the arm with a triangular bandage. No splint is needed.

Bring ends around the patient's neck.

Tie the ends in a square knot.

Place a second triangular bandage over his injured arm and around his chest.

Tie the ends with a square knot.

UPPER ARM FRACTURE. Use one padded splint only, slightly longer than distance from shoulder to elbow. Fasten it on the outside of the arm with two bandages.

Place the forearm in a narrow sling and tie the ends with a square knot behind the patient's neck.

Hold arm against the body with a second triangular bandage folded into a narrow band and tied behind his back.

FOREARM OR WRIST FRACTURE. Use something soft like a poncho to pad the stick splint. Be sure that the splint reaches from the elbow to the fingertips. Bind the splint and padding with two triangular bandages folded into a narrow band. Use square knots.

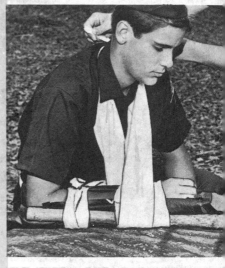

While the arm is resting on a support tie a sling around the patient's neck.

Check to be sure that the thumb is up and that the hand is a couple of inches higher than the elbow.

A seriously injured person should be moved by a first-aider only in case of extreme emergency, and then only after having received first aid and having had possible fractures splinted.

A fracture of the back or neck is the most dangerous fracture of all. An automobile smashup or a fall from a ledge or tree could cause this fracture. The person is in severe pain, is often unconscious. Legs and arms may be paralyzed. The slightest false move may cause the broken bone to cut into the spinal cord, killing the patient, or causing permanent crippling. *Wait for a doctor or ambulance!*

A patient who has suffered a minor accident and feels weak may be assisted to walk. Bring his arm up over your shoulder, holding onto his hand with one of yours, and place your free arm around his waist. If the patient is unable to walk yet is not seriously injured, you may be able to carry him piggyback.

When the patient has to be moved for some distance or his injuries are serious, he should be carried on a stretcher. A satisfactory stretcher can be made from two poles a couple of feet longer than the patient is tall. If you don't have blankets, use coats or shirts turned inside out and buttoned. Push the poles through the sleeves.

When you must pick up an unconscious person, make an accordion fold in a blanket. Pleat the blanket in folds about 18 inches deep. Place the blanket just beyond the victim's head so that the pleated blanket will feed out from the bottom when pulled.

While one man lifts and keeps the victim's head in line with his body slide the blanket under him.

With men kneeling on the blanket and holding the victim's shoulders and head, two men pull the blanket down.

Roll the blanket tightly until it fits the contour of the victim's body.

At a signal, the men on the sides pull back while the man holding the victim's head continues to hold the head in line with his body. The victim can be lifted 6 to 8 inches from the ground so that a stretcher can be slid beneath him.

For the blanket stretcher, place one staff on the blanket. Fold over almost half of the blanket. Place the second staff 6 inches from the edge of the folded-over part. Fold the short edge over the pole. Then fold longer bottom edge into the body of the stretcher.

Test the stretcher with an uninjured person before you lift and carry the victim.

268

RESCUE BLANKET is the name of a piece of survival gear that can fit into your shirt pocket. Naturally, it can't replace your sleeping bag or be as comfortable as a blanket, but it can perform some amazing functions just the same.

Spread the blanket out and fold a 4-inch hem at the top and the bottom. Place the poles on the blanket a third of the distance from each edge and fold the sides in.

With a fellow on the stretcher as heavy as the victim, make a test lift.

When you've thoroughly tested the stretcher, place the victim on the stretcher and carry him to the nearest place where aid is available.

269

14 HIGH ADVENTURE

ADVENTURE to a Cub Scout is sleeping in his own backyard. To the more experienced Scout, it's his first hike, his first overnighter, and then his first summer camp. The Explorer, who has done all these things, finds high adventure in reaching out for new places in more advanced activities.

Obviously, the key factor here is experience. For the inexperienced Cub, a canoeing and camping trip would be too much to handle. For the advanced Explorer, sleeping in the backyard is hardly an exciting or adventurous experience.

For trained Explorers, high adventure essentially involves experience and training. High adventure is backpacking in the wilderness where the chance of meeting another camper is remote. It's facing the challenge of white water with a canoe. It's paddling and portaging to an isolated lake where the fish will bite. It's taking extended trips to national parks, historical areas, even amusement and recreational centers.

This is frosting on the Scouting cake. It's one of those highlights that will linger in your memory throughout your life. Don't forget, though—the cake must be well done before you can add that frosting. High-adventure camping isn't for the novice. You must be proficient in basic Scouting skills to enjoy real high adventure. In many cases, you need training in the specialty you are undertaking. For example, you don't head for white water until you are expert where the water's smooth and slow.

And there's one more thing to remember—high adventure isn't only found in the wilderness. It's often high adventure to visit interesting "civilized" places in our nation—like national parks and recreation centers. Visiting other countries can also be exciting.

But whether you're miles away from civilization in the wilderness or right in the center of civilization in our nation's capital, training pays off. *Be Prepared,* and you can meet the challenge of high adventure.

backpacking equipment

In no area of Scouting is lightness and compactness more essential than in high-adventure backpacking. You'll probably need to carry everything you'll use during the entire trip, so even ounces are important. The load for each fellow should not be more than one-fifth of his weight. (A 150-pound backpacker should carry about 30 pounds in his pack.) When group gear is added to personal gear, you'll find serious overweight problems unless careful attention has been paid to the weight and importance of individual items.

CARRY ON YOUR PERSON
Essential
___Matches, waterproof safe
___Knife, pocket or sheath
___Compass, cased
___Survival kit (make)
___Nylon cord, 200-lb. test, 20 ft.
___Handkerchief, bandanna
___Money, identification, fishing permit in waterproof bag
___Pencil, notebook, pocket-size
___Toilet paper in waterproof bag
___Fire starters
___Map(s), topo or appropriate
___Sunglasses, case, safety loop
Optional
___Watch, waterproof preferable
___Documents for customs
___Camera and film, waterproof
___Water purification tablets
___Binoculars
___Head net or insect netting
___First aid kit, personal
___Flashlight, small; extra batteries

Extra eyeglasses
___Travel kit to carry items needed en route

WEAR
(Keep emergency or often-used items in pack pockets or near the top of the pack if not worn.)
___Shoes, hiking—ankle-high; broken-in but not broken-down
___Socks, medium wool
___Trousers, uniform
___Shirt, uniform
___Belt, uniform
___Poncho, lightweight, with hood
___Windbreaker, hooded, water-repellent
___Cap, visored

CARRY IN PACK
Clothing
___Wool shirt or sweater
___T-shirts (2)
___Socks medium wool (2-4 pr.)

__Handkerchiefs (2) or bandanna
__Camp shoes, sneakers, or
   moccasins

Sleeping Gear
__Sleeping bag (down pre-
   ferred); washable liner (Carry
   in stuffing bag or wrap in waterproof plastic.)
__Ground cloth, light nylon or
   medium plastic, size of sleeping
   bag
__Pajamas, sweat suit, or long
   johns (Choose for lowest
   temperature.)
__Cap, wool stocking, for night

Eating Gear
__Plate, bowl-type, plastic
__Cup, plastic
__Fork, tablespoon, water bottle,
   polyethylene

Toilet Articles
__Soap, floating, plastic bag
__Towel, small, plastic bag
__Toothbrush, in case
__Toothpaste/powder
__Shaving gear, plastic bag
__Toilet paper in waterproof bag
__Sunburn lotion and lip salve
__Insect repellent stick

Optional
__Fishing gear, very compact kit,
   telescoping rod
__Air mattress, 48-in.
__Moccasins or sneakers for camp
__Bible or Prayer Book

GROUP GEAR FOR BACKPACKING
Shelter—Lightweight, nylon tarp
   or improvise from 10 x 12-ft.

plastic sheeting rigged as "A"
tent or lean-to. Two men to
shelter plus extra for dining fly.

Cooking Gear
__Pots, 4-qt., lightweight (6)
__Frypans, 8-in. (2)
__Reflector ovens
__Spoon, large
__Can opener, small roll-type
__Spatula, small
__Scouring pads, stainless
__Soap, liquid in plastic bottle
__Cooking sheet, plastic, 4 by 4 ft.
__Sanitizing tablets

Camp Tools
__Saw, folding
__File, 5-in. ignition
__Shovel or large trowel
__Repair kit: cutting pliers,
   sewing kit, wire, nylon cord,
   adhesive, straps, etc.

Emergency and
Miscellaneous Gear
__First aid kit plus clinical oral
   thermometer, 3-in. elastic
   bandages (2), and tweezers
__Flashlight, spare bulb and
   batteries (2)
__Tote-litter bag with plastic
   liner

Optional
__Tongs, hot-pot
__Cooking gloves
__Ax, pack with sheath
__LP pack stove and fuel for
   areas without wood supply
__Snakebite kit
__Special gear for mountaineer-
   ing, conservation, and so on

canoeing equipment

When you backpack you carry everything you need all the time. When you travel by canoe you carry the canoe and everything you need some of the time. Indians were the first to recognize that short hauls of carrying everything was worth the effort, so they invented the canoe.

On open water the canoe carries you, your buddy, and a surprising amount of gear. There's a limit, of course, but you can make two or three trips at a portage to transfer your equipment and canoe around a dam or a rapid. You can take some luxury items along like air mattresses and roomier tents.

CARRY ON YOUR PERSON
Same as *Personal Gear for Backpacking*

WEAR
___Shoe, hiking—ankle-high
___Socks, medium wool
___Trousers, long, uniform
___Shirt, long-sleeved uniform

STOW IN PACK
___Shirt, long-sleeved wool, sweater, or jac-shirt
___Swim trunks or uniform shorts
___T-shirts (2)
___Underwear shorts (2)
___Shoes, sneakers
___Belt, uniform
___Socks (2-4 pr.)
___Poncho or rain jacket and hood or rainhat
___Handkerchiefs, bandannas (2)
___Cap, visored

Sleeping Gear
___Sleeping bag (down preferred); washable liner (Carry in stuffing bag or wrap in waterproof plastic.)
___Ground cloth, nylon or medium plastic, unless tents have waterproof ground cloths
___Mosquito net if tent is not netted
___Pajamas, sweat suit, or long johns (Choose for lowest probable temperatures.)

Eating Gear
___Plate, bowl-type, plastic
___Cup, plastic
___Tablespoon and fork

Toilet Articles
___Soap, floating, plastic bag
___Towel, small, plastic bag
___Toothbrush, in case

___Toothpaste/powder
___Shaving gear, plastic bag
___Toilet paper in waterproof bag
___Sunburn lotion and lip salve
___Insect repellent

Optional

___Air mattress, 48-in.
___Fishing gear
___Combination kneeling and
   shoulder pads
___Plastic sheet 2 x 3 ft. for
   protecting knees from rain
   while paddling
___Bible or Prayer Book

GROUP GEAR FOR
CANOE CAMPING

___Canoe—If rented, check con-
   dition thoroughly. Call attention of outfitter to any damage
   before you accept it.
___Paddles, 3 per canoe
___Life jacket for each man; in
   cases properly secured in canoe
   and readily accessible

Shelter

___Tent with sod cloths, netted
   door and vent (Voyageur
   recommended)
___Fly kitchen 12 x 16 ft. or
   10 x 10 ft., lightweight

Optional

___Poles, aluminum
___Pins, tent, steel

Cooking Gear (suit to group size)

___Pots, 10-qt., nesting, (2)
___Pots, 8-qt., nesting, (2)
___Frypans, 10-in., aluminum (2)
   or griddle, aluminum, large

___Reflector ovens
___Gloves and/or hot-pot tongs
___Mixing jars, screw cap, plastic,
   widemouthed (2)
___Spoons, large (3)
___Can opener, small roll-type
___Measuring cup, plastic
___Utensil bag
___Pot-and-pan bag
___Soap, liquid, plastic bottle
___Scouring pad, stainless/plastic
___Swab, dish, cellulose
___Scraper, rubber
___Canteen, 1-qt., per canoe
___4 x 4-ft. kitchen sheet, plastic

Camp Tools

___Shovel or large trowel
___Ax, three-quarter, and sheath
___Saw, folding or small bow
___File, 5-in. ignition
___Stone, sharpening
___Repair kit; canoe-repair mate-
   rials, parallel-jaw pliers with
   cutters, wire, tape, sewing
   kit, etc.

Emergency and
Miscellaneous Gear

___First aid kit, oral thermometer
___Waterproof supply of matches
___Toilet paper, waterproof bag
___Bucket, folding canvas
___Shock cord for securing gear
___Tote-litter bag with plastic liner

Optional

___Paper towels
___Dutch oven, aluminum
___Snakebite kit

canoe camping trip

As you start on the portage, don't try to throw the canoe up on your shoulders alone. A canoe mate or two can help set the craft on your shoulders before they load up with duffel.

The portage is the toughest part of a canoe trip, so don't wear yourself out by overloading. Unless the portage is exceptionally long, make two trips in preference to trying to be a human burro. Sometimes you can make your camp at the portage and spread the trek into the next day.

The pace during the portage should be comfortable and as untiring as possible. On a long overland hike, wrap extra clothing around paddle blades where they rest on your shoulders to prevent irritation.

At the end of your portage, repack your gear as carefully as you did at the trip's start.

Since most canoe camps are used for only a night, they should be very simple with a minimum of facilities. You'll need three basic areas—one for the latrine, one for cooking, and one for sleeping. You should pitch your tents if there's danger of rain, morning dampness, or an insect problem. Your canoes must be carried well up from the water's edge, and should be stowed upside down in an area that is safe from possible windstorm damage.

Shock cord is composed of a sturdy nylon covering over an elastic core, available in 1/8- and 5/16-inch diameters. It is generally tied (for smaller sizes) or clipped (for both sizes) in a circle for use. Large loops are used to secure equipment to a pack frame or cartop carrier. Loops of small shock cord do a good job in holding a tightly rolled sleeping bag. They can also be used to secure gear to the frame or to the pack itself. Once stretched in place, shock cord won't loosen en route.

A canoe camping pack needs to be of good size, heavy construction, and without sharp projections. In addition, it should be frameless, a frame just gets in the way. The Duluth pack has been popular for years in the Minnesota-Canada canoe country; because of its rugged construction and its neat fit in a canoe.

When carrying a heavy load on a short portage, use a tumpline with the pack. This is a strap that fits across the forehead and shifts weight from the shoulders.

Shock cord and bumper hooks are used in this photo to secure two canoes to a car top. The canoes are carried side by side on the car top by supporting the canoe edges with a frame and padding the spots where canoe and frame meet to prevent chafing.

On the water, most of your cargo is important only as it affects the trim of your canoe. The cargo and passengers in this photo are balanced from side to side and from end to end according to the weather and water conditions, and the canoeists' and the cargo's weights. Paddlers are in kneeling positions on mats. Packs are tied to center thwart with shock cord to prevent shifting.

The canoe-bearer carries the canoe, as shown here, with the craft tilted back on his shoulders and the flat of the paddle blades (the paddle yoke) resting on his shoulders. If there are two men to a canoe, the Explorer with the duffel leads the way. If there are three to a canoe, then the canoe is carried in the middle with one load of duffel in front and another behind.

This canoe is ready for the portage. The spare paddle is secured under the thwarts with shock cord, the two regular paddles are fastened on top of the middle thwarts to form a portage yoke, and the painter is tied down to prevent drag.

277

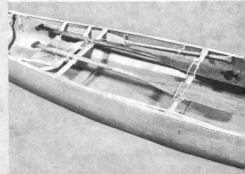

High-Adventure Bases

For tops in a once-in-a-lifetime activity for an Explorer post or troop leadership corps, consider one of the national high-adventure program bases—Philmont, Charles L. Sommers Wilderness Canoe Base, Northern Wisconsin National Canoe Base, or Maine National High Adventure Area. These are run by the Boy Scouts of America to offer a real high-adventure experience to those who might not be able to have it locally. Each of these programs offers the experience, the program, the leadership help, and the equipment necessary for a successful trip. Your council can provide detailed information on each of these high-adventure bases. It has brochures describing each base and can arrange for slides or filmstrips to help visualize the program and facilities available at any of these national high-adventure bases.

PHILMONT SCOUT RANCH. This photo reflects the great treasury of natural beauty found at Philmont. Located near Cimarron, N. Mex., the sprawling 137,000 acre ranch includes mountains and plains, streams and forests, wild birds, and animals. Miles of hiking trails connect base camps to special program features. A Philmont expedition is 12 days of he-man outdooring come-to-life in the Old West. Each group receives special training from a ranger who sticks with the group until he is sure it's ready to go it alone. Each group must be accompanied by its own adult leadership.

CANOE BASES AND MAINE AREA. Paddling to dinner at a campsite like this one can be a great experience at the canoe bases or Maine area. The Northern Wisconsin National Canoe Base is located on White Sand Lake near Boulder Junction, Wis. Hundreds of rivers, lakes, and small streams lie within range of this jumpoff point. Groups using this base should be kept to eight Scouts or Explorers and one adult leader. A training program is included in the trip fee. The Charles L. Sommers Wilderness Canoe Base is located in the Superior National Forest, 22 miles north of Ely, Minn. The base is in the heart of excellent canoe country with some 4,000 square miles of roadless wilderness. An experienced guide accompanies each group of 10 Scouts or Explorers and one adult leader. The Maine National High Adventure Area is based on Grand Lake Matagamon. The program features wilderness backpacking, camping, and canoeing. The program, length of stay, and group-size requirements are all flexible.

jamborees

The climax of your Scout camping and the most inspiring event in your Scouting life will come the day you travel cross-country to participate in a national jamboree of Scouts from every corner of America with guests from many other countries, or go overseas for a world jamboree of Scout delegates from all around the globe.

World jamborees are normally held every 4 years, national jamborees during the intervals between the world events. As many as 50,000 Scouts have taken part in some of these tremendous brotherhood gatherings.

Through these get-togethers of boys from around the world, the Scout movement is doing its part, in Baden-Powell's words, "to establish friendships among Scouts of all nations and to help to develop peace and happiness in the world and goodwill among men."

Tents cover the landscape at Moraine State Park in Pennsylvania where once strip mining changed the surface of the earth. This jamboree site is a model of what can be done to restore the beauty of America. The search for energy does not necessarily mean a ravaged environment.

Scouts and Explorer trade ideas. Here's the place to show others what you know, what you can do, and what you can cook up. Who said "Too many cooks spoil the broth?"

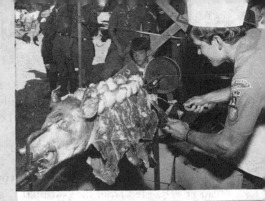

Jamborees don't stay put. America is big and wide. When you pitch your camp, the jamboree site may have mountains just beyond your reach and a bright blue sky overhead.

What do you do at a jamboree? Man, you wouldn't believe the fun you can have in a field like this. If you haven't crossed a monkey bridge you don't know what fancy footwork is.

If you were at Nordjamb-75 at Lillehammer, Norway, you might have met these Scouts from Canada, the Philippines and a hundred other countries.

281

National Eagle Scout Association

This association is for anyone who has achieved the Eagle Award. It provides an opportunity for all Eagles to retain an association with Scouting through service to their local council.

There is a registration fee based on your age and term of membership. Members will receive a subscription to the *Eagletter,* the association newsletter, and an attractive permanent membership card. Applications can be requested from the National Eagle Scout Association, Boy Scouts of America, P.O. Box 61030, Dallas/Ft. Worth Airport, Tex. 75261.

Advantages of joining the association are:
To continue active involvement with the national movement.
To maintain the many fine friendships made with other Scouts and leaders and to meet and enjoy additional friends of Scouting.
To reaffirm the pledge of service to others through Scouting.

The attractive symbol of the National Eagle Scout Association uses the miniature Eagle lapel pin against a red, white, and blue background.

Order of the Arrow

The tremendous potential for good in the idea of "cheerful service" can best be seen at a national Order of the Arrow conference. Held every other year, these great gatherings bring together Arrowmen from every State in the Union. If you're lucky enough to attend one of these conferences you'll have a high-adventure experience to remember the rest of your life. The main purpose of each conference is to train and inspire those taking part so they will be able to help make the Order of the Arrow idea more effective in their own local lodges.

Conferences include discussion groups and workshops on such a variety of subjects as ceremonies, service projects, all aspects of Indian lore, public relations, and conservation. Here you'll meet the great leaders of Scouting and the Order, and be thrilled at demonstrations and pageants put on by fellows who are the very best. But, most of all, you'll gain an appreciation of the power of thousands of young men from all over America—young men dedicated to helping now and in the future to make this a greater nation.

One of the most fascinating features of the Order of the Arrow is its wide use of Indian costumes. Local Order of the Arrow lodges are encouraged to study the customs of the Indian tribes that lived in their areas and to model their costumes after them.

In a huge candlelight ceremony each Order of the Arrow member rededicates himself to the ideals of brotherhood, cheerfulness, and service.

283

tours and permits

Your high adventure deserves official Campways BSA recognition. Special permits from your Scout office help you and your troop or post check out the important plans that ensure a successful trip. Federal and State park rangers are familiar with the system and will ask to see your permit when you check in and out. They are impressed by the permit because a group that carries it lives up to the Pledge of Performance that appears on the back of the permit.

Pledge of Performance

- We will use trucks only for transporting equipment—no passengers except in cab.
- We will restrict our maximum daily driving time to 8 hours of daylight travel.
- We agree to enforce reasonable travel speed (in accordance with State and local laws) in all motor vehicles.
- We will at all times be a credit to the Boy Scouts of America, and we will not tolerate rowdyism or un-Scoutlike conduct, keeping a constant check on all members of our party.
- We will respect the property of others, and we will not trespass.
- We will maintain high standards of personal cleanliness and orderliness and will operate a clean and sanitary camp, leaving it in a better condition than we found it.
- We will not bury any trash, garbage, or tin cans. All rubbish that cannot be burned will be placed in a tote-litter bag and taken to the nearest recognized trash disposal or all the way home, if necessary.
- We will be certain that fires are attended at all times.
- We will not cut standing trees or shrubs without specific permission from the landowner or manager.
- We will collect only souvenirs that are gifts or that are bought and paid for.
- We will use the Safe Swim Defense plan in any water activity.

- We will pay our own way and not expect any special concessions or entertainment from any individual or group.

- We will provide every member of our party an opportunity to attend religious services on the Sabbath.

- We will observe the courtesy to write thank-you notes to persons who assisted us on our trip.

- We will, in case of serious trouble, notify our local council office, our parents, or the Camping and Conservation Service, Boy Scouts of America, North Brunswick, N. J. 08902.

To be successful, a high-adventure activity must be preceded by days, weeks, and even months of careful well-thought-out planning. This is particularly true of all phases of travel experiences. Planning builds up anticipation that is the prerequisite of a good experience. Campways BSA should be your guide in all high adventure planning because well-thought-out plans ensure the full enjoyment of the trip for every person. Time will be allowed for relaxation as well as plenty of action and excitement. Delays, inconveniences, and accidents—caused by lack of knowledge of the situation or area or by lack of necessary equipment —are almost completely avoided by careful planning.

How about visiting historical spots to help develop an appreciation for our American heritage? You can walk the same ground as Washington, Grant, Custer, and lesser-known men whose lives helped shape the destiny of our nation. This type of trip will be enhanced by advance reading about the historic background of the area.

Planning helps your gang "get off the beaten path" and see and experience things that a poorly planned trip will miss completely. The main highway may be the fastest, but it is rarely the most interesting. Planning also gives every member of the group a definite responsibility and a stake in the success of the venture. Everyone understands and has a chance to express his opinion so that the trip belongs to every member of the group, not just to one or two.

Don't be in a hurry to outline your route on a map until you are certain it is the best one. Every trip offers a number of possibilities, and the possibilities need to be drawn on a map without marking it.

Use a clear sheet of plastic to cover the map of your trip. Trace possible routes on the plastic with a marking pen and rub them out or change them as new information becomes available.

The map with its plastic overlay is your trip-mapper. Place it on the bulletin board where it can be the center of attention as changes in the plan are redrawn.

Use two colors to plan the day journeys. Alternate the colors to show the number of travel days: black—the first and third days; red—second and fourth.

Mountaineering demands endurance, training, special equipment, and teamwork. The strange forms the ice makes as it melts away from the warmer rocks is just one of the sights Explorers can see close-up when they are prepared. The Sierra Club of the West and the Appalachian Trail Conference of the East are the experts in mountaineering.

Remember at this stage that many groups overtax themselves when determining how far they will go each day. Four hundred miles a day (450 miles on superhighways) is suggested as a maximum to travel. In going full speed ahead, you miss out on points of local and national interest that you could see if you cut your daily travel distance in half.

Use calipers and the map scale to determine each day's distance. Or make a trip-mapper gauge from a string tied with knots at 250, 300, 350, and 400 miles of the map's scale distance.

Keep the trip-mapper in operation until you are ready to apply for your tour permit, then mark the final route on your map.

If you're interested in rocks and minerals, birds and fish, or conservation, your interests may take you miles from home. Some Explorer posts have spent a year in planning and preparing for a trip to another part of the country to work on conservation in a terrain different from their home area. These trips are a lot more than just work since there's lots of free time for exploring the country, plus interesting things to see on the way to and from the project location. Contact local officials in the area you want to help. They'll work with you on plans.

Generations of Sea Explorers have taken part in short and long cruises on lakes, rivers, and oceans. They ship out with their own Skipper and apply the seamanship skills they learned at regular meetings. The cruise is usually on a ship large enough for the whole group. Naturally, Coast Guard regulations must be and are obeyed.

15 WINTER CAMPING

HAVE YOU ever heard some guy say "Go camping in the winter! Are you out of your ever lovin' mind?" Well, maybe, but only if you don't know how to camp in the summer and aren't prepared for the differences between warm- and cold-weather camping.

Summer weather is kind and forgives poorly prepared and trained campers, but winter is cruel and unforgiving. You can get by with improper gear and inexperience when the mercury is above 40 degrees, but it can be pretty miserable when it's below freezing.

Sounds like winter camping isn't so hot, doesn't it. Well, it isn't as far as the temperature is concerned, but it's real hot in the fun, adventure, and satisfaction that comes from knowing you can take care of yourself outdoors under extreme conditions.

Camping on the same site where you camped last summer is like going to a new spot. The leaves are off the trees, the woods are open, and you can hike through swampy areas that couldn't be explored last summer. If there's snow on the ground, you'll find transportation of gear easier by sled or toboggan, and best of all is the fun of skiing, skating, snowshoeing, sliding, tobogganing, and snowballing.

Keeping warm is no problem in this day of thermal underwear and footgear, of excellent down and synthetic sleeping bag materials, of properly designed tents and water-repellent, windproof outer clothing. Comfort in camp also means keeping off mosquitoes, flies, and similar critters that make life miserable. Here's where you can really shine in winter 'cause there just aren't any around to bother you. Save your insect repellents for next spring.

So, why say more? You don't have to stay at home when the temperature drops. You don't even have to plan your trips for some smoky old crowded cabin. Just train yourself for winter. Line up your clothing and equipment for comfort and head for the hills, the plains, or the woods, and be a year-round camper.

clothing

Personal comfort is the key to enjoyment for all types of camping. In the winter, this means just one thing—keeping warm day and night. Air is the great insulator that maintains body warmth in both clothing and bedding. That's why layers of material are warmer than just one thickness. Air is trapped between each layer. This air must be dry, however. Moisture in your clothing or bedding will chill you. Air insulates, keeping in body heat, but moisture conducts that heat away. Everyone is aware of moisture that comes from the outside—rain, damp snow, and puddles—but many don't know that inner moisture coming from the body can cause as much trouble in keeping warm as the more obvious outer dampness.

Waterproof outer garments and coverings for sleeping bags and blankets trap body moisture, making clothing and blankets damp and cold. The material covering you must be able to "breathe" so perspiration can pass away from your body and into the outer air where it evaporates.

Regulation of heat is important to winter comfort. If you become very warm through exercise or excessive clothing, your body will perspire. This moisture will dampen your clothing; then, when you slow down your activity, this moisture will conduct your heat away from you and you'll be cold. This is another reason for wearing layers of clothing in the winter. You can shed layers to keep from overheating when you are active, and add layers again when you are less vigorous. Heat regulation can also be controlled to some extent by the tightness of your collar or by the use of a parka. There is considerable body heat loss around your neck. Body heat rapidly passes out through your open collar, cooling the body. Control of the loss of heat in this area will help regulate your comfort. That's why scarves are important, and why a parka is such a wonderful piece of winter camping gear. With the hood up, there is very little heat loss around the neck, and what is lost helps to warm your face. The parka also keeps your head warm—a most important consideration in winter camping. Paul Siple, noted Antarctic explorer and Eagle Scout, studied the physiology of the body related to cold temperature and reported that the human head does not have a temperature regulating mechanism to shut off the flow of heat the way the rest of the body does. As a result, he states that keeping the head covered both day and night is essential in keeping warm.

Proper care of your feet is essential to winter camp comfort and well being. Dampness and tightness are enemies of warm feet. Your foot covering must be waterproof. Leather is cold and will absorb moisture unless heavily waterproofed. It's hard to beat the old shopac which is a rubber bottom with leather uppers. These worn over felt liners with wool socks will provide warmth and dryness in sub-zero weather. A pair of thin silk or cotton socks worn under the wool adds comfort. Rubber galoshes (the buckle type rather than zipper) with felt liners will serve the same purpose.

Now, how about the other enemy—tightness? You just can't take your normal shoe or boot and put on two pair of wool socks and have a comfortable fit. Winter boots need to be at least a size larger than normal to allow for the extra lining required.

Be sure to dry your boots, socks and liners every night.

Checklist for Winter Camping

Carry on Person or Wear
Long underwear
Wool trousers
Wool shirt
Sweater
Windbreaker (parka top)
Two pair of wool socks
Water repellent boots
Gloves
Mittens
Bandanna
Cap
Handkerchiefs
Toilet paper
Ration bar
Compass
Candle
Knife
Matches
Leather thong

Carry in Your Pack
Extra socks
Extra wool shirt
Extra long underwear
Mitten liners
Toilet kit
Sleeping bag
Ground cloth
Newspapers
Eating utensils
Extra boots
Canteen
Your share of group
   equipment

Optional
Winter sports equipment
Camera
Binoculars
Bible or Prayer Book

snow camp

The camp-of-the-month plan is a great way to get started as a winter camper. August—just like July, September—cool nights, October—chilly, November—skim off the ice, December—shake hands with Jack Frost, January—correct December's mistakes, February—practice what you learned in January, March—watch the wind, April—rain possible, May—beautiful. Between each camp go over every piece of equipment. Did you use it? No. Don't take it next month. Add the items that you could have used and repair any piece of equipment damaged.

Some camp-of-the-month campers just miss camping in snow. That might happen to you. Here's what you missed.

You can't move in soft snow without leaving a track. Animals, big and small, leave tracks that anyone can follow. You might say snow is the tracker's teacher. Pay attention to the snow and you'll discover the secrets of tracking.

Before setting up your tent, prepack the snow by tramping it down with skiis, snowshoes, or just by walking on it. You don't have to scrape away the snow down to bare ground.

In the snow camp, place "deadmen" instead of tent stakes. Dig a hole in the snow, insert the deadman with line attached, and fill in the hole again with packed snow. Loop the line through the ties on your tent to hold it down. If the ground is frozen and there isn't any snow, use large spikes for tent pegs.

In a snow camp you have a ready source of water, but it isn't quite as simple to get as it might seem. In a kettle over a fire, snow will actually scorch and burn unless it is stirred while melting. Purify by boiling for 5 minutes, just as you would untested water.

Don't keep your fire going all night. Instead, have tinder, kindling, firewood, and matches beside you in the tent. When you waken in the morning, stay in your sleeping bag. Lean out and build your fire. When the fire is blazing, put on your clothes in the sleeping bag. Then get up.

To warm or dry your boots hold them near the fire. If the heat is too much for your hands, it's too hot for your boots.

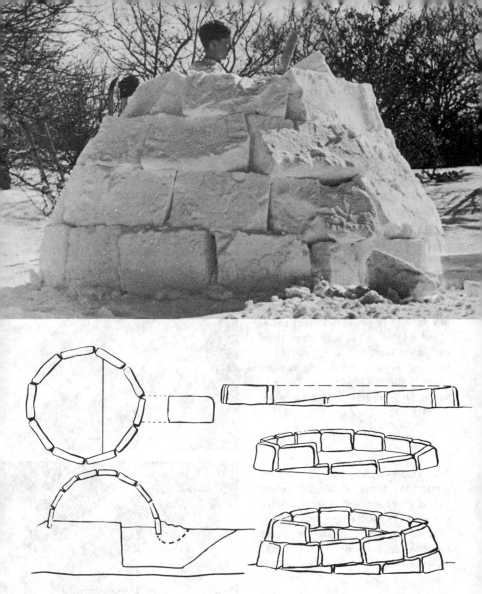

In deep-packed snow you can cut out blocks with a long knife to build an igloo. Make it a perfect circle and wedge shape the first quarter circle. Then spiral around, shaping the blocks with your knife so that the blocks pitch toward the center. Cap the top with a little help from outside. Dig the entrance tunnel and make your bed on the snow shelf.

- Choose camp long before dark. It takes longer to make a comfortable camp in winter than during other times of the year. Remember, too, darkness comes at a much earlier hour in the winter.
- Tests have revealed that a reflector behind a fire in front of a tent only increases the temperature inside the tent about one degree over that provided by a fire without the reflector, so it is of little value.
- Tents for snow country should have steep, slooping roofs to shed snow. A baker tent with its flat roof would collapse under a heavy snow load.
- Bank snow against the bottom of your tent. It will cut drafts.
- Undress and dress inside your sleeping bag. Put on fresh, dry underwear at night and sleep in it. Unless you perspire during the night, you can dress over it the next morning and wear it throughout the day.
- Mittens are warmer than gloves since there isn't a heat loss all the way around each finger. Carry gloves with you to wear when a job requires use of the fingers.
- Wrist coverings are important to warmth. They control heat loss in this area and protect you from the top of your mitten to the bottom of your jacket sleeve. Wrist coverings may be an extension of your mittens, part of your sleeves, or separate knitted wristlets.
- Many foods can be stored frozen. When using any of these in winter, freeze them ahead of time at home and they'll stay that way until ready to use in camp.
- Protect your water canteen from freezing by carrying it next to your body on the trail, hanging it near the fire in camp, and keeping it in your bedroll at night.
- Plan menus to avoid foods that can be damaged by freezing.
- Make up some kabobs, stew ingredients, hamburgers and onions with potatoes and vegetables at home. Wrap each meal in foil and freeze in your freezer. You'll save a lot of time in camp because all you have to do is thaw out a package and cook it.
- After your tent is set up, make your campfire lay in front. If your tent is the type that uses a single guy line in front, use two instead of one, spreading them out at an angle so there won't be a rope directly over your fire.
- After putting your ground bed in place, cover it with a ground cloth. Place several layers of newspapers on top of the ground cloth. Fluff

up your sleeping bag to put plenty of air in it, and lay it out on top of the newspapers. If you put the newspapers under your ground cloth, they'll become wet, soggy, and a problem for disposal at the end of your camp; but if kept dry, they can be easily burned.

- If you don't have a sleeping bag, you can make a warm bed of blankets, by folding them so there are no side or bottom openings and then using blanket pins to secure them so they won't come apart during the night. Tests show that when sleeping, 75 percent of heat loss is downward and only 25 percent up through the top of your bedroll. Therefore, to sleep warmly, you need three layers under you for every layer on top.

- A hooded sweatshirt will add to your nighttime comfort, just as a parka helps keep you warm during the day. It stops heat loss around your neck and from your head. Many campers put on dry underwear and socks at night before going to sleep. They also put on the parka-type sweatshirt over the underwear.

- If snow is not too deep, scrape it away down to bare ground where you plan to build your fire. Place stones or large logs on the ground as a fire base on which to build your fire. Heat from the fire will thaw the ground under the base, and will make a muddy mess unless you have a properly built fire base.

Open water attracts birds and animals.

cold-weather fun

Stalking is more fun in the winter because it's harder to hide: Leaves conceal your movements in the summer. Can you follow a buddy for a mile close enough to observe everything he does without him seeing you? How close can you get to animals and birds before they take off? You have two partners when you are stalking. The *wind* is your first partner—*keep it in your face*. If you don't, the wind will carry your scent to animals and warn them. The *sun* is your second partner—*keep it behind you* and in the eyes of the person or thing you're stalking.

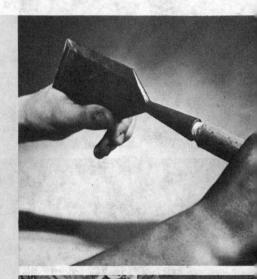

When the ice is more than 3 inches thick try fishing through the ice. You'll have to chop your own hole. That's easy with an ice chisel. Make one from a 2-inch wood chisel and a stout staff shaped to fit the socket. The water hole won't stay clear so you'll need a kitchen strainer to skim off the ice.

Experienced ice fishermen are smart. They rig a signal flag to their lines to let them know that fish are biting. This simple tip-up was made from a 1-inch dowel and a sharp triangle of plywood. The line is fastened to the base just to the left of the dowel. When fish bite, the flag flies.

297

Would you believe you could catch a fish with a mousetrap? Well you can. Here's how it's done. Nail trap to the middle of a long narrow piece of plywood. Solder a light piece of wire to the trap arm and put a little flag on the end. Nail a block with a U-shaped cutout over the bait holder. The block keeps the flag up.

Drill a hole under the bait holder. Bring the fishline through the hole and fasten it securely to the bait holder. A slight tug on the line and up flies the flag. You've caught a fish with a mousetrap.

Winter is the ideal time to develop a bird nest collection. With the leaves off the trees the nests are easy to spot, and there's no danger of taking a nest that is being used. When nest collecting, cut enough of the branch to show it attractively on a stand. Identification of type is more difficult since you won't see the bird that used it, but research should identify the builder.

298

ice rescue

There's water under that ice—cold water. Stay off ice that's under 3 inches thick. Ice is thin where current runs rapidly in bends of rivers and near dam gates in ponds. When you feel the ice bend beneath you, spread your weight by getting down on your stomach; then wiggle your way to shore snake fashion.

Very cold water—32°-38°—is paralyzing. Survival time is from 15 to 30 minutes.

Polar bears have claws that help them out of the water. Wise men who must travel on the ice make their own claws —ice awls. They are two pieces of wood with steel tips. If you carry ice awls in your jacket, you have a fighting chance to save yourself. See page 551.

If you fall in, kick your legs to level off and dig in with the ice awls to pull yourself out of the hole. Once out, roll toward stronger ice.

No rope or rescue equipment to use? No branch to hold out? Form a human chain to pull the man from the danger area. Remember, if you spread your weight, there's more ice support.

299

16 SURVIVAL

THE SECRET TO SURVIVAL IS PREPAREDNESS. While this chapter is specifically aimed at survival, almost every chapter in this book will help you to be prepared for survival should you ever be faced with that need. When you've camped every month of the year, you know what needs to be done to guard yourself from the cold. Preparedness brings confidence—confidence that you can lick any survival problem you face. An expert in polar life has said, "Morale is the single greatest factor in survival." Many who have survived trying circumstances echo this statement. You'll have that built in survival kit if you are prepared.

To survive means to "live on." Survival is a matter of life over death. It may begin with the suspicion that things are *not* going to wind up as you had planned: You are not going to stroll into camp with your string of big ones; you are not going to pull into the Desert Motel only a fast half hour away; you won't whip to a turn stop in front of the steps to the ski lodge; you won't lay smartly alongside the marina wharf; you won't just thank the stewardess and walk down the ramp.

Most of us, in doing fairly ordinary things, are close to disaster at one time or another. Mostly things work out fine and we blink away any sense of danger. But then up crops the broken ankle, the dry radiator, the turn of weather, wheels deep in sand, or the flapping rudder—and suddenly things are different. In itself it may not seem too serious, but things seem to snowball, and you realize you are alone, lost, adrift, cut off, wrecked, stuck, the radio is dead, or the electricity is gone for good. Now you are on your own . . . you need help.

How soon will help come? *Will* it come? Does anyone know? When will they start looking? How? Can you manage until they come? What are your urgent needs now and until help arrives?

Few people in a survival situation have had any training for it. But, you can survive if you are prepared—prepared physically, mentally, and morally, and if you know techniques to tip the odds in your favor.

responsibility

You know that your chances for early rescue improve if someone knows where you are going, where you should be, and will be alarmed if you don't show up or respond to a signal. Any time you go into a possibly hazardous situation, by all means arrange some way for checking out your position with the authorities—police, sheriff, ranger, warden, or camp personnel. This should make them happy, because they are the ones who will probably have to go in after you if you get lost. *The sooner someone knows you are missing, the sooner you will be found.* Now it may be the authorities' duty to rescue you, but it is *your* responsibility to anticipate the hazards of what you do and to take proper precautions. Do this, even if others scoff at your concern or try to minimize the dangers. After all, it's your neck.

In many cases, you will be warned: "If the weather on the mountain is bad, turn back before it is too late." "Last stop before desert—check your gas and water!" You are advised not to ski trails beyond your rated ability." These are *not* to be looked at as challenges to your daring or self-esteem. They are sober advice from those who probably have had much more experience than you—at least under local conditions. *Be alert to danger!* One survival school has a mock tombstone with these words: "On many graves the headstones glisten / of those who heard but wouldn't listen."

It's a matter of seconds or minutes to check tanks, ask weather conditions, see that chains and shovel are in the trunk, top off canteens, correct a map, see that the flares are in, stow an extra paddle, check with a ranger—it could be a matter of hours or days before rescue. Learn to check out the situation and your gear quickly and systematically. Don't let anyone talk you out of it. Stay in charge of yourself. If you do get lost, guilty feelings about your lack of preparedness will not help your morale, and *that's* your mainstay, remember?

"An ounce of prevention is worth a pound of cure." Agreed? Still, you can find yourself in a desperate situation you couldn't have prevented with any amount of preparation. OK, so it's not your fault. *Now* your responsibility is to survive, to help others to survive.

Let's look at some key problems in survival and some solutions that may help. There's no telling what may turn out to be useful.

In survival you must draw on your total resources, try every possibility until something works in your favor. It will help if you recognize the resources you have, such as those you're starting out with: your physical strengths, your mental store of facts, your powers of reasoning, and your emotional attitude. Now add to these some specially useful skills and equipment, and you have quite a bit going for you.

Then there are the resources around you—probably more than you'd think at first glance. If you're with others, you can see the wisdom of pooling your total inventory of physical things and mental assets. Don't forget, there's such a thing as *group morale*—probably the most important single factor in group survival. Your chances of survival are much better with a group, but this may have its own price, too.

Whether alone or with a group, there are things you must have and there are things around you. The trick is to fit them together so that the things you find will fit your needs. This is the part often more fun to read about or practice than to do in earnest.

Well, what are the things you must have? *Whatever is needed to get yourself found and to sustain life until that time.*

To tell you—right now—that the first thing you should do is this or that would be silly. No one knows what your situation will be. Surely your instincts will prompt you to check out injuries, stop the flow of blood, breathe good air, get away from possible explosions or fire, try to find others. Naturally you check out any other survivors and do what you can to aid them if they are injured or in shock. Serious injuries may complicate the entire situation—you will have to include them in your survival equation. You must survive until safe. So after sustaining life through first aid, STOP! *Try to figure out just what kind of a jam you are in.* Relax, if only for a few minutes, and fight off any feelings of panic. Saying a prayer might not be a bad idea.

Then see how these things might fit into the puzzle somehow: *signals* to searchers or possible rescuers; *shelter* to prevent injury from the elements; *fire* for signaling, cooking, and cheer or warmth; *water* to sustain life; *food* for cheer and energy; *tools* to obtain food, improve shelter, and afford protection; and finally, some *means of travel,* if that is your only hope. Keep first things first. Survive until safe.

signals

Early rescue is the goal. Air search is probably the means to this. It may be simple and swift once you are spotted. Because of the speed of aircraft, though, *you must make your position known as soon as possible.* Here's why—if your exact location is unknown, a systematic coverage of a large area will likely be started. Small sections of it will be flown one after another until the area is covered; if the search plane sees no trace of you in a section, that section is crossed off. If it happens you *are* in that section, you may have a long wait before they come back to it. So if you have reason to expect air search, *get signals out at once* to show your location and, if urgent, your condition.

Radio, of course, is best. *Smoke* is likely next best in daytime; *fire* at night. Much of our country is under constant watch by fire wardens, at least at certain seasons, and any unusual smoke will be investigated (probably by air) even if no one knows you are missing. But unless you think your area is covered by a manned fire tower or overflown by aircraft, maintaining a large smoke fire may prove a drag afterwhile. It may be better to keep a cooking or comfort fire going, with a large supply of fast fuel and smoke-generating material on hand for the moment you hear an airplane. It's a risk you would have to study. There are some signals that will work without your standing by; try them too.

Smoke may be your best daytime signal. Three fires, equally spaced apart, is standard distress signal; generate a dense smoke column by adding to a hot fire quantities of wet, green leaves, moss, or even water for white smoke—oil, oil-soaked rags, or rubber scraps for black smoke. Make a "Canadian smoke generator" from a 6-foot tripod with a chest-high platform for a ready, fast fire lay; thatch over top with green boughs—they keep kindling dry and ready for quick ignition. If planes are heard, touch it off.

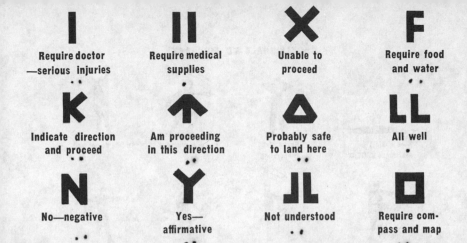

I	**II**	**X**	**F**
Require doctor —serious injuries	Require medical supplies	Unable to proceed	Require food and water
K	**↑**	**△**	**LL**
Indicate direction and proceed	Am proceeding in this direction	Probably safe to land here	All well
N	**Y**	**⌐L**	**□**
No—negative	Yes— affirmative	Not understood	Require compass and map

GROUND-TO-AIR SIGNALS. Make in open area near camp. Tramp out in snow or sand as big as you can. Line paths with boughs or stones for shadow and contrast. Burn grass, turn over sods, or lay out any material that might be seen—geometric design will catch attention of aircraft overhead. Such signals work even if you are asleep or ill when plane comes. Destroy upon rescue.

A long-distance signal device is a mirror (or even a bright can lid) to sweep the horizon *often* during daylight. It can be seen by aircraft too far away to be seen, even though it reflects only direct sunrays, which limits its scope. It is very effective at sea or on a large lake. Even on hazy days it may be seen by aircraft unseen from the ground.

Attention-getting devices that work whether you're on deck or not are good. Fly a large contrasting flag from a pole atop a tall tree. Spread an official Scout rescue blanket orange-side up on snow, silver-side up on grass or beach. Radar will pick up either side. If with a downed plane in snow, keep the upper surfaces clear of frost or snow so they will show the shape clearly. Do anything you can to disturb the "natural" look of the area *except* to start a brush or forest fire!

If, somehow, you are in contact with someone, you can talk even if widely separated by space or otherwise. Use Morse code to send messages by interrupted light or sound signals—flashlight, lantern, mirror, horn, whistle, spark coil, radio—or by flag. S O S is a simple distress call that will state your need for help. Semaphore is a two-flag code for daylight use. Body signals send direct messages to aircraft.

BODY SIGNALS TO AIRCRAFT

Need medical assistance URGENT

Our receiver is operating

Use drop message

All OK; do not wait

Can proceed shortly; wait if practicable

Affirmative (yes)

Negative (no)

Need mechanical help or parts—long delay

Pick us up— plane abandoned

Do not attempt to land here

Land here (point in direction of landing)

MORSE CODE FOR USE WITH LIGHTS, SOUND, OR FLAG

A · —	H · · · ·	O — — —	V · · · —
B — · · ·	I · ·	P · — — ·	W · — —
C — · — ·	J · — — —	Q — — · —	X — · · —
D — · ·	K — · —	R · — ·	Y — · — —
E ·	L · — · ·	S · · ·	Z — — · ·
F · · — ·	M — —	T —	
G — — ·	N — ·	U · · —	

NUMERALS AND COMMON SIGNALS

1 · — — — —	4 · · · · —	7 — — · · ·	0 — — — — —
2 · · — — —	5 · · · · ·	8 — — — · ·	HEY! · — · — · — · —
3 · · · — —	6 — · · · ·	9 — — — — ·	ROGER · — ·

HELP! · · · — — — · · · (repeat)

In using visual signals, try to contrast with background—dark or bright against snow, light or bright against green or brown. Send Morse by flag waved to *your left* for DASH, to *your right* for DOT. Steady radio signal may enable directional antenna of aircraft to "home" on you.

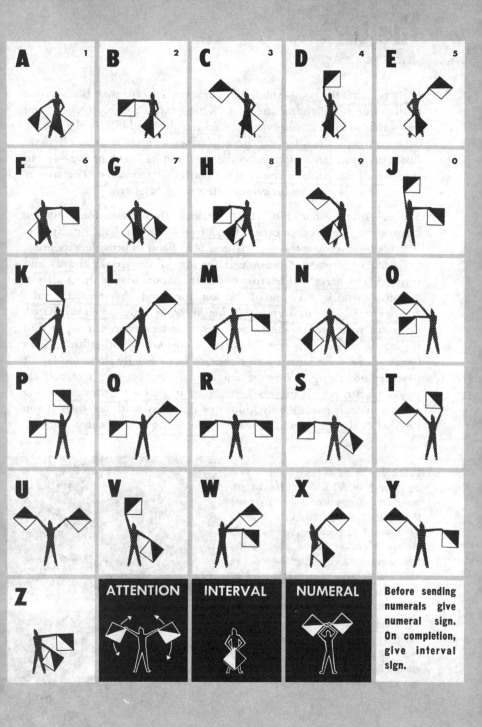

shelter

Early rescue is the goal—you have your signals set for that. But survival until rescue is the rest of the deal. What next? Probably *shelter.* You know that in some conditions the wind can chill and kill. In the searing desert, though, the wind can be a lifesaver—unless it dries off sweat faster than you can replace it. So the wind can be friend or foe—so can sun, rain, heat, cold, or snow. It's a matter of *too much.* The answer is *control over your environment*—in a word, shelter. POINT

Shelter—where, what kind, what with, and how are questions only *you* can answer. Use a rock, a cave, a log, a tree—your car, boat, or airplane, if that's how you got there—whatever is at hand to provide windbreak or shade or dryness. Grouse will fly into a snowbank; lizards and tortoises and hares will burrow under the sands. Maybe that's all *you* can do—so do it! Get out of the sun, the wind, the snow, the rain. POINT Below 10°F., *do not stay inside car or plane* unless well-ventilated. *Conserve your energy*—heat, cold, wind, and exertion can sap it. But if digging a hole is the price of survival, dig! On the other hand, don't knock yourself out building an elaborate Swiss Family Robinson layout —you're not going to be here longer than it takes to get rescued. If you're with a vehicle or vessel, stay near it—it's what they're looking for — unless it is absolutely hidden or destroyed with no trace. If you find better shelter elsewhere, leave a note or signals for sure. POINT

Lucky guy found a rarity—a tree root big enough to get under and good primary shelter from wind and rain (snow) if it doesn't change direction. Then he could use some screening. For now, he's playing it cool—no extra work to tire him. A fire will be cheering and ward off chill. His signal smoke will help ward off mosquitoes and gnats.

Get in out of that wind, anyway. Actually, snow is a good insulator and you will feel warmer inside. Brush snow off clothes to stay dry; put up some signal; run a vent hole out from roof.

Rocks, overhangs, or caves may offer shelter; add screening of boughs to improve it. Rocks will hold heat awhile. Ledge is not the best place to be in a lightning storm. Check on prior tenants in caves—they may resent sharing.

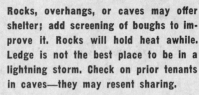

A large log or chunk of blowdown may screen one side of you and be high enough that you can snuggle under roof poles laid on it. Cover with leaved boughs, bark slabs, or grass thatch.

Luck may find you a tree broken off at head height so you can make an A shelter by breaking or cutting out the "inside" branches. Pile branches on outside for protection. Add other poles if branches are sparse on tree. Evergreens are best—but take what you get. If you can, make your own luck by chopping a tree nearly in two and bending.

A lean-to is more ambitious — justified only when nothing simpler is available or if you are with companions who can help and when sharing shelter is necessary or desirable. Use trees or two forked uprights to support a ridgepole. Lash or use dovetails to secure rafters slanted to ground and cross poles to hold boughs, bark, or grass thatch.

Thatch shelters with bundles of grass, palm leaves, or cattails by tying them to cross poles. Loose bark slabs can be shingled likewise, from bottom to top, by punching holes and tying them on.

fire

Early rescue is your best hope. Your best signal other than radio—a smoky fire. Best chance for this is a *dry* match from match safe, lost kit, or first aid kit. Run a damp match rapidly through your hair several times to dry it. Save your matches—use a fire starter, ample *dry* tinder and kindling, lay it up carefully, and keep it going. Try primitive fire starting *before* using all your matches; try several ways, the fastest first. Collect tinder when you see it —keep it dry. Pick up kindling as you walk around—keep adding to your reserves. Keep a small fire going; build several around you for warmth instead of one big one. Use judgment about steady smokes, but at least have a beacon or smoke generator all primed to touch off instantly. Take safety precautions.

POINT ABOUT MATCHES

Even with a lighted match you may have trouble finding dry tinder at once. A fire starter could make a big difference on a wet, cold, blustery day—or anytime. A waxed bundle of matches, waxed cardboard coil, a candle stub, a cube of wax-soaked insulating board are fine fire starters—waterproof, handy, hot-burning, safe. Do you pack any?

Getting a spark without matches isn't so hard—it's getting a fire from the spark. The answer usually is tinder: bone-dry, finely divided material to catch the spark, ignite readily, and blaze into hot flame. Try mouse nests, birch bark curls, bird nests, dry weed tops, cedar bark, scraped lint from cloth or cardboard, or charred cloth.

As soon as spark ignites tinder, catch it up between cupped hands and gently blow on the bright spot from below to make it hot enough to burst into flame, or whirl it at arm's length to fan it.

It takes fire to char cloth, so char some when you can and carry it tenderly wrapped and sealed (waterproofed). It will smolder the instant a spark hits it, a boon with the flint-and-steel method.

If struck smartly with a glancing blow, iron or mild steel will spark hotly on flint, quartz, and other hard rock. Position charred cloth to catch the spark. It may be over or under the rock. Wear safety glasses at all times when making fire by flint and steel to prevent fragments from hitting your eyes.

Have you some steel wool—a scouring pad, maybe? And a two-cell flashlight with live cells? Hold the two cells in one fist, top touching bottom in a firm contact. Shred out pad and tuck one end under the bottom cell. Touch the upper end of pad to the bright contact pole of the upper cell. It will glow and burn hotly. Catch in tinder.

You should know several ways to make fire with different materials since each requires materials you may not have. With the low voltage of dry cells you *must* have wire of about the resistance of steel wool for it to incandesce and produce flame. If, though, you have a live battery in a vehicle, you can easily put sparks into tinder by attaching any wires to the posts and scaping the ends together in the tinder. If you have a camera, binoculars, or anything with a convex lens to focus sunrays on tinder, you have a fast means to fire *if* the sun is high and bright. Clear ice can be shaped to a lens that will start fire! The fire drill also is made of natural materials, undoubtedly could be fashioned with a sharp stone—but a knife would be better, as shown on the next page. Try fastest way first, then others, before your matches are gone!

Shape a spindle of dry, dead wood with octagonal or other shape that will afford a grip by the thong, yet will rotate smoothly. Make a rounded point on upper end and a rather blunt shape at the lower; carefully smooth these.

A bearing for the upper end must be cut in the handpiece to hold spindle steady in the notch of the hearth and permit a downward pressure to be exerted, producing the friction that will cause fire. Hard wood can be used as shown, but bone or a pitted stone will work if smooth.

The bow moves the thong back and forth to turn the spindle. It must provide tension in the thong to do so and not stop or knock spindle by touching it. For thong, use shoelace or leather from belt, strapping, or hide. Plait a coarse non-slipping thong from cloth strips, unraveled webbing—anything that will grip and not stretch.

Hearth piece must be made of dry, dead wood, flattened for stability. In it, bore a round hole to receive spindle and hold it against side thrust. Wear it in slowly to match spindle end and make good contact—this is essential. Notch the edge of hearth at hole to allow hot coal to fall in tinder; this process does not produce real sparks.

Assemble drill as shown; hold hearth with foot, bearing in hand. Move bow smoothly back and forth, keeping tension on thong so rotation is continuous. Dump glowing coal into tinder.

While awaiting rescue, you may run into worse things than bad weather. Any area has hazards that are distracting, disabling, or deadly. Study the obvious ones before entering an area and take precautions; however, coping with them in survival conditions may be something else.

• *Biting or stinging insects* can be vile in good weather, making life really miserable. (A repellent may be ranked with knife, matches, and compass as basic survival tools.) Smoke deters them; smoldering punks or portable smudges may allow your moving around to work. Crushed ferns or wild onions can be rubbed on as a repellent. Treat bites and stings as instructed in chapter 13; *do not scratch*—secondary infection is the real enemy. Avoid scorpions and spiders by checking shoes and clothes before donning them; keep hands away from possible lairs. If stung, be calm and *lie down* until the pains ease, as with snakebite.

• *Sunburn* is a special risk on water, beaches, deserts, snowfields, and at high altitudes, even in cold weather or haze. Severe cases are crippling and dangerous. Bare feet are very vulnerable; swelling may prevent use of shoes. *Sunburn can poison you.* Seek shade or stay clothed; wear hat, neckerchief, and dark glasses. Make a parasol, desert-style headdress, or mask, as needed, to shield ears, neck, nose, and eyes.

• *Snow blindness* is very painful; recovery is spontaneous but slow. You can't afford to foul up early rescue or survival efforts while waiting. *Avoid it* with snow goggles, dark glasses, or improvised bark or cloth mask with slits. Soot around the eyes will cut glare somewhat.

• *Immersion foot* cripples feet constantly wet for a long time. Even at 50° F., wet feet react as if frostbitten. Dry your feet, socks, and shoes often. If below freezing, dry your socks by removing them (protect feet meanwhile); let socks *freeze,* then beat frost crystals out. Do not wear frozen shoes; thaw and dry! Tie cuffs over shoe tops to keep snow out; stay dry. Insulate loosely laced shoes or boots with dry grass or leaves. If your feet get numb, white, soaked, and wrinkled, you are in danger unless you find a way to get your feet dry and warm soon.

• *Improvise boots* from canvas or blanket to keep snow or sand out of low shoes. Make snowshoes of boughs or bark to go in deep snow.

• *Carbon monoxide* kills quietly; ventilate close quarters heated by *any* open-flame heater, even a candle or lantern. Vent near roof and floor.

water

Having done what you can to ensure early rescue and obtained immediate shelter from the elements, your next concern should be for your water supply. You need drinking water. Probably you've never been aware of just how much water you take in every day in normal life. For average efficiency, *you need about 2 quarts daily* (including water in food and beverages) even in cold climates—*a gallon a day in hot climates*. If you're sweating much, you need lots more.

Waste no time looking for food if your water supply is not assured— you can last for weeks without food, if your health is good; but water you *must* have in any circumstance. In desert heat, you must have it within a day or two at most. In any but desert conditions you should have little difficulty finding a safe supply. Take no chances with disease; *sterilize all water* by boiling for 5 minutes.

• The body cannot save water. Don't put off drinking. Drink as much as you need—don't sip and save. Find new sources immediately, for the body loses 1 gallon per day in summer and 2 to 3 gallons in the desert.

• Take all care to avoid loss of body water through wind dehydration and sweating. Wear clothing, even if uncomfortable. Stay in shade.

• Never, even in extreme circumstances, drink alkali water, sea water, or urine—they are poisonous. It *is* possible, however, to evaporate them and condense fresh water that is potable, using a makeshift still.

• Your sources of water are these: *ground water, rain, snow, ice, dew, succulent plants, sap of trees and vines,* and *fruit*—obviously depending on location and season. You will have to decide which are the sources most likely to yield the quantities of water you need daily.

In rocky terrain, look for springs, seepage, or pools of standing water. Limestones and porous lavas are likeliest formations to have water. Sandstones and granites may have seeps near cracks. Dig in dirt near any vegetation; see if water seeps in the hole. Don't bother digging with no sign of dampness or plants, except in streambeds or obvious dry springs. Along the coast, you may find water behind the first dune above high tide. In even dry swamps, you may get seepage in a hole dug near edge. In desert, you may be able to evaporate ground water with a solar still, illustrated. (Equipment to make several is worth taking on a trip through the desert.) Dig behind the first dune around an alkali water hole; the first water you find may be fairly fresh.

Rain, caught in clean containers, is potable without purification. Put out pans, shells, coconut shells, sails, awnings, bailing scoops, hubcaps, or wring from clothing, towels, or blankets. Seek out rock hollows, puddles, or tree crotches that may catch rain. Sudden showers sometimes occur in rather dry regions—store water, if possible. Heavy mountain showers sometimes send flash floods into desert regions suddenly. (For this reason, don't camp in dry gulches—such floods are bad.)

Snow and ice *are* water—but melt them; the air in snow makes you thirsty and the cold is hard on the stomach. Melting takes fuel which requires work which increases the need for water and food. Old, bluish sea ice can be used, but new, gray ice may be salty. Glacier ice is OK. Morning dew, mopped up, may be a good source of water in the desert.

point

Vines, such as grapes, can be cut and water drained from them. *Never drink milky sap of any sort.* Maple sap is delicious. Green coconuts yield good milk; split outer husk, puncture eyes of nut to drain milk. Notch joints of old, yellow bamboo to get at trapped water. Barrel cacti may contain water—cut off top or tap side. Prickly pears are moist.

SOLAR STILL. Dig a pit 4 feet wide by 3 feet deep. Put a shallow container in the center. If possible, rig a tube from this up to the edge of pit. Stretch clear plastic over pit, with a rock in the center to form a cone directly over container. (Split cactus stems laid around inside will improve yield.) Any kind of water poured around pit will help. Solar heat evaporates water that will condense on plastic and drip into pan. Draw water through tube to avoid disturbing still. Make several stills if these are your sole source.

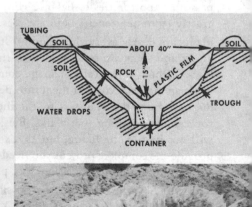

food

Early rescue, naturally, will relieve you of any great efforts to obtain food—actually, you can go for weeks without it if you have enough water. You'll get hungry before long—but this isn't quite the same thing as needing food. You're used to three square meals a day, but don't panic when mealtime comes and goes—the name of this game is Survival. You'll survive, so don't sweat it. *Conserve your energy!*

You can get food—but don't take any chances, either in getting it or in eating it. Frantic activity may use up more energy than you could possibly replace with the food you get.

If you have any food with you, ration it; figure a realistic possible time of rescue and ration two-thirds of your food for half that time, saving one-third for the rest. If someone is going to go for help, give him *double rations* as he'll have no time to hunt and will be using more energy than those staying put.

If water is down to a quart per day per person, don't eat dry, starchy, salty, or protein foods. If you have a choice, carbohydrates like candy are best. If water is no problem, drink all you can—more than you really want—it will cut your hunger *and* your need for food.

Wherever you are, there should be some sort of food—plant or animal. You may find it strange, may not like it, may get bored with it—but if it will sustain life, better eat it. You know what good diet is, so don't pass up opportunities to balance yours—but you're not likely to suffer greatly from deficiencies before a reasonable rescue time.

Plants are nearly everywhere and most are edible; but many you cannot digest and some are poisonous. An illustrated list of edible plants follows. Although you can't manage some plentiful plants, such as grass, other animals *can* convert them into flesh. As usual, your way of getting the best from the plants is to eat the animals. With few exceptions, you can eat anything that walks, flies, crawls, swims, or wiggles. Most will not be to your liking, but that's not the point. Only animals can provide the complete protein you need—some 3 ounces a day. Whatever it is, try to get food the easiest way possible. Conserve your energy.

You will have to scout out the possibilities and decide what the best value for the expense is likely to be. You know what your equipment is —let's hope you have a sturdy, sharp knife, if nothing else—and what materials are at hand. There are suggestions of primitive hunting and fishing gear further along. It would be silly, though, to sweat out making any elaborate implements when ample food, say shellfish, could be had for the picking up—or if there are no encouraging signs of animals or fish. (This is no time to get involved in a handicraft project or with busy-work, unless you're bored.) *Conserve your energy!*

Speaking of shellfish: probably the richest area you could be in, for food, lies between the breakers and high-tide mark on a beach—or around a freshwater swamp. (The least desirable areas are dry mountain ridges and deep forests.) Most edible plants and animals are where there are sunshine and water. Try to discover the food preferences and feeding habits of the animals you are hunting; the nature sections of this book will give you much information of value in this—check them.

Look for game trails to set snares and traps in; look for evidences of kills in woods, meadows, swamp edge, and beach; quietly observe pools and ponds for signs of life; likely the best time will be from dusk to dawn when other animals are hunting. (Your snares and traps that will work all night untended are probably a good bet for this reason.)

Primitive hunting and fishing gear will work, if well-made and cunningly used; but seasoned hunters and fishermen with the best of gear often know disappointment, so don't be discouraged quickly. You will see from the designs of equipment shown, that cord and wire would be great stuff to have along—a try at spinning native fibers will clinch it!

But take time *now* to practice these techniques. *Never leave traps set unless you are in an actual survival situation.*

Frogs, mice, lizards, turtles, and snakes are about your easiest quarries. Even poisonous snakes are edible, but obviously a risk. Frogs are a favored food and can be taken by hand, stone, spear, or hook; the whole thing is edible, but most of the meat is in the hind legs. Broil.

Maybe you *can* get bigger game than this, and maybe you are justified in taking whatever you can get for survival—but don't get carried away by the idea of being the mighty hunter (or by something bigger than you). Killing more than you need or can keep is senseless at any time. It may be possible in cold weather, or through smoking, to preserve meat or fish, but this seems a rather long-range kind of thing. Strict sanitary measures are of great importance to you—don't take chances with illness. You can get food—and you can go a long time without it. *Don't sweat it!*

hunting

Doubtless your best food possibilities are those requiring the least effort —shellfish, crawfish, frogs, and the like. But if there are none, you may have to go for whatever is around, probably small mammals, for your protein and fat. Again, elaborate preparation may use more energy than you'll get back. Hunting on foot, even with a gun, can make you very hungry and get you very lost (is *that* how you got here?). So don't get too hipped on the spear-and-arrow bit unless you're good at it. A snare is not too hard to make and will work without attention while you are conserving your energy by sleeping! Visit traps each morning.

Snares require tough, pliant, slippery cord or wire for the noose to work quickly and surely. If you have no cord or can't make any, you can try a deadfall trap if you can handle a big log or part of one. Be sure the log lies flat on ground when it falls.

Set traps in game trails; check for signs of browsing, droppings, footprints, tufts of fur, or signs of kills. Disturb area as little as possible, but lay brush to guide prey into noose. Areas near water holes, meadows, orchards, clearings, berry patches, or near swamps are probably most likely for trapping. Be wary of animals trapped but not killed.

Drag snare is simple: noose is attached to a drag stick that will catch in brush so animal's weight and speed draws noose about its neck, strangling it. Place in runway or trail; fasten or lay it up to permit spreading noose just large enough to accommodate head but not body or feet of animal. Bar alternate paths.

Deadfall kills by crushing. Log is held up by baited figure-four trigger which collapses when bait is wiggled. Notch trigger carefully for support and smooth action. Guide poles on sides keep log steady and in line with bait. Rig this with care—it's tricky.

Twitch-up snare uses spring of sturdy live sapling to haul noose tight and lift game off its feet. It will lift small game out of reach of predators; scale rig to size of game wanted. If noose can be spread in game trail, no bait is needed. Otherwise, choose a sapling near edge of woods and bait to attract game. Bait so that animal must put head in noose to get bait and dislodge trigger. Several kinds of triggers may be used. Here, a strong U-bar of green wood is thrust in ground to offset spring pole, with the holddown perched on an upright at one end so that any side motion will dislodge it. The noose is attached to the holddown. Other trigger arrangements are shown. BE EXTREMELY CAREFUL IN RIGGING. Spring poles are treacherous and pack a mean punch; don't get in their way at any time. WHEN YOU ARE DONE WITH THEM, DISMANTLE SNARES AND TRAPS!

Alternate trigger systems for twitch-up snare: left, if you have another sapling in the right spot, locking notches make a good holdfast; right, more usually you need a peg driven in at the proper spot, with the same holdfast notching engaging a block attached to the spring pole. Engage carefully.

319

fishing

Check chapter 19 for general information about fish, feeding habits, and fishing—but forget the techniques of fishing with conventional tackle. Food fishing is different from sport fishing—you don't throw 'em back if they're small! If they're too small to take a hook, herd them into shallows and grab 'em! Make a weir or trap of rocks or stakes to drive them into and spear them if they're big enough. For deeper water, though, you need *hooks, line,* and *sinkers* to get bait where the fish are. These are easily carried as emergency gear, but they can be improvised.

Setlines, like snares, work while you're not there and are especially good with *gorges* which must be swallowed to work. Attach setlines to overhanging branches by streams or ponds, or anchor to rocks on beaches. *Handlining* yields more food than anything except nets—which are too difficult to bother making, especially with handmade cord. The simple handline with live bait will work. You can *spear* larger fish, but if any frogs are around, go for them—you'll probably eat better.

You can make usable line from *bast*—the inner bark of trees—using the spinning technique shown. Basswood, slippery elm, American elm, Indian hemp, Osage orange, nettles, and yucca leaves yield good fibers. Your web belt or a strap, unraveled, yields fine fiber for spinning line.

Tie two equally wide strands of soaked bast in an overhand knot; start rolling them in the SAME direction between thumbs and forefingers. The tied end will start to twist itself in the opposite direction into a laid cord that will not untwist. Continue rolling until near end of one strand; twist on a new piece of bast and continue rolling. Do the same with the other as it ends. Space out splices for stronger cord. Make gorges of wood or bone; point ends, hole or notch center for line. Make hooks of wood, bones, claws, or thorns. Use stone for sinker.

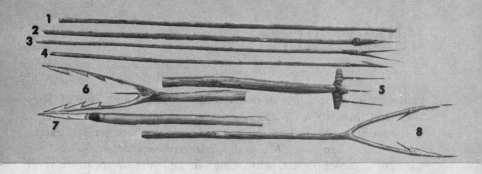

1. Blunt bird arrow; striking force kills birds, stuns small animals. 2. Bone-tipped bird arrow; sharp point penetrates deeply. 3. Thorn-tipped bird arrow; two or three large thorns bound on. 4. Thornbarbed and tipped arrow for fish or birds; barb prevents prey pulling free. (Points are all lashed on with bast. Arrows need not be feathered for accuracy at short range. A bow is easy to improvise, although suitable bowstring may be a problem.) 5. Thorn gig for frogs or fish; ash shaft was originally 3 feet long; crosspiece was wedged in hole in end of shaft, thorns bound with bast. 6. Thorn-tipped spear with wooden barbs for fish or large frogs, original length 5 feet. 7. Bone-tipped spear for use on game at close range; carved deer bone was stuck in 6-foot hickory shaft, lashed with bast. 8. Thorn tipped and barbed spear for fish and frogs; thorn points pushed in pithy center of ash sapling, barbs lashed; about 4 feet long originally.

Try to see what fish are eating (check stomachs of your catch, too) and offer them some more—or a close fake—if possible. Some fish will hit anything in the water. Live bait is best: worms, grubs, moths, crickets, grasshoppers, mice, crayfish, frogs, frog and fish bellies, and scraps of meat or fish. "Chum" the area with small scraps, then fish it. Slip a gorge endwise into bait; when the fish swallows it, the toggle lodges, catching the fish. Hooks must catch in fish as they take the bait—a light hand on the line will feel the action and set the hook with a jerk. Hooks must be needle-sharp (fishermen even hone steel hooks!). Make hooks carefully—clumsy ones can be wrecked by fish big enough to take them; small ones are hard to make. Simple spears will work well. Chumming helps when spearing fish, too—hold spear quietly *in* water over fish, then jab swiftly at *one* fish. A torch will attract fish, crayfish, and frogs at night. Sneak up on frogs for gigging in daytime. DO NOT EAT RAW FRESHWATER FISH (they may contain parasites!). You can eat saltwater fish raw—their flesh is a good source of water.

edible plants

Plants are a valuable part of man's food—some eat nothing else. They are found from tropics to arctic and from the sea to the mountaintops. You should be able to find some of these: fruits, nuts, cereals, starchy tubers, sugary saps, succulent stalks, potherbs, and salad greens. They are rich in carbohydrates, with some fats and incomplete proteins. *If your water is limited, stick with these foods.* Some are themselves watery, some add needed bulk, and many are rich in vitamins needed for good health. They supplement meat in good diet. Some plants are deadly and care must be taken to avoid them with others less poisonous or unpleasant. *Do not eat anything that tastes very bitter or bad to you.* A list of plants known to be good follows; carefully observe any cautions.

Common Alder (Alnus serrulata) grows in wet areas near swamp or shoreline; buds and young bark can be eaten raw throughout year.

Arrowhead (Sagittaria latifolia) is found growing in shallow water or at the water's edge throughout the United States. Use as potatoes. Tuber may be found as far away as height of the stalks from the base of the plant. They will float on the water after they are dug up.

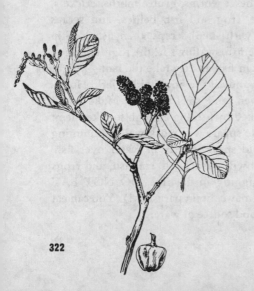

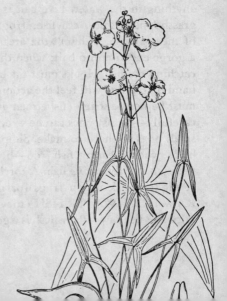

Basswood (Tilia americana). The red buds can be eaten raw or cooked the same as a green bean. The dried flowers can be used to make a tea. The fruit has been used to make a substitute for chocolate. The inner bark can be used to make excellent line or rope. One of the most useful trees; found from North Dakota to Texas and east to Maine.

Bulrush (Scirpus validus). The white base of each stem can be cut and added to a salad. The roots can be eaten raw, but can be roasted or dried to be ground later for flour.

Burdock (Arctium Lappa) shoots up to 3 inches long, can be cooked as asparagus; the young leaves, as a green. Roots can be peeled, sliced, and then boiled—they taste like parsnips.

Cattail (Typha angustifolia or Typha latifolia) is one of the best survival food plants. The spike and new shoots can be eaten raw or in salads; the yellow pollen can be added to flour. The white parts of the stalk can be eaten raw or cooked. The roots may be used as a vegetable or dried to be ground for flour. The stems can be sliced lengthwise and used for making baskets.

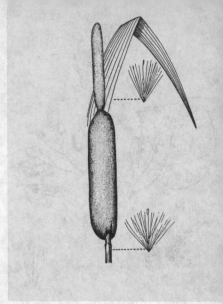

Common Chickweed (Stellaria media) can be used sparingly in salads or boiled as a green. In preparing, snap off the flowers or seeds.

Chicory (Cichorium Intybus). Young tender leaves are used in salads or boiled as greens. The roots may be dried and ground as a substitute for coffee.

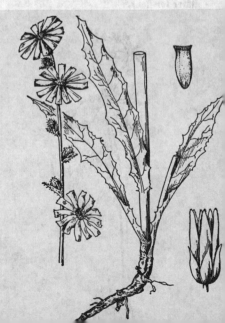

Hop Clover (Trifolium agrarium) or White Sweet Clover (Melilotus alba) or Yellow Sweet Clover (Melilotus officinalis). Both the young leaves and blossoms of members of the clover family can be eaten raw or in salads. The blossoms are sweet and enjoyable to chew. Limit the amount of young leaves you eat; too many can cause bloat. Can be cooked as a green or potherb.

Dandelion (Taraxacum officinale). Young leaves can be eaten raw or in salads. Leaves can also be cooked as a green. By baking the root until brown then powdering, a coffee substitute can be made.

Yellow Dock (Rumex crispus) leaves are used raw in salads and cooked as greens. Seeds are used as a grain, either boiled as cereal or ground into flour.

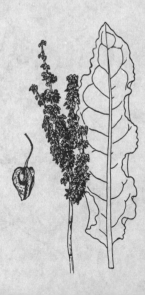

Goldenrod (Solidago). Young leaves are used in salads. Both the dried leaves and the dried blossoms will make a good tea—one spoonful of either to a cup of boiling water. Some member of the family grows in almost every area of the United States.

Wild Grape (Vitis californica or Vitis vulpina) tender shoots or ends of vines can be boiled. Blue or purple fruit is excellent raw. Several leaves can be used to fry meat or bake bread dough on.

Hawthorn (Crataegus). Fruit is edible either raw or cooked when ripe. Thorns can be used as needles or to make fishhooks.

Greenleaf Manzanita (Arctostaphylos) berries can be eaten raw, cooked, or dried to be used later as a cooked cereal.

Nettle (Urtica gracilis) leaves are gathered and cooked like spinach. Gather young, tender leaves (they taste best) all summer. Dried leaves can be used for tea. Stems supply excellent fibers for making fishlines or cord. Some members of this family are found in most States. CAUTION: Leaves and stems have prickly surfaces; no problem when cooked.

Wild Onion (Allium) plant and bulbs can be cooked by boiling or bulbs can be roasted over hot ashes. Onion soup made with meat stock is excellent; add onions to other soups or dishes. When rubbed on the body, the plant repels insects.

Pigweed or Lamb's-quarters (Chenopodium album). Use leaves of small plants for greens that taste like spinach. The seeds can be eaten raw or boiled as a cereal.

Pinyon Pine, two-leaved (Pinus edulis) or single leaf (Pinus monophylla) seeds are rich in protein and used raw or roasted as food by many people of the Southwest. Nuts can be ground and used as a flour or made into a gruel or soup.

Yellow Pond-lily (Nuphar) roots or tuber can be used as a baked vegetable. The seeds can be ground for bread or cooked in soups. The same is true of the white Fragrant Pond-lily.

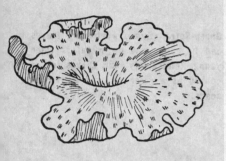

Rock Tripe (Gyrophora dillenie) can be scrambled like egg in a little water or fat.

Fourwing Saltbush (Atriplex canescens) seeds can be ground to make meal with which to cook. Leaves can be boiled like spinach when young.

Service Berry (Amelanchier), sometimes called Juneberry, can be eaten raw or cooked or dried for later use.

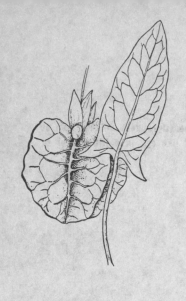

Sheep-Sorrel (Rumex Acetosella) leaves can be eaten raw or in salads when young. Refreshingly sour. Leaves can be cooked as a green or used to thicken soups.

Common Wild Strawberry (Fragaria virginiana or others). Young leaves and blossom petals can be eaten raw. The dried leaves can be steeped to make a tea. (During the Revolutionary War they were sold for this purpose.) The fruit contains sugar and can be eaten green; it is much better when red.

Shepherd's-purse (Capsella Bursa-pastoris) young leaves can be eaten raw or boiled; they taste like cabbage. The seeds can be roasted and eaten.

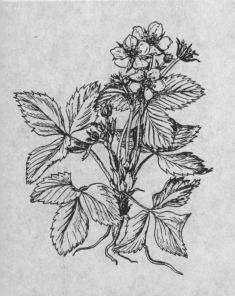

Watercress (Nasturtium officinale) can be eaten in salads and soups, as greens, or as a garnish with other foods. Use water purifier for rinsing, or boil.

Many plants are protected by federal and state laws. These plants should only be collected in an actual survival situation.

In addition to the pictured plants, there are many more—either less common, or of such great variety that it would take too much space to list each. Fruits and berries are examples of this. Here is an additional listing. For identification and use, look them up in books on edible plants. You may wonder why some well known edible plants are left off the list. Some plants have edible parts such as roots or leaves, but other parts of the same plant are poisonous. Similarly any edible plant that might be mistaken for a poisonous plant has been omitted because of the danger of mistaken identity. It's better to go hungry than to eat a poisonous plant. If you don't know it's safe—don't eat it!

Bracken fern	Greenbrier	Pennyroyal
Cat's-claw	Honey locust	Pigweed
Evening-primrose	Jerusalem-artichoke	Purslane
Fireweed	Mustard	Rice (wild)

morale

If morale is your strongest weapon in your fight for life, probably the greatest defense you can have against adversity and despair will be your reliance on inner strengths developed through your religion. Many men have, indeed, spoken of their experiences in the wilderness as being a sort of spiritual revelation. Their faith has sustained them despite thirst and hunger and disappointment and pain. A beautiful expression of this feeling was given to us by the psalmist David who sang:

> *I will lift up mine eyes unto the hills,*
> *From whence cometh my help.*
> *My help cometh from the Lord,*
> *Which made heaven and earth.*
> *He will not suffer thy foot to be moved;*
> *He that keepeth thee will not slumber.*
> *Behold, he that keepeth Israel*
> *Shall neither slumber nor sleep.*
> *The Lord is thy keeper;*
> *The Lord is thy shade upon thy right hand.*
> *The sun shall not smite thee by day,*
> *Nor the moon by night.*
> *The Lord shall preserve thee from all evil;*
> *He shall preserve thy soul.*
> *The Lord shall preserve thy going out and thy coming in*
> *From this time forth, and even for evermore.*

You may have learned other Scripture that will remind you and your companions of the power of faith in men's lives. If you have committed such passages to memory, fine—they will stand you in good stead. If you have not, *now* might be a good time to make such preparation. Go to your religious counselor and ask him to suggest to you some appropriate words that could help to renew your strength in times of need. Write them down and tuck them in your wallet—just knowing they are there to remind you could be a comfort. This is not to suggest any mystical value in the possession of such a paper, of course—it is a convenience. The value will be in your understanding and acceptance of the words . . . words that will inspire you to faith and give you strength to *live* by means of that faith.

To survive means to "live on." It is a matter of life over death. It is serious business. A coward might read some of this chapter and say, "No, sir! Not for me—you'll never get me into the woods again!" Well, maybe he's better off, then. But *you*—you like going into the woods and the open spaces. You know what Be Prepared really means and you know that the effort of being prepared makes life more worth the living—you get more out of it because you put more into it.

You know, too, some ways to stay out of trouble, some ways of getting out of trouble quickly, and some ways to make the best of it, if somehow you're forced to stay put awhile. You check out your regular and emergency equipment; you check the hazards; you let people know your plans (including plan B). Prepared, you don't panic if you tear it.

You know about *early rescue* and *signaling,* your need for *shelter* and *protection* in some situations, and how *fire* may help fill these needs. You know how important *water* is and how *conserving your energy* usually makes better sense than scurrying for *food. But* you know ways to get food by *hunting* or *fishing* or finding *edible plants.*

You know your chances of survival are great if you go into the struggle physically strong, mentally awake, and morally straight. That last item is important—it means (among other things) that *you don't kid yourself* or other people, that you can be relied on to do your best when things get rough. It's the basis for *morale,* and you know that this is the most important single factor in survival.

You *know* that one match is worth hours of hunting flint or quartz—or sweating over a bow drill—so you carry waterproof matches. You see how a sharp knife beats a sharp rock all hollow—you carry a knife. If you've tried it, you know how hard it is to make a little bit of cord. Hard, compared with having some in your pocket! You can *practice* the survival hunting techniques but they must not be used except in an actual survival situation.

Then you'll know how valuable these basic things are—and how nice it would be to have some of them in your pocket. Chapter 24 has a list of things to put in your "survival kit." Probably you'll start right in to make one—a good idea. Then you'll probably start carrying it anytime you *could* get lost. It's part of being prepared—to "live on!"

17 WORLD OF NATURE

YOU'LL HAVE MORE FUN on hikes or camping trips if you learn to do one important thing—live *with* nature instead of trying to change nature to fit your ideas. Think of yourself as a part of the world of nature, rather than as an observer apart from it somehow. Most things on earth have been in existence longer than we humans. Many changes have taken place since the beginning, many changes are happening right before our eyes, and many more changes will take place. As you hike or camp, try to see for yourself how things work, how nature operates in a place that has taken millions of years to develop.

First, look at the countryside where you hike or camp as a "natural community" that can be compared in some ways with the human community in which you live. Consider it as a community of plants and animals living together in a very close interrelationship with each other and their environment. In somewhat the same way a supermarket is important in your human community, plant life plays a vital role in the natural community. Green plants, in a sense, can be compared to factories using sunlight as power, that change air, water, and minerals into stuff animals can eat—which is something animals can't do for themselves. Just as each person has a part to play in a human community, so each plant and animal has its place in a natural community. As you think of yourself as a part of a natural community, first look at the community as a whole rather than any one of its parts. In other words, look at the forest, not the trees.

Almost any story you read builds up to a high point—a climax—and soon ends. The story of nature in action also builds up to a climax, but it doesn't end—it goes on and on. In nature, this climax community has taken many, many years to develop; once in existence, though, it will stay as it is unless destroyed by wind, fire, or man—or unless the climate changes. When you see a sagebrush desert in Nevada or a pine forest in New Mexico or California, when you look at a tall-grass prairie in Kansas or a short-grass prairie in Colorado, when you see a beech-maple forest in New York or a spruce-fir forest in Oregon, you're looking at a natural climax community. What you see may be the last of a long series of changes, where one community replaced another, until the climax is reached. Here is how it may happen.

Start with an area of bare soil: Once there were plants growing there, but they were destroyed by fire, disease, plowing, or some other cause. That area of soil won't stay bare long. First, annual weeds will spring up and grow and in a year or more cover the area. Next, other plants will grow and help set the stage for another group of plants.

If that patch of soil were in the East, shrubs of various kinds would get started in a few years, and than some trees. Finally, after many years, a climax would be reached. The trees growing there then would reproduce themselves and a more or less stable condition would exist. If that patch of soil was in Kansas, grasses would form the climax community.

In the mountains of the West or in parts of Alaska (depending upon altitude and other factors), the climax community might be a pine forest, spruce-fir forest, or other group of coniferous trees. This process in which plant communities change until the climax is reached is called *plant succession.* It is a natural process that conditions the soil and creates an environment enabling successive plant stages to grow.

Basically it is the soil and climate in an area that determines which plants will grow there naturally, for each plant has its own requirements of soil, temperature, and moisture. But plants also have individual requirements of light—sunlight that reaches them directly or indirectly. Some plants will grow only in direct sunlight. Others can get started only in open shade or even dense shade. There are many variations in between. But it is this process of plant succession that makes it possible for plants that start to grow in the shade to grow into the forests or prairies that become climax communities.

As you hike or camp, then, take a look at the natural community and try to figure out what stage it is in. Figure out what happened to it in the last 100 years or so, and think what might happen in the next 100 if the area is undisturbed. Many Scout camps are on what once was farmland. Others are in forests where the climax trees were cut sometime in the past. Still others are located in prairie or desert country where trees do not grow naturally. The first step in living *with* nature is understanding the natural community and why it is what it is.

plant communities

All along the Atlantic, Gulf, and Pacific coasts are large areas of salt marsh. They are in a state of constant change. Some are just being formed, others are changing form to a dry-land community. Besides having distinctive plants and animals living in them, salt marshes and their nearby waters are important as "nurseries" of ocean life.

Hardwood forests extend from the Atlantic coast west to the great plains. They grow where rainfall averages from 25 to 50 or more inches a year, and where there are distinct winter and summer seasons. Beech, maple, birch, oak, hickory, basswood are the dominant trees in much of this forest. Animals here include the white-tailed deer, black bear, bobcat, fox, raccoon, ruffed grouse, and the wild turkey.

Water communities from the oceans and tidal bays to inland rivers, streams, lakes, and ponds have a wide variety of animal life living in them. The largest animals that ever lived on earth swim in our oceans, and our most important fur-bearing animals live in or close to water. Fish of all kinds, many birds, reptiles and amphibians, snails, clams, crayfish, and many insects all live in or near the water.

Marshes and swamps all represent a stage in plant succession between open water and dry land. A marsh is a wet area dominated by sedges and grasses, while a swamp contains some trees and shrubs. Animal life is abundant in many of these areas. Some of our most spectacular birds: herons, egrets, and ibises nest in or near swamps and marshes, as well as ducks, geese, and other birds.

Natural grasslands or prairies grow where rainfall averages 10 to 30 inches a year, where summer temperatures are high, and where there are periodic droughts. Wildlife of the grasslands include the bison, antelope, jackrabbit, ground squirrels, gophers, prairie dogs, badgers, coyotes, quail, pheasants, burrowing owls, and other birds.

338

There are different kinds of deserts from the State of Washington to Texas. Rainfall is low and the temperatures of air and soil are extremely high by day and cold at night. Some typical desert plants include sagebrush, greasewood, saltbush, bitterbrush, creosote bush, and cactus. Animals include mule deer, antelope, jackrabbits, coyotes, badger, kit fox, rats, mice, and many birds.

Coniferous forests cover the northern edge of the continental United States and parts of Alaska, with arms that extend down along the top of the Appalachian Mountains and the sides and tops of the Sierra Nevadas, Cascades, and Rockies. These forests grow where the climate is cold and where rainfall ranges from 20 to 40 inches a year. Wildlife of this forest includes moose, deer, wolves, foxes, otters, mink, fishers, porcupines, snowshoe rabbits, spruce grouse, horned owls, and other birds.

The plants and animals that live above timberline resemble those of the Arctic tundra. The growing season is short and strong, cold winds prevail at all seasons of the year. Elk, mule deer, bighorn sheep, and mountain goats spend the summer here, but move to lower elevations in winter. Marmots sleep out the long winter, but the interesting little pika stores grass during the summer for winter food.

339

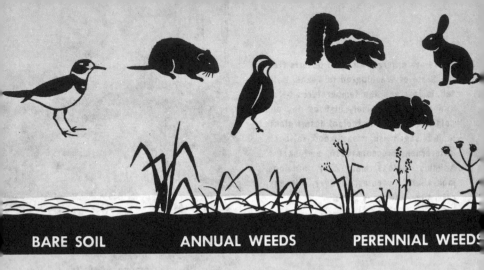

BARE SOIL   **ANNUAL WEEDS**   **PERENNIAL WEEDS**

Plant succession is a process of plants replacing each other as each creates certain conditions favorable to the growth of the next stage. Animal life changes along with the plants. The climax is the last stage to grow and will continue to grow if undisturbed. The more important climax formations in North America are (1) tundra, the area between northern limit of trees and perpetual ice and snow or the area above timberline on mountains; (2) forest, coniferous and deciduous; (3) the broadleaf evergreens in Florida; (4) scrub, chaparral, or desert shrubs; and (5) grassland or

PRAIRIE POND   **EMERGING VEGETATION**

SHRUBS   **CLIMAX FOREST**

prairie. In these illustrations you see plant succession from bare soil to hardwood climax forest and from prairie pond to climax prairie. Naturally, as the plants change so does the wildlife. Above are killdeer, vole, quail, skunk, mouse, cottontail, opossum, woodchuck, deer, squirrel, woodpecker, and raccoon. Below are sunfish, bass, frog, duck, muskrat, redwing blackbird, shrike, jackrabbit, meadowlark, badger, sage grouse, pronghorn, and rattlesnake. Plant succession, of course, also takes place in the Arctic, on mountaintops, in Florida, and on the deserts.

WILLOW FRINGE   **CLIMAX PRAIRIE**

animal needs

Think of the elements that make up your home, and you have an idea of what animals need to live and maintain their numbers.

First, animals need a "dining room," a place where they can find the food they need all year round. Some animals need drinking water too. Others get the moisture they require from their food.

Next, animals need protection. They need a "bedroom" where they are protected from the weather and safe from their enemies. They need a place where they can raise their young in safety.

They also need a "living room" or living space. Some animals roam for miles while others live out their lives in a much smaller area. But they need space where, according to their species, they are not crowded.

This combination of needs of animals—food, shelter, and living space—determines what biologists call "carrying capacity." This means that at any time, a given area of land or water can supply the needs of just so many animals of a given kind. It means that if the numbers of one or more animals are greater than the ability of the land to support them, the surplus will die or move away. It means, also, that different places, depending upon soil, climate, and plant life, will differ in their ability to support animals. It means, too, that to a large extent man can influence animal numbers by what he does with the land and its plant life. There are also natural forces at work that have an influence on animal numbers.

There are many animals that eat plant life as the main part of their diet. There are insects, fish, reptiles, birds, and mammals that eat plant materials in one form or another. In each natural community there are animals that eat other animals. Thus animals have an influence on the community through their food preferences.

In each case, though, the small forms of life are the most numerous, and as you go up to the higher forms, their numbers become fewer.

In the world of nature, generally, the lower forms of animals that live on plants produce many young—many more than can survive. This overproduction is the food supply for the next higher form of animal life. Since it is generally the surplus that the higher animals eat, the overall numbers are not affected much in the long run. The meat-eaters high up the ladder do not wipe out their own food supply. Since they help keep

	10,000—11,000 FT.	ALPINE FIR
	8,000—10,000 FT.	SPRUCE FIR QUAKING ASPE
	7,000—8,000 FT.	GAMBEL'S OAK PONDEROSA PINE
	6,500—7,500 FT.	JUNIPER PINON
	6,500 FT. GRASSLAND	PINON JUNIPER

Climbing a mountain is much like going north as far as plants are concerned. Changes in altitude produce changes in climate. The climate (and plant life) at 6,000 feet on one mountain may be similar to that at 4,000 feet on a mountain farther north. Here from top to bottom the wildlife is (1) marmot, pika, and wood rat; (2) red squirrel, chipmunk, crossbill, and Canada jay; (3) porcupine, golden eagle, gray fox, and black bear; (4) bobcat, deer, and Lewis's woodpecker; (5) kangaroo rat, jackrabbit, burrowing owl, and pronghorn.

343

Life in the water is based upon the water's ability to support microscopic plants. In this food chain of interdependence plankton and algae form the base, then fish eggs and fry, aquatic insects, crayfish, and minnows. Frogs eat minnows, insects, and crayfish and all are food for the largemouth bass and snapping turtle. Man depends on the chain for food and recreation.

PLANKTON AND ALGAE

the plant-eaters from becoming too numerous, the plant-eaters do not destroy their food supply.

Thus a kind of ever-changing balance exists so the plan may continue to work. When the animals at the top have an easy time finding food and their numbers increase, along comes "carrying capacity" as well as another natural control. Food may be plentiful but living space or lack of shelter will limit their numbers. Disease also may spread and take care of the surplus.

The numbers of animals change constantly, going up and going down. There are annual cycles with the seasons and longer cycles over several years. One animal may be numerous this year, and low 2 years from now. Then another animal may be up in numbers. This all happens within certain limits, and those limits usually come from the ability of the land to meet the needs of animals.

Much the same thing happens in a lake, pond, stream, or river Bodies of water, too, differ in their ability to support plant life, and thus animal

Plant life is the base of any food chain. Animals depend on plant life; the plant-eaters provide food for the meat-eaters. This is a typical food chain in a hardwood forest. Squirrels eat acorns. Land snails and earthworms live on decayed vegetation; beetles and mice eat plants. Toads, shrews, snakes, and birds eat insects; and with the squirrel provide food for the red-tailed hawk.

life. In waterways, as on land, there is a food chain that starts with plant life. Plant life in a lake depends upon the basic fertility of the water, the temperature, and other things. Some waters are much more fertile than others, and can support a greater population of animals. In other words, some waters have a greater "carrying capacity."

Plant life then is the base of a natural community, where plants and animals live together in a close relationship to each other and to their environment. Within that community, there are natural forces at work that tend to control animal populations.

Here again is a tremendously interesting field of observation while hiking or camping. Trace food chains for yourself from green plant to hawk, owl, or fox. Find out what plants are preferred food for deer, rabbits, grouse, wild turkey, or quail. In a stream or lake, see for yourself how a meat-eating bass, trout, or mink really depends upon plant life for food. When you see these things and understand them, you will really be living *with* nature.

18 PLANT KINGDOM

A GOOD STARTING POINT in finding out about plants is the knowledge of how plants are classified. This will help you in identification and also in understanding more of how nature works in any natural community. Scientists have divided the plant kingdom into four groups called phyla. Plants belonging to the first phylum are the simplest, while those represented in the fourth phylum are the most highly developed. Any plant you find will fall into one of the following four groups.

THALLOPHYTA. First, are plants such as bacteria, yeast, mold, mildew, rust, mushrooms (fungi); diatoms, seaweed and pond scum (algae). These lowly plants have no stems, roots, or leaves. They range from microscopic in size (bacteria and yeast) to more than 200 feet long (giant kelp). The thallophytes are divided into two classes; the *algae* and the *fungi*. The *algae* are largely plants that live in water or damp places. They have chlorophyll, and can manufacture their own food. They occur as a single cell, or masses of cells, all appearing similar. Some algae form the base of the food chain in lakes, and they supply food for both insects and fish. The second class of thallophytes are *fungi,* such as mushrooms, puffballs, and bracket fungus. They depend on living or dead animal or plant materials for their existence. They cannot manufacture their own food. Mushrooms reproduce by spores as do all fungi except bacteria. Lichens are also thallophytes; they are plants containing algae and fungi. The alga manufactures the food and the fungus stores water and supports the plant. Lichens are the first plants to fasten to rock and slowly break it down to form soil.

BRYOPHYTA. Second, are plants such as the *mosses* and *liverworts.* These are relatively small plants, at most a few inches in length, having simple leaves and stemlike and rootlike parts. *Liverworts* are little, green plants with ribbonlike leaves growing flat on the bark of trees in moist places, on wet rocks, or on the surface of the water. The rootlike structure of the liverwort consists of only one cell. In *mosses,* though, the structure consists of many cells. They get their food and water through these rootlike, hairy structures. Mosses grow on trees, rocks, and soil in either wet or dry places. They grow close together.

PTERIDOPHYTA. Third, are the *ferns, horsetails,* and *club mosses.* During geologic time fossil remains show that this phylum represented prominent plants attaining the size of forest trees. Pteridophytes have true roots, stems, and leaves and produce spores, not seeds. They have true woody tissue which enables them to grow tall. *Ferns* grow in many different kinds of places, but most of them grow in shady, damp woods. They have feathery leaves, some growing 4 to 5 feet high. When you find a fern you see the leaves only, the stem is underground with the roots. The tree ferns of the tropics do have stems above ground. *Horsetails,* as the name implies, resemble a horse's tail and, generally, grow in moist places. Some, however, do grow along roadsides where it is dry. They are also called "scouring rushes," because these plants contain a glassy material and were once used to scour pots and pans. They have no real leaves, but the green hollow stem produces the food. The *club mosses* look a lot more like mosses than ferns. They are classified with ferns because of their structure and ways of reproduction. Club mosses, commonly called ground pine, creep over the ground.

SPERMATOPHYTA. Fourth, is a large group that includes all grasses, wild flowers, shrubs, vines, cacti, and trees. This group, known as seed producing plants, are considered the "highest" and most complex. They range in size from a fraction of an inch (duckweed) to 300 feet tall (redwood), some dying in one season (annual) and others living year after year (perennial). Some spermatophytes grow on land, such as trees; some in wet places, like cattail; and others completely submerged, like pondweeds. None grow in the open seas. Seed plants have roots, stems, and leaves but produce seeds, not spores. This group is divided into two parts. In the first group, *gymnosperms,* are plants such as pines, firs, and spruces which have unprotected seeds that are usually borne in cones. Gymnosperms that produce cones are called conifers. In the second group, *angiosperms,* are plants such as oaks, grasses, and wild flowers. The plants of this group produce seeds that are enclosed in some kind of covering, usually called a fruit. Flowers produce the enclosed seeds; consequently, the angiosperms are referred to as flowering plants. The flower in most of these plants is easily recognized but there are some that you might not notice, like grasses.

DICOTS

MONOCOTS

ANGIOSPERMS

GINKGO

GYMNOSPERMS

CONIFERS

CYCADS

SPERMATOPHYTA

HORSETAILS

FERNS

PTERIDOPHYTA

CLUB MOSSES

MOSSES

BRYOPHYTA

LIVERWORTS

ALGAL FUNGI

LICHENS

CLUB FUNGI

FUNGI

SAC FUNGI

SLIME MOLDS

BACTERIA

THALLOPHYTA

RED ALGAE

BROWN ALGAE

GREEN ALGAE

ALGAE

BLUE GREEN ALGAE

DIATOMS

ANCESTRAL PROTOPHYTA

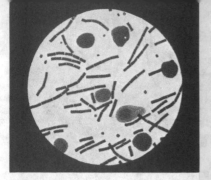

Bacteria are the smallest of plants—probably the smallest living things. They are seen only through a microscope. Some cause disease; others are valuable to man. The swellings on the roots of clover, lespedeza, or peas are masses of bacteria.

There are four groups of algae: blue-green, green, brown, and red. Some are microscopic but some, such as seaweeds, are more than 200 feet long. Pond scum is a common freshwater algae.

Algae grow in a wide variety of waters from the Arctic to hot springs where no other plant can grow. More than 14,000 kinds have been discovered.

Lichens are composed of algae and fungi living together. The fungus lives on the food produced by the alga and, in turn, supplies moisture for the alga. Reindeer moss is a lichen and an important wild-life food in the Arctic.

White pine blister rust is a fungus that grows on currants and spreads to white pines. The disease usually kills the pine tree, and may completely destroy all the pines in an area.

Puffballs are fungi that live on decaying plant material in wooded areas or open fields. They vary in size from a few inches through, to a foot or more.

Fly amanita are beautiful mushrooms with a 6-inch cap, yellow to orange in color. They are found during the summer in the open or in the woods. They are deadly poisonous.

Fairy ring mushrooms are usually found in rings in grassy fields, on lawns, or in orchards from spring to fall and often in the same place. If you find them, measure the size of the circle. Check again next year to see if the circle is larger.

Liverworts are usually found in moist places or on the wet rocks of gorges. Some live on tree bark. These plants are of little economic importance. Some grow well in terrariums.

Sphagnum moss is a bog-builder. It will gradually replace water in a pond. When dry, it may be burned as a fuel. It is also used in soil conditioning. The sphagnum of millions of years ago is today's coal.

Common fern moss is found over much of North America, growing best in moist, shaded places. It grows in dry places too and on tree trunks. It forms large mats.

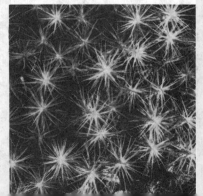

Hair-cap moss grows over much of North America from sea level to high in the Rockies. It grows in dry places, in sand, or on rocks. It has been used for stuffing in furniture.

Common club moss (called ground pine or ground cedar) grows over much of North America in open fields or in woods, commonly on poor soils. It has been used in Christmas decorations, but is slow growing and cannot survive too much collecting.

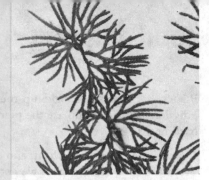

Scouring rush is a horsetail that is found over most of the United States and Canada. It grows along streams in moist places, on dry banks, and on railroad embankments. It was used to scour pots and pans by our pioneers.

Bracken fern grows from the Atlantic to Wyoming in open woods, generally in dry places. It grows to about 3 feet high with wide spreading fronds. The young fronds are edible if gathered when they are not more than 8 inches high.

Sensitive fern grows over much of the United States in swamps, wet fields, and roadsides. It grows to about 30 inches high. The brown fronds with the hard "beads" produce the spores that grow into new ferns.

353

seed bearing

Plants that bear seeds make up the most important group in the plant kingdom. In this group are the plants that provide us with many of our basic needs.

Included here are corn, wheat, and oats which supply much of our food. From the cone-bearing trees we get timber for shelter and pulp for our paper. Cotton and flax (linen) have enabled us to clothe ourselves. From other plants we derive some of our medicines, rubber, and many other highly useful products.

This group is divided into two parts: First are those plants such as sago palm (an ornamental tree that originated in Java), the ginkgo (a "living fossil" tree imported from China), and the more common conifers. Second are flowering plants such as oaks, maples, and wild flowers.

The ginkgo or maidenhair tree is a native of China and Japan. It is called a "living fossil" because of the many millions of years it has been on earth. It is grown as an ornamental or street tree.

The sago palm is a native of Java, but has been planted as an ornamental in the South. It grows to 8 or 10 feet high, with palmlike branches 2 to 6 feet long.

Probably the oldest and largest living things in the world are members of this group of trees—the giant redwoods of the west coast. They reach heights up to 300 feet with diameters from 8 to 12 feet.

But "evergreen" trees of one kind or another grow over a large part of the country or have been planted as ornamentals, for windbreaks, or as a future supply of pulp or timber. Most trees in this group hold their leaves (needles) over the winter months, some even for several years. The seed-bearing cones sometimes grow to 12 inches or more in length.

Because they grow high and upright, these trees supply most of our lumber. They also provide paper pulp, turpentine, and resin. The pines, firs, hemlocks, spruces, cedars, junipers, redwoods, yews, and cypresses are common cone-bearing trees.

Ground hemlock is a low-growing member of the yew family that is found from Iowa east to Virginia and north to Canada. It grows in shaded areas usually under other conifers. It has a red berrylike fruit, the seed of which is poisonous.

White pine grows to 200 feet and is found from the Atlantic to Minnesota and in mountains, south to Georgia. Its needles are in clusters of five. It has been planted widely. The western white pine grows at sea level in Washington and to 10,000 feet in California.

355

Pitch pine grows from Canada to Florida and eastern Tennessee on sandy or poor soils. Its needles are in clusters of three, and are 3 to 5 inches long. The seeds are eaten by birds and squirrels. The cones may remain on the tree for many years.

Red pine, also called Norway pine, is a tall forest tree that grows from Minnesota east to Maine along the northern edge of the country. Its needles grow in clusters of two. It grows on light, sandy soils and has been planted widely for the production of timber.

Longleaf pine, called southern pine, grows in sandy soil from Virginia to Texas through Florida. Needles grow in threes and may be 18 inches long. It is an important timber tree and is used for pulp, paint, and turpentine.

Ponderosa pine grows from Canada to Mexico and from the Pacific to South Dakota and New Mexico. Its needles are in threes from 4 to 11 inches long. The cones are prickly. This is a very important timber tree of the West.

356

Lodgepole pine grows from Alaska to California and east to the Dakotas. Its needles are in twos, 1 to 3 inches long. The cones are 1 to 2 inches long and prickly. In the mountains this tree grows to 90 feet, but is smaller on the coast.

White spruce grows across the northern edge of the country, from the Atlantic to Alaska. Its needles are ½ to ¾ inches long and are arranged around the twig. They are blue-green in color. The tree grows to 60 or 70 feet and is used for pulp, timber, and Christmas trees.

Norway spruce grows from Maine to Virginia and west to Kansas, where it has been planted. The needles are dark green and about 1 inch long, sharp pointed, and four sided. The cones are 4 to 7 inches long. The wood has been used for oars and pulp for paper.

Sitka spruce grows from Alaska to northern California close to the coast. This is the largest of all the spruces and grows to 150 feet. The needles are long, flat, and sharp pointed. The cones are 2 to 4 inches long.

Larch or tamarack grows in wet and moist soils in the northeast, west to the Lake States, and across Canada to Alaska. The soft needles, which grow ¾ to 1 inch in tufts on old growth, fall off in winter. The cones are small.

Firs grow across the northern edge of the country and down the mountains to Virginia in the East and New Mexico in the West. Balsam fir grows in the East; white fir, grand fir, and alpine fir in the West. Needles are flat. Cones stand upright. Balsam fir is widely used as a Christmas tree.

Eastern hemlock grows from the Atlantic to Minnesota and south to Alabama. Western hemlock grows from Alaska to California and east to Idaho. Needles are ¼ to 1 inch long, flat, and seem to grow on opposite sides of the twig.

Douglas fir, from Canada to California and east to the Continental Divide, grows 200 feet high—an important tree for timber. Used in the East for windbreak and ornament, its needles are ¾ to 1 inch long and grow on all sides of the twig.

Bald cypress grows in swamps from Delaware to Florida and west to Texas. It has been planted in California. It sheds its needles each winter. The needles are about ¾ inches long, flat, and thin. The wood, resistant to moisture, is used for cabinet production.

Redwood grows from sea level to 3,000 feet elevation in western California and Oregon. It grows to 350 feet in height and 12 to 15 feet in diameter. Needles are flat and stiff, ¼ to 1 inch long. Wood is used for many purposes in house construction.

Common juniper grows over much of North America in a wide variety of habitats and forms. The redcedar that grows from the Atlantic to North Dakota and Kansas is a close relative. The fruit is eaten by many kinds of birds. Wood from the redcedar is used for fenceposts and cedar chests.

White cedar grows in swamp areas in cool places from Quebec to Pennsylvania and in the mountains to North Carolina and west to Minnesota. In the West it grows from Alaska to California, east to Idaho and Montana. Leaves grow in a fernlike pattern.

359

grasses

Grasses are eaten by more people than any other food. Wheat, corn, and rice are all in the grass family, as is sugar cane. Animal life, which provides meat, milk, and leather, is dependent on grassland.

Grass is the main plant life over large areas of the world. In America, grasslands now make up about 60 percent of the land.

Grass is important in ways other than food. It is very important as a ground cover to protect the soil from washing or blowing away. Sugar is used to make alcohol which in turn is used in plastics, explosives, paint lacquer, and many other products.

Big bluestem, or turkeyfoot bluestem because of three flowering branches, is a native, tall, perennial bunchgrass, often forming colonies. Young shoots are flattened, the leaves are rolled in the bud; lower sheaths and leaf blades often with silky white hairs. Used for range and hay.

Wild rice grows from the St. Lawrence River to North Dakota, south to Kansas and Louisiana and along the coast. It grows in shallow water in mud. It is important as food for wildlife.

Crab grass, a native of Europe, is found over all of the United States, growing commonly in fields, gardens, and lawns. It may grow to 4 feet in height and may be a pest.

Foxtail is another grass from Europe that is now established over most of the country on cultivated lands. The flowering clusters resemble a foxtail.

Canary grass is found from Maine to Alaska, south to Virginia, Kansas, and California. It grows to 3 feet in height and the flowering head is a dense spike about I inch long. The seeds are fed to canaries.

Timothy grows in managed pastures and hayfields growing best in the Northwest and Midwest. The fruiting head is a slender spike about 5 inches long. It is grown as feed for cattle and horses.

Fescue is a native of Europe, and several kinds are cultivated in hayfields and pastures and for lawn grasses. The leaves are flat to ½ inch wide and grow to 4 feet in height.

Bluegrass appears over much of the country. The stems grow on the ground before becoming upright. Kentucky bluegrass reaches 3 feet and is used as a pasture and lawn grass.

Bromegrass grows from Ohio to Oregon and south to Kansas. The flower head is about 10 inches long and the flowers purple in color. It is used in improving worn-out land and is important pasture grass.

Buffalo grass grows on dry plains from Minnesota to Montana, south to Iowa, Texas, Louisiana, Arizona, and New Mexico. It forms a heavy sod. Early settlers used the sod for houses and it is an important food for grazing wildlife.

wild flowers

Wild flowers of one kind or another grow in woods, the deserts, swamps, marshes, fields, or along roadsides. They grow in water and in the melting snows high on mountaintops. Some start blooming early in the spring; others bloom right up to frost in the late fall.

Study them where you find them in their native environment. Add a magnifying glass and field guide to your pack, plus a notebook and pencil.

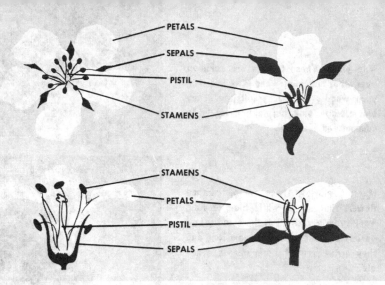

PETALS

SEPALS

PISTIL

STAMENS

STAMENS

PETALS

PISTIL

SEPALS

First, though, you should know the parts of a flower—the petals, sepals, pistil and stamens — because this enables you to tell one flower from another more quickly.

The pictures on the following pages show representatives of major groups of wild flowers. Only those groups with wide distribution across the country are shown. When you find a flower you do not know first try to place it in the right group, then use a field guide to determine the species.

Bee-balm. These are tall flowers in the mint family that range in color from lavender to scarlet. Many of them grow in dry places such as along roadsides and in fencerows. They bloom in summer and early fall.

Trilliums. These are beautiful plants of the lily family that bloom in early spring. They range in color from white to pink to deep red and grow in moist woods of the East and in the mountains of the West.

Wild pinks. These flowers are common over all of the country and grow in fields, open woods, and rocky hillsides. They bloom white, pink, purple, and scarlet in summer and early fall.

Morning glories. These are bell-shaped flowers that may be white, blue, or pink. They grow across all of the country in a variety of places. The stems are long and they twine around other plants. They bloom in summer.

Clovers. These flowers may be red, pink, yellow, or white and from a few inches high to 2 or 3 feet. They are legumes, meaning that their roots add nitrogen to the soil. They bloom from spring to fall and are important food for some birds and other animals.

Columbines may be scarlet, yellow (in the East) or blue or red (in the West). In the Northwest is a white species. They grow from 1½ to 3 feet high in open woods and fields. They flower in spring and early summer.

Mallows grow in a variety of places from salt marshes to prairies and mountain meadows. They range in color from purple, pink, and yellow, to white. They bloom in spring and summer.

Fireweeds grow on burned-over ground and are common in northeastern and northwestern wooded areas. They are purple in color, grow to 5 feet in height, and flower from June to August.

Thistles grow in fields, pastures, and along roadsides, and are known for their prickly leaves and stems. The flowers may be white, purple, pink, or yellowish and grow to 4 feet or more in height. They flower in spring and summer and attract bees, butterflies, and goldfinches.

Orchids of many kinds grow over most of the country. Most of them grow in moist, rich soil in woods or bogs. In color, they range from purple to pink to orange, yellow, and white. They bloom in spring and summer.

Geraniums grow in open areas or in woods and are lavender, pink, or white. They are from 1 to 3 feet in height and bloom from spring to early fall.

Fleabanes grow in fields and meadows and along roadsides. They grow from a few inches to 2 feet high and are purple to reddish in color. Dried plants were supposed to ward off fleas.

Milkweeds are tall plants with flowers that may be pink, red, or white. All parts of the plant contain a white, sticky sap. They grow in fields, meadows, marshes, and along roadsides. They bloom in summer and fall.

Asters of many kinds grow all across the country in a variety of places—from the woods, swamps, or roadsides to open fields and meadows. The best known kinds are purple or blue, but some are pink or white. They bloom in late summer and fall.

Vetch grows as a vine in cultivated fields and field borders. The flowers may be purple, blue, or white, and the plant blooms from summer to fall. Vetch, like clover, is a legume.

Penstemons grow in many kinds of places from moist soils to rocky spots at timberline. They grow from a few inches to 3 feet high, and the flowers are blue to purple, though some may be red, yellow, or white. They bloom in spring and summer.

Violets are well-known spring and early summer flowers that grow in moist fields, wooded areas, or along roadsides. They are low-growing plants with flowers that may be purple, blue, white, or yellow.

Lobelias bloom in summer and fall, and the flowers are generally blue to purple. They usually are found in moist places, along streams or in wet fields and meadows. They are from I to 2 feet in height.

Blue toadflax blossoms in summer or fall and grows in open fields in dry soils. It grows from 5 to 18 inches high.

Bellflowers are found in summer or fall in moist, shady places. The flowers are blue, and the stem has a milky sap. They may be from I to 2 feet high.

367

Chicory grows commonly in pastures and along roadsides and waste places. It blossoms in summer and fall and grows from 1 to 3 feet high. The flowers generally are blue.

Gentians grow generally in moist places such as wet meadows or woods. The common ones are purple to blue and they grow from 1 to 2 feet high. They bloom in late summer or fall.

Camas, also called wild hyacinth, blooms in the spring. The flowers are blue to white, and the plant grows in rich, damp soil and moist fields.

Blue-eyed grass grows in open areas and moist meadows. The flowers are blue with yellow centers and bloom in spring and summer. They are about 12 inches high.

Lupines may be found in the East and West but not commonly in the Midwest. They grow from 1 to 2 feet high and may be blue, purple, white, yellow, or pink. The common one in the East is blue.

Wood sorrels, with leaves that resemble clover, blossom in spring and early summer. The flowers may be yellow, lavender, or pink. They grow in gardens, fields, or waste places.

Sunflowers are tall, yellow flowers that grow in open fields, along roadsides and ditches. They bloom in summer and fall, and the seeds are important food for some birds.

Coneflowers resemble daisies and grow in dry areas, along roads, and in waste places. They are yellow with brown "cones" in the center. They may be from l to 4 or 5 feet high and bloom in summer.

Hawkweed grows best in dry places, open fields, or pastures. It may be orange, yellow, or reddish and grows from l to 3 feet tall. It blooms in summer or fall.

Buttercups generally are yellow and grow in a wide variety of places, from marshes to dry fields. They bloom from spring to fall. The petals are shiny.

Goldenrods grow generally in dry open fields and along roads. They may be from 2 to 4 feet high and generally are pale to deep yellow. They bloom in summer and fall.

Yellow orchids, such as the yellow lady-slipper, grow in moist, rich, generally shaded places. They bloom in the spring and the summer.

Primroses are generally yellow and vary in size. Some open in the evening and close the next morning. They may grow from I to 4 feet high. They bloom in the summer.

Cinquefoils grow in open fields, pastures, and along roadsides. The leaves resemble the leaves of strawberry plants. The most common ones have yellow flowers, but they may also be purplish or red. They bloom in summer.

Mulleins grow in dry areas and waste places. The leaves are large and hairy and the flower stalk is quite tall. The pink, yellow, or white flowers may be found in summer and fall.

370

Meadow rues have small white or greenish star-shaped flowers. They grow tall, and are found in fields, woods borders, and pasture edges. They bloom in summer or early fall.

Solomon's seal has whitish bell-like flowers that hang under the slender stalk. They bloom in spring, and the flowers become blue berries by summer. They grow in open woods.

Chickweed is a common weed of gardens, lawns, and fields. The flower is white with deeply notched petals. It is a low-growing plant that blooms in spring.

Yarrows have lacelike leaves and white, flat flowers. They grow in open fields or along roads and may be from 1 to 2 feet tall. The flowers are found in summer and fall. The crushed leaves are aromatic.

Daisies are common early summer flowers in fields and along roadsides. The flowers are white with yellow centers and may be from 1 to 2 feet high. The plants grow in clumps.

trees, shrubs, vines

Shrubs, trees, and some vines are generally called woody plants. This means that the stem or stems of these plants are woody. Trees are defined as woody plants having a single, erect perennial (persisting for several years) main stem or trunk at least 3 inches in diameter at breast height, and having a crown with a head of branches or of foliage, and a height of at least 12 feet. Shrubs are woody plants that are smaller than trees but with several stems growing together to form a clump. Certain shrubs become trees if moisture and good soil are available. Many trees may be large shrubs in poor soil. Some are shrubby in the northern part of their range and treelike in the southern part or vice versa. Botanists consider woody vines as being shrubs. These vines have a woody stem that is too slender, flexible, or weak to hold themselves erect. In nature the vine supports itself by climbing over other plants or objects by tendrils (slender, spirally, coiling organs) or by twining or extending itself horizontally by running along the ground.

Woody plants occur in all sections of the country, from the low elevation deserts to the high mountains. In our prairie States where grasses are dominant, trees and shrubs grow along water courses.

Trees are divided into two groups; coniferous and deciduous. Conifers are mainly cone-bearing and keep their leaves after the growing season. Deciduous trees shed their leaves at the end of the growing season. Some, however, are persistent. Do not confuse the name evergreen with conifer. An evergreen refers to any plant that retains its leaves including all conifers and members of the deciduous group such as holly, rhododendron, laurel, ivy, and most tropical plants.

Woody plants are of inestimable value to the well-being of our country. As plants, their roots hold the soil; falling leaves, branches and, upon death, the plant itself helps build soil incorporating humus. These plants reduce the force of raindrops and the vegetation holds water where it falls. Woody plants, along with grasses and herbs, make up part of plant communities in which wildlife seeks food, shelter, cover, and homes. Without food and cover provided by shrubs, wildlife could not survive. Man, too, is provided food from woody plants, fruits and nuts from trees, berries from shrubs, and grapes from vines. The products from trees is a long list from paints to plastics, from lumber to paper.

Willows generally grow along stream-banks or other wet places. Leaves are long and narrow, and in some the flowers are "pussies." Some are shrubby in growth, but some grow to be large trees.

Cottonwoods grow generally along waterways, except where they have been planted. They become large spreading trees with deep furrows in the pale bark. Leaves are more or less heart shaped.

Quaking aspen grows in the mountains of the West and across the northern part of the country. The leaves are round on a flattened stem, so they quake in the slightest wind. Young trees have greenish bark. Makes good kindling wood.

Bayberry is a shrub or tree and grows in moist places. The berries and leaves are very fragrant, and the wax from the berries is used in making candles. Many birds eat the berries in winter.

Black walnut grows in rich, open woods in the eastern part of the country. It may be a large tree up to 90 feet high. The nut is good to eat, and the wood very valuable for furniture and veneer.

373

Pecan grows from Indiana to Georgia and west to Kansas. Noted for its long pointed nuts, it may be a large tree with deep furrows in the gray-brown bark. It grows best in rich soils.

Shagbark hickory is a native of the eastern half of the country. Its gray bark has long, loose scales. The nuts have thick husks, but the shell is thin. It grows in rich soils in open woods or fencerows.

American hornbeam is often called muscle-wood because of its musclelike growth. The bark is gray and smooth. The wood makes good fuel and tool handles. Grows in the East.

Yellow birch is a northern or mountain tree of the East. The bark curls into yellow or silvery strips. The inner bark smells like wintergreen. It may be a large tree and grows in rich, open woods.

Gray birch is a northern tree with white bark. The leaves are shaped like triangles. It grows in open fields and along roadsides. The bark from dead trees makes good tinder.

American beech is a large tree with smooth gray bark. It grows in the eastern part of the country in rich soil in wooded areas. The nut is important wildlife food, and the wood is good for fuel.

White oak has light gray bark and leaves with rounded lobes. It grows to 100 or more feet in rich soil. Acorns are pointed in shallow cups. They mature in 1 year. Wood is hard and heavy and used for furniture and boats.

Red oaks grow in the eastern part of the country, sometimes to 100 feet or more. The inner bark is reddish. They grow on well-drained soils. The wood is hard and makes good fuel. Acorns are large and round in shallow cups.

Live oak is a tree of the South and remains green all year-round. The leaves are oval shaped and leathery. Acorns are small. Wood is hard. It grows best on moist, sandy soil.

American elm is a native of the East but has been planted over some of the West. It is a large vase-shaped tree, commonly found in towns and villages, along streets and roadsides.

Tulip tree or yellow poplar grows as a tall, straight tree. The yellow flowers resemble tulips. The wood is soft, straight grained, and good for whittling. It grows in rich soil.

Sassafras, with its three or four different leaf shapes, is well known in the East. The bark is fragrant. It grows in acid soils in fields, hedgerows, and roadsides. Generally, it is not a large tree.

Spicebush is a shrub of the moist woodlands of the East. The bark, leaves, and fruit are fragrant when crushed. Birds eat the fruit. The wood will burn when green—a good thing to know.

Sweetgum, with its star-shaped leaf, grows in low, damp woods of the East and Southeast. It may become a tall, straight tree. The fruit is a dry, round ball covered with spines.

Sycamores become large trees in wet woods and along streams. Bark is a mottled white and green or brown. The fruit is a ball about 1 inch in diameter.

Shadbush has several other names, including serviceberry and June cherry. It is a shrub or small tree of the dry woodlands of the East. The red fruit, ripe in June or July, is edible.

Black cherry may grow to 100 feet in rich woods or open areas. The red wood is valuable for furniture or veneer, and the fruit is edible for man and wildlife.

Locusts are native in the East but have been widely planted for erosion control. They grow in woods and along hedgerows. The fruit is a long, flat pod with oval seeds. The wood is hard and durable.

Redbud or Judas tree is a shrub or small tree native in the East. Because of its flowers, it has been widely planted as an ornamental. The fruit is a flat pod, pointed at each end.

Sumacs are shrubs or small trees that grow in fields, fencerows, or roadsides. The fruit heads are red and grow upright. The bark is eaten by rabbits. Some birds eat the fruit.

Poison ivy may be found as a low-growing plant or a shrub or vine. It has three, shining, green leaflets, usually with course teeth. In the fall, the leaves turn bright red—then yellow.

Poison sumac grows as a shrub or small tree and grows in damp places. It is related to poison ivy, and has compound leaflets and white drooping berries. Unlike sumac, its leaflets are smooth and grow in a V-shape from the midrib.

Poison oak, closely related to poison ivy, has three to seven lobed leaflets that are hairy underneath. Poison oak is common in the South.

American holly is a native of the East, but has been widely planted as an ornamental. It grows best in moist woodland. The leaves have sharp spines and are evergreen. The berries are red and eaten by birds and squirrels.

Bittersweet is a climbing vine that may reach high into trees. It is native to the East in rich soils, woods, or along roadsides. The flowers are greenish, and the berries are orange.

Broad-leafed or Oregon maple is a native of the West, growing in the mountains from Oregon south. It is planted as a shade tree, and the wood is useful as fuel for the camper.

Red maple is a native of the East and extends to Nebraska and Texas. The young trees have gray, smooth bark; the older ones have rough, dark bark. Red maple grows best in moist areas and is a good fuel.

Sugar maple, largest of the maples, grows west to North Dakota, Iowa, and Texas. The young trees have smooth, gray bark; the older trees have ridged, grayish bark. The wood is hard and heavy, good for fuel. The sap is used for making syrup.

Basswood is a native of the East. Growing best in rich soil, the inner bark is fibrous and useful for making lines. The whitewood is excellent for whittling. It is a good browse plant for wildlife.

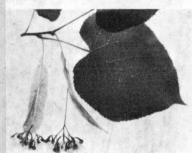

Dogwoods are found over much of the country. Some are shrubs; some are trees. All but one have opposite leaves and branches. The fruit is important as wildlife food. They are planted widely as ornamental trees.

379

Laurels are evergreen shrubs of acid woodlands. They have attractive flowers and are used as ornamentals. Turkey hunters make a call from the leaves. The wood is hard and heavy. The green parts are poisonous.

Huckleberries of one kind or another grow over most of the country, generally in acid soil in swamps or woods. The fruit is edible by man and is important as a wildlife food.

Ashes are native to the East and grow west to Minnesota and Texas. They are usually straight, tall trees that grow in rich soil or swamps and wet places. The leaves and branches are opposite.

Catalpa has been widely planted. The leaves are heart-shaped and the fruit is a long "bean." The wood is durable and is used for fence posts.

Viburnums of several kinds are found over much of the country. They are woodland shrubs, generally, and the fruit is important as wildlife food. Some are used widely as ornamental shrubs.

380

Elder is a shrub that grows along road-sides and in rocky places over much of the country. Its flowers are white and the fruit is a red berry.

Wild grapes grow over much of the country in hedgerows, woods borders, and along streams. They grow as climbing vines and may reach high into trees. The fruit is an important wildlife food.

Alders are generally shrubs that grow in damp places in the East and West, but not in the Plains States. Red and white alders of the west coast may become trees. The fruit is a woody cone.

Magnolias are native to the Southeast and generally grow in wet, rich soil. They have large, white, waxy flowers that are most fragrant. The large leaves are dark green and leathery.

Eucalyptus is a native of Australia, but is widely planted in California. The bark peels off in long strips, leaving a smooth trunk. The leaves are thick and leathery.

381

cacti

Cacti are succulent (having fleshy and juicy tissues), thickened spiny plants without green leaves that occur most commonly in desert regions. They have reserves of water in the fleshy stems and a very thick "skin" which reduces water evaporation. A few kinds are found in the East, but the greatest number grow in the West. Cacti usually have prickles, spines, or stinging bristles coming out of the stem, usually in stars or clusters.

Cactus flowers are showy, solitary, and sessile (flower stem absent) or growing from the prolonged part of the ovary (future fruit). The fruit is usually a fleshy, juicy berry containing many seeds. Cactus is eaten by a large variety of animals from small rodents to livestock.

Cacti have most of their roots in the upper few inches of soil. These may spread in all directions from the plant. This allows them to take advantage of any light rainfall even though the water does not penetrate deeply into the soil.

Saguaro cactus grows in Arizona and southern California and may grow to 40 feet in height. The flowers are white with a yellow center and about 4 inches long. The fruit is edible.

382

Barrel cactus. A barrel-shaped cactus covered with spines which are used by Indians for fishhooks, so sometimes called fishhook cactus. The Indians cut off the top and pound the pulp and squeeze it to get juices. This moisture has saved lives in the desert.

Cholla cactus. Pronounced choy-ya. A jointed, twisting shrub growing to 6 feet tall. The main stem and large branches are brown, the new twigs are pale green. The entire plant is covered with clusters of yellowish barbed spines an inch or more long. Yellow, cup-shaped fruit develop from magenta flowers. The fruit remains on the plant for several years.

Prickly pear cactus of one kind or another grows from Massachusetts to Florida and over much of the western United States.

Pincushion cactus. A small cactus that grows singly or in colonies. It is characterized by the long, black, hooklike spine that grows from a cluster of smaller spines. The flowers are pink, the fruit a deep red and edible.

383

desert shrubs

The hot deserts from southern California to Texas are characterized by creosote bush, giant cactus, mesquite, and ocotillo. The creosote bush is the most common plant of the warm desert. It is a many-branching evergreen shrub 3 to 4 feet tall and is aromatic. Like sagebrush, creosote bush is notoriously deep-rooted. The roots of this plant find the permanent moisture in the soil at any level if it is present. That is why this plant survives in the desert and is classified into a group called drought enduring species.

Creosote bushes appear evenly spaced across the desert between 15 to 30 feet apart. In between, much of the area is bare ground. Another shrub growing with creosote bush is bur sage. Other desert shrubs are yuccas, the Joshua being a tree-like yucca, ocotillo, century plant, and paloverde. The paloverde is a spiny shrub or small tree with bright green twigs. The century plant has a cluster of large leaves at the ground level, but no stem. In 10 to 25 years it sends up a tall flower stem and as the seeds mature the plant dies.

The unifying factor of the warm desert is the creosote bush. It occurs in all the lowland areas. The only exception is the Tamaulipan Desert at the southern tip of Texas. Here, creosote bush is missing and mesquite is the prominent shrub or small tree.

Sagebrush is the most common shrub in North America. Best known as an aromatic shrubby plant with grayish-green downy-covered leaves, common in desert and semi-arid regions of the West.

Mesquite is a dry-land shrub or tree that is a native of parts of the West. It grows to 20 feet. Flowers appear in late spring; beanlike fruit ripens in the early fall. It provides food and cover for wildlife.

Creosote bush is an evergreen desert shrub with fragrant dark green leaves. The flowers are large and yellow and produce white furry balls.

Yucca or Spanish bayonet grows naturally from South Carolina southward around to western deserts. It has been widely planted elsewhere. The flower spike may grow to 10 feet. The leaves are sharp pointed.

Greasewood. Known also as chamise. Grows to 10 feet tall. One species, abundant in the higher coast ranges and the Sierra Nevada Mountains of California, bears heavy clusters of small, whitish flowers. Another species in southern California has fewer leaves and larger flowers and is very fragrant.

Bitterbrush. This low-growing shrub is commonly known in the West as antelope-brush, deer-brush or buckbrush, as it is a chief browse plant for deer, elk, antelope, cattle, and sheep. Found growing with dry-land plants on arid plains, foothills, and mountain slopes usually on southerly exposures.

Ocatillo. Often called flaming sword in the spring because red flower clusters appear on the stem tips. It has no main stem but several branchless stems that are covered with thorns.

385

projects

There are many hike or camp projects that are not only fun but from which you find out more about plants and how they grow. Making collections is a good place to start, but make collections that have a purpose. Instead of collecting on a hit-or-miss basis, plan ahead of time how you will use your collection and what its purpose will be. You might collect the leaves of the important timber trees in your area or of the wildlife food plants. As you mount them in a notebook, write down the use of the tree—for construction, furniture, pulp, or other use. Or indicate which animals eat the plant and what part—the bark, buds, seeds, or leaves.

See how many different flowers you can find in a mile of roadside or 5 acres of woods or field. But be sure that the flowers you collect are growing in reasonable abundance. Some flowers in some places are becoming rare.

A seed collection can show you the many ways that tree and other seeds are distributed over the landscape. Some, such as oak or walnut, are carried away and buried by squirrels. Others are attached to miniature parachutes and float away on the breeze. Some are inside "stickers" and become attached to your clothing or to wild animals and are spread in that way. Poison ivy is spread by birds that eat the seeds and deposit them in the droppings up to many miles away. Witchhazels are spread by an "explosion" of the seedpod when it is ripe.

Wood samples can be helpful. Many people can tell trees from the bark, leaves, or twigs; few can identify a board in a lumberyard. You wouldn't cut down a 6-inch tree just to get a wood specimen. Use trees already cut for campsite development or road construction or trees that have blown down or are diseased and will die anyway. Sometimes a low-growing branch can provide a specimen.

Make notes of interesting observations in the field. On a winter hike, you might see a flock of winter finches eating the catkins of a birch or tearing apart the cones of a spruce to get at the seeds inside. Make a list of the different plants in a bog, deep ravine, or on a mountain slope or top. Observe one tree at regular intervals for a year and record the date it flowered, when its leaves first appeared or started to fall. There are many kinds of collections which can help you learn about plants.

Cut newspapers to fit in a heavy loose-leaf notebook. Carefully place the leaves of a tree or shrub between the sheets of the newspaper with notes on the kind of tree, the date, where it was collected, and other important information.

Use a belt or strap to hold the notebook securely shut to keep the leaves flat until they dry. Or lay heavy weights on the notebook when you return home.

Attach a pressed leaf to unlined loose-leaf notebook paper with clear tape or glue. You can put more than one leaf on a page but be sure they are the same kind. Attach a label to the bottom right-hand side of the page. The label should include the name of the tree, location, date of collection, and the name of collector. Keep your collection in a hard-cover loose-leaf notebook.

Clear plastic, which you can buy by the yard in a hardware or department store, can be used to mount leaves permanently.

In collecting wild flowers, insert them carefully between the sheets of newspaper; place in a notebook that has a stiff cover. Place them in a plant press when you get home until they dry.

Galls, those swellings on plant stems and leaves caused by insects, make an interesting collection. Cut a few open and examine the insect larva inside.

If you arrange the twigs from a number of trees or shrubs on the ground, you'll soon begin to recognize that each has special characteristics. Select the ones you want to mount and label for a permanent display.

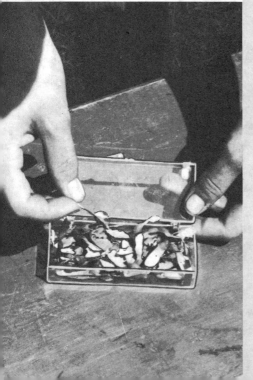

Use small plastic boxes or discarded plastic pill bottles to collect and store tree seeds. These boxes or bottles are light in weight and do not take much space in your pack.

A troop or post wood collection is a useful device for learning to identify trees. It may take time to assemble a collection because you would not want to cut a tree just to get one specimen of wood. Watch for trees being cut along highways or for housing developments and other new construction. Sometimes trees are cut as part of a woodland improvement project in camp or on private land.

Cut 3- to 5-inch-diameter pieces, 10 inches long, as shown here. Sand the surfaces smooth and then varnish them so they do not turn gray or dark.

When pruning branches from a tree, use a sharp saw. First cut upward from under the branch about one-quarter of the way through, as close as possible to the bark.

Then cut down from above being careful not to injure the bark. The undercut prevents the bark from peeling when the branch falls off.

A young tree should be planted at the correct depth, about ¼ inch deeper (never higher) than in the nursery. It is easy to see the old groundline on the tree.

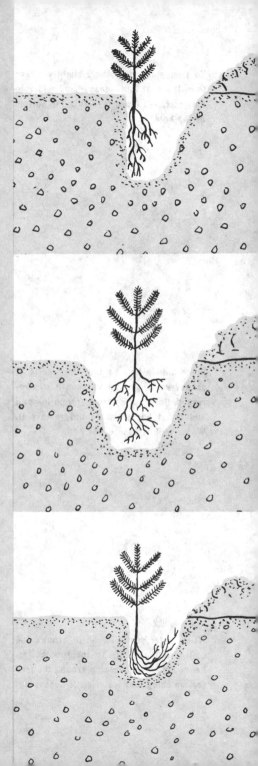

Be sure the main roots are nearly straight, not doubled or sharply bent. This is very important.

If this tree lives it will take a long time to recover from a poor transplanting job. Don't crowd the roots or bend them. If you put a kink in a garden hose, the water shuts off. Roots are like that.

Dig the hole a little wider so that the roots are free to spread. Water. Push the soil around the roots and press down. Fill almost to ground level. Tamp the soil down around the tree and water again.

393

To transplant, dig a hole slightly larger than the root ball—deeper and wider in diameter. Put loose topsoil in the bottom of the hole.

Place ball in hole so that the tree is at same level of ground as when it was removed. Untie burlap from around the ball and lay it back, but do not remove it. Water well at base of the ball.

When water soaks in, fill in around the ball with topsoil up to the root collar. Leave a slight depression around the tree for mulching and watering if necessary.

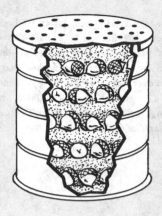

Some trees or shrub seeds must be "stratified" before planting. Here is an easy way to stratify acorns or other nutlike seeds: Punch small holes in the bottom of a coffee can. Place a layer of sand, a layer of seeds, a layer of sand, another layer of seeds until the can is full. Punch holes in the top.

Bury the can a foot or two deep and leave over the winter. In spring, plant the seeds in suitable locations. Get advice from a forester or county agent.

terrarium

Use a widemouthed gallon jar or fish tank to keep a collection of small native plants. Place a layer of gravel on the bottom and cover with sand, then charcoal. Cover the charcoal with a good layer of some soil in which plants are growing. Some forest plants will grow for years in such a terrarium.

If you like the smell of the woods, make a terrarium. Then some icy day next winter, remove the top and take a good "whiff." You'll think you are back out in the wilderness.

For your terrarium, use a goldfish bowl, a fish tank, or even a half gallon or gallon jar, but use some container that can be covered. Put a layer of gravel, then sand on the bottom, and a half inch of charcoal on top of that. Then add 2 or 3 inches of good woodland soil.

On your next hike, collect a few, low-growing ferns, partridgeberry, wintergreen, or other small ground plants. Be sure to get ample roots. Plant them in the terrarium and moisten the soil well. Place the cover on and keep it in a shady spot. For added fragrance, put in some crushed pine or spruce needles.

Make a "grab-bag terrarium." While on a winter hike, dig up a small patch of woodland soil. Take it home intact, and put it in the terrarium. Keep the soil moist for a few weeks and watch to see what comes up.

measuring trees

A forester must know how to estimate the volume of lumber or other products a tree will produce. He does this by measuring the tree. First, he measures the "dbh" (diameter at breastheight)—$4\frac{1}{2}$ feet above the ground. Then he measures the height. By using a prepared volume table, he estimates the volume of the tree in board feet.

To measure the diameter of a tree, the forester uses a special tape measure. You can make one easily. Use the back of an ordinary tape measure or any strip of cloth about I inch wide and 5 to 6 feet long. Starting at one end, use the scale provided here or measure $3\frac{1}{7}$ inches with a ruler and draw a line across the tape. Mark this line "I." From that line measure $3\frac{1}{7}$ inches more and draw a line. Mark this line "2" and so on to the end of the tape.

Measure around the tree trunk at breastheight, just as if this were a regular tape measure. You can read the diameter of the tree, in inches, directly from the numbers you marked on the tape.

1" ←——— 3 1/7" ———→

Foresters often use a cruiser stick to measure tree diameters and heights. This is a combination tool—one side is a Biltmore stick for measuring diameters; on the other side is a hypsometer for measuring height. Make it from a carpenter's rule using the scales on the following pages.

To use your Biltmore stick, hold it horizontally against the tree at breastheight and exactly 25 inches from the eye. Line up the zero end with the outside of the tree. Then, without moving your head, glance at the other side of the tree and read the graduation where your line of sight crosses the stick. That figure is the diameter of the tree.

Diameters measured with a Biltmore stick usually are not as accurate as those measured with a diameter tape.

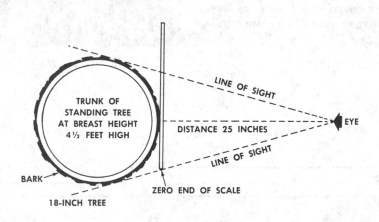

LINE OF SIGHT

TRUNK OF
STANDING TREE
AT BREAST HEIGHT
4½ FEET HIGH

DISTANCE 25 INCHES

EYE

LINE OF SIGHT

BARK

ZERO END OF SCALE

18-INCH TREE

To measure the height of a tree, stand 25 feet from the tree. Hold the hypsometer vertically, 25 inches from your eye. Line up the bottom of the hypsometer with the bottom of the tree. Without moving your head, sight to the top of the tree. Read the number on the hypsometer where your line of sight crosses it. This is the height of the tree in feet. If the tree is more than 24 feet high, stand 50 feet from the tree. Multiply each number on the hypsometer by 2 to find the height in feet. For still larger trees, stand 75 feet from the tree, and multiply each number of the hypsometer by 3. In other words, for each 25 feet you stand from the tree multiply by one higher number.

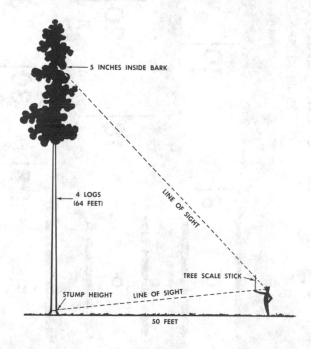

5 INCHES INSIDE BARK

LINE OF SIGHT

4 LOGS
(64 FEET)

TREE SCALE STICK

STUMP HEIGHT · LINE OF SIGHT

50 FEET

THE POCKET BILTMORE STICK
25-INCH REACH

INCHES

6

16   14   12   10   8

26   24   22   20   18

40   38   36   34   32   30   28

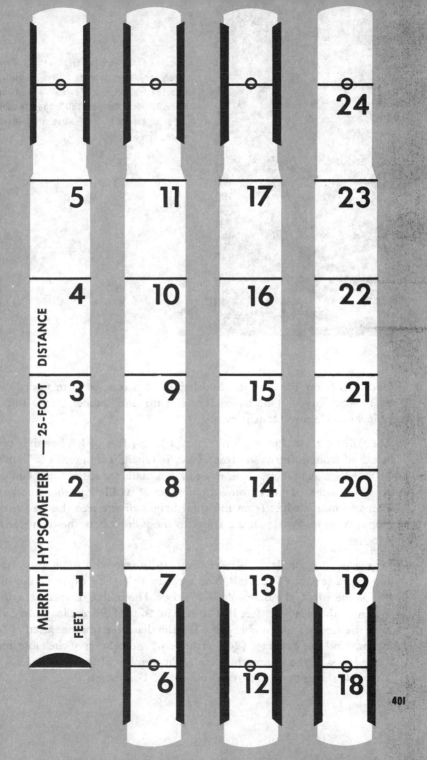

Loading sawlogs is no trick with modern machinery. Here a crane hoists a sawlog into the trailer ready for delivery to the sawmill. How do you think they loaded logs in the old days when they used mules and horses?

Once you know the diameter and height of a tree, you can figure the board-foot volume. One board foot is a piece of lumber 1 inch thick, 12 inches wide, and 12 inches long.

The volume table shows the number of board feet of lumber that can be sawed from different size trees. Note that height is in terms of usable 16-foot logs. A usable sawlog must have a diameter at the small end of at least 8 inches. To determine the number of usable logs in a standing tree, you must deduct from the total height of the tree the estimated length from its top down the trunk to the point where the diameter is 8 inches.

Let's take an example. You have measured a tree with the hypsometer and found it to be 66 feet tall. You estimate that 10 feet down from the top of the trunk, the diameter is 8 inches. The usable or merchantable height of the tree is 66 feet less 10 feet or 56 feet. Since a log is 16 feet long the tree has 3½ usable logs. Say the diameter you measured is 24 inches. Find this diameter (24) in the left-hand column of the table and move across to the column headed by the number of usable logs (3½). The table shows that your tree contains 708 board feet.

The figures in this table are averages determined from the measurements of many trees.

Amount of Saw Timber in Trees

Diameter of Tree at Breastheight (Inches)	Volume (Board Feet) According to Number of Usable 16-Foot Logs								
	1	1½	2	2½	3	3½	4	4½	5
10	39	51	63	72	80				
11	49	64	80	92	104				
12	59	78	98	112	127	136	146		
13	71	96	120	138	156	168	181		
14	83	112	141	164	186	201	216		
15	98	132	166	194	221	240	260		
16	112	151	190	223	256	280	305		
17	128	174	219	258	296	325	354		
18	144	196	248	292	336	369	402		
19	162	222	281	332	382	420	457		
20	181	248	314	370	427	470	512	546	580
21	201	276	350	414	478	526	575	616	656
22	221	304	387	458	528	583	638	685	732
23	244	336	428	507	586	646	706	761	816
24	266	368	469	556	644	708	773	836	899
25	290	402	514	610	706	779	852	922	992
26	315	436	558	662	767	849	931	1,008	1,086
27	341	474	606	721	836	925	1,014	1,100	1,185
28	367	510	654	779	904	1,000	1,096	1,190	1,284
29	396	551	706	842	977	1,080	1,184	1,289	1,394
30	424	591	758	904	1,050	1,161	1,272	1,388	1,503

19 ANIMAL KINGDOM

DID YOU KNOW that any living thing is either plant or animal? This means that worms, snails, ants, fish, and birds, as well as mammals, are animals. Those having similarities are placed in a large group called a phylum. The phyla are arranged from the simplest forms of animal life to the highest or most complex.

PROTOZOA. Mostly microscopic one-celled animals including the amoeba, paramecium, and volvox.

PORIFERA. A few sponges occur in freshwater, but most in the sea. Used for cleaning purposes.

COELENTERATA. Jellyfish, sea anemones, and coral make up this group. Jellyfish have the ability to sting. Coral produce lime deposits.

CTENOPHORA. These are free-swimming marine animals resembling jellyfish called "comb jellies."

PLATYHELMINTHES. Soft, flat, ribbonlike worms of which some are parasites. Flukes and tapeworms live upon animals and humans.

NEMATHELMINTHES. Roundworms include trichina that infects pork, hookworms that bother people, and vinegar eels that swim in cider.

ECHINODERMATA. The spiny-skinned animals contain the starfish, sea urchin, sea cucumber, brittle star, sand dollar, and sea lily.

MOLLUSCA. Animals with soft unsegmented bodies are *cephalopods*—squid and octopus; *bivalves*—oysters, clams, and mussels; and *gastropods*—snails.

ANNELIDA. Segmented worms are the common earthworm, freshwater leeches, and saltwater sandworms and clam worms.

ARTHROPODA. Arthropods are named for having several pairs of jointed legs. Besides *insects* the following classes are members. *Crustaceans* are animals with a hard shell including lobster, crab, shrimp, crayfish, barnacle, and pill bug. *Arachnids* are spiders, scorpions, mites, and ticks. *Myriapods* are centipedes and millipedes.

CHORDATA. The vertebrates (animals with a backbone) form the largest part of this phylum: fishes, amphibians, reptiles, birds, and mammals.

ARACHNIDS

 **INSECTS**

ARTHROPODA

 MYRIAPODS

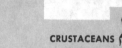 **CRUSTACEANS**

 CEPHALOPODS

 ANNELIDA

MOLLUSCA

 **BIVALVES**

 NEMATE–HELMINTHES

 **GASTROPODS**

CTENOPHORA

 PLATY–HELMINTHES

COELENTERATA

INVERTEBRATES

 PROTOZOA

ANCEST

MAMMALS

BIRDS

REPTILES

AMPHIBIANS

VERTEBRATES

FISHES

CHORDATA

LOWER CHORDATES

ECHINODERMATA

INVERTEBRATES

OTOZOA

PORIFERA

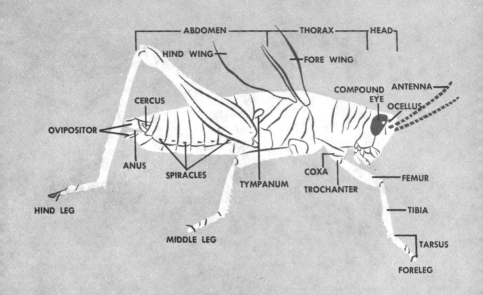

ABDOMEN — THORAX — HEAD

HIND WING — FORE WING

COMPOUND EYE — ANTENNA

CERCUS — OCELLUS

OVIPOSITOR

ANUS — SPIRACLES — TYMPANUM — COXA — FEMUR

TROCHANTER

HIND LEG — TIBIA

MIDDLE LEG — TARSUS

FORELEG

Insects

Wherever you hike or camp at anytime of the year, you can have fun watching or collecting insects. Insects are found everywhere and more than 600,000 kinds have been described. It has been said that anyone can find 1,000 different kinds almost anywhere, if he looks for small ones as well as the large insects that are more easily seen. To get the most fun out of watching or collecting insects, you should know which insect you see. At least you should know the general type of insect even if you cannot determine the exact species.

First of all, though, what is an insect? How does it differ from other forms of animal life? Take along a magnifying glass on your next hike, catch an insect and see for yourself. Simply, you will see that an adult insect always has six jointed legs and a jointed body. When not yet an adult, an insect may be a caterpillar, a wood-boring larva, or an underwater creature that darts around like a miniature fish. But when full grown, it has three pair of legs and its jointed body is divided into three parts: a head, a middle body or thorax, and an abdomen. Some insects have wings, some such as the walking stick do not.

All insects start out as eggs, layed by the female on leaves, in the ground, on trees, or in the water. But insects become adults in different ways. Insects, such as the beetles, butterflies, moths, flies, bees, and others, go through four stages. The egg hatches into a caterpillar or larva which feeds actively and grows. When the larva reaches its maximum size, it weaves a cocoon around itself. Within the cocoon the tissues are changed into those of the adult. Finally, the adult breaks from the cocoon and emerges as a moth or other insect.

Some insects, such as the dragonfly, go through only three stages. The eggs are laid in water or on water plants. The eggs hatch into nymphs that live underwater and breathe through gills. The nymph grows, and as it grows it molts—sheds its skin and grows a new one. When the nymph is full grown, it climbs out of the water. Its skin splits open, and the adult insect emerges.

Insects, such as grasshoppers and praying mantises, go through two stages. The eggs hatch into miniature replicas of the adult. The insect grows, molts, grows, and molts until it reaches full growth.

Only adult insects have wings. These wings appear at the end of the last molt. When an insect has wings, you can be sure it has grown as much as it ever will. Thus, small bumblebees flying through the flowers will never become larger bumblebees, or small flies annoying you as you hike will never become large flies.

By looking carefully at the head of an insect, you can get an idea of what it eats. Butterflies and moths have sucking tubes for taking nectar. Plant lice and squash bugs have sucking beaks with which they get plant sap. Grasshoppers have jaws for chewing leaves and praying mantises have jaws for eating other insects. As you watch or collect them, try to find out more than just an insect's name. Try to see what it eats and how it lives.

relatives

The nymphs of insects that live in ponds and streams are fun to collect, take home, and watch. Some are quite ferocious looking and acting little creatures, and may eat others in your aquarium or jar. Stone flies, mayflies, damselflies, dragonflies, water bugs, dobsonflies, water beetles, and crane flies are some to look for. At this stage they hardly look like insects.

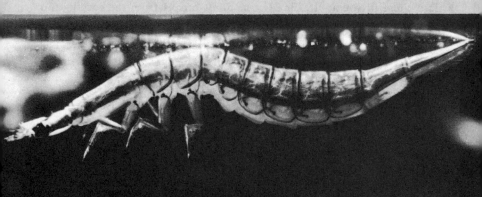

Millipedes, found in damp places and usually in decaying vegetation, are not insects. They have two pair of legs on most of their body segments. Some are one-tenth of an inch long while others may be 4 inches.

Centipedes, not insects either, have quite long antennae and one pair of legs on each segment of their body. They have claws behind their head to kill their prey. They eat insects and spiders.

Spiders are different from insects in that they have four pair of legs and two body segments. All spiders can spin webs to protect their eggs or capture food. They eat insects.

Crayfish, distantly related to insects, live in water or wet meadows. They are from 3 to 6 inches long, have a hard outer shell with five pair of legs. The front pair have claws for catching food.

411

insect groups

When the early biologists divided the insect kingdom, they chose the wings as the mark of distinction. They placed many insects into groups called "orders." For example, the name "hymenoptera" was given to the order that have membranelike wings. Insects in this order have four wings, the two pair of wings lock together so that they act as a single pair when the insect flies. Bees, wasps, and ants are in this group.

There are eight main orders and a number of minor ones. Probably 90 percent of all the insects you will find belong to one of these eight orders. When you can place an insect in the correct order, you are taking an important step in finding its name or species. The following orders are arranged according to the names of species they contain.

Beetles. Typical of this group is the june beetle which is frequently heard droning around streetlights or dashing against window screens at night. Others in this group are tiger beetles, ground beetles, water beetles, and lady beetles.

Bees and Wasps. Well known in this group is the bumblebee most frequently seen darting through fields of clover in search of nectar and pollen. Others in this group are ants, sawflies, and ichneumons. The most highly developed insects are in this group.

Butterflies and Moths. The attractive patterns on the wings of these insects are produced by tiny shinglelike scales that rub off when you handle them.

412

Flies. This group includes many pests of man and beast. Mosquitoes, houseflies, fruit flies, botflies, midges, and robber flies belong in this group. Maggots are larvae of flies.

True Bugs. These insects have a sucking beak. Their wings fold flat over their back. True bugs include water striders, giant water bugs, chinch bugs, ambush bugs, squash bugs, stinkbugs, and bedbugs.

Grasshoppers and Crickets. Insects in this group have mouth parts formed for chewing. Grasshoppers and crickets eat plant materials. Mantises, also in this grouping, eat other insects.

Dragonflies. These are strong-flying insects that eat other insects. They capture their prey on the wing. Some dragonflies may live as long as 3 years as underwater nymphs before they emerge as adults.

Aphids. Small and mostly wingless, these tiny sapsuckers are preyed upon by many larger insects. They survive by their rapid rate of reproduction.

413

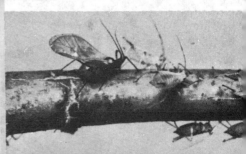

insect pets

One of the most dramatic things that you are apt to see in watching insects is the emergence of a butterfly from its cocoon. The cocoons of some butterflies may be taken home and watched until the butterfly emerges. Place the cocoon between a window and a screen on the shady side of the house. When the adult emerges, feed it a mixture of sugar and water in a sponge. The butterfly will uncoil its proboscis and insert it in the holes to feed upon the syrup.

Several kinds of insects can be captured alive, taken home in small cages or collecting boxes, and kept quite successfully. You can have a lot of fun and learn more from watching live insects.

The larvae of several butterflies and moths can be kept quite easily, if you pay attention to their needs. Be sure to note what plant or tree a larva is feeding on when you find it. Keep feeding it the same food. It can't change diets and frequently starves to death rather than change to another food. The larva can be kept in a shoebox covered with netting.

Use a lamp chimney covered with screen or cheesecloth and a can or flowerpot filled with soil to make an insect zoo.

An ant house is easy to make, and an ant colony is easy to collect. Watch them for a few weeks and you will see why ants are among the most highly developed of all insects.

414

A tin can set in the ground and baited with meat or fish makes an effective beetle trap. Beetles fall in and cannot climb out.

Hold an umbrella under a shrub, while you beat the branches with a stick. Insects will fall into the umbrella where they are easily captured.

If you are not sure whether you have a moth or a butterfly, keep the larva in a box with a layer of earth on the bottom. Moths, many of them, transform from larvae to adults in the ground. When you are digging in the earth you may discover these pupa cases which can be placed in sphagnum moss and sprinkled with water from time to time until the adult emerges.

Grasshoppers, katydids, praying mantises, and crickets make good pets and provide their own kind of music as well. Feed them lettuce and other greens with small bits of meat or bone meal. The bone meal is important, because without it or meat the crickets will eat each other. The praying mantis eats other insects but will eat raw hamburger as a substitute.

Several kinds of beetles and true bugs may be kept as pets as long as you feed them the same plant leaves where you found them. Whatever insects you try to keep, watch them for a few minutes each day. Try to learn all you can about them. There is still much that is not known about some of our most common insects.

collecting insects

Without any equipment at all, you can have fun watching insects, finding out what they eat, how they eat, how they use their legs to walk, where they lay their eggs, and what they look like in various stages of development. But if you want to start collecting, you will need several pieces of equipment, most of which you can make or easily acquire.

COLLECTING NET. You can buy collecting nets or make one for yourself. All you need is a 3-foot section of broom handle, a 5-foot piece of heavy wire, some strong tape, and a 3- by 5-foot piece of mosquito netting.

KILLING BOTTLE. Insects should be killed quickly after capture. Use a widemouthed jar, with cotton in the bottom. Dampen the cotton with nail-polish remover. Put a piece of cardboard over the cotton, and insert a layer of dry cotton covered by another piece of cardboard.

A PAIR OF TWEEZERS. You need these for handling insects without damaging them. Perhaps you have a pair in your first aid kit.

A COLLECTION OF JARS AND PILL BOTTLES. These are for storing insects in the field and for carrying them home.

A NOTEBOOK. Keep accurate notes on what you observe and on what you collect. Later you will want to label each insect with the date and place collected and any interesting information about it.

A MAGNIFYING GLASS. This may be an inexpensive magnifier or a more expensive 5-7-10 power pocket lens.

SPECIMEN BOXES. At first, make these of cigar boxes with corrugated cardboard on the bottom. Later on, you may want to buy better cases.

INSECT PINS. Buy insect pins from a biological supply house or hobby shop. They are thinner than common pins and will not rust or corrode.

SPREADING BOARD. You can buy a spreading board or make one from two pieces of cedar clapboards, two pieces of furring strip, and some plywood.

DIP NET. If you want to collect insect larvae in the water, you will need a stronger and differently shaped net. You can buy or make them.

PAPER TRIANGLES. Make a dozen or two of these to take with you in the field. Use them to protect butterflies and moths until you can mount them in a specimen box.

Storage bottles

Magnifying glass

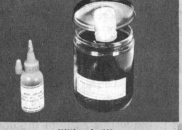

Killing bottle

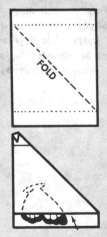

Dip net

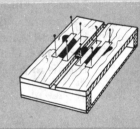

Spreading board

Paper triangles

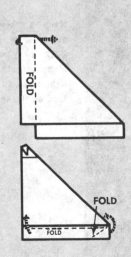

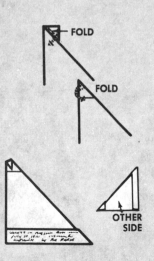

collecting hints

Instead of walking around and looking for insects, sometimes you can make them come to you. You do it by putting out bait that attracts them. Interestingly enough decaying animal and plant materials make the best bait. Fermenting grapes and apples are excellent baits. Mash the spoiled fruit and place on tops of stumps or rocks in a place where you have seen butterflies. Visit the bait from time to time with your net.

Moths can be attracted in much the same way. Mash some peaches or dried apricots and set them in a warm place until they ferment. Then mix them with some sugar until you have a paste.

Use a paintbrush to apply this paste to the downwind side of several tree trunks. Do this about dusk. Pick trees on the edges of woods or hedgerows. After dark, visit the baits with a flashlight and net and look for moths. Other insects will visit the bait during the day. Another trick is to collect cocoons and wait for them to hatch. Select a female

Hang a sheet from a clothesline. At night, shine a strong light behind it. Back away and watch what happens. Many insects will be attracted to the light and can be easily caught as they land on the sheet.

You can find out what your captured insects prefer to eat in this food preference box. Put a different food in each compartment and let the insects go from one compartment to another. What food did they eat first? What did they prefer?

Before you pin an insect for a specimen collection, study this illustration. Each order of insects has a different body structure, therefore, be careful so that the least damage will be done. The illustration shows where to place the pin in each order. Dermestid beetles become part of your collection and destroy it if you don't keep one or two mothballs in the box.

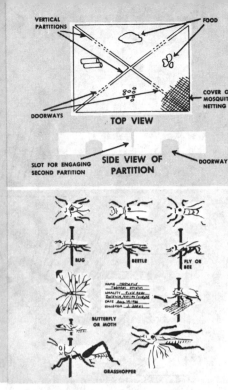

moth and place her in a wire-covered box. Place the box out in the open. Many times male moths will be attracted by the female moth.

In removing a struggling butterfly from a net, you can quiet it and prevent it from damaging its wings by giving the thorax a sharp pinch. In handling butterflies and moth specimens use tweezers to grasp a leg or the antennae.

Often the abdomen of a dragonfly breaks off when the insect dries out. Before the body hardens, insert a slender pin or bristle from a brush from the tip of the abdomen forward into the thorax.

If you cannot put butterflies or moths on a spreading board immediately, and they become dry and stiff, place them in a tightly covered box or jar containing a piece of moist blotter paper or cotton. In 24 hours, they should be relaxed enough to place on the spreading board.

As you collect insects remember to write down all you can about their habits—how they fly, their favorite resting places, their favorite food, and similar information. It will help you in future expeditions.

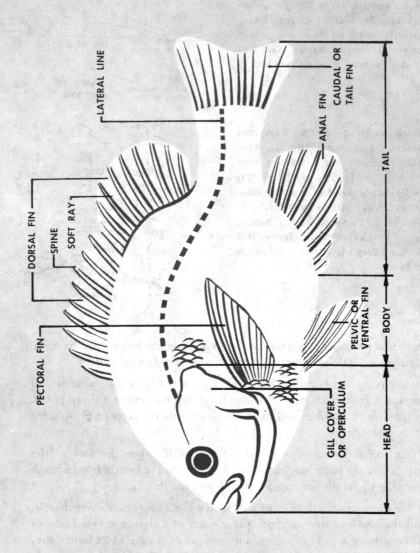

LATERAL LINE

ANAL FIN

CAUDAL OR TAIL FIN

TAIL

DORSAL FIN

SPINE

SOFT RAY

PELVIC OR
VENTRAL FIN

BODY

PECTORAL FIN

GILL COVER
OR OPERCULUM

HEAD

Fish

Judging by the number of people who go fishing each year, fish are the most popular of all animals. It is doubtful, though, that many fishermen are concerned about fish as animals. They are attracted by the fun of fishing and partly by the enjoyment of eating self-caught fish.

But many people are interested in fish for a different reason—money. Commercial fishing is an important industry from Maine to Hawaii and from Alaska to the Gulf of Mexico. Sport fishing is the basis also, of an even greater industry—that of supplying tackle and other equipment to fishermen.

Fish, however, can be tremendously interesting as animals. The naturalist, studying the world of nature, can have many fascinating hours finding out how fish live and something of their relationship to other animals, to plants, and to their environment.

But first it is important to know something about fish in general and how they differ from other animals. Many of these things you may know already.

Fish are cold-blooded animals with an internal skeleton. They live in water and breathe by means of gills, using oxygen that is dissolved in the water (not the O of H_2O). Most fishes have two pairs of fins and three single fins. (The word "fishes" is used to refer to two or more species, while "fish" refers to two or more of the same kind.)

Fish may be placed in five groups—those that live in freshwater but spawn in salt water (eels); those that live in salt water and spawn in freshwater (Pacific salmon and shad); those that live in salt water only (bluefish, albacore, or codfish); those that live in freshwater (black bass, pike or channel catfish); those that live in the brackish water part of the time and in freshwater or salt water part of the time (white perch).

Fish are affected by water temperature, light, amount of oxygen in the water, differences in chemicals in the water, depth of the water, currents, and the amount of silt or other pollution. Fish, such as trout, need clear, cold water and abundant oxygen. Carp, on the other hand, can live in warm, muddy water with much less oxygen. Most fish have definite temperature requirements for spawning.

Fish have been classified by scientists into groups according to similarity of structure: mouth, teeth, skeleton, and scales. The major groups are illustrated and described below and on the next three pages.

Sharks and Rays. These primitive fishes have changed little in 100 million years. They do not have bones. They have skeletons of cartilage. They live in salt water.

The Herring Family. These are fishes with forked tails, fins without spines, pelvic fins on the abdomen and no adipose fin. As a group, they are the most important of all fish caught commercially. Generally, they live in salt water, and some spawn in freshwater.

Salmon and Trout. Several kinds of Pacific salmon live in the ocean until they return to freshwater to spawn. Various kinds of trout live in clear, cold streams and lakes. Note adipose fin behind dorsal.

422

Whitefish. This group related to salmon, also lives in clear, cold water, both in lakes and streams. Smelt live in salt water close to shore migrating into streams to spawn.

Eels. These fish, that look more like snakes, were a mystery until fairly recently. The American eel spawns in the ocean south of Bermuda. Young eels live in bays, rivers, and lakes until old enough to spawn. There are no spines in their fins, and their tiny scales are embedded in the skin.

Suckers. This is a large family of fish that is widely distributed in freshwaters of the United States. Generally, they feed on the bottom and have thick lips. They have large, coarse scales. They eat both plant and animal materials. They spawn in the spring.

Minnows. This is the largest group of freshwater fishes. Although most minnows are small, carp may grow to 3 feet and squawfish to 5 feet. Dace, chubs, and shiners serve as food for many other fishes and for several kinds of birds.

Catfish. There are more than 30 species; most have smooth bodies without scales and long barbels around the mouth. Their dorsal fins have spines. They eat both plant and animal materials.

Pike, Pickerel, Muskellunge. This is a small but popular group, with long narrow jaws and sharp teeth. Their dorsal fins have no spines and they have large anal fins. Most of them are important as game fishes. They eat smaller fish, crayfish, and sometimes young ducks.

Killifish. These are small fishes, 2 to 4 inches long, that live in ponds, streams, and salt marshes. Their tails are rounded or square and their scales large. They have small mouths and feed on insect larvae and small plants. Some are important as destroyers of mosquito larvae.

Codfish and Haddock. These saltwater fishes generally live in deep, cold water. They have three dorsal fins, and two anal fins. They feed on small fish, crabs, and other saltwater animal life.

Flounders and Halibut. These are bottom fish that swim on their sides. Both eyes are on the same side of their head. They have a long dorsal and anal fin without spines. Flounders may weigh 7 or 8 pounds. Most are smaller. Halibut, important as a commercial fish, weigh from 20 to 400 pounds.

Mackerel, Tuna, Bluefish. This is a famous group of saltwater game fishes. In it are albacore, bonito, marlins, sailfish, swordfish, and others. They have deeply forked tails.

Perch and Walleyes. These freshwater fishes are also sought after by fishermen. They have two dorsal fins, with spines. Yellow perch generally are small, but weigh a pound. Walleyes may weigh up to 10 pounds. These fishes eat insects, smaller fish, and crayfish.

Bass. Members of this group live in both salt and freshwater, and include sea bass, striped bass, groupers (salt water) and white and yellow bass (freshwater). They too are important as game fish. They closely resemble the sunfish family.

Sunfish. This group includes the sunfishes, crappies, and the so-called black basses, most of them game or pan fishes. They generally prefer the warmer lakes and streams. They have a single, spined dorsal fin. Sunfishes generally have small mouths, bass large mouths, with crappies coming in between.

425

things to do

Fish are not so easy to observe as birds or other animals, and at first you might think you cannot do much about fish except catch and eat them. But there are other things to do that will help you find out more about the fishes of your locality and how they live.

Visit a fishing tackle shop or talk with an old-time fisherman. Ask your conservation officer for information. Find out what fish are caught locally. Then read about the life history of these species. Find out the temperature at which they spawn, feed, and generally are most active. Find out the depth at which they usually live, and what they eat. Find out all you can about them.

Go out to a stream or pond and try to see fish. Early in the morning, late in the afternoon, and after dark are good times. During the day, conceal yourself in shrubbery or a small tent and watch the shallows. Fish may come in to feed or you may see schools of young fish or small fish swimming by. At night use a strong light. Sometimes in a small pond, you can throw grasshoppers or crickets out in the water, and see fish jump for them.

Look, too, for fishnests. Bass and sunfish build a saucer-shaped nest on the bottom in water from 1 to 6 feet or more deep. The males guard the eggs and the young in the nest. If you find a nest, with an adult fish over it, drop a piece of wood on the water or any other small object that floats. Watch to see what happens, but don't let the fish see you or your shadow.

Check the water temperature at different depths with a thermometer. See if there is any relation between fish activity and water temperature. Walk along in the shallow water of a stream or lake with a rocky bottom. Turn over the rocks carefully and see what insects or other animals you find that fish may eat.

Keep a careful record of any fishing trips you take, with notes on time of day, the weather, the air and water temperatures, how many and what kinds of fish you caught, where you caught them, what kind of bait and how deep, and other important information. After several trips, you may be able to discover why you did better at some times than at others. You may improve as a fisherman.

Make or buy a minnow trap made of hardware cloth. Bait it with uncooked oatmeal or bread crusts. Place in a muddy place in a lake or stream. It is an easy way to catch small fish. Check conservation laws first to find any limitations for minnow traps.

Make or buy a "fishscope" or "fish glass." If you make one, cut a hole in the bottom of a 5-gallon can and cement a piece of glass over the hole. Paint the inside black. Hold it with the bottom a few inches underwater, and look for fish and other water animals.

finding fish

Bass, pickerel, and pan-fish rest and feed along the shore near logs and in weed beds of lakes and ponds.

DEEP WATER

PICKEREL

BASS

PANFISH

In streams, fish rest downstream of rocks and feed in the swift water where food is carried by the current.

RESTING FISH

FEEDING RAINBOW

FEEDING BROWN

429

internal structure

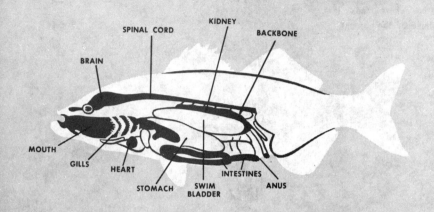

The next time you catch a fish—any small fish—try to find out what it has been eating. In the process, look at and try to identify some of its other internal organs. Finding out what fish eat at any particular time may help you catch more.

Use a sharp knife and slit the fish up the belly very carefully. The knife point should be no deeper than necessary to cut the skin. Hold the fish open with your fingers or two short pieces of stick and use a pointed match or toothpick to locate the heart, stomach, swim bladder, and kidneys. Carefully pull out the stomach and cut it open.

You may find small bits of insects, either adult or nymph; other small fish; crayfish or small bits of plant materials. You may not be able to identify the food exactly, but you will get an idea of what the fish has been eating.

If you are a beginning fisherman, using an inexpensive cane pole outfit with live bait is a good way to start. You can catch sunfish, perch, crappies, bass, and some saltwater fishes. But even experts sometimes still-fish with a cane pole as the best way of catching some fish.

Still-fishing from a boat with a cane pole outfit or a rod and reel with bobber and live bait is fun. You can cover more water, weed beds, rocky areas, or drop-offs that you can't reach from shore. Trolling is another way of fishing for both freshwater and salt water game fish. It takes specialized tackle, but the biggest fish caught with rod and reel are captured in this way. Lake trout, pike, and muskellunge are caught by trolling in freshwater, while sailfish, tuna, swordfish, and albacore are caught in salt water.

Real sport comes from being skilled with a spinning outfit. You cast your lure to the spot where you hope a big fish waits and hope he is in a feeding mood. When he hits, you have a fight on your hands that you will remember for years to come.

431

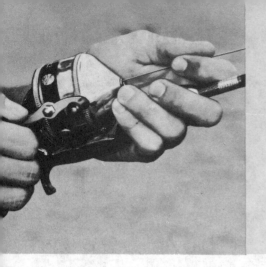

Spin casting is a modern version of bait casting. The advantage is that you do not get backlashes and you can cast much lighter lures. There is a fixed reel seat for the spin-casting reel. An 8 to 15-pound test monofilament line is recommended.

Fishing is a sport enjoyed by many million Americans each year, for there are fish of one kind or another nearly anyplace in the country where there is ample unpolluted water.

How much fun you have fishing depends largely on your attitude. If your only objective is fish in the frying pan, there will be many days when you will not have much fun. But if you enjoy being outdoors, on the water, and look at fishing as a sport whether you catch fish or not, you will have fun and will soon belong to the fraternity of millions of other followers of Izaak Walton.

The fellows who have the most fun catching fish are the ones who use the lightest tackle possible, consistent with size of the fish they expect to catch. For example, you could use a stiff cane pole and heavy line with a worm for bait and catch a 6-inch sunfish. You could also use a light flyrod with a very fine nylon leader and dry flies for lures, and then catch the same fish. Which would be more fun? A 2-pound bass caught on very light tackle and artificial flies can provide all the excitement of a 100-pound tuna on much heavier tackle. The thing that is fun is the fight the fish puts up, and you cannot appreciate that fight if your tackle is too heavy and cumbersome.

Contrary to what you might think, fishing may be poor in a lake or pond

One form of fishing that requires a high degree of skill, to be consistently successful, is fly-fishing. A skilled fly-fisherman catches fish that weigh as much as 40 pounds on a rod that weighs a very few ounces and leaders that have a breaking strength of 5 pounds.

because there are too many fish instead of too few. The reason is this: Fish lay a great many eggs, some of them way up in the thousands. One study of a northern lake showed an average production of a half million young fish per acre per year. Naturally, a great many must die if a few hundred are to grow to large size. Otherwise, there wouldn't be enough food to go around.

The rate of growth of a fish depends upon how much it eats, provided temperature and other conditions are favorable. A 2-inch bass and a 10-inch bass, for example, may be the same age. Well-fed fish keep on growing as long as they live. Poorly fed fish stop growing.

A lake or pond may have in it more fish than its food supply can support. Thus there would be many fish that were not growing—many fish that would not be much fun to catch. There would be a few big fish— but they would have an abundant food supply (the smaller fish) and would not be attracted by your lure or bait. That is the situation in some lakes that are said to be "fished out."

One partial solution is to fish the lake more heavily and remove as many small panfish as possible. Biologists help solve the problem in other ways. They treat the lake with chemicals that kill large numbers of fish, in an attempt to get the fish population in balance with the food supply.

how to clean

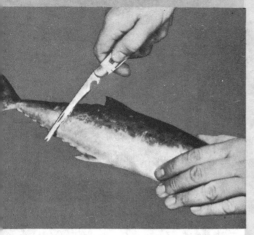

First, scale the fish, unless you intend to skin it. Some knives have scalers on them, or you can use a special scaler made for that purpose. Try skinning some fish. You may be surprised how different they taste.

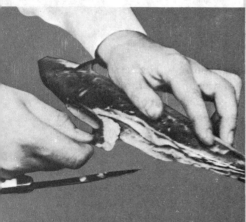

Next, remove the dorsal fin by cutting along both sides of the fin and removing it and the bones that are attached to it. Remove the pelvic fins at the same time.

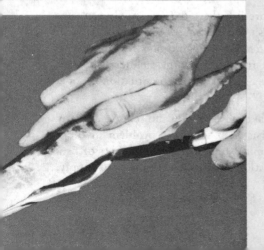

Slit the fish from vent to throat, with the knife point just under the skin. Do not cut internal organs. Place the fish on its belly and cut through the spine just behind the head and gills. Hold the body in your left hand and pull the head off with your right. The internal organs will come out at the same time. Wash thoroughly inside and out.

age and population

If you fish frequently in one small stream or pond, take a pair of shears and try fin clipping. When you catch a fish, cut off one of the paired fins. This will not bother the fish to any great extent if you do not cut into the body. By fin-clipping and carefully returning a known number of fish to the water, you can get a rough idea of the number of fish present. For example, if 10 percent of the fish caught in the next few months are fin-clipped, there are roughly 10 times the number of fish of the size that you marked. This method is not exact, but it will tell you whether most of that size of fish are being caught or whether you are catching only a small number of all the fish of that size.

Fishery biologists can tell the age of some fish by examining the scales under a microscope. Scales get larger as the fish gets older, and rings are formed on the scale. During the winter, most fish do not feed as much, and temporarily stop growing. The interruption in growth is marked by a dark band. This scale is from a fish that is 3½ years old.

Reptiles and Amphibians

What are reptiles and amphibians? How do they differ from other animals? For one thing, they are cold blooded and have internal skeletons (vertebrae). For another, as adults they breathe air with lungs.

Amphibians start out life in water or at least in moist habitats. Adults, in general, live on land. There are some exceptions. Frogs, salamanders, toads, and newts are amphibians. And so is the mud puppy shown at the left.

Reptiles—snakes, lizards, and turtles—are born or hatched on land. At birth they resemble their parents. They all have scales, plates, or horny shields. The alligator, of course, is a reptile.

Because of their habits and dependence upon definite types of habitats, certain reptiles and amphibians may be characteristic of one section of the country while they are rare or lacking in another. Thus, the salamanders, which depend very largely upon moist conditions, are especially abundant in forested regions. Frogs have a somewhat similar distribution, although toads can stand drier conditions and live in deserts. Turtles are most abundant in the East, because they need moisture, while lizards are plentiful in the Southwest because moisture is not so important to them. The alligator ranges along the coast from the Carolinas to Texas and north in the Mississippi Valley to Arkansas. The crocodile is found in the United States only south of Lake Worth, Florida. Our amphibians and reptiles are most common in the South.

Long before you try to collect these animals, be sure you can identify the four groups of poisonous snakes. If you are in the Southwest, be sure that you know the poisonous gila monster, which is a lizard. Study color pictures in a book on snakes, and better yet, visit a museum or zoo and look at live or mounted specimens. Then check with your conservation officer and other experienced outdoorsmen to see what amphibians and reptiles that you may see where you live and where you camp. Know too, and know well, first aid for snakebite.

Red-Spotted Newt. The olive-green adults are found in ponds, lakes, and marshes. The red eft, or land form, is bright orange. The newt and eft have red spots circled in black.

Tiger Salamander. The adult stage is easily recognized by its yellowish markings against a dark background. It breeds in ponds, lakes, stock tanks, and temporary water. Some greenish larvae remain and breed in the water, never reaching the land stage.

Two-Lined Salamander. A dull brown salamander with a lighter, yellowish band on the back from the snout to the tail. It is marked by a dark line on each side and spots along the back. It is found along brooks, under stones and logs in the moist soil. It is at home in the water, but occasionally is found in drier sites.

Toad. Thirteen different species are found in the United States. They all appear somewhat similar, having dry, warty skins. Toads hop rather than leap and seek protection by burrowing. They eat a variety of insects and other small animals. They breed in water, laying eggs in long, jellylike strings that hatch into black tadpoles.

Gray Tree Frog. Commonly called hyla or tree "toad." The tree frog and the spring peeper live in shrubs and low trees near the water. The sticky pads on their toes enable them to cling and climb.

Bullfrogs. This largest frog is green above and white below. It lives along the edges of lakes, ponds, and marshes. Both male and female have loud voices. Source of commercial frogs' legs.

Leopard Frog. A brown or green frog with two or three rows of dark spots with light borders. Commonly called a meadow frog because it inhabits moist, grassy meadows. Leopard frogs range over much of the country exclusive of all but small areas of the Pacific States. Often used as a laboratory animal for biology study.

Chuckwalla. A large lizard of the rocky desert regions in the Southwest. The chuckwalla feeds on the fruit and flowers of cactus. If discovered in a crevice, it can inflate its body and becomes hard to dislodge. The adults are usually dull brown above and reddish on the abdomen, some have dark bands on the tail.

Horned Lizard. Commonly called "horned toads." This little lizard lives in the West and gets its name from the spines on its head and sides. They are active in the heat of the day eating pill bugs, spiders, and ants. If kept as pets, they require high temperatures to stimulate feeding. Some lay eggs, while others bear living young.

Glass Lizard. This legless lizard is commonly called a glass "snake." It has movable eyelids and external ear openings that a snake does not have. The brittle tail grows back, if broken.

439

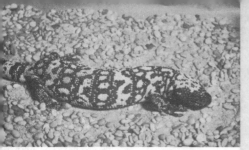

Gila Monster. Pronounced heela. This is our largest and only poisonous lizard. It lives in the desert regions of the Southwest. Clumsy looking, but can move swiftly. Feeds at night.

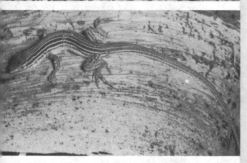

Six-Lined Lizard. Commonly called racerunner. Widely distributed from Delaware to Arizona and likes dry, sandy areas. It burrows for night shelter and feeds during the day on insects, worms, and snails. The six pale lines run the length of the dark brown body. The abdomen is white or bluish white.

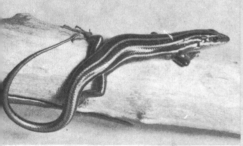

Five-Lined Skink. When young, this lizard has a blue tail and distinct yellow lines running the length of its black body. So, it is known as a blue-tailed skink. Later, the stripes fade, the body turns dull brown, the tail turns from blue to gray; and males develop a reddish head. These fast-moving lizards are widely distributed.

Hognose Snake. This harmless snake is commonly called puff adder because it hisses and puffs when it is molested. If that act does not fool the tormentor, it rolls over and plays dead. Its hard, turned-up nose enables this snake to burrow in search of toads. Ranges from New Hampshire to Arizona.

Black Snake. There are two. One is the aggressive black racer with a little white on the throat. The other is the pilot snake that nests in hollow trees.

Bull Snake. A big snake averaging 5 feet long found on the prairies. Its cousin in the East is the pine snake, and in the West the gopher snake. Eats rodents.

Snapping Turtle. A large dangerous turtle that can inflict a painful wound with its powerful jaws. They live in the water and feed on fish, other aquatic life, waterfowl, and some vegetation. The snapper may live in any body of freshwater and may enter brackish water. It ranges from the Atlantic in the East to the Rocky Mountains in the West.

Pacific Turtle. The only freshwater turtle of the Pacific region. It lives in mountain lakes and slow streams, is shy and remains in the water most of the time. It suns itself on logs and rocks, and drops into the water when alarmed. Feeds on small aquatic animals and vegetation.

Box Turtle. A land-dwelling turtle that can close its shell tightly when alarmed. It prefers woodland or damp areas and feeds on berries, vegetation, insects, snails, slugs, and earthworms. The eastern and western species make good pets and will eat chopped meat, fruit, and greens or lettuce.

Gopher Tortoise. This slow-moving land turtle prefers dry, sandy areas in which it can dig the burrows where it lives. Many other animals live in these "gopher" burrows, including owls.

441

poisonous

Rattlesnakes may occur in every State except Alaska and Hawaii. The diamondback is the largest and the pigmy rattler the smallest. Between are the massasauga, timber, and prairie rattlers.

Next widest in distribution is the copperhead. They are found from New England to Kansas and south to Texas and Florida. The name comes from the bronze or copper colored top of the head. They may grow to 4 or 5 feet but the average is half that size.

Water moccasins, as the name implies, live in or close to water. They are also called cottonmouths because of the white color inside the mouth. These snakes, in general, are fighters and frequently stand their ground as you approach. Most non-poisonous snakes will retreat.

Coral snakes are the smallest and most brightly colored of the poisonous snakes. If you see a snake with red and yellow bands that touch each other, it is a coral snake. They are found from North Carolina to southern Arizona.

442

collecting hints

Be alert at all times. If you are not, you may step on a poisonous snake or miss seeing a valuable specimen. Never go into the field without a first aid kit and a certain knowledge of how to use it. Always go with a companion. He may help you catch a specimen you might not be able to capture alone, and he could help you in an emergency.

Look under flat rocks, boards, logs, and in rotten logs or stumps for specimens. Almost all kinds of reptiles and amphibians seek shelter in such places. But, do not lift rocks or boards with your bare hands, or do not poke your hand into a hole in the ground or under rocks. Use a lever or collecting hook.

Remember to replace all rocks and boards where you found them. When stepping over logs, or stone walls, look first. When climbing a ledge, look first before you reach up with your hands. Wear high boots in poisonous snake country. Be careful or cautious for two reasons. First, because you can avoid snakebite; and second, you can be more successful in collecting specimens.

Collect only the number of specimens that you can care for and feed properly. Before you start collecting, have cages, terrariums, and aquariums all ready for your specimens. Do not put too many specimens in one container. Reptiles and amphibians do not do well when crowded. Before you collect live specimens know what they eat, and have the proper food ready for them.

Check the conservation laws of your State. In some places, turtles and frogs are protected in one way or another. Your sporting goods store or conservation officer can give you a copy of the game laws.

Spring in most parts of the country is the best time to look for reptiles and amphibians. They are just coming out of hibernation, and are hungry. Most of them are hunting for mates at this time of year and are more active.

Fall is the next best time, until cold weather sets in. Turtles, water snakes, and frogs may be found in summer, but many kinds avoid the hot sun. They hide in the daytime and are active at night.

Keep careful and accurate notes on what you see and what you collect. Record the date, place, description of habitat, and weather.

A plastic or glass aquarium tank can be made into a terrarium for keeping lizards or toads. With water in one end and rocks in the other, turtles, salamanders, or frogs may be kept alive. Small snakes may also be kept in a terrarium. Cover the top with a piece of glass.

Widemouthed gallon jars make good temporary quarters for small specimens. Be sure to keep all cages or aquariums clean at all times. Do not put in more food than an animal will eat at one time.

A hole in the ground makes a good turtle pit in camp. Dig it large enough so the turtle can move around, and deep enough so it cannot climb out. Fill in the hole when you leave camp.

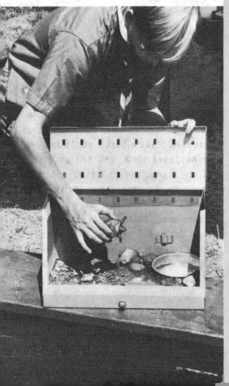

The small-animal cage shown here is one that you may purchase. If you make a cage for keeping snakes at home, use glass on the sides and fine mesh screening on the top and over ventilation holes. Attach some sort of catch so that the top cannot be opened accidentally or forced open by the snake.

food for pets

You'll be more successful feeding captive amphibians and reptiles if you feed them with their natural food. When that is not possible, you'll have to experiment with various foods. Keep notes on when you feed them, what they ate, and how much they ate. Variety of food and regularity of feeding is important. Recognize, too, that in wintertime many specimens should be allowed to hibernate.

FROGS AND TOADS   Live, soft bodied insects, such as mealworms or other soft grubs; small moths or flies. Will also eat small earthworms, or pieces of worm.

To make a trap for small snapping or other water turtles, start with four pine or spruce logs, 4 inches in diameter. Notch the logs, and nail them together in a square. Make a basket of chicken wire or hardware cloth, and nail on bottom of log frame. Set in water, and mark waterline as logs float. Drive large nails I inch into logs at waterline, 2 inches apart. Place trap in water and use dead fish or old meat as bait. Turtles can crawl into trap, but have difficulty climbing out because nails catch the bottom of their shells.

SNAKES	Usually fussy about their food. Some will eat chopped raw fish or meat, earthworms, grubs, mealworms, or other insects. Others want live mice, toads, small snakes, or lizards, or very small eggs.
POLLYWOGS	Microscopic life in fresh pond water, and on small water plants.
TURTLES OR SMALL ALLIGATORS	Raw meat or raw fish, ground into hamburger, with a bit of cod liver oil or bone meal added. Place food at edge of water. One or two meals a week is adequate.

Make a snake collecting stick from a length of broom handle and a 4-inch angle iron. You can also buy them from scientific supply houses. They are handy, too, for turning over rocks and boards.

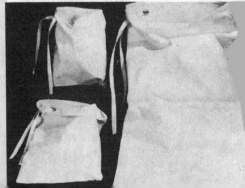

Make or buy a dozen bags made from a tightly woven material. Wash them well before using. These are used to carry specimens of snakes or turtles from the field. Tie a knot in the neck of the bag to keep the snake from escaping.

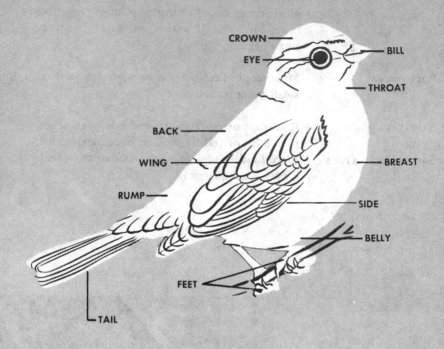

CROWN

EYE

BILL

THROAT

BACK

WING

BREAST

RUMP

SIDE

BELLY

FEET

TAIL

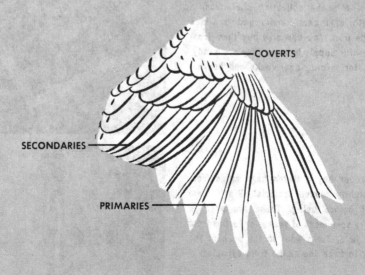

COVERTS

SECONDARIES

PRIMARIES

Birds

Bird-watching may easily be the highlight of any hike or camping trip. For anywhere you go, at any time of the year there will be at least a few birds to observe. You may be the one to make a discovery or interesting observation of real importance to science. There is still much that is not known about many birds.

But what is a bird? How does it differ from other animals? Birds are warm-blooded animals, with internal skeletons, and whose bodies are covered partly or wholly with feathers. Their young are hatched from eggs. Most birds are capable of flight.

A pair of binoculars or field glasses is very important in studying birds as is a good field guide to birds. Keeping accurate notes is helpful in checking up on a bird you do not recognize. Generally, birds are compared in size to a sparrow, a robin, or a crow. You probably know those birds already. The next step is to describe color. Learn the parts of a bird so that as you keep notes or refer to a guide you know the breast from the belly or the rump from the back.

Where you see birds is also helpful in telling one from another. With a little practice you will find that birds usually are found in definite kinds of places. You would look for meadowlarks in a field, for example, or ducks in a marsh.

How birds perch in a tree or on wires, whether they walk or hop, and how they fly are other ways of telling one from another. Some birds fly in an up-and-down pattern, while others may fly in a straight line. The first step in identification is placing a bird you see in the correct group. Scientists have classified birds into groups according to similarity of bills, feet, and wing forms. Other points of similarity are not too important in identification. On the next few pages you will find pictures of representative birds from the main bird groups that you are likely to see. When you place a bird in the correct group, then use your bird guide to find out which species it is.

Loons and Grebes. Usually seen swimming or diving. Fast flying. Legs are set far back. Loons have long, pointed bills. Grebe bills are slender and pointed. Loons and grebes nest in marshy areas on edge of ponds and lakes.

Herons, Egrets, and Bitterns. These are wading birds found in swamps and marshes. They have long legs, long necks, and long, pointed bills. They fly with neck pulled in and legs extending beyond tail; the wing beat is slow. Usually seen flying over or near water or stalking fish and frogs in shallow water.

Ducks and Geese. Strong-swimming and generally fast-flying birds. Geese and ducks, such as mallards, feed by tipping up and dabbling in shallow water. Others, such as mergansers, dive for food. Generally, the bill is broad and flat. Some ducks nest in tree cavities, but most nest on or near ground in swampy or marshy areas near water.

Cranes, Rails, and Coots. These are birds of the marshes that fly with their necks extended. Coots are usually seen swimming and diving. Rails may be seen flying over a marsh or wading on mud flats. They are more often heard than seen.

Shorebirds. Sandpipers, plovers, snipe, and woodcock are in this group. They are small to medium wading birds found along streams, ponds, mud flats, or the ocean beaches. Some kinds live in fields and prairies. Generally, they have long, pointed bills and are fast flying.

Gulls and Terns. These are long-winged, strong-flying birds usually found near large bodies of salt or freshwater. Gulls are sometimes seen on garbage dumps or feeding in newly plowed fields. Herring and ring-billed gulls are found in the East, while western Franklin's, and California gulls are found in the West. Black, common, and least terns are probably most often seen.

Hawks, Eagles, and Vultures. Generally large birds, with hooked bills and strong feet. They feed on small animals, such as mice, ground squirrels, amphibians, snakes, fish, or birds. Vultures eat dead animals. Usually seen soaring overhead or perched on a dead snag from which they watch for prey. Sparrow hawks and sharp-shinned hawks are robin size.

Grouse, Turkey, and Quail. These are land birds that scratch for their food like chickens. They have short, heavy bills and strong feet. Wings are short and rounded and they are fast-flying birds. Some of these birds are seen throughout the country.

451

Doves. Related to and resembling the domestic pigeon. These birds have small heads and slender bills. Their legs are short. The mourning dove is most often seen flying over open fields or perched on wires along roadsides.

Owls. Small to large birds with strong, hooked bills and rounded heads. They have large eyes and strong feet with hooked claws. Owls feed on other animals, usually mice or birds, but some will eat rabbits. Burrowing owl of Florida and western prairies nests in a hole in the ground. Others nest in tree cavities or nests built high in trees.

Cuckoos. Long, slender birds with curved bills and long tails. Middle tail feathers are the longest. Feed on insects, but the roadrunner of the Southwest and West may feed on small snakes and lizards.

Swifts and Nighthawks. Swifts are small birds resembling swallows. Long, slender wings and short tails. Chimney swifts may nest in abandoned chimneys. Whippoorwills are in this group, and like nighthawks, have long wings, short bills, and wide mouths.

Hummingbirds. Very small birds with long, needlelike bills. Usually seen hovering over flowers darting in to probe the blossom with their bill for food. Ruby-throated only species in the East. Several kinds may be seen in the West.

Kingfishers. Long, heavy, pointed bill and large head with crest. Small feet. Usually seen flying over water or sitting on dead limbs over water. Kingfishers dive for small fish and nest in holes in banks of streams and rivers.

Woodpeckers. Small (sparrow sized) to large (crow sized) climbing birds, with strong, pointed bills adapted for digging grubs out of trees. Tail feathers are stiff and pointed. Usually have four toes—two in front, two in back. Their flight pattern is up and down. Flickers, downy and hairy woodpeckers, and red-bellied, and Lewis's woodpeckers are the most often seen.

Perching Birds. This is the largest bird group and all the following birds are in this group. These are all land birds and vary in size from tiny kinglets to ravens that are larger than crows. All have four toes—three in front, one in back. Some walk and some hop.

453

Flycatchers. Small birds that perch on bare twigs and powerlines. From their perch they pursue flying insects and return to the perch after each flight. Kingbirds and phoebes are common birds of this group.

Swallows. Small birds with long, slender wings seen most often flying gracefully over fields or water feeding on flying insects. Some, such as martins or tree swallows, nest in boxes. Others nest in or on barns and houses.

Jays. Generally, jays are birds of the woodlands with loud, raucous calls. They are large birds with long tails and are bluish or grayish in color. Blue jays are found in the East; and the magpies, California jays, and Stellar's jays are found in the West.

Chickadees. Small woodland birds whose call gave it its name. It frequently visits feeding stations and can be tamed so that it will feed from the hand. They nest in holes in trees.

Thrushes. This group includes the robin, bluebird, and thrushes. Except for the bluebird, most are generally brownish on the back with speckled breasts. They are all known for their beautiful songs and are usually seen feeding on or near the ground.

Warblers. Small, brightly colored, insect-eating birds with slender bills and flitting habits. Generally, they are birds of the woodlands and brushy roadsides, usually seen at the top of trees or on the tops of branches or shrubs. Some of the more common ones are the yellow warbler, black and white warbler, myrtle warbler, and Audubon's warbler.

Blackbirds. These birds are found in several kinds of wildlife communities: bobolinks, meadowlarks, and cowbirds in fields; orioles high in trees; grackles in marshes or woods and redwings in marshes. Most are brightly colored and all have distinctive songs.

Finches and Sparrows. Birds in this group all have strong, cone-shaped bills, adapted for crushing or cracking seeds. They are found in several wildlife communities. Cardinals, grosbeaks, sparrows, towhees, and juncos are all in this group.

455

watching birds

Knowing where to look, when to look, how to look, and what to look for are all important not only in finding different birds, but in finding out more about one particular bird.

Brushy roadsides, hedgerows, edges of fields or forests, edges of campsites, and woodland openings; marshes along streams, rivers, lakes, and bays are all good places for birds. Look for places where there is a large variety of different kinds of plants. Look, too, in those places where birds find the kind of food they prefer.

During the spring and fall, when birds are migrating, you will usually see more different kinds. But there is some bird activity at any time of year, and seeing large numbers is not always the sign of a successful bird trip. Finding out more about one bird and its habits can be just as interesting and many times more important.

Early morning, generally, is the best time of day for bird-watching, but late afternoon may be a good time too. But if you are concentrating on one bird, you will want to watch it frequently during the day.

When looking for birds, walk slowly and quietly, make no sudden or jerky movements. If you see a bird, do not point at it. Describe its location by the shrub or tree it is in and the height above the ground. Walk with the sun at your back, so that it shines directly on the bird. Colors stand out better that way.

When you see a bird, even at a distance, stop and watch it. Try to identify it. Watch to see what it is doing. Then move slowly toward it, stopping every few feet to look again. In this way, even if you frighten it and it flies away, you will have had a look at it.

With practice, you will find that certain places where you hike or camp are best for birds. Many times in the summer or early fall, after a rain, birds will gather at a puddle in the road or trail to bathe and drink. Spring holes in the woods are often good places. But you won't find many birds in the deep woods or forests.

Studying the habits of one kind of bird can be fascinating. There are many things to watch for. What birds eat and how they feed; where they build nests; what materials are used for nest building; and whether both male and female work together in nest building are fun to see.

Sometimes you may bring birds in quite close to you by "kissing" the back of your hand and making a squeaking noise. It resembles the sound made by young in the nest and attracts the attention of adult birds.

Hang some short pieces of string and brightly colored yarn on shrubs around the campsite, so that they move in the wind. Some birds will use them as nesting material. When birds are through nesting in the fall, try to find nests containing the string or yarn.

Learning the songs, calls, and alarm notes of birds will help you identify them, and also be helpful in telling you more about the birds and their habits. Some birds establish definite territories and sing to warn others to stay away. Alarm notes may tell you that a hawk is nearby or that a snake is approaching the nest. Your library may have phonograph records of birdsongs.

attracting birds

There are several ways of attracting more birds to your campsite or to a place where you go on hikes. You know already that like all animals, birds need certain things to live—nest sites, water, food, and cover. You can help provide some of these things by planting a few shrubs and trees.

Clump plantings of conifers such as cedar, pine, and spruce will provide cover for some birds as well as nest sites. Dense plantings of shrubs, such as autumn or Russian olive, highbush cranberry, silky dogwood, tartarian honeysuckle, and others provide food and cover.

Talk with your local Soil Conservation Service officer, county agent, or State conservation department officer to see which plants are best in your area, and how to plant them.

Building brush piles will also provide cover. Putting up bird boxes will also attract some birds, and digging out spring holes or digging holes in wet places will help provide birds with water.

Closeup observations of birds are often possible if you use a device called a blind. It hides you from the bird; place near water hole or nest. Here's how to make it: (1) Four 4-feet-long, 2x2 poles are needed. (2) Sew sleeves in burlap or other cloth to hold upright poles. (3) Push poles into sleeves. (4) Drive poles into ground to hold blind upright. Frame top with 1x2's. Fasten top with safety pins. Cut slots large enough for camera lens.

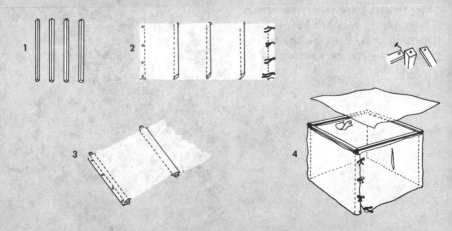

what birds eat

It is fun and interesting, too, to find out what kinds of foods birds prefer. Make two or three food trays as shown below, and take them on your next hike along with a supply of different kinds of seed.

At your local seed dealer or at a garden supply store or even at a supermarket try to get a half pound or so of five or six kinds of bird seed—sunflower seed, cracked corn, millet, kaffir corn, buckwheat, or hemp.

Place the trays close to the ground or on fenceposts. Put a different kind of seed in each cup. It may take a few days for birds to find the food. But try to find out if any one kind of seed is preferred over the others, and if so, which one and by which kind of birds.

Try the same project with natural foods. While on a hike or in camp, collect as many kinds of natural foods as possible, but keep them separate. Collect weed seeds, tree seeds, fruit from shrubs and vines, and small nuts. Place them in separate cups and find out which one is eaten first.

To make a food preference tray, drill holes in a board and insert waxed paper cups. Put a different kind of seed or natural food in each cup. Check a few hours later or even the next day to see which food birds eat first.

When you know which kinds of seeds birds eat first, try this: Dye the preferred seed several different colors with vegetable dye you can get at a supermarket. Use yellow, green, blue, red, orange, and black. Place the dyed seeds in the tray and see if one color is eaten more than the others.

459

water

In summer and early fall, particularly if it has been a dry season, many birds can be attracted to water, if there is no natural water close by.

A simple birdbath is easy to set up in camp or other place where you may go on hikes. A shallow tin pan, a metal washbasin, a plastic dish, or a trash-can lid all make good bird-watering devices. Place them in a shallow hole in the ground or on a pile of rocks so that they are sturdy and will not tip over.

It is well, too, to have a rock or two inside, or a shrub nearby for birds to perch on as they dry off.

A drip can over the bath is a good idea, too, since birds are attracted by the dripping water. The bath should be placed near shrubbery or a tangle of vines where birds can find cover.

In addition to attracting birds that you might not otherwise see, a watering device gives you a chance to watch birds close at hand.

Birds are frequently attracted by dripping water. Punch a small hole in the bottom edge of a large can. Whittle a stick to fit the hole and insert it in the hole. Fill the can with water and adjust the stick so that water drips out very slowly. Hang the can over a birdbath, or even a water hole or puddle where there is no movement of water. Back away and sit quietly as birds come to drink.

homes for birds

More than 50 kinds of North American birds have been known to nest in boxes. Most of them are birds that normally would nest in tree cavities or abandoned woodpecker nests. Many of them, too, are birds that are commonly found around campsites.

A good winter project is this: Make a few bird boxes suitable for birds you know are found on your campsite. Take a winter hike or camp trip and set out the boxes. Do this before late February.

Then on spring and early summer camp trips, check up on the boxes to find out how many were used and by what kinds of birds.

If you find an occupied box, you might set up a blind nearby, and watch the bird activity for an hour or two. Be careful, though, that you do not frighten the adults and keep them from the nest.

But as you watch, try to see what the adult birds feed the young. How long are they away from the nest to get more food? How many trips do they make in half an hour or an hour? If they feed their young one insect each trip, how many insects do they capture in a day?

Wood duck boxes have been responsible for increasing the number of these birds in some parts of the country. Check to see if wood ducks nest in your area, and if so, make boxes and set them out.

Bluebird boxes, too, have been very effective in increasing the numbers of these attractive birds in many places. One Michigan troop has made and set out hundreds with excellent results.

461

Birds, like people, are particular about their houses. Bird boxes must be built to specifications or birds will not use them. Make nest boxes for specific birds: wood ducks, chickadees, or bluebirds. Make the hole fit the bird. Do not use tin cans because the sun may heat the can and bake the young birds. Make any bird box so that it is well ventilated and drained. Slits under the roof provide air circulation and a few small holes in the bottom provide drainage. Do not set up too many boxes. As a general rule, three or four to the acre, widely separated, are the most that will be used. They should be placed in the open or in open shade. Finally, clean out the houses after each season; therefore, make any bird box so that it is easily cleaned.

	Box Floor	Box Height	Hole Above Floor	Hole Diameter	House Above Ground
Bluebirds	5x5 in.	8 in.	6 in.	$1\frac{1}{2}$ in.	5-10 ft.
Wrens	4x4 in.	6-8 in.	1-6 in.	1 in.	6-10 ft.
Chickadees	4x4 in.	8-10 in.	6-8 in.	$1\frac{1}{8}$ in.	6-15 ft.
Swallows	5x5 in.	6 in.	1-5 in.	$1\frac{1}{2}$ in.	10-15 ft.
Flycatchers	6x6 in.	8-10 in.	6-8 in.	2 in.	8-20 ft.
Flickers	7x7 in.	16-18 in.	14 in.	$2\frac{1}{2}$ in.	8-20 ft.
Wood ducks	10x10 in.	22-28 in.	15-20 in.	3x4 in. (oval)	6-20 ft.

Bluebirds like their houses facing south and they are particularly fond of fenceposts. *Chickadees,* nuthatches, titmice, and downy woodpeckers like bark-covered houses; and the downy will feel more at home if you put wood chips in the bottom of the box. *Swallows* like their houses on top of posts. *Flycatchers,* like chickadees, prefer bark-covered houses. *Flickers* want a wall-to-wall wood-chip carpet. *Wood ducks* are even more particular; their carpet must be a 4-inch pile of sawdust and they need a screen stairway for the young ducks to climb out.

Many times you do not know that a bird has nested near your campsite until you actually come close enough to see the nest or the bird. By learning nests, you can tell what birds nest in a given area.

When you find a nest, there are several things to notice: Where is it located? How large is it? What is it made of? Are there any unusual things about the nest; are the eggs layed on the bare ground? What kind of bird would have oyster shells near its nest?

Sometimes you can find out what plant materials were used in the nest or what the birds have been eating by collecting a nest and keeping it damp in a shallow pan of water. Sometimes seeds from plants used in building the nest will sprout and grow.

You may find small bundles of fur beneath pines and spruces. Open them carefully; you may find the bones and skulls of mice or other small animals that the owl swallowed. The bundle is the pellet that the owl spit out after his meal.

463

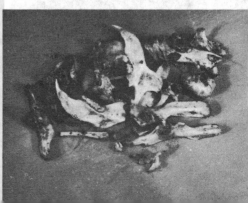

Mammals

Observing mammals in the wild is not as easy as finding other forms of animal life. Perhaps that is one reason why these animals are so interesting to many outdoorsmen. It takes real skill and practice to find them and study their habits.

Mammals have highly developed senses of smell, hearing, and sight, and many can "sense" you first and keep out of your way. Some can run swiftly and escape your notice, while protective coloring helps others blend into the foliage so that you miss them completely. Then too, many mammals are active only at night.

If you do not see mammals when you hike or camp, it does not necessarily mean that they are not there. Some, like mice, may be present in unbelievable numbers, while others may not be so abundant.

Every natural area from the oceans and their coastal marshes through forest, prairie or desert, river or lake, to high mountaintops, has certain mammals living in it. There are several kinds of wild mammals that live successfully in towns and villages.

But before starting seriously to study mammals and their habits, it is well to know what mammals are and how they differ from other forms of animal life. First, like birds, mammals have internal skeletons and are warm-blooded. But unlike birds, their bodies are partly or wholly covered by hair. Mammals bear their young alive and have glands that produce milk.

Mammals typically have four limbs with toes that end in nails, claws, or hoofs. In some cases these take different forms. The front limbs of whales or dolphins are flippers. The limbs of seals have developed into fin-like flippers. Bats, the only mammals that really can fly, have front limbs that have developed into wings.

Mammals have been on earth for about 190 million years. They were not an important group of animals until the dinosaurs died out about

70 million years ago. Since that time many ancient mammals have died out and others have changed until they have become the animals we know today. There are some 350 species of mammals in this country and Canada. Some of them are sure to be found where you hike or camp.

Scientists place all mammals in groups called *orders*. In each order are those mammals which have certain characteristics that show they are closely related to others in that order. Some of these characteristics that show relationship are similarities of teeth, bone structure, and reproduction.

Mammals of the world are classified in 19 orders. Eleven of these orders have representatives in this country. Placing a mammal in the correct order is an important first step in identification. Here are the orders of mammals with representatives in this country:

Pouched Mammals. The female has a pouch in which she carries her young. The young are born undeveloped. The opossum, the only member of this order in our country, is found in the East.

Moles and Shrews. These are small mouse-sized animals that live under ground and eat insects. Water shrews swim and dive easily and feed on water insects, small fish, and other water life. Moles and shrews are found throughout most of the country.

Bats. These are the only mammals that truly can fly. They are active at dusk and at night when they fly about locating insects with a built-in "radar system."

Flesh-Eating Mammals. Bears, raccoon, marten, weasels, mink, skunks, badgers, otter, foxes, coyotes, wolves, mountain lions, and bobcats generally eat the flesh of other animals.

Seals and Sea Lions. Found only on the west coast and the extreme northeast coast, these are mammals with flippers developed for swimming. They feed on fish. Their young are born on land.

Rodents. This is the largest and most widespread order. Porcupines, beavers, jumping mice, squirrels, woodchucks, pocket gophers, rats, and mice are some of the animals in this group. Some live in holes in the ground, in trees, or in water.

Hares, Rabbits, and Pikas. Snowshoe hares, jackrabbits, common cottontails, and pikas are in this group. Hares are long-legged and their young are born open-eyed and well-furred. Rabbits are born blind without fur. The short-eared pika lives in the western mountains.

Hoofed Mammals. Bison, bighorn sheep, mountain goats, antelope, moose, deer, peccaries, and elk are in this group. Deer live in many parts of the country.

467

Armadillo. This odd mammal lives only in parts of the South. Except for their ears and legs they are covered by bony plates. They have no teeth, and feed on insects. They try to escape their enemies by digging a hole in the ground.

Manatee (Sea-Cows). These mammals live only in southern Florida and along the gulf coast. They live only in water but come to the surface to breathe. They feed on aquatic plants and grow to be 10 feet long and may weigh a ton.

Whales, Dolphins, and Porpoises. These are all mammals that spend all their life in water. They breathe air and must come to the surface to breathe. Blue whales are the largest animals that ever lived. Whales, dolphins, and porpoises may be seen along our ocean shores.

how to see mammals

One of the easiest ways to see some mammals is to walk along a woods road or trail at night, carrying a powerful spotlight. Shine the light into treetops, holes in trees, on the trail ahead of you, and into dense brush. Many times, skunks, foxes, deer, raccoons, opossums, or porcupines may be caught off guard.

Using a canoe or small boat at night frequently results in your seeing mammals. Quietly sit near a beaver dam or muskrat house. When you hear the slightest noise, aim your light toward the sound.

In the morning, look along the shore for tracks in the mud or sand. The tracks will show where mammals come to drink. The next night, row to a point off shore from where you saw the tracks. Sit quietly and at the slightest sound, aim your light toward it.

Several kinds of mammals may be attracted to bait. First, make a tracking pit. Remove the sod or leaf litter on a flat area about 10 feet square. Soften the earth so that when you walk on it you sink in about 2 inches. In the center of the area place your bait. Rake the area smooth. At night, sit about 50 feet away and watch and listen. Better yet, climb a tree so that you are about 10 feet off the ground. At any sound, aim your light toward the bait.

Rabbits, deer, and opossums may come to eat cut-up apples. Corn will attract mice, deer, or raccoons. Bacon fat will attract flying squirrels, opossums, foxes, porcupines, or maybe a bear. Meat or fish will attract bears, foxes, raccoons, or opossums. You might want to try one of the commercial baits used by trappers. Even if you don't see the animal itself, it will leave its tracks in the pit for you to identify the next day. Another good trick is to look for hollow trees. Pound on the trunk with a stout stick. An owl may look out, but so may a squirrel, a flying squirrel, a raccoon, or an opossum.

If you find a burrow or hole in the ground, first see if it is occupied. Poke some pencil-sized sticks in the ground at the entrance so that an animal coming or going will knock them over. If you find that the hole is used, then find a comfortable place to sit and watch. Woodchucks, badgers, ground squirrels, mink, otter, and foxes are some animals that live in holes in the ground.

signs and signals

Many times the only way you know that wild mammals live where you hike or camp is by the signs they leave, the sounds they make, or by their scent. Being able to read signs of the wild takes skill and practice. But once you can do it, you will get much more enjoyment from the outdoors.

DENS, NESTS, BURROWS. Some mammal homes are easy to find and identify. Beaver dams or lodges, muskrat houses, or squirrel nests are easy to detect. Holes in the ground may be a bit more difficult, but generally the size, location, and shape give you a clue. Woodchuck burrows are often found in open fields and if you look carefully, you will find two holes, one with a mound of dirt nearby and the other without the mound. A red fox burrow resembles a woodchuck's but the tunnel is larger and the location is rarely near buildings or roads used by man. Fox burrows, too, often have two entrances. Skunks many times move

Woodchucks, like some other animals, use the mound of earth at the entrance of the burrow as a lookout point. Sometimes a sharp whistle will cause a woodchuck to sit up and look around.

Sometimes muskrats build dens in holes in banks of ponds and lakes. When they live in marshes, they build houses of marsh plants. These houses have an underwater entrance and a dry platform well above water level.

470

Squirrels build summer homes of sticks, twigs, and leaves high in trees. Sometimes they take over an old bird nest, build a roof over it, and reinforce the base. In winter they move back to hollow trees or stumps where they get more protection from the cold.

Beavers sometimes fell unbelievably large trees to get the tender bark on the higher branches. Such feeding signs are unmistakable evidence, even though you may never see the animal.

into abandoned woodchuck or fox burrows, and rabbits will also use a woodchuck hole for their home.

Prairie dog burrows resemble miniature volcano craters. The mound around the entrance is used as a lookout post, and also keeps surface water from running down the hole. Coyotes, ground squirrels, some mice, gophers, and moles also live in holes in the ground. Bears use caves, hollow logs, undercut banks, and space under uprooted trees for their dens. In the high-mountain country of the West, mountain goats and cougars use caves or niches in the rocks for their homes. Bats are noted as cave dwellers.

TRACKS AND SCENT TRAILS. As they move about on the ground, most animals leave two kinds of trails—tracks from their feet, and scent trails left by scent glands or by its feet or fur touching the ground, grass, trees, or shrubs. It takes another animal to follow the scent trail, but many a skilled outdoorsman can follow tracks. Prints are easy to find. Look along the beach, around puddles in country roads, in mud along streams and rivers, in the snow, or in other places where the earth is soft enough for a foot to make an impression.

Sometimes, you may not see tracks as such; but as the animal uses one route night after night to get to water or to feed, it leaves a trail sometimes worn down to mineral soil. By following a trail you can "read" some interesting animal stories. You may see where a rabbit stopped to nibble clover or to browse on tree bark; where he was frightened and bounded in a zigzag manner to find shelter in a woodchuck hole or bramble patch. You may see where a fox walked; stopping occasionally to sniff the air, to dig out a mouse nest, or where he warily stalked a chipmunk or rabbit. You may follow the tracks of deer and find what it browsed on in its search for food (about 7 pounds of food a day). You may see where a bear wandered in search for food.

There are many things you can tell from animal tracks. But first, you should be able to tell the front from the rear footprints. With foxes this is difficult, because their hind feet come down in the tracks of their front feet. But with rabbits, squirrels, raccoons, mice, and opossums the hind foot is larger than the front.

The next thing to look for is how far apart the prints are. This tells you two things—the size of the animal, and whether it was walking, bounding, running, moving slowly or quickly for its size. The depth of the track and whether it is deeper in the front than in the back tells you whether the animal was moving slowly or quickly.

Careful study of the track will show whether the animal walks flat-footed or on its toes. This gives you a clue to its identity. Skunks, raccoons, beaver, porcupines, bears, and man walk flat-footed. Foxes, bobcats, cougars walk on their toes while deer, antelope, moose, and elk walk on their toenails.

Squirrels leave tracks in which their front feet are side by side, while in rabbit tracks the front feet are usually one in front of the other. Deer mouse tracks show paired front footprints, while in meadow mouse prints the front feet are on the diagonal.

FEEDING SIGNS. Because all animals must eat in order to survive, feeding signs often tell us which animals live in a given area. In many cases, these signs are very different from each other.

Signs of feeding take many forms. Gnawed bark on trees, browsed twigs or branches, shells of acorns and other nuts, bits of fur or feathers,

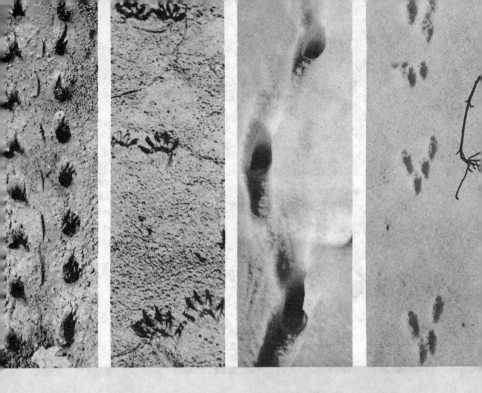

At every season of the year, damp ground and mud retain the tracks of animals. Was the animal at the left a skunk? The next print is easier; it's a raccoon. In winter, new fallen snow records the passage of a deer and a rabbit. Mud and snow are not the only record keepers; dust can tell a tracking story, too.

skeletons or carcasses, holes in the ground, floating vegetation on a lake, closely clipped grass, ridges in the earth—are all signs.

Signs of animals that eat plant life are usually easy to find if you know what to look for. Rabbits will often browse on low-growing shrubs, nipping off the new growth on the end of a shoot. They will also eat bark on young saplings, sometimes killing the tree. Deer, too, browse on the tender buds and twigs of certain trees and shrubs. Mice will sometimes eat the tender bark of a young tree or shrub.

Beavers will cut down entire trees, then cut them into shorter lengths and store the branches on the lake bottom where they can reclaim them

Plaster casts of the tracks you find come in handy when you try to identify different animals. Surround the print with a cardboard collar, pour in plaster of paris about as thick as melted ice cream. Let it set, then clean it off.

during the winter when they feed on the bark. Muskrats eat the tender parts of some water plants, discarding the tougher parts which float to the surface of the lake or pond. Porcupines eat tree bark, and often you may see the top of a pine stripped all the way around. Porcupines will also gnaw on the handle of an ax or canoe paddle.

Several kinds of animals eat the fruits of plants, such as blackberries or wild cherry. The droppings of animals, such as raccoons and bears, frequently show their food preferences. But some animals eat other animals. Muskrats will eat mussels and other water life leaving piles of shells on a rock in a lake. Skunks and foxes will dig out mouse nests, leaving telltale holes in the ground or snow. Mink and otters eat fish, and you sometimes find neatly-cleaned fish skeletons along a stream or lakeshore.

OTHER SIGNS. There are other signs that are not related to feeding or to animal homes. Buck deer in the spring, for example, find a favorite tree to use as they rub the "velvet" from their new-grown antlers. In the process, they sometimes rub the bark off the tree at the same time. In

A large birdhouse placed high in a tree may be used by gray, red, or flying squirrels. Small wooden boxes or wren-sized birdhouses placed in high grass along a hedgerow, or low to the ground in the woods, may be taken over by mice.

Where hollow trees are scarce and where there is food to meet their needs, raccoons sometimes will nest in nail kegs or boxes placed in the crotch of a tree. If raccoons live around your camp, see if they will move into a box.

any case, they rub a smooth spot on the tree bark which you can find.

Bears have signposts which they use regularly; special trees which they visit. They sniff around the tree, then reach up and scratch the bark with their sharp claws. Sometimes, they bite the tree and tear out chunks of wood. Bears have been known to tear apart power poles where they mistook the hum of the wind blowing through the wires for the hum of bees in the pole.

Sometimes as you walk through woods or fields you can see where animals bedded down for the night, leaving matted grass or leaves as a sign of their night's sleep. Near lakes or streams where beavers live you can sometimes find canals built to float logs and branches to the lodge or dam. These same animals have places along pond banks or stream edges where they leave a message for others to read. They make small mud pies which are scented with castoreum from their scent glands. Other beavers can read these "letters in the mud." These signs may not be easy to find, but it always pays to look carefully whenever you are outdoors.

tracks

(I) Cats—house cats, wildcats, lynxes, and cougars—place their hind feet in the tracks of the forefeet. Claw marks do not show in the tracks. When walking, a house cat's tracks are 6 to 10 inches apart, and 10 to 12 inches apart when the cat is running. (2) Dogs aren't as careful as cats when they walk; sometimes the hind foot is placed almost in the track of the forefoot, but usually it is to one side. When

(4) Rabbits, as you might expect, make large tracks with their hind feet and smaller tracks with their forefeet. They leapfrog along placing their hind feet in front of the fore. Hopping along, a rabbit may cover 1 to 2 feet. When something frightens him,

476

a dog runs the tracks are clearly separate—one track a little ahead of the other. Claw marks are visible in the dog's track. (3) Foxes, coyotes, and wolves are as careful as cats when they walk, placing their hind feet in the tracks of their forefeet. Like dogs, the claws of these animals show in their tracks. An irregular pattern of three develops when foxes, coyotes, and wolves run.

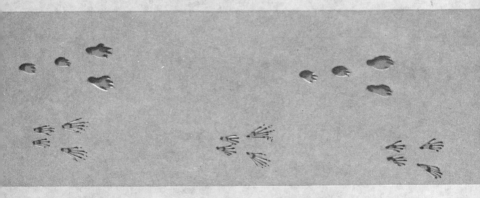

he will cover 6 to 7 feet at a single bound and the forefeet track one behind the other. (5) Squirrels and chipmunks run very much like rabbits; but unlike rabbits, their forefeet do not change their position when a squirrel speeds to safety.

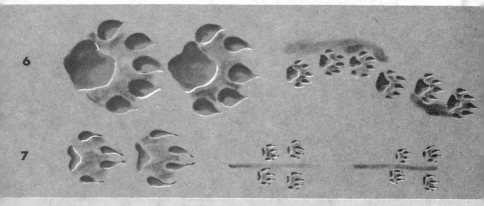

(6) Otter have webbed feet that make a light impression between their toes. When they walk, the otter's tracks weave back and forth. When the otter runs, he bounds along throwing his hind feet close behind his forefeet making paired prints in the

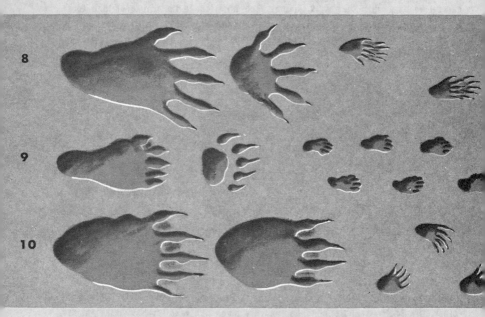

(8) Raccoon's tracks overprint when they walk and separate into the leapfrog pattern when they run. (9) Skunks walk deliberately and their distinct prints are regular and easy to follow. When they run, the pattern is unlike other animals

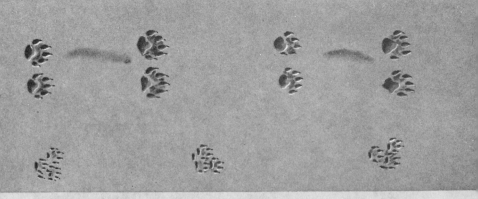

track. (7) Mink, weasels, and martens make smaller tracks than the otter. When they walk, their pattern is similar to a running otter. When they run, their tracks overprint often showing three prints.

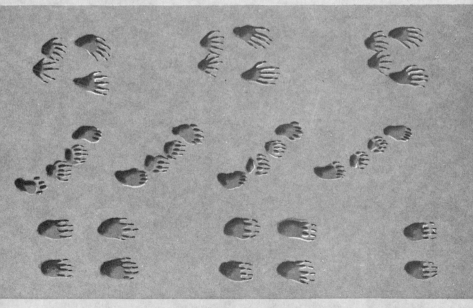

because only the left leg is ahead of the forefeet. (10) Porcupines walk pigeon-toed; when they run, if they ever need to, the track is the typical paired print that most other animals make.

20 CONSERVING RESOURCES

WHEN YOU SEE a vapor trail streaming behind a speck in the sky or hear the countdown for a new space vehicle, stop and think—would these out-of-this-world things be possible without the natural resources of our earth—its air, water, minerals, soil, plants, and animals?

Sure, we live in a space age. But our necessities of life come from the earth—we are still earthbound. And our high standard of living and strength as a free nation are due largely to our bountiful supply of natural resources. Conserving these resources of the earth is something that should concern each of us—which is why conservation is an important part of the program of the Boy Scouts of America.

Conservation simply means the intelligent use of our total environment —using our natural resources so we'll have the things we need for as long as possible. It means restoring resources we have abused: worn-out soils and polluted air and waters. It means planning for the best use for the most people for the longest time of *all* of our resources.

Conservationists put all resources in two categories: nonrenewable and renewable. In the first are such things as coal, gas and oil, and minerals that once used up are gone forever. These must be used carefully. The second group includes such resources as forests, wildlife, water, and soil. These may be renewed with proper use and management practices. Many problems exist because men don't fully understand the actual relationships existing among all resources or because they interfere with or interrupt one or more of these relationships.

For the outdoorsman, conservation often means *not* doing something— *not* ditching tents, *not* digging holes, *not* overusing a campsite. *Not* hacking or carving trees may mean healthy trees for years to come.

Conservation also means doing things *correctly,* too. Before you try to undo damage, be sure you will not just exchange one kind for another— nature's balances are very delicate and easily disturbed. Good intentions are not enough. Hard work can be a total loss if it is misguided.

Sometimes conservation projects are enthusiastically carried out where there isn't the slightest need, actually. Brush roosts for quail don't make sense in an area quail don't inhabit. Wood duck boxes are not of much value in locations where "woodies" wouldn't nest.

You may read that pruning trees improves their quality, and thinning is beneficial to a forest—but check with a local forester for expert advice on the pruning of different species, the proper time of year, the maximum size beyond which pruning is useless. Learn to select the trees to be thinned with regard to location, value to remaining trees, possible utility of wood in the culls, and so on. You should be practical about such matters—will it all be worthwhile in the end?

This goes, not just for forestry projects, but for stream improvement, wildlife management, and the other things we can do to try to make the best use of the world we live in. Projects must have *real meaning*— and professional conservationists will be glad to assist you. Just ask. Then follow their suggestions about conservation projects in your area.

One excellent water conservation project is to clean up trash and litter along streams, lakes, and other waterways. In doing this, you are making the area much more attractive, safer, and a more pleasant place to swim or fish. If you find any numbers of dead fish, report them to your conservation officer.

It is estimated that 140 gallons are used each day for each person, not counting that used for transportation or hydroelectric power. The conservation of water to meet the need is a serious and growing problem.

The problem can be divided into two broad areas: *quality* and *quantity*. Pollution, in the form of mud and sewage from cities and factories, has made much of our water unusable without expensive treatment. And, then, we don't always have *all* the water we need, *where* we need it, *when* we need it—there may be floods in one part of the country while a severe drought ravages another.

If you work for the Soil and Water Conservation or Environmental Science merit badges or read the merit badge pamphlets, you will find out more about this problem that affects us nationally.

There are several things you can do about water conservation while hiking or camping, such as these projects:

Plant grass, shrubs, or other plants along streambanks and lakeshores to help check erosion. Muddy water is unpleasant for swimming or boating and may be harmful to fish.

483

soil

The loss of topsoil through wind or water is serious. It takes good top-soil to grow the food and fiber that we use each day or to grow the grass that feeds the animals that supply us with meat, milk, or leather. But—nature, alone, may take hundreds of years to build up one inch of new topsoil. In addition to erosion, much soil is being lost each day to housing developments, highways, and such construction.

Good soil is important, too, on a campsite. Good productive soil is needed to grow the grass, the shrubs and vines, and the trees that make a campsite a pleasant place. Wildlife, too, is dependent on the productivity of the soil.

You can help build up the topsoil on a campsite by having the soil tested and then adding lime or fertilizer, or both, as needed. Other things you can do are:

If gully erosion is taking place on or near your campsite, get the advice of a soil conservation expert on how to control it. First, check or divert the water that causes the gully, then build structures that help the gully fill in and heal over.

If erosion is a problem on a trail, first relocate trail so that it follows the level contour of the land as far as possible. Then place water bars in the old trail to slow up the water running down the trail and divert it off the side. Plant grass or shrubs in the old trail.

484

Campsite erosion is a common problem. First, rotate the use of a campsite so that the ground cover is not worn off. Slick and clean sites such as this are the sign of an inexperienced camper. When it rains, such a site is muddy; when dry, the site is dusty.

Keep a cover of grass or leaves on your campsite. It protects the soil from becoming packed hard and helps water to soak in rather than runoff taking soil with it.

plantlife

The conservation of grasses, shrubs, trees, and other plantlife consists chiefly of using plants and managing them so that you have the plants you want in such a condition that they are continuously productive.

In a pasture, for example, it means a balance between the number of cows and the rate of growth of the grass so the cows get enough to eat without depleting their food supply. In the case of some forests, it means cutting only the number of board feet per year equal to the annual growth of the forest.

On a campsite, plantlife conservation means keeping the best kind of plant cover on the ground to protect the soil, to provide those plants that give food and shelter to wildlife, and provide the needs of camping —fuel, open shade, and wood for campcraft uses.

In the Plant Kingdom section are some projects you could carry out. Others are:

Be careful with fire. Check first to see if an open fire may be built on your campsite. Check to see if you need a written permit. Then always build your fire in a safe place and in a safe way. Keep your fire small. Do not leave an open fire unattended. Be sure the fire is dead out before you leave.

Insects and diseases destroy an unbelievable number of trees each year—more than any other cause. Check with a forester to see if you can help with this problem. Sometimes, collecting twigs and leaves from dead or dying trees, near where you hike or camp, can be helpful to a forester.

Use your ax and knife only for those purposes for which they were intended—hacked trees and carved initials are signs of greenhorns. They can cause disease to get started and kill the tree. At the very least, they aren't attractive.

In some cases, carefully pruning lower branches from timber species may help the tree produce better lumber in future years. Meantime, it may open up your campsite and permit better air circulation. Do NOT do it, though, without the specific advice of an expert.

487

fish

In fish conservation, the job is to provide those things that fish need to live and thrive. As with any animal, this means food, a place to nest and raise young, and living space. While reptiles, birds, and mammals get the oxygen they need from the air, fish get it from the water, and sometimes lack of enough oxygen dissolved in the water limits the kind of fish that can live there. Temperature of the water, too, has a lot to do with what kinds of fish will live in a stream or lake. Another important factor is the kind of bottom. Some fish can spawn only on gravel or sand; they can't spawn on a mud bottom.

Some fish, too, need clear water. They cannot survive in muddy, silted streams or lakes. With those things in mind, here are some things you can do in fish conservation, but first get the advice of a professional conservationist.

Prevent erosion along stream and lake banks, by riprapping the bank with rocks. This prevents silt from washing into the water where it may clog the fish's gills, cover its eggs, or cover its food on the bottom. Other stream improvement devices include small, low dams that create small pools and also add oxygen to the water, as the stream flows over the dam.

V-shaped dams are designed to use the flow of a stream to dig a hole in the bottom where fish may hide. The pools created by these dams also make collecting places for food, and the fall of the water keeps the oxygen content higher than it might otherwise be.

Plant willows or other moisture-loving shrubs along streambanks or lakeshores. Planting willow shoots about 2 feet apart will result in a heavy cover in a few years that will check erosion and also shade the stream, helping to keep the water cool.

wildlife

Wildlife conservation projects consist of providing food, cover, and water for those birds or mammals that you want to live in or around your campsite. If you camp on your council campsite, there may be a conservation plan already in progress which will give you some ideas of what to do. If you have your own campsite, talk to the owner about what he would like done to improve his property for wildlife. It would be well, too, to get some ideas from your conservation agent.

There are several wildlife projects that will show results in a short period of time. Others take longer to accomplish their purpose.

Build brush piles for shelter for birds and small mammals. Start with a base of log cribbing, a stump or a pile of rocks. Place large branches down first, then smaller branches on top. Last, place some heavy branches or use wire fastened to stakes to keep the brush pile from blowing over. Be sure there is lots of open space underneath. A good brush pile should be 10 to 15 feet in diameter and 6 feet high.

Plant some annual food plots consisting of corn, sorghum, millet, wheat, sunflowers, and other seeds. These will provide fall and early winter food for birds and game animals.

Dig out spring holes or seeps so that, when the holes fill with water, wildlife will have a place to drink. You will be surprised at how fast animals find the water and use it.

Planting cover plants such as pines or spruces and food shrubs such as autumn olive, dogwood, or Tartarian honeysuckle is a project that takes time to achieve results. But it is worthwhile and in a few years provides food and cover for wildlife for a long time to come.

outdoor manners

The Outdoor Code is your guide to good outdoor manners. Other people's bad manners out-of-doors *is* a matter for our concern—not only is it a great expense to clean up roadsides, parks, campsites, trails, and waterways, but many choice areas have been closed to all for the sins of a few. Besides ordinary courtesy, show these considerations and you will earn for yourself or your group a hearty "welcome back!"

• Seek permission before going on private land; either you're a guest or a trespasser—you have no "rights"—only privileges granted to you.

• When you get permission to use such lands, offer to render some service to the owner, such as help with a conservation or other useful project.

• Leave gates open or shut as you find them. Don't disturb livestock. Don't walk over cultivated lands. Fruits and vegetables are usually a cash crop for a farmer; leave them alone unless told to help yourself.

• When hiking, stick to existing trails; don't cut across hillside switchbacks or bypass the regular trail except in soggy spots.

• Obey regulations for firebuilding and cutting fuel or other wood.

• When near lakes and rivers in park areas, check to see if they are zoned for different uses. People enjoy the water in many ways—fishing, swimming, skin diving, water-skiing, boating, or just sitting by the water's edge. Don't let *your* way of enjoying it interfere with others'.

• When camped in a public site, keep noise down and observe an early curfew—many campers are early to bed and early to rise. Respect these and other rights to privacy. Self-discipline will earn goodwill.

• Take pride in leaving a campsite better than you found it. Don't leave trash; burn what you can, carry what you can't—you brought it. Clean up your site before you leave, even trash left by others. Leave no signs of fire except leftover wood neatly stacked for the next fellow.

• Washrooms, tables, fireplaces, shelters, exhibits, trail signs, and other conveniences are established for your use—treat them as if they were really yours and take the best possible care of them.

• Live up to the spirit as well as the letter of fish and game laws. If you need a license, get one. Observe seasons and limits strictly. Don't take more fish or game than you need or can use. Be a good sport.

OUTDOOR CODE

AS AN AMERICAN, I WILL DO MY BEST TO —

BE CLEAN IN MY OUTDOOR MANNERS

I will treat the outdoors as a heritage to be improved for our greater enjoyment. I will keep my trash and garbage out of America's waters, fields, woods, and roadways.

BE CAREFUL WITH FIRE

I will prevent wildfire. I will build my fire in a safe place and be sure it is out before I leave.

BE CONSIDERATE IN THE OUTDOORS

I will treat public and private property with respect. I will remember that use of the outdoors is a privilege I can lose by abuse.

BE CONSERVATION-MINDED

I will learn how to practice good conservation of soil, waters, forests, minerals, grasslands, and wildlife; and I will urge others to do the same. I will use sportsmanlike methods in all my outdoor activities.

21 THE EARTH

UNDER your feet, no matter where you are, lies our earth.

You may go up in a plane to the stratosphere—eventually you'll have to return to *terra firma*. Unless we take off on a space flight, most of us are bound to good old Mother Earth to the end of our days—to this globe that has been spinning through the universe for possibly 3 billion years at more than 200 miles a second!

There have been many guesses about the beginning of the earth. A recent theory suggests that a large star, passing by our sun, attracted and drew a great stream of matter out of the sun. After the star had passed, this streamer eventually broke apart and formed the planets.

There's no doubt that the earth was once a seething hot mass. Its surface cooled, became a solid crust. Air seeped out and formed a layer around the earth. Water condensed on its surface.

OUR CHANGING WORLD. Many forces then went to work, changing the earth's surface.

Earthquakes cracked and twisted the surface layers. In some places these layers were wrinkled into mountain ridges. In other places, layers that were deep down were pushed to the top. Parts of our country rose. What was under the sea became dry land. Traces of seashells have been found in rocks as far inland as Oklahoma and Wisconsin. Other sections sank—maybe a few feet every million years.

Volcanoes poured melted rock out over large sections of the earth. In our own country, thousands of square miles of the States of Idaho, Oregon, and Washington have a foundation of lava.

The heat of summer and the cold of winter broke open the solid crust of the earth. Wind and water ate into it. Water dug the Grand Canyon as the Colorado River gnawed its way through 5,000 feet of rock, taking about 2 million years to do the job. Ages ago a large sheet of ice, moving from the far north down over the Northern States, ground off the tops of mountains and hills, giving them a rounder outline than those farther to the south. Along our coast, to this day constant change is taking place as waves batter the shores, cutting down cliffs, building up beaches. Water also carries sand and mud down rivers to the ocean where they settle as sandbars and flats.

Time, time, and still more time has gone over our earth, bringing new changes for each swing it took around the sun.

The crust of the earth as we know it today is made up of minerals, rocks, and decayed vegetable and animal matter.

MINERALS ARE CHEMICALS. Minerals are chemicals that exist in nature. Each mineral is made up of certain elements such as aluminum, magnesium, silicon, oxygen, calcium, carbon, and others, always in exactly the same proportions in any given mineral.

Some minerals form beautiful crystals. Quartz and feldspar, for example, you may find in many sections of our country as white or pinkish, glassy crystals.

Minerals are told apart, among other things, by their hardness, the way they can be cracked, their color, and their weight.

ROCKS ARE MIXTURES. Rocks are solid masses, made up of a mixture of tiny mineral pieces, sometimes only of one kind of mineral, more often several kinds. Many mineral particles make up a rock in the same way as many trees form a forest.

Rocks often crop out of the earth as one solid mass. But generally they are surrounded by loose pieces of cracked rock in the form of boulders, stones, and pebbles.

We divide rocks into three main groups: igneous, sedimentary, and metamorphic.

Igneous rocks were once molten masses, melted by terrific pressure deep in the ground or poured out of spurting volcanoes. Lava, basalt, and granite are samples of igneous rocks. Those that cooled quickly, such as lava, are often glasslike. The ones that cooled slowly—granite and others—consist of small mineral crystals.

Sedimentary rocks are formed from sediment, that is, small particles

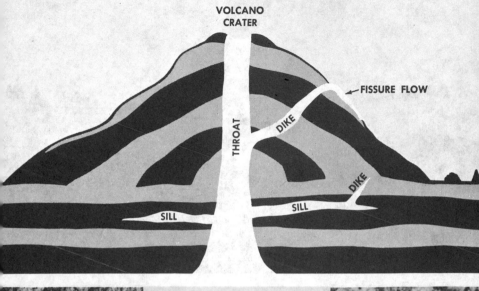

VOLCANO
CRATER

← FISSURE FLOW

THROAT

DIKE

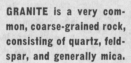

DIKE

SILL   SILL

BASALT is usually fine-grained and dark gray. It is true lava that has erupted from a volcano.

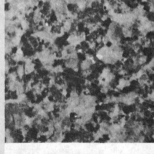

GRANITE is a very common, coarse-grained rock, consisting of quartz, feldspar, and generally mica.

DIORITE is coarse-grained like granite, but of a darker color and without any quartz in it.

OBSIDIAN, dark gray or black, is a glasslike rock. Indians used it for making arrowheads.

sedimentary rocks

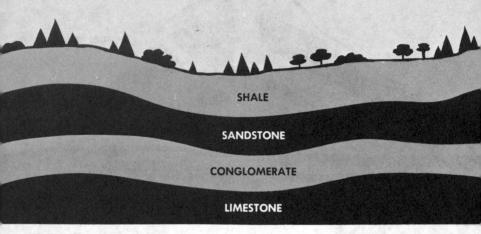

SHALE

SANDSTONE

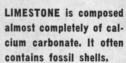CONGLOMERATE

LIMESTONE

SANDSTONE is made up of grains of quartz sand cemented together. It may be yellow, red, or brown.

LIMESTONE is composed almost completely of calcium carbonate. It often contains fossil shells.

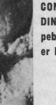

CONGLOMERATE or PUDDINGSTONE consists of pebbles cemented together by filling of fine sand.

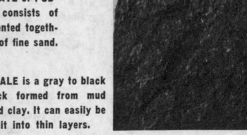

SHALE is a gray to black rock formed from mud and clay. It can easily be split into thin layers.

metamorphic rocks

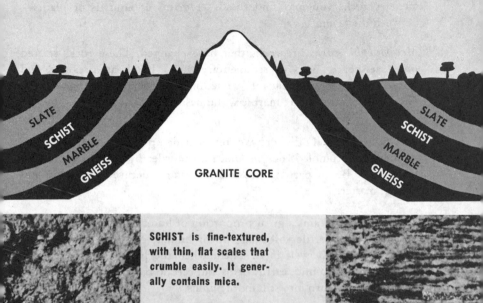

GRANITE CORE

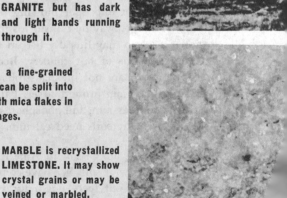

SCHIST is fine-textured, with thin, flat scales that crumble easily. It generally contains mica.

GNEISS (pronounced nice) looks much like GRANITE but has dark and light bands running through it.

SLATE is a fine-grained rock that can be split into layers, with mica flakes in the cleavages.

MARBLE is recrystallized LIMESTONE. It may show crystal grains or may be veined or marbled.

499

that have settled on top of each other. Layer was built upon layer, and eventually the pressure of the upper layer squeezed the bottom layers into solid rocks. Layers of sand grains became sandstone. Clay turned into shale, pebbles into conglomerate or puddingstone. Millions of tiny shells of sea animals hardened into limestone. In some of the sedimentary rocks you may find fossils—remains of animals or plants—between the layers.

Metamorphic rocks are rocks that have changed. These rocks started out as either igneous or sedimentary rocks; but heat, pressure, and water finally turned them into something else. Slate is changed shale. Gneiss once was granite; marble was limestone.

THE SOIL. The soil on which we step is made up of tiny particles. Some of them are crumbled rock ground into powder by the forces of wind and water. But a part of the soil is humus—decayed vegetable and animal matter.

The best soil contains a great proportion of humus. Loam, for example, is a fine, rich, fertile soil made up of humus, clay, and sand. Plants grow wonderfully well in it. Then, when the plants wither and die, and fall to the ground, earthworms and certain bacteria go to work and change them in turn into still more humus.

A farmer who has good soil takes good care of it. The farmer who must till poorer soil, does his utmost to keep what he has and improve it. He knows that improper plowing of the soil may cause the fertile layer to be swept away by rainstorms in erosion or cause it to dry into dust that a storm may literally lift up and carry off—as has happened in several sections of our country. Because elements in the soil vital to plant growth are not inexhaustible, it is necessary to restore them in order to maintain ground cover. Farmers use fertilizers to put back the nitrogen, potassium, and phosphate that plants consume. In addition to fertilizer, many soils need calcium.

We are learning our lesson in America, learning from bitter experience how to save our soil. We have come to appreciate more deeply the riches that lie at our feet—our natural wealth of minerals, rocks, and the good earth.

Soil erosion is the saddest thing you can see on a farm or on public lands. As topsoil washes away, the poor underlying subsoil is exposed and the land is riddled with gulleys. Result is small crops. In case of drought, soil may blow away in a duststorm.

Modern soil management employs contour plowing and strip planting. By plowing along the contour lines, rain cannot wash away the topsoil. Strips of grass or other planting between crops add further protection.

"EVERYBODY talks about the weather, but nobody does anything about it."

Of course, the reason "nobody does anything"—except a few scientists —is quite simple. There isn't much we *can* do.

Our weather is caused by three things playing together: the air, the sun, and the movement of the earth.

We live at the bottom of an ocean of air that rises above us, gradually thinning out, until at about 200 miles above the earth there is almost no air left. The air contains a number of gases (oxygen, nitrogen, carbon dioxide, and others), moisture in the form of invisible water vapor, and a lot of fine dust.

The air rests on the earth with a weight of about 15 pounds to a square inch at sea level and exerts a pressure equal to this weight. When air over a certain place heats up, it expands. As it expands, it gets lighter and the cooler air that surrounds it flows in under it. As the warm air rises there is less air above to press on it, and so its pressure becomes lower. Differences in temperature cause differences in pressure, and these pressure differences in turn cause the air to move. And air that moves over the earth's surface we call *wind*.

It is, of course, the sun that heats the air—mostly by first heating the earth, which then heats the air above it.

But the sun doesn't heat the air evenly. The air over desert land gets hot quickly; it takes the air over the ocean longer to warm up. At the equator, it's very hot; at the poles, it's very cold.

Since, generally speaking, cold air masses push warm air masses out of the way, you might think that the wind would always blow from the North Pole to the equator. But, because the earth rotates from west to east like a top around its own axis, air movements are thrown off their direct courses. The final result is that in northern Alaska the polar easterlies prevail while in the continental United States, north of the 30° latitude, the prevailing westerlies move the air from the Pacific to the Atlantic. States that extend below 30° latitude are influenced by the northeast trade winds for part of the year. Hawaii, Puerto Rico, and the Virgin Islands are in the northeast trade winds all year round. In the prevailing westerlies, the weather moves across our country at an average speed of 500 miles a day during the summer and 700 miles a day during the winter.

From time to time the prevailing westerlies are interrupted by whirlpools of air flowing counterclockwise around areas of low air pressure. Some of these low-pressure areas are very small—a tornado is an example. Other low-pressure areas extend over many miles. When the wind shifts from the southwest to the south, one of these interruptions in the normal weather pattern is approaching. The wind will continue to change direction from south to east, east to north, north to west, and finally back to southwest as the disturbance moves out.

The Weather Bureau of the U. S. Department of Commerce follows these movements closely through more than 400 stations scattered throughout the country.

Each day these stations report the local weather conditions and send in the readings of their various instruments. One instrument is the *barometer* which tells the pressure of the air, and shows when it gets higher and lower. Another is the *thermometer* that gives the temperature. The *hygrometer* measures the moisture (humidity) in the air.

On the basis of this information and photos from satellites, the Weather Bureau makes its daily weather reports and predictions. These predictions, in spite of the fun some people make of the "weatherman," hold true about 85 percent or more of the time on the average. But local conditions may upset the predictions.

TELLING THE WEATHER YOURSELF. When in camp, you won't have much chance to study weather maps. And yet, if you intend to go on a hike or take a canoe trip, you'll want to be sure that the good weather will hold. There are several things that will help you to forecast the weather—the wind, for example.

The west wind, that is a wind coming from the west, almost always brings clear, bright, cool weather (except in California and west Florida

atmospheric phenomena

Northern lights or aurora borealis may look like the dawn or a forest fire—or may be a wild display of colored rays, streamers, or moving curtains in the northern sky.

Tornado is the proper name for the dreaded "twister." It is a violently whirling and destructive column of air.

Rainbows are caused by sunlight being broken up by raindrops that act as prisms to disperse the colors.

where it carries in moisture from the sea). East of the Rockies, the east wind generally brings rain. The north wind brings a clear cold; the south wind, heat and often quick showers.

In winter, when the wind shifts to northeast, there's snow ahead; in the summer a rainstorm is on its way. The northwest wind brings cold waves in winter, cooler weather in summer.

The wind from the southwest is warm—in the summer often scorching. The wind from southeast is the wettest of them all.

The wind itself carries the heat. The water that falls as rain or snow comes from clouds brought in by the wind. When warm air gets cooled by ascending and expanding—as by blowing over high mountains —or by being pushed up after strong heating on the earth, for instance—some of its invisible moisture condenses into tiny droplets and clouds form.

To describe the shape of clouds, we use Latin words. There are three general types of clouds: (1) *cirrus,* featherlike; (2) *stratus,* in a layer; (3) *cumulus,* in big heaps. *Nimbus* is any cloud from which rain falls. Sometimes these descriptions are combined, such as cirrostratus (cirrus cloud in layers). If the word *alto* (high) is put in front of the name it indicates a formation high up in the atmosphere.

Some of these clouds follow each other in procession when a storm is brewing. First feathery, wind-blown *cirrus* clouds ("mare's tails") appear in the sky. They often warn that the fair weather is over; rain is coming in 24 to 48 hours. Now the clouds seem to get closer together in a layer that lies like a thin veil across the face of the sun: *cirrostratus.* The clouds come closer to the earth, the sun gets duller as *altostratus* sweeps before it like a gray curtain. Then a blanket of *stratus* covers us, completely

clouds

The clouds lower and these alto-cumulus clouds make the sun look as if it were shining through ground glass.

When stratus clouds darken and release their moisture they become nimbostratus clouds. The word "nimbus" means rainstorm.

shutting off the sun. Rain is ahead, within 6 or 7 hours. *Nimbostratus,* black and threatening, brings it in. This sequence of cloud forms will likely produce a long siege of moderate precipitation but no violent storms. There may be brief squalls as the front moves by, heralded by fast-moving low scud.

But there is a great difference between the gray blanket of nimbostratus covering the sky and the truly frightening blackness of a gigantic cumulonimbus or group of such clouds that may cover thousands of square miles in one vast storm system. These last clouds produce the killer storms with lightning, hail, tornadic winds, flash floods, and other dangers to life and property. They usually pass swiftly, even though they may occur daily or seem to be continuous, and are considered local compared to our overall weather pattern. However, if you sight them to windward, be prepared!

In the summertime, your predictions based upon the clouds may not always come true. There's an old saying: "All signs of rain fail in dry weather." The cirrus cloud may be swept off the sky by a hot sun. The sun may disperse the stratus. So you'll have to take other things into consideration.

There are clouds that appear in the sky in good weather that foretell bad weather to come—as we have seen previously—but there will be no actual precipitation from cirrus, cirrostratus, or altostratus clouds, though they may be part of a storm sequence. And there are other clouds that can be called fair-weather clouds even when there may be a spatter of rain or dusting of snow from them on occasion; unless there is a rapid wind-direction change, fair weather will likely hold.

The *altocumulus* is a typical cloud of the summer sky. It looks like a flock of white sheep drifting lazily across the sky. Sometimes it is broken into

Altocumulus are fair-weather indicators but seldom last long.

Stratocumulus clouds appear gray and dull. They may turn to rain clouds, nimbostratus.

Cumulus "fair-weather" clouds are welcomed by all outdoorsmen.

Cirrocumulus is the mackerel sky preceding change in weather.

In hot weather, the cumulus fair-weather clouds may bunch together and begin to rise, forming impressive but ugly thunder-heads or cumulonimbus, often in afternoon.

smaller clouds, *cirrocumulus,* that look like the scales of a fish ("mackerel sky"). They mostly indicate fair weather, but may bring unsettled weather with quick showers. *Stratocumulus* are rolls of clouds of darker color. The most beloved of clouds is the *cumulus,* huge masses of white fluff like a woolpack in the sky. But beware of the cumulus when on a hot summer's day it gets overgrown and becomes the *cumulonimbus* or thunderhead, the breeder of violent storms.

Difference between wet-bulb and dry-bulb readings	Temperature of air, dry-bulb thermometer, Fahrenheit							
	30°	40°	50°	60°	70°	80°	90°	100°
1	90	92	93	94	95	96	96	97
2	79	84	87	89	90	92	92	93
3	68	76	80	84	86	87	88	90
4	58	68	74	78	81	83	85	86
6	38	52	61	68	72	75	78	80
8	18	37	49	58	64	68	71	71
10		22	37	48	55	61	65	68
12		8	26	39	48	54	59	62
14			16	30	40	47	53	57
16			5	21	33	41	47	51
18				13	26	35	41	47
20				5	19	29	36	42
22					12	23	32	37
24					6	18	26	33

TABLE OF RELATIVE HUMIDITY – MEASURING MOISTURE

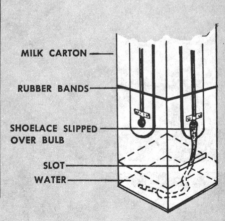

MILK CARTON ——

RUBBER BANDS ——

SHOELACE SLIPPED OVER BULB ——

SLOT ——
WATER ——

WET-BULB HYGROMETER. Comparison of readings on the wet-bulb thermometer with those on a dry-bulb thermometer will show relative humidity by using this table. For instance, if the difference between dry- and wet-bulb thermometers is 6 degrees, and the dry bulb reads 70 degrees, the relative humidity is 72.

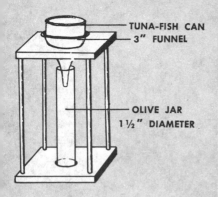

TUNA-FISH CAN
3" FUNNEL

OLIVE JAR
1 ½" DIAMETER

RAIN GAUGE. You can measure very small amounts of rain in this simple rain gauge. The ratio is 4 to 1 which means that 1 inch of water caught in the glass jar represents ¼ inch of rain on the ground. The tuna can, minus its top and bottom, is a splash guard to capture all of the rain that falls on the funnel.

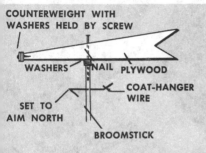

COUNTERWEIGHT WITH
WASHERS HELD BY SCREW

WASHERS   NAIL   PLYWOOD

COAT-HANGER
WIRE

SET TO
AIM NORTH

BROOMSTICK

WIND VANE. Weather vanes must be perfectly balanced and pivot on a bearing, in this case a washer. The downwind feather part must be longer and lighter than the arrowhead part. When the wind blows the arrow points into the wind and indicates which direction the wind is coming from.

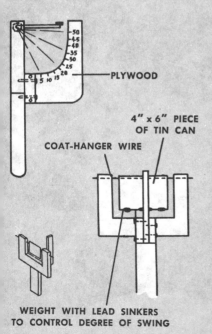

PLYWOOD

4" x 6" PIECE
OF TIN CAN

COAT-HANGER WIRE

WEIGHT WITH LEAD SINKERS
TO CONTROL DEGREE OF SWING

ANEMOMETER. Set the scale on your anemometer by holding it outside the window of a car on a windless day. Have the driver hold at a steady 5 miles per hour and mark the degree of swing on your blade. Increase car speed to 10 miles per hour and mark. Repeat at 5-mile-per-hour intervals. If the blade swings to its top limit at low speeds, weight with lead, test again, and make new calibrations.

23 THE HEAVENS

WILL YOU STAND ON THE MOON someday looking back at the earth and up to the stars? Who knows? Someone will, and it could be you. What will the constellations look like from that vantage point? Well, except for extra brilliance, you won't see any difference. They'll still have the same familiar shapes you learned on earth. Distances in the universe are so vast that changing the angle of view by the 200,000 plus miles from earth to moon doesn't change the position of the stars making up the constellations. So study the stars—learn the constellations and their relationship to one another. They'll be familiar friends to guide you when you explore the lunar landscape.

"CON"—TOGETHER; "STELLA"—STARS. For thousands of years people have grouped the stars together into figures—"constellations." The custom probably goes back to the times when men spent many of their nights under the stars, watching sheep or tending cattle. The shepherds thought they could see pictures of heroes, kings and queens, men, maidens, and monsters in the stars. They noticed, for example, two bright stars close together and got to thinking of the story of Castor and Pollux, twin brothers who loved each other dearly. Castor was killed in battle, and Pollux in his great grief asked Jupiter to let him share the same fate. So what was more appropriate than that the great god Jupiter should take pity on him and put the Gemini twins up in the sky where they could be together for all time?

CONSTELLATIONS AROUND THE POLE. To learn some of the constellations, all you need is a good starting point. And you can't ask for a better one than the *Big Dipper*. So find it in the northern sky.

There it is: The four stars that form the bowl of the dipper, and the three that make up the handle. Three, did we say? Not so fast. Look again at the second star in the handle. If you have good eyesight, you'll see that it is really two stars: one larger one with another, smaller, next

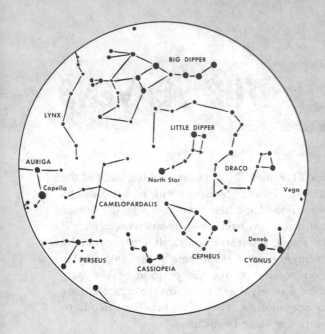

Circumpolar constellations are above the horizon every night of the year as they revolve around the North Star, although their positions differ daily. They are useful guideposts to other constellations and stars, including the pole star or North Star.

to it. The Indians used the two to test the sight of their children. They called the large star the *squaw,* the other on her back the *papoose.*

Now, let the pointers of the Big Dipper—those two stars farthest from the handle—guide you to the *North Star.* Look around it, and you'll notice that the North Star belongs at the end of the handle of a smaller dipper. So there's your next constellation: The *Little Dipper.* Between the two Dippers dangles *Draco,* the *Dragon,* a long wandering line of not-too-bright stars.

Back to the Big Dipper again. Continue from the pointers through the pole star in a curved line across the sky till you strike a crooked W formed of five stars. This is *Cassiopeia,* the *Lady in the Chair.* The lady's husband, King *Cepheus,* is close by. He looks more like a square house with a triangular roof than a king.

Next imagine a line across the line between the Big Dipper and Cassiopeia, crossing it at the North Star. In one direction along this line (the same direction in which the handle of the Big Dipper lies) you'll see a bright star that seems to have a rectangle of four smaller stars hanging on to it. This bright star is *Vega,* in the constellation the *Lyra.*

In the opposite direction from the North Star is another bright star with three faint ones near it. It is *Capella,* the She-Goat, with the *Kids.* They belong in *Auriga,* the *Charioteer,* a five-sided figure.

So far, so good. Only keep in mind that Vega dips under the horizon when Capella is high in the sky, and vice versa. The reason is that the stars seem to turn around the earth every 24 hours in the same direction as the sun, from east to west. It isn't the stars that move, but the earth turning on its axis. If that were the only movement of the earth, then the same stars would be out each night at the same time. But since the earth moves around the sun, the star schedule is upset. The result is that a certain star rises 4 minutes earlier each night, until—after a year —it rises again at the same time. As seasons change, you'll see different stars overhead and to the south. The stars directly to the north will be the same, but those *above* the North Star at one season will be *below* the North Star at the same hour of the evening 6 months later.

The Great Bear, or Ursa Major, contains the Big Dipper, perhaps the best-known skymark in the Western Hemisphere. The Big Dipper makes up about one-quarter of Ursa Major. The Greeks and the North American Indians saw this star grouping as a large bear in the sky looking for a place to hibernate.

A time exposure of the stars around the North Star show star trails of light. This photo was made with a 4-hour exposure with the lens set at infinity.

summer constellations

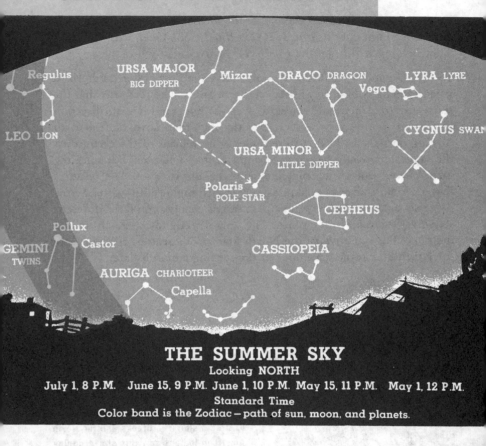

Regulus   URSA MAJOR   Mizar   DRACO DRAGON   LYRA LYRE
BIG DIPPER   Vega

LEO LION   CYGNUS SWAN
           URSA MINOR
           LITTLE DIPPER
       Polaris
       POLE STAR   CEPHEUS

Pollux
GEMINI   Castor   CASSIOPEIA
TWINS
    AURIGA CHARIOTEER
       Capella

THE SUMMER SKY
Looking NORTH
July 1, 8 P.M.   June 15, 9 P.M.   June 1, 10 P.M.   May 15, 11 P.M.   May 1, 12 P.M.
Standard Time
Color band is the Zodiac — path of sun, moon, and planets.

SUMMER STARS. On a summer's evening, locate the stars that swing around the North Star: the Dippers, Cassiopeia, Vega, Capella.

This time, follow the pointers of the Big Dipper in the opposite direction from the North Star till you locate the sickle-shaped *Leo,* the *Lion,* with the star *Regulus.* Between the Regulus and Capella are the *Twins* —Castor and Pollux; between Capella and Cassiopeia, the three-armed figure of *Perseus;* between Cassiopeia and Vega five stars form a wide cross—*Cygnus,* the *Swan,* or *Northern Cross.*

Back to the Big Dipper. Follow the curved line of the handle until you reach *Arcturus,* the brightest star in a constellation that looks like

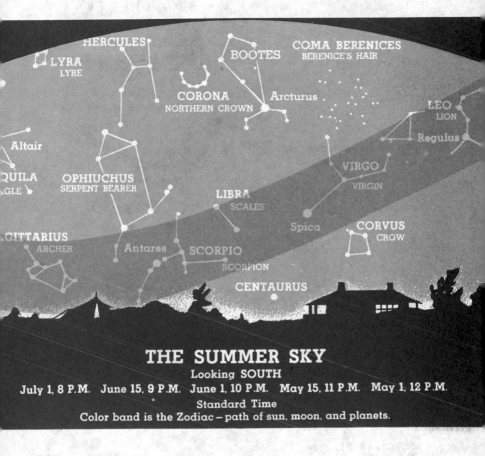

THE SUMMER SKY
Looking SOUTH
July 1, 8 P.M.   June 15, 9 P.M.   June 1, 10 P.M.   May 15, 11 P.M.   May 1, 12 P.M.
Standard Time
Color band is the Zodiac — path of sun, moon, and planets.

a big kite: *Boötes,* the Herdsman. Next to Boötes, you can make out a half circle of not particularly bright stars: *Corona Borealis,* the Northern Crown. Continuing, you see *Hercules,* shaped like a lopsided H, and then find yourself again at Vega.

Now look south. Right in front of you is *Scorpius.* Its tail swings toward the horizon, its head points toward *Spica,* the bright star of *Virgo,* the *Virgin.* Behind the Scorpion follows *Sagittarius,* the *Archer,* almost buried in the Milky Way, and above him in turn flies *Aquila,* the *Eagle.* It actually looks somewhat like a bird with wings spread. The brightest star of Aquila, the Eagle, is *Altair* which with Vega and *Deneb* in the Northern Cross form a large right triangle.

517

LYRA, the Lyre, is decorated by the brilliant diamond Vega—the brightest summer star.

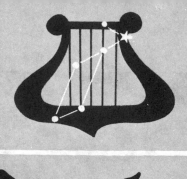

CYGNUS, the Swan, flies down the Milky Way. Deneb is her taillight or the head of the Northern Cross.

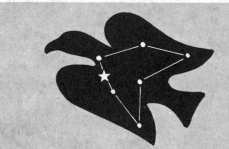

AQUILA is the Eagle of the ancient world. Altair in the Eagle's breast is the third star in the triangle with Vega and Deneb.

SAGITTARIUS, the Archer, between Capricorn and Scorpio in the Zodiac will look to you more like a teapot than a bowman.

HERCULES, the Superman of old, wore a poisoned shirt that killed him so Jupiter placed him in the sky.

518

CORONA, the Crown, is between the strong men of the sky — Hercules and Bootes.

BOOTES, the Herdsman, drives the Great Bear. The handle of the Big Dipper stretches toward golden-yellow Arcturus.

SCORPIO is a Scorpion in the Zodiac and rules the southern sky. Antares, as red as Mars, is the Scorpion's brightest star.

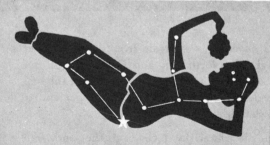

VIRGO, the Virgin, in the Zodiac is marked by Spica south of Arcturus and west of Antares.

LEO is the Lion that prowls along the Zodiac. Regulus is at the foot of a backward question mark.

winter constellations

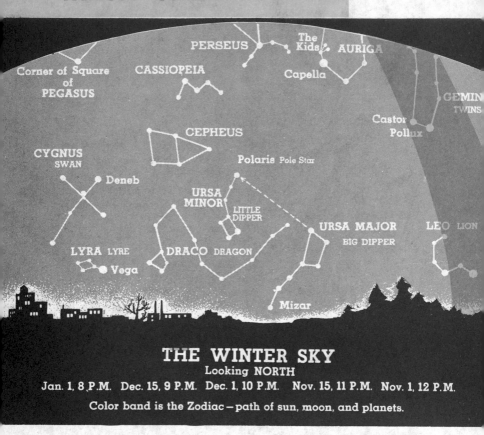

THE WINTER SKY
Looking NORTH
Jan. 1, 8 P.M.   Dec. 15, 9 P.M.   Dec. 1, 10 P.M.   Nov. 15, 11 P.M.   Nov. 1, 12 P.M.
Color band is the Zodiac — path of sun, moon, and planets.

WINTER STARS. On a winter's evening, start again from the Big Dipper. Follow the pointers through the North Star and Cassiopeia till you strike a line of three stars: *Andromeda.* The star at one end of the line, with three more, form the famed *Pegasus* square. The other end of Andromeda points toward Perseus, almost overhead.

The finest group of stars in the winter sky is *Orion* to the south. The Irish say O'Ryan is the greatest Irishman in heaven! Two bright stars —*Betelgeuse* and *Bellatrix*—make up his shoulders, three small ones form his triangular head, two more his legs—*Saiph* and *Rigel.* Three stars are his belt, three more his sword. Look at the sword through field glasses to see Orion's great nebula. Because Orion's belt is near

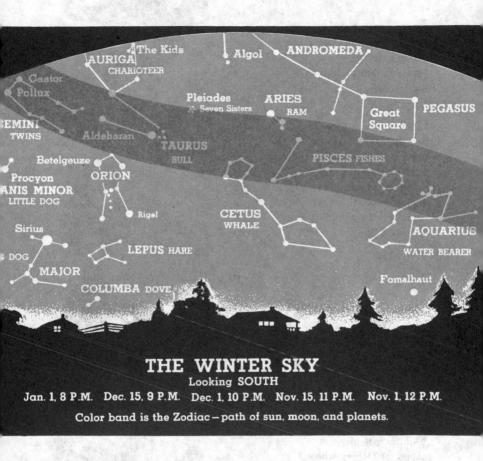

THE WINTER SKY
Looking SOUTH

Jan. 1, 8 P.M.   Dec. 15, 9 P.M.   Dec. 1, 10 P.M.   Nov. 15, 11 P.M.   Nov. 1, 12 P.M.

Color band is the Zodiac – path of sun, moon, and planets.

the celestial equator, it can help you find directions. The first star in the belt, the one to the right, rises due east and sets due west. Orion's sword points in a southerly direction.

Draw a line upward through Orion's belt. First you come to the red star *Aldebaran,* the "eye" in the V-shaped head of the *Bull.* Continuing further you find the *Pleiades* or *Seven Sisters.* If you have good eyesight, you can count six. In a telescope, you'll see more than two hundred. If you don't have a telescope, use field glasses.

Back to Orion again. This time follow the line through his belt in the opposite direction till you hit *Sirius.* Next to our own sun, it is the brightest star in the sky.

521

GEMINI, the Twins — Castor and Pollux are the two bright stars. The constellation is in the Zodiac.

CANIS Major and Minor, the Dogs — the Little Dog's star, Procyon, is a neighbor only a few light-years away. The Big Dog's star, Sirius, is the brightest star in the heavens.

AURIGA, the Charioteer, is a five-sided figure. Capella, the Goat Star, has three little stars nearby called the kids.

ORION, the Hunter, out-shines all others with Betelgeuse and Bellatrix in his shoulders and Saiph and Rigel at his knees. The right-hand belt star marks the celestial equator.

TAURUS, the Bull, has two star groups: the V-shaped Hyades with the red star Aldebaran and the Pleiades.

PERSEUS, the Champion, cut off Medusa's head and rescued Andromeda. Algol in Medusa's head varies in magnitude.

ANDROMEDA, the Chained Lady, is a constellation and a part of another — Pegasus. When you recognize it look for the nebula near her right hand.

PEGASUS, the Winged Horse, gallops across the sky upside down. You can find one corner of the Great Square by drawing a line from Polaris to Cassiopeia and extending it that distance again.

PISCES, the Fishes, are tied together and appear at the sides of the Great Square of Pegasus. A circle of stars represents one of the fish in the Zodiac.

AQUARIUS, the Water Bearer, in the Zodiac is near the circle of Pisces. The bright star is Fomalhaut.

stars by compass

Using the tables below, you can identify the bright stars with your compass. As you know, Polaris is almost directly over the North Pole, so if you face Polaris and take a compass reading, you should be able to see for yourself what correction you must make to adjust for variation. If your reading is 350°, you must subtract 10°, if your reading is 010°, you must add 10° to each direction value below. While it is not essential to know exactly how high above the horizon a star is, altitude will help you know where to look. One way to measure altitude makes use of the Silva compass held on edge. Face Polaris, hold the compass housing in your left hand with the index finger over the letter N and

summer stars

Date		July 1		June 15		June 1		May 15		May 1	
Standard Time		8 P.M.		9 P.M.		10 P.M.		11 P.M.		12 P.M.	
STAR AND		55° LATITUDE		45° LATITUDE		35° LATITUDE		25° LATITUDE			
MAGNITUDE		Dir.*	Alt.†	Dir.*	Alt.†	Dir.*	Alt.†	Dir.*	Alt.†		
Vega	0.1	088°	48°	078°	45°	068°	45°	058°	38°		
Arcturus	0.2	190°	54°	190°	65°	200°	72°	Overhead			
Altair	0.9	096°	15°	095°	14°	090°	15°	088°	15°		
Spica	1.2	202°	22°	202°	32°	205°	40°	210°	50°		
Antares	1.2	—	—	155°	15°	155°	22°	150°	32°		
Pollux	1.2	298°	15°	300°	10°	—	—	—	—		
Deneb	1.3	060°	35°	055°	38°	050°	25°	048°	18°		
Regulus	1.3	260°	24°	265°	25°	268°	25°	272°	25°		

*Direction †Altitude

your thumb over the letter S and sight over your thumb to the horizon. Keep your left hand steady and twist the plastic plate upward until you can see Polaris above its edge. Now read the degree opposite the *direction of travel*. That reading is the altitude of Polaris and the approximate latitude of where you are.

Notice that Betelgeuse varies from brighter than Procyon to dimmer than Aldebaran. Stars as bright as these, that you cannot account for, are probably the planets: Venus, Jupiter, Mars, or Saturn.

For the dates and time listed Sirius is not visible in Alaska but is 20° above the horizon and due south the first week in March at 8 p.m. Fomalhaut is visible in Maine and Oregon 15° above the horizon and is due south at 8 p.m. the first week in November.

winter stars

Date		Jan. 1		Dec. 15		Dec. 1		Nov. 15		Nov. 1	
Standard Time		8 P.M.		9 P.M.		10 P.M.		11 P.M.		12 P.M.	
STAR AND		55° LATITUDE		45° LATITUDE		35° LATITUDE		25° LATITUDE			
MAGNITUDE		Dir.*	Alt.†	Dir.*	Alt.†	Dir.*	Alt.†	Dir.*	Alt.†		
Sirius	−1.6	—	—	122°	08°	120°	14°	118°	18°		
Capella	0.2	095°	65°	075°	63°	058°	60°	045°	54°		
Rigel	0.3	142°	20°	138°	28°	135°	34°	128°	42°		
Betelgeuse	0.1 1.2	124°	30°	118°	35°	110°	38°	104°	42°		
Procyon	0.5	102°	14°	098°	15°	095°	18°	092°	18°		
Aldebaran	1.1	142°	48°	132°	54°	120°	60°	104°	64°		
Pollux	1.2	085°	31°	078°	30°	074°	28°	068°	24°		
Fomalhaut	1.3	—	—	—	—	—	—	230°	12°		

*Direction   †Altitude

solar system

THE STARS ARE SUNS. Yes, our sun is a star with the rest—and, to us, the most important of them all.

The reason it is large and hot and brilliant is simply because it is so much closer than the others. The sun is some 93 million miles away. One of the nearest stars, Sirius, is 25 times as bright, but 50 trillion miles away. Can't grasp the immense distances? Then think of it like this: If we let this dot · represent the earth, the sun will be over there ◗ about 100 *feet* away, Sirius more than 10,000 *miles* away.

How big is the sun? 109 earths could be placed in a line side by side across the surface of it. They wouldn't remain there long, though. The terrific heat would turn them into vapor in a flash.

Without the heat and the light of the sun, there would be no life on earth. Besides, the sun gives us day and night and the seasons of the year. By the sun we tell the time, and ships at sea determine their exact position with its help at high noon.

THE PLANETS. Our sun has a family. The earth belongs to this family, but so do other bodies that swing through the sky.

The earth is a planet, a cold body that has no light of its own but reflects the light of the sun. Between us and the sun are the planets *Mercury and Venus.* Farther away from the sun than we are *Mars, Jupiter, Saturn, Uranus, Neptune, Pluto.* Between Mars and Jupiter whirl the *asteroids,* 2,000 or more baby planets, some of them only a couple of miles in diameter.

Venus, Mars, Jupiter, and Saturn you can see with the naked eye as bright spots in the heavens. Occasionally, Mercury is visible also in early evening or early morning.

Although the planets travel in the Zodiac and always close to the ecliptic (path traveled by the sun), they do not keep the same position relative to the stars, but seem to wander among them. Early astronomers noticed that their paths were not straight but contained loops they had trouble explaining. A study of those loops finally gave the clue to the fact that the sun is the center of our system, not the earth, as people thought at one time.

OUR SOLAR SYSTEM is made up of bodies re-
volving around the Sun—the planets and leftovers called asteroids. Pluto is farthest away—
so far the Sun would look like a bright star. And
yet our whole solar system tucks into a small
corner of the galaxy to which we belong.

PLUTO is 3.61
billion miles from
the Sun.

NEPTUNE is closer
—some 2.79 bil-
lion miles.

URANUS, fourth
largest, is 1.78
billion miles.

SATURN is only
886 million miles
from the Sun.

JUPITER, biggest,
is 484 million
miles out.

SUN, our star, a
whirling furnace
of hydrogen and
—source of our
energy.

EARTH. We are
92.9 million or so
miles out.

MARS, our neigh-
bor, 142 million
miles from Sun.

ASTEROIDS, cos-
mic dust, 200—
400 million miles.

ERCURY, only
million miles
m the heat.

VENUS is a mere
67.2 million miles
from our Sun.

THE MOON. Some of the planets have several moons. The earth has only one, as you know.

Our moon is 240,000 miles away from us. Yet, by a queer coincidence, its size is such that it almost exactly covers the sun when it happens to pass before it at times of sun eclipses. Another coincidence: The moon turns around its own axis with precisely the same speed it moves around the earth. That's the reason that it always shows the same face to us.

The moon itself gives off no light. The light we get from the moon, like the light from the planets, is reflected sunlight. When you look at the moon, you see darker and lighter patches. To some people they take on the shape of a "man in the moon." They are simply the mountains and plains of the moon reflecting the sunlight differently. Look at the moon through field glasses. It will appear round and very much like the pictures on the next page.

Besides lighting up the earth at night, the moon has the tremendously important effect of causing (with the sun) the tides—the rise and fall of the waters in the ocean twice each day.

SHOOTING STARS. If you look at the sky after midnight and later—on a bright August night, especially around August 11—you may see a number of "shooting stars." Since they look as if they come out of the constellation Perseus, they are called the *Perseids*. You may see shooting stars at other times, too, but August is the big month.

Shooting stars are not stars at all, but *meteors*—bodies of various metals and minerals that fly through the universe. When the earth gets close to their paths, it attracts them; and, as they fall through the air, friction causes them to heat and glow and most of them burn up in bright streaks. It is estimated that 20 million meteors—not counting those visible only in telescopes—enter our atmosphere everyday. Many of them reach the earth without burning up and traces of them are found from time to time. They usually contain varying amounts of iron and nickel as well as many rocklike components. Those that reach the earth's surface are called *meteorites*.

LEARN MORE ABOUT THE SKY. The deeper you get into star study, the more you'll want to know of especially interesting stars, of the *Milky Way,* and of numerous other signs in the sky. The more you know, the better will be your understanding of the universe.

moon phases

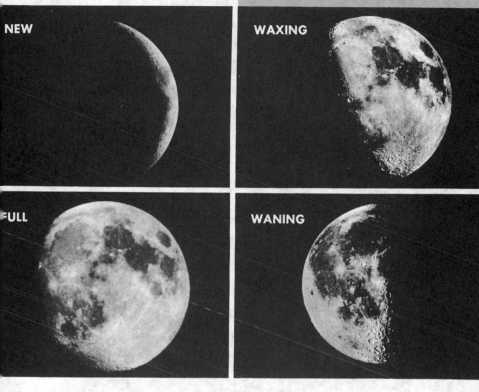

NEW

WAXING

FULL

WANING

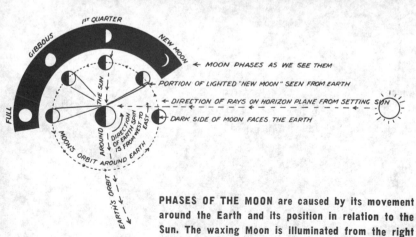

← MOON PHASES AS WE SEE THEM
← PORTION OF LIGHTED "NEW MOON" SEEN FROM EARTH
← DIRECTION OF RAYS ON HORIZON PLANE FROM SETTING SUN →
← DARK SIDE OF MOON FACES THE EARTH

PHASES OF THE MOON are caused by its movement around the Earth and its position in relation to the Sun. The waxing Moon is illuminated from the right and the waning Moon from the left.

52

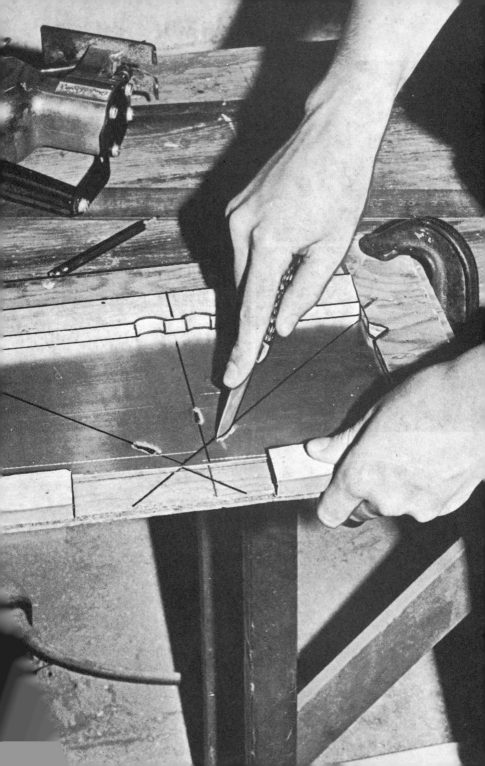

24 BETWEEN ADVENTURES

GREAT ADVENTURES are not accidents. Just as in a contest the players make the breaks. They do it by thinking through each situation and deciding what they should do in that event. Then they practice until the right move is automatic.

You've sailed through some easy weather camping and Old Man Winter may have taught you a thing or two. By now, you may be an expert outdoorsman. If you are, you're still looking for the best pack, the easiest riding pack frame, the lightest reflector oven, the surest way to keep from getting lost, and a thousand other things. That's the funny thing about experts: The more they know; the more they want to know. So, between adventures, sharpen your skills as well as your ax.

You've used topographic maps before and you know how tough it is to keep them from fluttering in the wind. If you fold them, the creases become worn and dirty. That's not all, often the spot that you're mainly concerned with is just off the map. High-adventure area topographic maps are easier to use when they are mounted on cloth. They'll last longer because the cloth folds, allowing the printed map portions to remain flat. Mounting maps has another advantage: You can combine them to include areas that appear on more than one quandrangle. You can't buy mounted maps. You must do the job yourself and it goes a lot faster if you do it with some other fellows. What's more, it's as easy to mount a dozen maps as it is one. As a matter of fact, if you do a good job, you could go into the business and mount maps—for a price. This is what you need: yardstick, pencil, wallpaper paste, *cotton* cloth, 2-inch brush, two pots or pans—one for paste and one for water, newspapers, pinking shears, and room to work.

If you divide the map into equal panels, the mounted map will have a Z-fold. While this fold is acceptable, the U-fold is better because middle panels can be folded out. To use a middle panel in the Z-fold, you must open the map as you would open a book.

mounting maps

To provide for a U-folding as well as a Z-folding map, divide each map using as guides the 5-minute markings for 15-minute maps and the 2½-minute markings for 7½-minute maps. Divide panels I, 2, and 3 above the crossmarks; panels 7, 8, and 9 below; panels I, 4, and 7 to the left; and panels 3, 6, and 9 to the right of the crossmarks.

Making the middle panels larger than the others permits the map to be folded down to any one of the nine sections. If the panels are all the same size, only the outside panels will show in the map case.

Spread newspapers on your worktable and cover the papers with a cloth. Mix some wallpaper paste into a pint of water until the mixture looks like canned applesauce. Dip a piece of cotton cloth into the water. Let it hang—don't wring it. Spread the wet cloth on the table and brush paste into the cloth.

Cut out panel I, wet it in the water, brush paste on the back, and place on the cloth. Read a word to be sure you have it right side up. Repeat for panel 2 and position ⅛ to ¼ inch from panel I.

Continue the process for the other panels being sure that they are right side up and are equally spaced to allow for straight folds, horizontally and vertically.

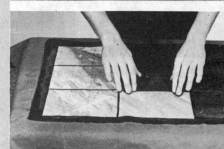

Brush a light coating of paste over the map panels which will provide a transparent protective covering when dry.

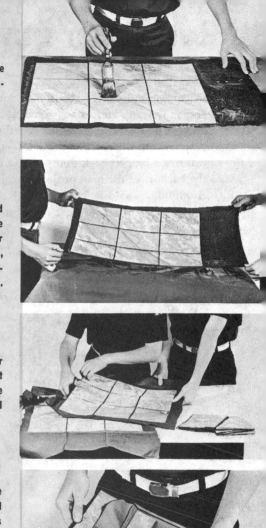

Pick up the cloth by the corners and transfer it to a flat newspaper pad. Be sure that it is out of the sun. An hour later, pick up the cloth by the corners, turn it over, and press out the air bubbles. Turn the map faceup and let it dry.

Trim the edges and fold. Place under some heavy books overnight. The next day, mark in India ink the name of the quadrangle, scale, date of issue, and magnetic declination.

For heavy-duty, wet-weather use make a map case from frosted acetate and heavy cloth or leather. A number of cases can be made from one sheet of acetate. You can make pencilled notes on the frosted side of the acetate and erase them later. The flap tucks in to keep the map in place. Sew with nylon fishline.

If you find it difficult to keep compass north and map north separated, rule in compass north lines on the acetate.

backpacker's oven

When you must carry all of your equipment, ounces and space become very important. Here are two ovens, each fit into an envelope and weigh only 15 ounces. One oven fits together by sliding the reflector and rack tongues into the slots of the sides—this oven is rigid. The other model features a hinged back that lets you reposition biscuits in comfort from the back. Like the map project, this job has possibilities for production. Aluminum is sold in 36- by 36-inch sheets—enough for three ovens. Of course, if you prefer larger ovens you can make only two.

Make a tray jig for the side pieces. The jig should extend beyond the bench and be large enough to clamp securely to the bench. Frame the sides with lath or scrap plywood, but leave an opening in the front for the saber saw. Drill holes for the saw blade and cut slots in the jig. Make stop marks on the frames for the saw guides.

The top reflector pivots on a threaded rod that is rolled into the top edge. When the oven is taken apart, thread the nuts on the rod. The nails, trapping the tongues in the slots, are not needed because they can be replaced by small pointed sticks.

The rigid oven has no moving parts. If you must change the position of a biscuit, you must either move the oven or work close to the fire. There are no small parts to pack.

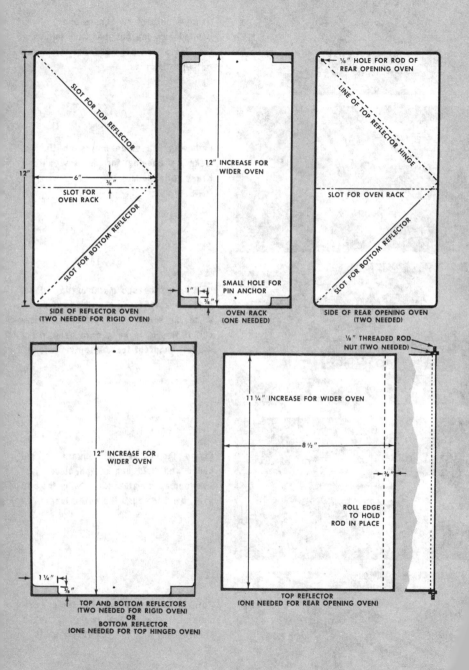

SLOT FOR TOP REFLECTOR

12"

6"

⅜"

SLOT FOR OVEN RACK

SLOT FOR BOTTOM REFLECTOR

SIDE OF REFLECTOR OVEN
(TWO NEEDED FOR RIGID OVEN)

12" INCREASE FOR WIDER OVEN

1"

⅜"

SMALL HOLE FOR PIN ANCHOR

OVEN RACK
(ONE NEEDED)

⅛" HOLE FOR ROD OF REAR OPENING OVEN

LINE OF TOP REFLECTOR HINGE

SLOT FOR OVEN RACK

SLOT FOR BOTTOM REFLECTOR

SIDE OF REAR OPENING OVEN
(TWO NEEDED)

12" INCREASE FOR WIDER OVEN

1¼"

⅜"

TOP AND BOTTOM REFLECTORS
(TWO NEEDED FOR RIGID OVEN)
OR
BOTTOM REFLECTOR
(ONE NEEDED FOR TOP HINGED OVEN)

⅛" THREADED ROD
NUT (TWO NEEDED)

11¼" INCREASE FOR WIDER OVEN

8½"

⅜"

ROLL EDGE TO HOLD ROD IN PLACE

TOP REFLECTOR
(ONE NEEDED FOR REAR OPENING OVEN)

Using a carpenter's square and a sharp pointed awl, lay out the parts following the diagram on page 535. Cut the pieces out with tin snips.

Following the guide marks on the jig, make an opening for the saw with a heavy knife blade.

Using a nonferrous metal cutting blade, guide the saw along the line to the stop V on the frame. Repeat for the center cut. If this is to be a rigid oven, make the left-hand cut for the top reflector.

Clamp the carpenter's square to the bench and hold one of the pieces just overlapping the steel edge. Using the ball peen, bend the edge the entire length.

Turn the piece over and tap the edge to square it. Leave the two long edges square bent on the rack to stiffen it.

536

On all other pieces flatten the bent edges. Don't peen the tongues and cheeks of the rack and reflectors.

A five-piece reflector oven isn't much good if a piece is missing. Besides, it needs protection—nothing elaborate—a simple cloth envelope does the job.

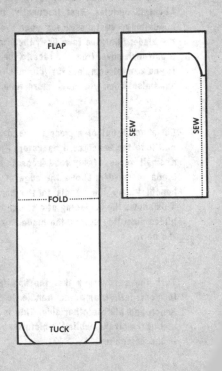

Put the parts together and place them across a piece of cloth a yard wide. Fold the material over the parts, tuck the top edge under, and bring the bottom edge over as a flap. The tuck can be 4 or 5 inches and the flap 6 or 7, depending upon cloth width. Mark the sides with chalk. Cut out the strip. Sew the sides. Turn inside out and round out the tuck with pinking shears.

ax conditioning

If you follow these directions, you can trim branches in a single stroke that usually took two or three strokes. You can use your ax as a woodsman's plane to smooth a log for a clean worktable. You can, if your eye is true, cut the dovetail notch (pages 80 and 81) with two strokes of your ax. The toe of your ax can be used as a chisel while you tap the butt gently with a chunk of wood. These wonderful promises can begin to come true when you can file your ax straight back making a bright half-moon on the blade (page 70). Remember that a file is a one-way tool—it's designed to cut when it's pushed. Push the file forward with just enough pressure to bite into the steel. Lift it up, return to the starting point, and push again.

How many strokes did it take on this side of the ax to make that pile of filings? About 15 minutes. Rest frequently, tired hands make mistakes. Keep your eye on the blade, filing the face first, then bring a half-inch bevel from the face to the bit. If you cannot complete the job, mask the ax, finish when you have more time.

Cut a notch out of a piece of wood and nail it to the bench as a backstop. Place a small piece of plywood beneath the blade to raise it above the edge of the bench. Clamp the handle to the bench. This shows the beginning of a stroke that glides smoothly across the blade toward the butt.

Turn the ax over so that the handle is to your left. Clamp the handle to the bench and file the other side. This is the end of the stroke, while the picture above is the beginning.

What's good for a big ax is good for a small one. On this model you do not need to file the face. Begin the stroke here and file straight back. Work for a half-inch bevel.

Turn the hand ax over and work the other side. This picture shows the stroke nearing its end. Lift the file from the ax and return.

Hone your ax with a hard, fine grit stone. Hold the head of the ax in your left hand and rub the stone down the ax edge from toe to heel, tipping the stone forward. Honing will turn the wire edge that develops when the ax is filed.

Cradle the head of the ax in your left hand. Now stroke the ax edge from heel to toe with the stone, thereby cutting off the wire edge that was bent to this side.

To be sure that you have removed the wire edge, draw the bit across a piece of wood. Look directly down at the ax edge, dull spots will show up as reflected light. A sharp bit is almost invisible.

tent pole pack frame

Double-duty equipment lightens your load. When you must carry tent poles, put them to work and take credit for carrying their weight. You'll need: a saber saw, an expansive bit, some cloth and plywood, ¾-inch webbing, 10 feet of nylon cord, monofilament 6-pound test nylon fishline, a fine needle, long tacks or sheet metal screws.

In scrap plywood, test drill until you find a setting of the expansive bit that snugly fits the bottom of the tent pole. Drill the holes halfway through the base and crosspiece. Adjust the expansive bit and test drill to find a setting that snugly fits the first shoulder on the pole. Complete the holes for the tent poles in the crosspiece. Cut out the base and crosspiece with a saber saw. Tack or screw the webbing tightly around the base and crosspiece. Sew the taper or strap angle in the straps and tightly sew the straps to the crosspiece, sewing into the edges of the webbing at the taper and at the top of the crosspiece.

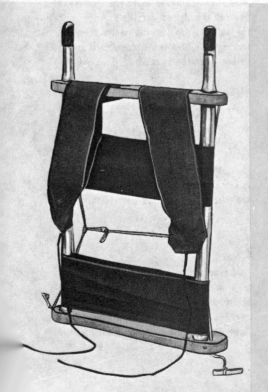

The straps and back protectors are made from several thicknesses of cloth. Department or dry goods stores may have ends of bolts of cloth that you can buy inexpensively. Any tightly woven cloth will do. The broad straps spread the weight over your shoulders making the load easy to carry. The knobs extending from the tent poles add length to the frame and protect the bag's support ears or pocket. The guy line, holding the frame together, has a toggle at one end and a smaller stick stopper tied 5 inches from the toggle.

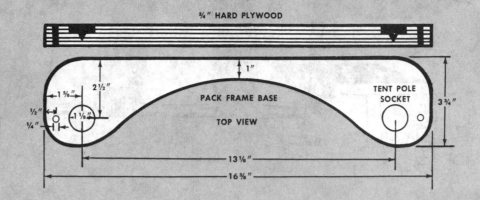

¾" HARD PLYWOOD

PACK FRAME BASE

TOP VIEW

TENT POLE SOCKET

1"

2½"

1⅝"

½"

¼"

1⅛"

3¾"

13⅛"

16⅝"

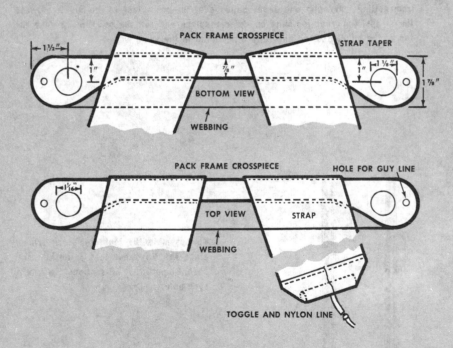

PACK FRAME CROSSPIECE

STRAP TAPER

1½"

1"

1⅛"

1"

⅞"

1⅞"

BOTTOM VIEW

WEBBING

PACK FRAME CROSSPIECE

HOLE FOR GUY LINE

1⅛"

TOP VIEW

STRAP

WEBBING

TOGGLE AND NYLON LINE

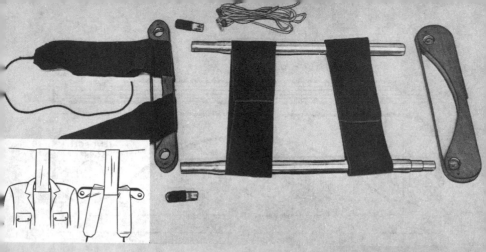

The frame comes apart easily. The poles go to work holding up the tent. The knobs, straps, bands, and base so far have nothing to do until the return trip—unless you need some coat hangers. Put the knobs in the crosspiece holes (just to keep them from getting lost), slip one of the bands over the crosspiece to the middle between the straps. Put your jac-shirt on the crosspiece and run the guy line through the top of the band. Use the base and other band in the same way.

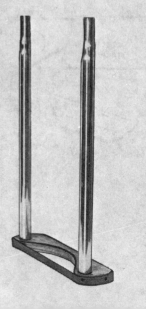

To assemble the tent pole pack frame, place the Voyageur tent poles into the base. Be sure that all sections are within each pole.

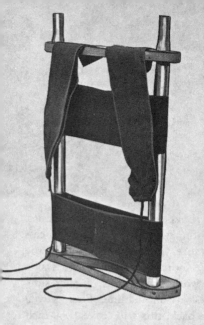

Place both protecting bands over the upright poles, then drop the crosspiece over the ends of the poles and push down until it stops. When you make the back protectors, fold several thicknesses of cloth into a 4-inch band. Wrap it around the poles and pin into the position. Chalk a line where the edges overlap. Take out the pins. Overlap the pieces making it tighter than when it was pinned to the frame. Tuck in the raw edges and tightly sew with monofilament fishline.

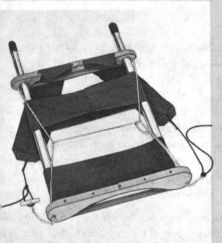

Run the loop end of the toggle line through the base at the left until the stopper hits the base. Thread the loop through the crosspiece at the left. Run the line over the crosspiece on this side of the poles and down through it—and through the base. Pull the line tight and tie an overhand knot in a bight. Bring the free end back upon itself and tie a taut-line hitch, pull tight, loop the free end around the left line and draw together until tight. Secure with two half hitches.

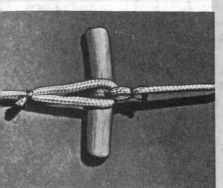

Strong nylon toggle lines are easy to make because you can whip the ends of the line by melting them in a match flame. You can sew the line together with monofilament fishline. Easy to sew—tough to break. Wrap line around your waist four times, make a loop in one end and put a grooved-stick toggle in the other.

trail pack

Big, modern, easy-to-make, the trail pack fits all standard pack frames. It takes only 2 yards of denim-weight cloth. Ask a dry cleaner to process the cloth to make it water-repellent before you lay it out. Chalk the layout on the cloth and cut only where indicated. Decide which side you wish to have on the inside—then work your seams on that side, sewing with monofilament 6-pound test nylon fishline. First, sew a 40-inch nylon cord along the fold at the back, this will leave 12½-inch tielines at the corners of the bag. Sew the bottom sides to the side pocket creases.

Then sew the front to the sides. Turn the bag right side out. Taper the unsewn edge of the side pocket, turning the raw edges in as you sew. Sew an 8-foot nylon cord into the top fold, and through the back crease at the top of the pack frame support pocket. This will provide 40-inch cords at the top of the bag to lash a sleeping bag to the top if the tent pole pack frame is used. When not on the frame, the ties can hold the pack against a tree. Crease the back top corners of the bag and double sew the pack frame support pocket seams securely. Working right side out and turning the raw edges in, sew the top corners. Hem the raw edges of the top and sew in cords for tie-downs.

Make a corded hem in the rim of the bag. Sew a 12-inch zipper to the bottom and top of the front pocket pieces. Sew the center pocket to the side beginning at the left 5 inches down from the top of the bag. Sew until you reach the bottom corner of the pocket. Now sew the other side to the bag in the same way. Take the pins from the corner, crease the other way to make a right triangle. Loop a 7-inch piece of nylon cord over the triangle and sew the ends inside, leaving the loop outside of the pocket for a tie-down. Fold the raw edges in and sew across the top and bottom of the pocket to a narrow crease that you put into the bag as you sew. Attach the flaps to the side pockets in the same way.

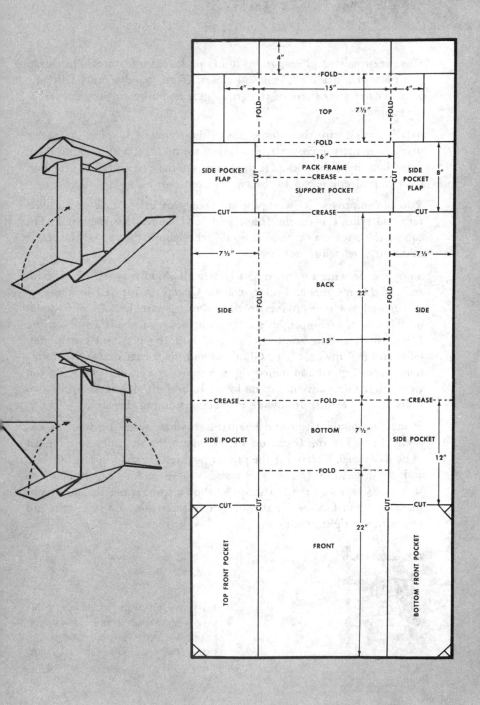

ely pack frame

This inexpensive and easy-to-make Ely pack frame features a hip strap that takes the strain off your shoulders. It can handle practically any pack to carry your share of the group gear and all your personal camping equipment.

Attach a pack with shoulder straps to the frame by looping the pack's straps over the top crossbar, drawing them up tight and hooking them to the bottom of the pack. Tie the D rings to the first and third crossbar. Lash your sleeping bag to the two bottom crossbars.

You can improvise by wrapping all your gear in a plastic or a canvas tarp and tying this on the frame with a diamond or spider hitch. The top of the pack may extend several inches above the top of the frame or about even with your head.

Study the drawing carefully. Cut to size all wooden parts. Notch both ends of the uprights and the crossbars. Clamp the hip-rest brackets together and saw five grooves in them 1 inch apart. Drive eight staples on the side of each upright, starting 6 inches from the top and leaving 1 inch between the staples. Glue and nail the plywood crosspieces. Glue and nail the crossbars. Glue and nail the corner braces. All joints must be well-glued and nailed tight. Keep your eye on them while you work, tightening any that come loose. Round off all edges. Apply two coats of spar varnish following instructions on can. Let dry.

String the shoulder rest and wrap the shoulder straps on without stapling them. Try the frame on to see where the shoulder straps need to be shortened. Determine the proper position for the hip-rest brackets and the hip strap (below the waist, square on the hips). Sew the shoulder straps and the hip straps as shown using a needle and monofilament nylon fishline for thread. Staple the straps and string the hip rest with the light nylon cord.

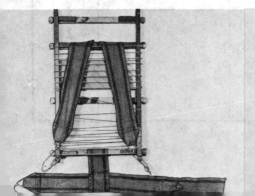

Tested on the trails at Philmont, this easy-to-make pack frame carries man-sized loads easier, because the hip strap shares the work with your shoulders.

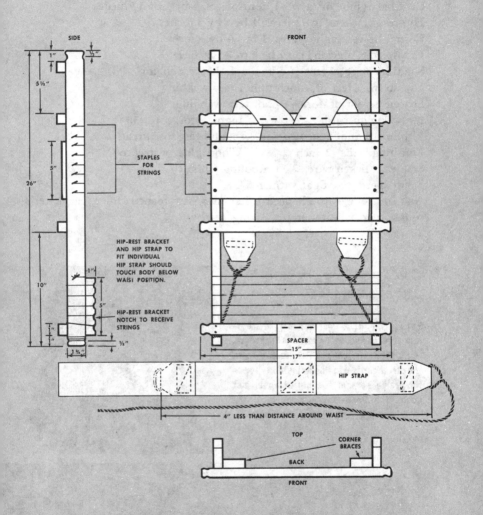

SIDE

1"

½"

5 ½"

26"

5"

STAPLES
FOR
STRINGS

HIP-REST BRACKET
AND HIP STRAP TO
FIT INDIVIDUAL
HIP STRAP SHOULD
TOUCH BODY BELOW
WAIST POSITION.

1"

10"

5"

HIP-REST BRACKET
NOTCH TO RECEIVE
STRINGS

1 ¾"

½"

FRONT

SPACER
15"
17"

HIP STRAP

4" LESS THAN DISTANCE AROUND WAIST

TOP

CORNER
BRACES

BACK

FRONT

Uprights (straight-grained, clear pine or spruce), two pieces, 1 by 2 by 26 inches

Crossbars (pine or spruce), four pieces, 1 by 1 by 17 inches

Hip-rest brackets, two pieces, 1 by 1 by 5 inches

Corner braces, eight pieces, 1 by 3/4 by 3 inches

Crosspiece (plywood), 1/4 by 5 by 15 inches

Shoulder strap, 4 feet of 4-inch upholstery webbing

Hip strap, 3 feet of 4-inch upholstery webbing

Spacer, 1 foot of 4-inch upholstery webbing

Heavy nylon cord, 8 feet   Light nylon cord, 30 feet

Fishline, monofilament nylon, 6-pound test for thread

Finishing nails, 2 inch   Wood glue, waterproof

Staples, chicken wire   Roofing nails, 1½ inch

Sandpaper   Spar varnish

And, of course, you'll need a hammer, saw, pencil, ruler, carpenter's square, pocketknife, and a sewing needle.

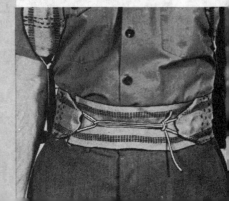

Notice that the spacer supports the bottom crossbar when the strap is turned up. In this photo, the position is too high, the strap cords must be adjusted to lower the frame so that the hip strap is just above the pockets. Then much of the pack's weight will ride on the hips.

You can adjust the tension of the strap by tightening the hip lash. The extra webbing protects your stomach. The top of the strap should be even with the top of your belt.

pail and basin

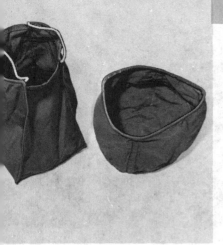

Water for cooking and washing provides some of the comforts of home on the trail as well as in camp. Using a yardstick and chalk, lay out the pieces on canvas or waterproofed cloth. Only one side is shown for the pail and basin, but two are needed. For the bottom of the basin — chalk a rectangle 10½ by 14 inches, cut out, fold in half, then round off the corners evenly.

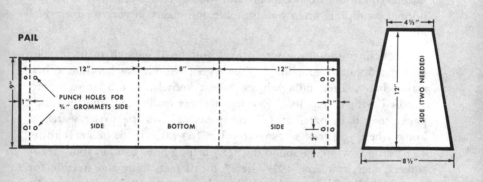

PAIL

12" 8" 12"

9"

1"

PUNCH HOLES FOR
¾" GROMMETS SIDE

SIDE   BOTTOM   SIDE

2"

4½"

SIDE (TWO NEEDED)

12"

8½"

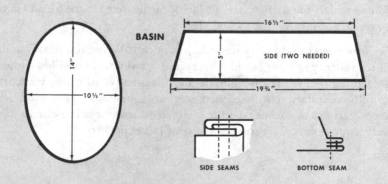

14"

10½"

BASIN

16½"

5"   SIDE (TWO NEEDED)

19¾"

SIDE SEAMS   BOTTOM SEAM

survival kits

Every good woodsman always carries a knife, matches in a waterproof container, a compass, and a few adhesive bandages in his pockets. Under normal conditions that's enough. But you're prepared for more than just normal conditions when you assemble and maintain your own survival kit.

The container should be waterproof and small enough to fit in your pocket. It should contain: (1) emergency food like bouillon cubes, ration bar, malted milk tablets, wheat kernels; (2) matches waterproofed with nail polish; (3) fire starters made from tightly rolled paper soaked in paraffin; (4) compass; (5) whistle to let searchers know where you are—saves your voice; (6) razor blade or small knife; (7) fishline, nylon, 25-pound test; (8) fishing lures good in your area— sinkers, flies, spinners; (9) wire, 5 to 10 feet, light and flexible for snares; (10) adhesive tape, 1 inch wide and 6 to 12 inches long; (11) pencil and paper for messages; (12) aluminum foil, two sheets 12 inches square to make drinking and cooking utensils; (13) bandages; (14) iodine tablets to purify water; (15) list of the items in the kit and dates to replace or inspect items 1 and 10.

Ice fishermen should carry ice awls just in case. When you're swimming in icy water, you want out in a hurry and it's almost impossible without something like an ice awl. Simple and inexpensive to make, yet worth a million dollars. Use hardened steel masonry nails—the kind that carpenters use to anchor wood to concrete or masonry. These nails have very sharp points. Carry ice awls in your jacket pockets.

Don't try to saw the head off, instead put the nail in a vise and snap the head off by striking it with a hammer or working it back and forth with a wrench.

Make a handle from a piece of hardwood. Smooth it down and drill a 1/8-inch hole in the end. If you use a piece of green hardwood from a branch, oven dry the wood for an hour.

Clamp the nail point down in the vise. Tap the handle to drive the headless part of the nail into the drill hole. Drive the handle all the way down to the vise jaws.

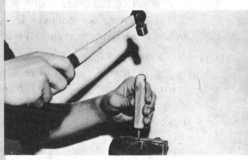

The million dollar do-it-yourself rescue kit won't be much good if the handle splits out the first time it's used. Therefore, whip the end of the awl handle to ensure your investment.

Cut two short pieces of the same wood. Drill a shallow hole in each one to mask the awl point. Drill 1/4-inch holes through the top of the handles and fasten a nylon cord to both awls.

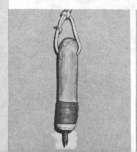

lifetime career

The greatest adventure is finding the right career for you. Now, Scouting means fun and fellowship, but it can mean much more. Did you know that throughout America over 4,000 men and women enjoy working in Scouting full time?

As you know, a pack, troop, or post is chartered by an organization such as a church, synagogue, civic club, business, school organization, or group of citizens. To administer the program in your area, there is a voluntary association that includes representatives from the groups using the program. The association is called a council, and it is staffed by a small number of professionally trained leaders who guide these volunteers.

If you like to work with people, helping them make Scouting available and effective for more young people, Scouting cold be your profession. There are over 400 councils in America, each with its local leadership, office, camp, and professional staff.

Your council office is listed under "Boy Scouts of America" in the white pages of the telephone directory. Your executive would like to talk with young people who are interested in Scouting as a career. Don't think that you are too young, because you can start now to learn how Scouting operates and how you can prepare yourself for this great adventure.

Books Have the Answers

AQUATICS

Basic Canoeing. American Red Cross.

Basic Outboard Boating. American Red Cross.

Basic Rowing. American Red Cross.

Basic Sailing. American Red Cross.

Boys' Life reprint pamphlets: *Boats and Canoes, Swimming and Waterfront Activities.* Boy Scouts of America.

Canoeing. Carle W. Handel.

Merit badge pamphlets: *Canoeing. Lifesaving, Motorboating, Rowing, Small-Boat Sailing, Swimming, Water Skiing.* Boy Scouts of America.

Swimming and Water Safety. American Red Cross.

CAMP ACTIVITIES

Book of Indian Crafts and Costumes, The. Bernard S. Mason.

Book of Indian Crafts and Indian Lore, The. Julian H. Salomon.

Complete Book of Campfire Programs. LaRue A. Thurston.

Dances and Stories of the American Indian. Bernard S. Mason.

Golden Book of Indian Crafts and Indian Lore, The. W. Ben Hunt.

Merit badge pamphlets: *Archery, Athletics, Indian Lore, Orienteering, Pioneering, Signaling.* Boy Scouts of America.

Scout Songbook. Boy Scouts of America.

Universal American Indian Sign Language. William Tomkins.

CAMPING AND HIKING

Be Expert With Map and Compass —The Orienteering Handbook. Bjorn Kjellstrom.

Complete Book of Camping. Leonard Miracle with Maurice Decker.

Golden Book of Camping and Camp Crafts, The. Gordon Lynn.

Jack-Knife Cookery. James Austin Wilder.

Merit badge pamphlets: *Camping, Cooking, Cycling, Hiking, Orienteering, Skiing, Surveying.* Boy Scouts of America.

New Way of the Wilderness, The. Calvin Rutstrum.

Outdoor Chef, The. Paul W. Handel.

Wildwood Wisdom. Ellsworth Jaeger.

CITIZENSHIP

American Adventure, The. Bertrand M. Wainger.

American Heritage Book of Great Historic Places. Editors of American Heritage.

Boys' Life reprint pamphlets: *Bill of Rights, Law and Justice, Our Heritage of Freedom.* Boy Scouts of America.

Merit badge pamphlets: *Citizenship* series; *American Heritage.* Boy Scouts of America.

Your Life as a Citizen. Harriet Fullen Smith.

Youth Faces American Citizenship. Leo J. Alilunas and J. Woodrow Sayre.

NATURE—GENERAL

American Southeast, The. H.S.Zim.

American Southwest, The. H.S.Zim and N. N. Dodge.

Animal Tracks and Hunter Signs. Ernest Thompson Seton.

Basic Mountaineering. Edited by Henry I. Mandolf.

Birds. H.S.Zim and I.N.Gabrielson.

Birds in Our Lives. Edited by Alfred Stefferud and Arnold L. Nelson.

Birds of North America. H.S.Zim, Robbins, Chandler, Bruun and Bertel.

Butterflies and Moths, H.S.Zim and R.Mitchell.

Fishes. H.S.Zim.

Flowers. H.S.Zim and A.C.Martin.

How To Attract, House, and Feed Birds. Walter E. Schutz.

Insects. H.S.Zim and C.A.Cottain.

Life of the Cave, The. C.E.Mohr.

Life of the Desert, The. A.Sutton.

Life of the Forest, The. J. McCormick.

Life of the Marsh, The. W.A.Niering.

Life of the Mountains, The. Maurice Brooks.

Life of the Ocean, The. N.Berrill.

Life of the Pond, The. W.Amos.

Life of the Seashore, The. W.H. Amos.

Mammals. H.S.Zim and D.F.Hofmeister.

Merit badge pamphlets: *Astronomy, Bird Study, Botany, Environmental Science, Fish and Wildlife Management, Fishing, Forestry, Geology, Insect Life, Nature, Reptile Study, Soil and Water Conservation, Weather.* Boy Scouts of America.

Reptiles and Amphibians. H.S.Zim and H.M.Smith.

Rocks and Minerals. H.S.Zim and P. R. Shaffer.

Rocky Mountains, The. H.S.Zim.

Sea Shells of the World. H.S.Zim.

Seashores. H.S.Zim and L.Ingle.

Stars. H.S.Zim and R.H.Baker.

Trail and Camp-Fire Stories. Julia M. Seton.

Trees. H.S.Zim and A.C.Martin.

Using Wayside Plants. Nelson Coon.

Web of Life. John H. Storer.

Where There is Life. Paul B. Sears.

Wild Animals I Have Known. Ernest Thompson Seton.

Zoology. H.S.Zim, H.I.Fisher, and R.W.Burnett.

NATURE—GUIDEBOOKS

Audubon Land Bird Guide. Richard H. Pough.

Audubon Water Bird Guide. Richard H. Pough.

Complete Field Guide to American Wildlife. Henry Hill Collins, Jr.

Field Guide to Animal Tracks, A. Olaus J. Murie.

Field Guide to Reptiles and Amphibians, A. Roger Conant.

Field Guide to Rocky Mountain Wildflowers, A. J.J.Craighead, F. C.Craighead, and Ray J. Davis.

Field Guide to Rocks and Minerals, A. Frederick H. Pough.

Field Guide to Shells of the Pacific Coast and Hawaii, A. Percy Morris.

Field Guide to the Birds, A. Roger Tory Peterson.

Field Guide to the Birds of Texas and Adjacent States, A. Roger Tory Peterson.

Field Guide to the Ferns, A. Boughton Cobb.

Field Guide to the Shells of Our Atlantic and Gulf Coasts, A. Percy A. Morris.

Field Guide to the Stars and Planets, A. Donald H. Menzel.

Field Guide to Trees and Shrubs, A. George A. Petrides.

Field Guide to Western Birds, A. Roger Tory Peterson.

Field Guide to Wildflowers of the Northeastern and Central States, A. Margaret McKenny and Roger Tory Peterson.

Game Birds. H.S. Zim and A. Sprunt.

Insect Guide. Ralph B. Swain.

Wild Flower Guide. Edgar T. Wherry.

PHYSICAL FITNESS

Boys' Book of Physical Fitness, The. Hal G. Vermes.

Boys' Life reprint pamphlet: *Toughen Up.* Boy Scouts of America.

How To Be Fit. Robert Kiphuth.

Merit badge pamphlets: *Athletics, Hiking, Orienteering, Personal Fitness, Swimming.* Boy Scouts of America.

SCOUTING HISTORY

Baden-Powell: The Two Lives of a Hero. William Hillcourt with Olave, Lady Baden-Powell.

Scouting for Boys. Lord Baden-Powell of Gilwell.

SERVICE TO OTHERS

Emergency Service. Boy Scouts of America.

First Aid Manual. American Red Cross.

Lifesaving. American Red Cross.

Merit badge pamphlets: *Emergency Preparedness, Firemanship, First Aid, Public Health, Safety.* Boy Scouts of America.

SURVIVAL

Deadly Harvest. John M. Kingsbury.

Emergency Care, Edited by Robert H. Kennedy, M.D.

Survival. Department of the Air Force. AFM 64-5.

Wilderness Survival merit badge pamphlet.

MAGAZINES

Boys' Life, Boy Scouts of America.

Curious Naturalist, The. Massachusetts Audubon Society.

Exploring. Exploring Division, BSA.

Nature and Science. American Museum of Natural History.

PHOTO CREDITS

Appreciation is expressed for the illustrations made available by these photographers and agencies; they are identified by page number and, where necessary, by code letters (reading from left to right or top to bottom).

The American Museum of Natural History 425A, 468B

The New Britton and Brown Illustrated Flora 322-31

L. W. Brownell 355A, 357B, 367C, 374CDE, 376C, 463AB

Hank Bruns 434

Lynwood M. Chace 439B

G. A. Clarke 505C, 507C

Cook Observatory, University of Pennsylvania 529ABCD

Allan J. de Lay, The Oregonian 308B

E. Ross Allen Florida Reptile Institute 436B

Ewing Galloway, N.Y. 502

Wendler from FPG, endpapers

Faust Photo Service 285

Gottscho-Schleisner, Inc. 4, 337A, 338AB, 350B, 368B, 369C, 373A, 378A, 413E

Hayden Planetarium from painting by D. Owen Stephens in Buhl Planetarium 515A

Hedrich-Blessing 402

Jim Hosmer Photo 286

Humphreys 509C

International News Reel 505B

Jack McManigal, Agricultural Photographs 501A

Don Wooldridge from Missouri Conservation Commission 431B

F. Gerard Moran 7, 32, 39, 43D, 47A, 53A, 58BC, 61B, 78ABC, 79AF, 96 background, 308A

National Audubon Society:
Arthur Ambler 368D, 370D

G. Ronald Austing 454A, 466C

Alfred M. Bailey 383B

N. E. Beck, Jr. 410A

Art Bilsten 493

Mitchell Campbell 422C

Lynwood M. Chace 411D, 425B, 463D

Allan D. Cruickshank 450BCD, 451B, 452D, 453CD, 454B, 455CD, 461B, 467CE, 471B

Treat Davidson 423ACE

Walter Dawn 354B

William Dawson 339C

Jack Dermid 359B

Gladys Diesing 381E

John H. Gerard 354A, 355B, 356B, 357C, 359A, 374A, 375B, 376E, 378E, 380D, 381B, 383C, 384B, 411C, 451C, 470AB

Samuel A. Grimes 457C

Grant M. Haist 353D

Hugh M. Halliday 452C, 455A, 464

Hal H. Harrison 350C, 411AB, 424D, 436A, 440B, 441C, 452B, 453A, 455B, 466A

John Hendry, Jr. 424A

Robert C. Hermes 438E

Clarence J. Hylander 383A

William Jahoda 366B

Verna R. Johnston 339B, 356D

H. W. Kitchen 385E, 424B, 425D

Pat Kirkpatrick 339A

Bob Leatherman 467A

Norman Lerner 270

Les Line 378B

Jesse Lunger 376B

Karl Maslowski 452A

Henry M. Mayer 369D, 373B

Chuck Meyer 468C

Charles J. Ott 383D, 450A, 451D

George Porter 337B

Leonard Lee Rue III 454D, 466B, 468A

W. J. Schoonmaker 467D

Diamon T. Smithers 356C

Hugh Spencer 360B, 375A

Alvin E. Staffan 423D, 453B, 467B

John O. Sumner 375D, 381C

John K. Terres 377B

Gunther A. Wachter 451A

H. D. Wheeler 454C

Jeanne White 366C, 367D

Don Wooldridge 369E

National Aeronautic and Space Administration 512

New Mexico State Tourist Bureau 300

New York Zoological Society Photo 422A, 423B, 424C

North Carolina Wildlife Resources Commission 431A

Phillips Petroleum Company 366D

Gayle Pickwell 507DE, 509BDE

H. Armstrong Roberts 238ABD

Roche 350D, 351BC, 352ABCD, 353ABC, 358CD, 359D, 363BC, 364ABCDE, 365BCD, 366A, 367AB, 368AE, 369AB, 370ABCE, 371ABCDE, 373DE, 374B, 375E, 376AD, 377ACDE, 378D, 379E, 380ABE, 381AD, 385B

Joseph Coburn Smith, Colby College 515B

Prof. Carl Störmer 505A

Edwin Way Teale 408BC, 412ABC, 413CD

Chet Ullin x

Union Pacific Railroad Co. 494

USDA — Soil Conservation Service 360AC, 361ABCE, 362AB, 385A, 501B

USDA — U.S. Forest Service 334, 356A, 357AD, 359C, 361D, 365AE, 368C, 373C, 375C, 379ABCD, 380C, 413A

USDC — Weather Service 507AB, 509AC

USDI — Bureau of Land Management 338C, 384A, 385CD

USDI — John VanOosten from USDI Fish and Wildlife Service 435

Robert F. Patton, University of Wisconsin 351A

Ward's Natural Science Establishment, Inc. 413B, 414B, 417BCD, 447B, 497BCDE, 498BCDE, 499BCDE

Zoological Society of Philadelphia 438ABCD, 439ACDE, 440ACDE, 441ABDE, 442ABCD

The original *Scout Fieldbook* (1944-59) was written by William Hillcourt, then national director of Program Resources. He took most of the photographs for that book. Many of these pictures appear in this edition of the *Fieldbook*. Other uncredited photos were taken by members of the national staff.

INDEX

BOY SCOUTS OF AMERICA

ORIENTEERING DISTANCE COMPUTER

If you know anything about slide rules, you will recognize this as a simplified version. If you don't, it won't take you long to find out how it works. The scale is the only thing that is tricky. The number 11 can be 11 or it can be 110 or 1,100 depending upon the problem. This won't throw you when you get the hang of it.

Measure 100 feet. Pace the distance. Begin with your left foot and count each time your right foot hits the ground. Rotate the inner circle so that the pace arrow points to the number of paces it took to cover 100 feet (30.48 meters). Make a pencil mark opposite the little arrow to the right of 30 on the scale. From now on, the scale will read in meters opposite that mark.

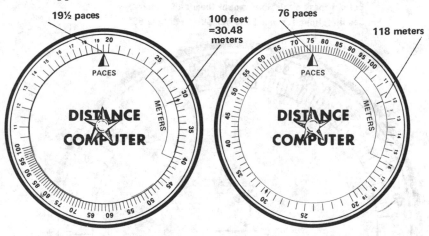

Suppose you covered 100 feet in 19½ paces. Set the dial like this and make your mark in the meters box opposite the little arrow to the right of 30. That represents 30.48 meters or 100 feet.

If you have to go 118 meters, set the dial so that your mark is to the left of 12 on the scale. That's 118. Then read paces opposite the big arrow. That's 76 paces. Also could be 1180 meters and 760 paces.

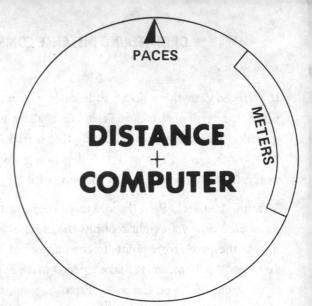

DISTANCE
+
COMPUTER

Cut out these circles and mount them on stiff paper.
See directions for using the computer on page 565.

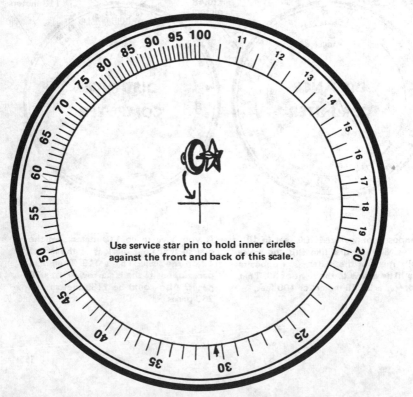

Use service star pin to hold inner circles
against the front and back of this scale.